Applied Social Science Research in a Regional Knowledge System

Balancing validity, meaning and convenience

Edited by
Hans Christian Garmann Johnsen, Elisabet S. Hauge, May-Linda Magnussen and Richard Ennals

Routledge
Taylor & Francis Group
LONDON AND NEW YORK

First published 2017
by Routledge
711 Third Avenue, New York, NY 10017

and by Routledge
2 Park Square, Milton Park, Abingdon, Oxon OX14 4RN

Routledge is an imprint of the Taylor & Francis Group, an informa business

Library of Congress Cataloging in Publication Data
Names: Johnsen, Hans Chr. Garmann, 1955- editor.
Title: Applied social science research in a regional knowledge system : balancing validity, meaning and convenience / edited by Hans Chr. Garmann Johnsen, Elisabet S. Hauge, May-Linda Magnussen, Richard Ennals.
Description: New York, NY : Routledge, 2016. | Includes bibliographical references.
Identifiers: LCCN 2016020669| ISBN 9781472487827 (hbk) | ISBN 9781472487841 (ebk)
Subjects: LCSH: Social sciences—Research—Norway. | Research, Industrial—Norway. | Research—Economic aspects—Norway.
Classification: LCC H62.5.N6 A67 2016 | DDC 300.72/0481—dc23
LC record available at https://lccn.loc.gov/2016020669

ISBN: 978-1-4724-8782-7 (hbk)
ISBN: 978-1-315-41141-5 (ebk)

Typeset in Sabon
by Swales & Willis Ltd, Exeter, Devon, UK

MIX
Paper from responsible sources
FSC www.fsc.org FSC® C013604

Printed and bound by CPI Group (UK) Ltd, Croydon, CR0 4YY

Contents

Figures

Tables

Preface

There are questions relevant for applied social science researchers around the world, and challenges where one region has a lot to learn from others. In this book, the case is the Agder region, the southernmost region in Norway. In the book's chapters, researchers working in the regional research institute Agder Research, some in association with researchers at the University of Agder, reflect on their research practice. The book builds on *Creating Collaborative Advantage* (Johnsen & Ennals 2012) and *The New Natural Resource* (Johnsen 2014).

The book illustrates how applied social scientists and their research are integrated with stakeholders and practitioners in a local/regional setting, and how knowledge development is a mutual concern, made in, and dependent on, ongoing dialogue. It is relevant for both policy makers and researchers and will help them reflect on the type of mutual competence building that applied social science research implies, and depends on, in a regional knowledge development process. It represents a voice on how to understand the development of the knowledge society at regional and global levels.

Most of the cases presented in this book have been research and development projects at Agder Research. Many of them are documented in project reports. These reports contain more references and data, as well as description of sources of data, than is presented here. Some chapters make references to such reports. For others, the project reports can be obtained through the web-page of Agder Research: http://www.agderforskning.no.

This book has developed through a series of seminars and discussions. The first seminar was in June 2013. Draft chapters were presented at 5th NORSA conference, Kristiansand, Norway, in January 2015. We should like to thank reviewers and authors for their participation. We would also like to thank Agder Research for providing resources to develop this book, Kristine Miland, who helped with finalising the text, and the editors at Taylor and Francis for constructive comments during the process.

Hans Christian Garmann Johnsen, Elisabet S. Hauge,
May-Linda Magnussen and Richard Ennals
Kristiansand/London, March 2016

Contributors

Jørn Cruickshank is Associate Professor at the Department of Planning and Global Development, at University of Agder, Norway. He is a senior researcher at Agder Research(*), Norway.

Richard Ennals is Professor at the Department of Working Life and Innovation at University of Agder(*), Norway. He is also Professor in the Department of Skill and Technology at Linnaeus University, Sweden, and Emeritus Professor at Kingston University, UK.

Eugene Guribye, PhD, is head of Innovation in the Public Sector and Senior Researcher at Agder Research, Norway.

Hanne Haaland is Associate Professor at the department for Global Development and Planning at University of Agder, Norway. She is also associated as Senior Researcher at Agder Research(*), Norway.

Elisabet S. Hauge is a senior researcher at Agder Research(*), Norway, and Post Doc at the University of Agder, Norway.

Tor Helge Aas is Associate Professor at the Department of Management at University of Agder, Norway, and Senior Researcher at Agder Research(*), Norway.

Arne Isaksen is Professor at the Department of Working Life and Innovation at University of Agder, Norway, and Senior Researcher at Agder Research(*), Norway.

Hans Christian Garmann Johnsen is a professor at the Department of Working Life and Innovation at University of Agder, Norway, and a senior researcher at Agder Research(*), Norway and Professor at Norwegian University of Science and Technology (NTNU), Gjøvik, Norway.

Geir Jørgensen is former Head of Industrial Development and Innovation Management at Agder Research(*) and is at the present time Head of Strategy and Business Development at NorgesEnergi.

James Karlsen is Associate Professor at the Department of Working Life and Innovation at University of Agder, Norway, a senior researcher at Agder Research(*), Norway, and has an affiliation to Orkestra-Basque Institute of Competitiveness, Spain.

Sarah Holst Kjær is Senior Researcher at Agder Research(*), Norway. She is also an assistant professor at the Department of Ethnology, History of Religions and Gender Studies, Stockholm University, Sweden.

Ingunn Kvamme is a former researcher at Agder Research(*) and PhD Research Fellow at University of Agder, Norway.

Nina Kyllingstad is PhD Student at the Department of Working Life and Innovation at University of Agder, Norway, and Researcher at Agder Research(*), Norway.

Karen Landmark is PhD Candidate at the Department of Working Life and Innovation at University of Agder, Norway, and Senior Project Manager at The Eyde Cluster, Norway. She is a former researcher at Agder Research(*), Norway.

Miren Larrea is a senior researcher at Orkestra-Basque Institute of Competitiveness, Spain, and Lecturer at the University of Deusto, Spain.

May-Linda Magnussen, PhD, is Senior Researcher at Agder Research(*), Norway and post doc at the University of Agder, Norway.

Roger Henning Normann, PhD, is acting Managing Director at Agder Research(*) and Head of Department, Department of Working Life and Innovation, School of Business and Law, University of Agder, Norway.

Ellen K. Nyhus is Professor at the Department of Management at University of Agder, Norway, and Senior Researcher at Agder Research(*), Norway.

Rómulo Pinheiro is Professor at Department of Public Policy and Administration at University of Agder, Norway. He is also Senior Researcher at Agder Research(*) Centre for Advanced Studies in Regional Innovation Strategies (RIS), Norway.

Michael Ricke is Senior Project Manager and Researcher at Agder Research, Norway.

Sissel Strickert is Researcher and Senior Project Manager at Agder Research, Norway.

Christine Svarstad is Political Scientist and Researcher at Agder Research, Norway.

Stina Torjesen, PhD, is former Senior Researcher at Agder Research(*) and Associate Professor at School of Business and Law, University of Agder, Norway.

Part of this development towards a knowledge society is that, increasingly, public sector and businesses rely on research in their decision making and development processes. It has become more common that public programmes are evaluated by researchers, or that new policy documents are "evidence-based", meaning that research institutions provide background knowledge or verify information. This works differently in different countries. In the UK, for instance, evaluation and research are often conducted by major private sector management consultancies. In the EU research programme *Horizon 2020*, however, it is often a requirement that research institutions co-operate with enterprises or public institutions. A *knowledge society* depends on *applied research*.

The authors of this book share an interest in regional development, aiming to make a region more socially, economically or environmentally sustainable. Our institutional setting is applied social science research in ongoing social and economic processes that provide knowledge to stakeholders. This happens in space and also in real time, as challenges are identified, and the need for more or other kinds of knowledge triggers demand for applied research. The key challenge facing today's society is to find ways to develop better knowledge in areas where there are no fixed solutions to society's challenges.

This book discusses the role and methodological challenges of *applied social science research*. Our argument is that this form of research plays a role in a dialogical and discursive interaction with practice. Beyond the individual research project, there is the overall effect of increased applied research in society. By looking at a particular region, and at a multitude projects in a single region, we might be able to detect the overall effect of this research on regional development. We argue that this research is part of what we have chosen to call a *regional knowledge system*. Most of the individual research projects describe, understand, explain and engage in changing practice. However, some projects presented in this book are more aimed at describing, some at understanding, explaining and changing practice. We have therefore grouped the chapters in this book into these four categories that form the four parts of the book, based on the projects they present.

Key to our discussion is what we mean by *knowledge*, and what kind of knowledge is developed through different kinds of applied social science research. We acknowledge the social dimension of knowledge: The production of knowledge is a social process. Production of knowledge happens at a certain time in history, and within a certain geographical space. Knowledge is also produced by people. Knowledge is, as we will argue, what is perceived to be correct at a certain point in time and space and by certain people. This means going beyond saying that knowledge is socially warranted opinions, adding that people's possibilities to make their knowledge count in economic and social processes are unevenly distributed in all known societies. We go deeper into the question of what this implies for applied social science research.

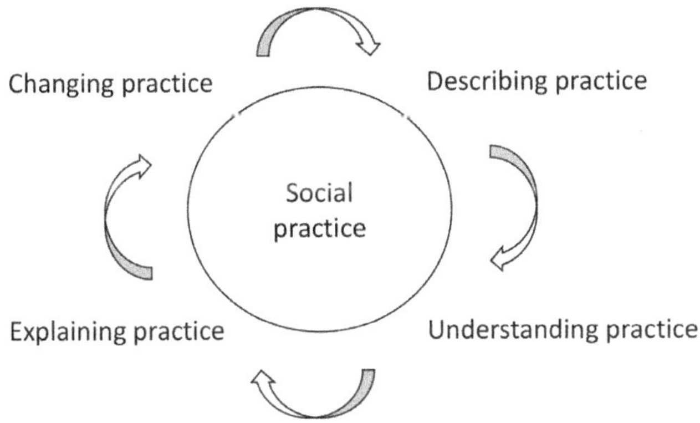

Figure I.1 Different roles of applied social science research in relation to practice

We look at how applied social science research and more accurately, how geographically specific knowledge that is part of what we call a regional knowledge system becomes social knowledge. We start from the observation that contemporary applied social science research engages with stakeholders, and argue that it has to balance validity, legitimacy and relevance issues in order to be socially accepted. This is the *methodological problem* of the book, and we see it in a comprehensive perspective. We are interested in both the more traditional issues of what is considered true knowledge, and also the social and institutional conditions under which this knowledge is developed. In this introduction, we outline our perspective on these methodological challenges and how we define a regional knowledge system.

Positioning our book in the sociology of knowledge

The meta perspective in this book is that applied social science research projects influence social practice, not only at a single project level but also in society at large. This book has chapters that represent different traditions and disciplines within social science, but we have positioned the overall argument of the book in what we may roughly call *the sociology of knowledge* (Johnsen 2014). We will go on to present positions within sociology of knowledge that we draw upon in the book.

Sociology of knowledge is a wide field that includes anthropological, epistemological and sociological positions. However, the core claim of sociology of knowledge is that social organisation influences what is perceived as knowledge. A strong claim would imply that all knowledge is a function of social organisation, a weak claim would argue that social organisation has some influence on what is regarded as valid knowledge. A complete rejection of the sociology of knowledge means arguing that knowledge is universal or a priori in relation to a specific social context. A weak claim, a perspective followed by this introductory chapter, will accept some aprioristic and some universality of knowledge, but still argue that social organisation influences what is regarded as valid, interesting and as social facts. The interaction between agents, institutions and knowledge forms is what we describe as a knowledge system.

When we use the term *knowledge system*, we indicate that our main focus is on knowledge development beyond the individual actor and the individual organisation. The term builds on the concept of social system commonly used in social science. While some thinkers reject the usefulness of the term altogether (i.e. Smith 2005), many find it useful for identifying and understanding social organisation. Central thinkers conceptualise the term differently, and here we position our use of the concept in this theoretical terrain.

One of the most comprehensive discussions of social systems is found in the works of Niklas Luhmann (i.e. Luhmann 1996). He sees social systems as autopoetic, self-referential social entities, and argues that knowledge is a main factor in differentiating social systems. He defines science as such a system, as well as disciplines within science. Social systems in general can be defined as internal communicative processes, creating the form of meaning that differentiate the system and give it legitimacy. Luhmann sees this as a systemic process beyond individual agency. However, agency can be included in a definition of a social system. James Coleman's famous bathtub model combines a system and an individual level of analysis. In this model, there can be changes at a system level and interaction between system level and agents (Coleman & Coleman 1994).

In his *The Constitution of Society* (1984), Anthony Giddens argues that social sciences, different from natural sciences, contribute to the meaning construction of society at a given time and place. He refers to this as mutual knowledge, which is understood as integrated into the common sense of everyday social life. In Chapter 6: Social integration of refugees and Chapter 7: Comparative reflection of this book, there is a discussion about scientific knowledge in relation to common sense, everyday knowledge. Mutual knowledge is a concept that resonates with our concept of knowledge system. In our use of the concept, however, we do not only include social meaning construction but also the institutional set-up of the social system. Common to the two concepts is that social sciences are not above or outside a knowledge system, but part of it.

Pierre Bourdieu in his book *The Logic of Practice* (1980) has a stronger focus on the institutional and historical dimension in social and knowledge development. His concept of *social field* and analysis of social capital (habitus), represents a framework that allows us to see how power and position play a strong role in the knowledge development within a social entity. His argument is that knowledge development is situated in a social situation of historical conditions. He writes:

> Because the *habitus* is an infinite capacity for generating products – thoughts, perceptions, expressions and actions – whose limits are set by the historically and socially situated conditions of its production, the conditioned and conditional freedom it provides is as remote from creation of unpredictable novelty as it is from simple mechanical reproduction of the original conditions.
>
> (Bourdieu 1980, p. 55)

Jürgen Habermas, who is a proponent of a *dialogical* approach to social development, in his *Theory and Practice* (1974) argues in more social epistemological terms. He says:

> There is a systematic relationship between the logical structure of science and the pragmatic structure of the possible applications of the information generated within its framework. . . . Therefore the technical and practical interests of knowledge are not regulators of cognition which have to be eliminated for the sake of the objectivity of knowledge; instead they themselves determine the aspects under which reality is objectified, and can thus be made accessible to the experience to begin with. They are the conditions which are necessary in order that subjects capable of speech and action may have experience which may lay a claim of objectivity. . . . The underlying "interests" establishes the unity between this constitutive context in which knowledge is rooted and the structure of the possible application which this knowledge can have.
>
> (Habermas 1974, pp. 8–9)

Subsequently, when we present our concept of a regional knowledge system, we use many of these arguments. The theories presented earlier are to some extent conflicting. Still, we argue that it is possible to take a pragmatic position and put many of these competing arguments together. As a meta perspective it is fair to argue that our approach is close to what Steve Fuller (2002) has described as the *dialectical approach of social epistemology*. Fuller describes the dialectical approach in this way:

> The basic concepts and principles of social epistemology are developed and justified in the actual context of knowledge production that concerns the social epistemologist. Thus, one starts in *medias res*, treating current knowledge production practices as empirical constraints on the possible directions that future knowledge production can take. There is no clear distinction here between pure and applied, because it is not presumed that knowledge has an essence that can be accessed independently of recognised cases of knowledge. Instead the relevant questions are whether we wish the future to continue certain tendencies of the past, and if so, which ones. The answer to these questions

> are to be found by deciding what we want (a political issue centring on the definition of "we") and evaluation of the consequences of those practices accordingly."
>
> (Fuller 2002, p. xvi)

Our book can be regarded as a case study in *dialectical knowledge development*, even though we take a pragmatic approach, and include dialogical arguments in our meta perspective. We still think the description by Fuller gives a relevant reference to the study we present here; our point of view is not that of an outsider, studying a regional knowledge system in this respect, but of insiders in that knowledge system, as researchers engaged in practice.

Applied research and the methodological challenges

The development towards a knowledge economy, and a knowledge society within which academic institutions have a more active role, requires more multidisciplinary kinds of knowledge. This argument has been described as a new production of knowledge (Gibbons et al. 1994), rethinking science (Nowotny, Scott & Gibbons 2001) or triple helix (Deiaco, Hughes & McKelvey 2012; Etzkowitz & Leydesdorff 2000). At the same time, these same studies reveal that in spite of this trend, the counter trend of maintaining traditional disciplinary boundaries at university level is still very strong (see Chapter 17: Universities' external relations in this book), and that the trend towards multidisciplinarity has not progressed at fast as one could have expected. There are paradoxes in the governance system of academic institutions, stimulating academic knowledge to be more relevant and at the same time evaluating academic knowledge according to traditional, disciplinary criteria. Chapter 1: Developing a sustainable business model in a changing economy and Chapter 16: Commitment to sustainability in Agder in this book give data from Norway that support some of these general observations.

This book contributes to this debate in three ways. First, the case is a multidisciplinary research institute, producing research close to practice, with a university as its main owner. The book can be seen as a case study into how such research institutes operate. Thus, it gives a more concrete and practical content to the role of academic institutions in the knowledge economy. Second, the book addresses the development of knowledge in the interaction between research and practice, and addresses the particular methodological challenges for this kind of multidisciplinary, practice-close research, including the challenges of evaluation of knowledge in this situation. Finally, the book contributes to the understanding of how applied multidisciplinary research contributes to knowledge development in a knowledge society.

We consider how applied social science research plays a role in developing knowledge in a regional context. Regional social science research institutes are supposed to deliver applied research, often with relevance for the region, although they also engage in national and international research projects.

We divide applied research into *commissioned* and *contributory* research. These differ when it comes to funding. Most applied research institutes in Norway have basic funding. Although this is targeted for the institute, it gives the involved researchers some freedom in designing the research. It is therefore called contributory research. At the same time, most institutes compete in open calls for proposals. These projects are called commissioned research, because the objective and the design of the research is much more restricted, seen from the researchers' point of view. There are also projects developed and applied for through partnerships with actors from the field of practice. These are neither as "free" as projects financed with basic funding, nor as restricted as projects initiated and defined by such actors.

In Norway, applied research institutes are often linked to universities. In the current process of restructuring higher education and research, some have been made into university departments. Compared with US cases, one can see these as the equivalent of extension activity of US universities. Applied research institutions have both the ambition to be academic in the sense of delivering papers to research seminars and articles in scholarly journals and have PhD students, as well as being relevant for society more generally, and being practical in the sense of contributing to social, economic or environmental change. In Chapter 1, the dilemmas between these tasks are discussed. We argue that applied research is executed in the tension between validity, meaning and convenience.

The idea of *applied research* dates back to the philosophy of the French social scientist Auguste Comte. Around 1840, Comte developed the philosophy of positivism, by which he meant social thinking in which development in society is based on science (Comte 1988). He argued that science should replace religion as the foundation of society. He was impressed by how natural science had made fundamental insights into scientific laws, insights that later on were applied in developing technology and thereby industry. He thus developed concepts of what he called concrete science versus abstract science, and saw the development of science as the development towards abstract theories. For Comte, the objectivity of science was defined by its ability to come up with abstract explanations.

At the same time, Comte saw that abstract science could develop into concrete research. In his mind, there was a linear relation between abstract (basic) research and concrete (applied) research. All aspects of society and life should therefore be developed along similar, linear models. In spite of the fact that many have questioned the linear model of science and positivism as a philosophy, much of Comte's thinking is still a reference point in discussions on knowledge development, both at a national/international level and at a regional level. As is discussed in Chapter 2: Why Norway has to develop its own innovation policy in this book, there is a strong tendency to argue that we need basic research for developing new knowledge, and then applied research to implement this basic research insight in practice. It should also, however, be mentioned that Comte regarded the study of

Table I.2 Overview of the chapters in the book

Chapter	*1*	*2*	*3*	*4*	*5*	*6*	*7*	*8*	*9*	*10*	*11*	*12*	*13*	*14*	*15*	*16*	*17*
Funding																	
contributory	x	x	x		x	x	x		x			x					
commissioned					x	x		x		x	x		x	x	x	x	x
participatory				x			x	x		x				x		x	x
Initiated/organised																	
researcher	x	x			x	x		x	x	x							
board, administration					x		x				x		x	x	x	x	x
part of a larger programme			x	x								x					
Use of results																	
politics/change of policy	x	x					x					x					
for research purposes			x				x	x					x				
problem resolution				x	x	x				x	x			x	x	x	x
public debate						x			x							x	

into research questions and strategies, theoretical and methodological choices have to be made. These choices have impacts on the knowledge provided by the research project and affect the context where the research was initiated. We do not regard these challenges as restricted to the research project itself: we focus on how this research affects the regional knowledge system. We can term this a *comprehensive perspective* on methodological challenges.

We consider not only the isolated decisions made by the researchers but also see these decisions as part of a dialogue with stakeholders. By understanding the methodological challenge in this way, it becomes possible to discuss the type of social knowledge creation process of which applied social science research is part. This book presents some cases of applied social science projects. These cases demonstrate what type of context the research took part in, the choices on research strategy made by the researchers, the theoretical reflections the research initiated and the use of the results both by practitioners and researchers.

The cases and projects described in this book touch upon issues of who initiated/organised the project (researcher/board administration/part of a larger programme) and how the results were used (politics or change of policy/ for research purposes/problem resolution/public debate). Table I.2 shows how the research in the 17 chapters in this book vary in this respect.

The table tells us something about the strategies and methodological approaches chosen by the projects presented in the different chapters. Some do research close to practice, with practice and even within practice. Others choose more of a spectator's view. This research also influences practice and is in dialogue with practice on topics of their research, and in presenting findings and results, but their way of gathering data is more detached. The chapters in part II of this book argue for producing knowledge that may challenge the established knowledge in their fields. All these chapters build upon extensive studies, including PhD dissertations, and the knowledge that is presented in this section to a large degree originates from or elaborates on "basic research". This is decisive for the ability to both understand the hegemonic knowledge and how to produce alternative knowledge. The ambition is for this knowledge to gain influence in the social world. We then need to tease the researcher out from their desks to relate to the world of applied research, where reality "happens". We also need to stimulate funders and policy makers to be curious of alternative conceptualisations, rather than fearing diversity.

The applied researcher can approach the part of social reality they research, including their relations to stakeholders, differently. Even if researchers aim to go beyond the individual, and say something about society at large, the focus and the entry point may vary. While some pay a great deal of focus to the social activities of individuals, others give more focus to the organisational/institutional level. Table I.3 presents a typology of research practise.

This book exemplifies these research methodologies. We find examples of high levels of researcher involvement in the field, as in Chapter 6: Social

Table I.3 Research strategies and areas of research

Part of society studied/degree of personal involvement of the researcher	*Individual*	*Social*	*Structural*
Involved	Researcher is involved and influences practice	Researcher having a normative agenda towards practice	Not meaningful
Engaged	Researcher observes situations/relations involving individuals	Researcher looks at social processes from within	Researcher makes meaning out of structural dimensions
Observer	Not meaningful	Researcher observes social processes	Researcher describes the social system

integration of refugees and Chapter 7: Comparative reflection. We also find examples of more of a spectator approach, like in Chapter 16: Commitment to sustainability in Agder and in Chapter 17: Universities' external relations. There are differences between these chapters concerning how data are collected (experiences, surveys, statistical data) and how they are processed (with practitioners, in the reflection of the researcher, using statistical tools). In the concluding chapter, we discuss some of the experiences concerning these issues. However, our main interest is to see these in a sociological perspective; that is, to see the research presented in the book as part of a larger knowledge production process.

The book's overarching theme cuts across the different disciplinary perspectives and themes of the chapters. It is not a problem that there is great variation in these themes. Based on the cases we present, we discuss the construction of regional knowledge in social, economic and environmental development. In normative terms, we are interested in the role of applied social sciences in the regional knowledge system, and how collaboration between research and regional institutions can help develop a sustainable society. In more descriptive terms, we are interested in how applied researchers practise theory and theorise practice, bring practice into theory, interpret practitioners' problems, make sense of social change in real time and space and if they are sometimes too close to practise.

A regional knowledge system

In order for us to make the argument about how applied social science research contributes to social knowledge development beyond the individual project, we introduce the concept of a *regional knowledge system*. A regional knowledge system is a perspective for analysing how different kinds of knowledge influence different parts of society. We will next explicate what we put into this perspective. We start by explaining what we mean by regional.

The region

The discussion in this book to some extent builds on arguments developed in other books that the editors and authors have been involved in. In *Creating Collaborative Advantage* (Johnsen & Ennals 2012), the regional dimension in economic development was explored. Cases from eight different countries and three continents threw light on how collaboration at a regional level can contribute to social and economic development. In another book, *Higher Education in a Sustainable Society* (Johnsen, Torjesen & Ennals 2015), the argument is that the building of mutual competences is a key to sustainable social development. Higher education has an important role to play, in order not to create a divide between those with and without education.

In public policy in Europe, the regional dimension has gained renewed attention over the last 20–30 years. Regions are substituting the national level in areas that call for local solutions. This has been supported by concepts like learning regions (Florida 1995) and regionalisation (Storper 1997). Politically, it has been supported by, for example, the Lisbon agreement (Rodrigues 2002).

Norway has a long tradition of local self-government, both at a county and at a municipality level. This matches to some extent the situation in other Nordic countries, although Finland, Sweden and Denmark have had regional reforms in order to develop larger regions and municipalities. Regional borders are not fixed, and Norway is now in the process of developing larger regions. This also influences the regional dimension of a regional knowledge system.

Regionalisation can be seen as decentralisation, based on acknowledging that responses to globalisation are best based on regional characteristics. Developing regional characteristics, in the sense of particular advantages or competences, can be a good response to the national challenges of globalisation. Regions transcend national boundaries, and form more natural areas of development. Building institutional capacity to take on the role of development dynamics implies increased attention towards research and higher education.

There has been a call for new forms of interaction between public sector, university, research and business. Nowotny et al. (2001) have talked about the new production of knowledge, implying a new institutional relation between business and academia: They are expected to collaboratively produce the type of innovative economic development that the new knowledge economy demands. Lydesdorff (2006) argues that the so-called triple helix between public administration, university and industry is a key motor in knowledge development. Godin and Gingras (2000) strengthen the argument that the pattern of interaction in research development is changing in the direction of more research being done in collaborative and network structures between university and the field of practice.

Development over recent years of financial crisis and austerity has influenced this institutional development in many European countries, towards more applied research, financed by regional stakeholders and with a clear development purpose. Chapters 1 and 2 in this book both give an overview of the Norwegian research system, and position this in a European context. In spite of national differences, the policy of enhancing applied research is steadily strengthening throughout the European area. In line with this, the EU report *Challenging Futures of Science in Society – Emerging trends and cutting-edge issues* (EU 2009) talks about science in terms of "innovation oriented research", "responsible development" and pressures for "sound science". Furthermore, it argues for five dimensions in science's contribution to society:

> The innovation dimension: ensuring economic competitiveness in the global marketplace, providing innovation and contributing to wealth, and economic growth;
>
> The quality of life dimension: contributing to health, education, welfare, and a viable social order;
>
> The political dimension: contributing to relevant debates, especially concerning future developments involving science and technology, as well as giving expert advice to policy makers and the public;
>
> The cultural dimension: respecting cultural diversities, conserving cultural heritage, developing communication skills and intercultural dialogues;
>
> The intellectual dimension: thinking about a "good society", the future of human nature and sustainable development, contributing to the quality of life.
>
> (EU 2009, p. 15)

In normative terms, this signifies new ways of organising knowledge development processes between universities and businesses. In descriptive terms, we can see the emergence of new governance structures, new organisational forms between universities and businesses and more practice-based ways of organising education. This implies overcoming traditional dilemmas related to roles (such as the role of the researcher) and institutional understanding (such as the role of the university or new arenas for university/business collaboration) in the regional context. Related to this, there is increasing demand for knowledge management in organisations.

Organisations now formulate knowledge strategies, and discuss what knowledge resources they possess.

How can we conceptualise this relation between research and practice? Cooke and Leydesdorff (2006) argue in terms of whether the region can develop specific, competitive advantages from its unique forms of knowledge:

> We consider the history of the idea that knowledge is an economic factor, and discuss the question of whether regions provide the relevant system of reference for knowledge-based economic development. Current transformations in university-industry-government relations at various levels can be considered as a metamorphosis in industry organisation.
>
> (Cooke & Leydesdorff 2006, p. 5)

Our intention is not to argue for specific innovation outcomes of applied social science research in the regional knowledge system. This book mainly focuses on *the indirect processes of knowledge development* that is; societal changes that are indirectly influenced by research. It is necessary to understand these processes even if our intention were to study innovation. Here, we discuss this at a system level, in line with Etzkowitz and Leydesdorff (2000). They argue that:

> This network of relations generates a reflexive subdynamics of intentions, strategies, and projects that adds surplus value by reorganising and harmonising continuously the underlying infrastructure in order to achieve at least an approximation of the goals. . . . Innovation systems, and the relationships among them, are apparent at the organisational, local, regional, national, and multinational levels. The interacting subdynamics, that is, specific operations like markets and technological innovations, are continuously reconstructed like commerce on the Internet, yet differently at different levels. The subdynamics and the levels are also reflexively reconstructed through discussions and negotiation in the Triple Helix. What is considered as "industry", what as "market" cannot be taken for granted and should not be reified. Each "system" is defined and can be redefined as the research project is designed.
>
> (Etzkowitz & Leydesdorff 2000, p. 113)

This *"subdynamics reflexively reconstructed through discussions and negotiation in the Triple Helix"* is our point of interest. A region, in geographical terms, can refer to both large and small areas (i.e. the Nordic countries will for some form a European region). Our use of the term refers to the fact that there is a proximity dimension between institutions and actors. A region, in our use of the word, is thus an area containing a set of actors and institutions that have a major influence on social and economic development, are related to each other and communicate or at least are part of the same discourse.

A knowledge system

Burkart Holzner (1968) and Holzner and Marx (1979) argue for a sociology of knowledge that "investigates the socio-cultural processes which shape the construction of reality, identifies the effects of modes of reality construction on social structure, and looks into the distribution of reality constructs in the social structure" (Holzner 1968, p. 18).

Holzner furthermore, and in line with Berger and Luckmann (1991), deliberately argues for a position on the construction of social reality (or sociology of knowledge) that draws on phenomenology (like Schütz [1972] and Merleau-Ponty [1994]). Holzner (1968) argues that we should avoid the larger debates on the development of our perception of reality as such, but rather have a more limited agenda of situational analysis of the formation of everyday, practical, reflective, contextual, learning based, how-to-do-it-knowledge and knowledge building. We can discuss which type of knowledge is constructed in society, and in specific situations. This allows us to look at socially constructed knowledge without implying a complete epistemology.

Holzner's argument is similar to Bourdieu (1980) that society, deliberately or indirectly, controls actions. The constructions of knowledge are a product of constraints in interactions. Holzner argues that knowledge has a controlling effect on action, so controlling knowledge is a way to regulate society. There are three main areas of control: orientations, situations and communication. Orientation is controlled through cultural socialisation, education and rules. Situations are controlled through rituals and norms and expectation related to different roles: what is appropriate to do at work, in the church or in class? Communication is controlled both directly, in limiting information flows, but also indirectly, through the type of normative references inherent in the language. The concepts by which we address issues are themselves inherently formed by our perceptions and beliefs. In a technical sense, we can talk about a hermeneutical dimension to our perception.

These control mechanisms have to be seen in relation to the underlying theory of how we as humans learn and are socialised. The micro process Holzner refers to is that of social and development psychologies, where rewards, punishments and recognitions are the main factors in forming the child's social orientation. As adults we meet these mechanisms again, as cognitively developed frames of references that we reproduce in our actions. Networks and epistemic communities are regulative systems that presuppose compliance with rules and norms. They develop in parallel with identity formations, and there is a sort of self-closing, auto-poetic process by which social structuring is reinforced.

The term knowledge system has increasingly been used in organisational studies. The point made by Tsoukas (1996) is that our understanding of the organisation as a knowledge system draws on research at societal level. At the same time, we might argue that we can apply to the societal debate some of the insights from the discussion at an organisational level. Tsoukas argues:

> Recently, Spender . . . has suggested a "pluralistic epistemology", seeking to capture the different types of knowledge that organisations make use of. For him knowledge can be held by an individual or a collectivity. Also, knowledge can be articulated explicitly or manifested implicitly – namely, it is, respectively, *more or less abstracted from* practice. Thus, there are four types of organisational knowledge: conscious (explicit knowledge held by the individual); objectified (explicit knowledge held by the organisation); automatic *(preconscious* individual knowledge); and collective (highly context-dependent knowledge which is manifested in the practice of an organisation).
>
> (Tsoukas 1996, p. 14)

We will argue that these four knowledge forms are relevant to our discussion:

- conscious (explicit knowledge held by the individual)
- objectified (explicit knowledge held by the organisation)
- automatic (preconscious individual knowledge)
- collective (highly context-dependent knowledge which is manifested in the practice of an organisation).

Of course, a key issue is how these varieties of knowledge are changed. Here, Tsoukas refers back to social theory. He argues:

> Attempting to synthesise the work of Parsons, Bourdieu, and of several ethnomethodologists, . . . has suggested that social practices be viewed as consisting of three dimensions. First, the social position or role dimension, namely the normative expectations that are associated with the carrying out of a particular role. [. . .] Secondly, the dispositional dimension, namely the system of mental patterns of perception, appreciation, and action, which has been acquired by an individual via past socialisations and is brought to bear on a particular situation of action. . . . Finally, the interactive-situational dimension, namely the specific context of a social activity within which normative expectations and the *habitus* are activated. This dimension is similar to Goffman's . . . "interaction order" and . . . it is what gives social interaction its open-ended character.
>
> (Tsoukas 1996, pp. 17–18)

We think these are important dimensions to be considered in our own discussion:

- the social position or role dimension
- the dispositional dimension
- the interactive-situational dimension
- the institutional dimension.

Table I.4 The knowledge system

	Power: the social position or role dimension	*Beliefs: the dispositional dimension*	*Position: the interactive-situational dimension*	*Institutions: the knowledge-institutionalisation dimension*
Individual, explicit knowledge	What are the dominant strategies	What values are underlying dominant strategies	Who are gatekeepers for dominant strategies	What institutions exist
Collective, explicit knowledge	What is the social position of the organisations – their ability to influence	What is considered relevant	Who are the influencing institutions	What is the strategy of the institution
Individual, implicit knowledge	Who has the knowledge	How do persons interpret	What are people's positions and personal networks	How do institutions preserve knowledge forms
Collective, implicit knowledge	Who is in power to decide over knowledge	What is the nature of social deliberation	What is the network structure	How inflexible are the institutions

This book takes a pragmatic perspective on different positions within the sociology of knowledge. The perspective we present below build on a combination of the theories we have presented in this introduction. Table I.4 presents a framework for how to understand the different dimensions of knowledge in a knowledge system. We exemplify what these different dimensions mean with relevant questions.

The argument that can be read from this table is that what eventually comes out as knowledge is somehow illustrated by the questions in the table. A knowledge system can be divided into a set of sub questions. We have put emphasis on power*: the social position or role dimension*, in Part I. The chapters in this part will illustrate how the formation of knowledge is defined by the institutional arrangement and political priorities of the region. Part II of the book has chapters that illustrate beliefs; *the dispositional dimension.* The chapters in this part discuss how applied social sciences challenges established beliefs in the region. The chapters in Part III have a focus on position; *the interactive-situational dimension.* Chapters in Part IV focus on institutions: *the knowledge-institutionalisation dimension.*

The 16 different positions in the table give us a set of dimensions, factors and questions that cover the main issues in this book, and thus help explain how knowledge is developed in a certain social context. What the table tells us is that this development is multidimensional, dependent not only on the knowledge itself, but on who presents it, what other beliefs it relates to and the context of power and position for the new knowledge. These sub questions, and the dimensions they relate to, tell us about how adaptive a knowledge system is to new knowledge, and who is in a position to change knowledge. We use this framework throughout the book and in the concluding chapter, where we summarise some findings from the chapters and reflect on the learning from this book project.

The context of our case

We present projects from one case: the Agder region of Norway. The Agder region is the southernmost region in Norway, with some 250,000 inhabitants. It is a region without a long academic tradition, and got its first university in 2007. In this respect, it is a rather young region in adapting to what we can call the knowledge society. Chapter 13: The Mittelstand gives an overview of the business structure of the region.

Over recent decades, there have been several waves of establishing a knowledge infrastructure in Norwegian regions. A first wave came in the 1970s, when regional colleges were established. All regions got their own college. A second wave of this development came in the 1980s and 90s, when regional research institutes focusing on economics and social science were established. Again, all regions in Norway got their own regional applied research institute, often co-financed by the state, counties and local industry and businesses. Agder Research is an example of this development. Although consultancy firms could respond to calls, collaborating with applied research institutes, there was a political intention to develop semi-public research institutes that would accumulate and apply knowledge in social and economic processes in the region.

Part of this regional turn was to develop the regionally located research institutions. These had to balance being locally specific and nationally relevant, without weakening national education and research institutions. Regional colleges exemplify this. In Norway, this development contributed to a long historical discussion about centralised versus decentralised solutions to social and economic development.

Regional research institutes, although mostly funded by public and private regional actors, received basic funding from the state. Chapter 1: Developing a sustainable business model in a changing economy in this book gives more details on this financial structure. These institutes often have a large proportion of their research and development work related to the local region, are part of the policy instruments in the region and are seen as part of the regional institutional infrastructure. Chapter 3: Knowledge transfer in different regional contexts and Chapter 12: Regional knowledge infrastructure try to explain how this concept of an institutional infrastructure has been developed further in recent years, labelled as the regional innovation system, the regional research system, the triple helix or the regional incubator system.

After 2000, three of the regional colleges in Norway were allowed to become universities. Among those were Agder University College. There is an ongoing debate in Norway, as in most European countries, about the structure of higher education, and what roles different institutions should have. Strong voices still want differentiation between national and regional institutions. There is also an ongoing debate about the structure of the applied research sector in Norway, and a strong push towards fewer, bigger and more international research communities, something Chapter 1 also touches upon.

We present this context, even though this book is not supposed to present a comprehensive study of the region. Rather, the different chapters represent aspects and themes that have had priority in the regional development discourse or ought to be there. Our main interest, however, is to try to understand what goes on in knowledge creation in a region. We therefore look for some of the more general learnings that can be extracted from the different studies and across the different studies and cases. In line with this we can reformulate the research question that this book will be addressing as: *how is knowledge developed in a reflective reconstruction within a regional context, and what is the role of applied social sciences in this process?*

The structure of the book

The contributions to this book have been grouped into four parts. The following outlines the methodological issues that are addressed in the chapters:

In Part I, describing regional practice, we present the context – the region and studies that deliberately aim at influencing regional policy. These studies relate to the policy frameworks and discourses in the region. Chapters 1, 2 and 3 discuss structural/institutional preconditions for knowledge development in a region. Chapters 2 and 3 argue that institutional arrangements influence the learning capacity, and development dynamics, in regions.

Part II is mainly about understanding regional practice. The chapters present studies that predominantly have an interpretive perspective. Several chapters in this book, particularly Chapters 4, 5 and 9, address conflict. The problem of power is explicitly discussed in Chapters 5 and 9. Chapter 7 argues for the need to see people as humans and as complex individuals, rather than categories. This idea of research as conceptualising practice is also discussed in Chapters 11, 13, 14 and 15.

Part III of the book presents studies that mainly aim to explain regional practice. Common to these studies is that they have a proactive ambition to be able to say something about causes, and important and decisive dimensions for social development. Power in more indirect forms is discussed in Chapters 6, 7, 10 and 14. Chapter 6 links to the discussion in Chapter 5, on the role of researchers in being critical, redefining research questions and challenging existing knowledge.

The fourth part of the book presents studies that mainly aim to influence and change regional social practice. Common to these studies is that they have a strong, normative objective. In the concluding chapter of this book, we pull together some of the insights from the discussions in the chapters, and return to some of the overriding questions we have addressed here in the introduction.

Part I

The spatial dimension of knowledge development

In this part we present chapters that give insight into both the institutional set up of Norwegian regions, as part of what we later in the book discuss as The Norwegian Model, and a discussion of concepts that can help us understand knowledge development in the region. The chapters aim to describe regional practice. They also aim to influence and change practice; however, we emphasise here their descriptive dimension. This part of the book will help the reader understand some of the institutional set-up and processes of knowledge development that we find in a Norwegian region. All four chapters in this part make comparison to other regions of geographical areas.

Chapter 1: Developing a sustainable business model in a changing economy presents the regional paradigm. It divides applied research into three types: commissioned, contributory and participatory. It demonstrates how regional research institutes receive both contributory and commissioned funding, thus developing applied research in general, as well as contract research. The chapter also demonstrates how academic credibility has become more important in applied research.

Chapter 2: Why Norway has to develop its own innovation policy argues that the region can be understood in different ways in terms of modes of innovation. This calls for a contextualised understanding of innovation, on how research can support innovation. The main argument is that Norway in general has a more learning mode of innovation than found in other countries that rank high in innovation indexes. This is partly due to the fact that incremental, learning and social trust and interaction are difficult to measure in international rankings.

Chapter 3: Knowledge transfer in different regional contexts tries to develop a typology of regional institutional setups. It divides between institutional thin and thick regions and diverse or specialised regional innovation systems (RIS). It connects this to forms of knowledge exchange, where there is a divide between static and dynamic, and between formal and informal. This typology places Agder in the category of thick and specialised regional innovation system.

Chapter 4: Collective knowing argues that regional innovation is a matter of collective knowing. Based on cases from Spain and from Agder, Norway, the argument is that knowledge development happens as a process over time and is dependent on building trust and developing a common language.

compelled to develop without the support of the long-existing scientific and academic traditions which the national institutions in the major cities have. In this early phase, most of the institutes were financed by national and regional authorities, both general financing of institutional activities and project financing. This provided financial predictability.

In the 1990s, RCN's regional policy was the driving force in the further development of the regional research institutes.[1] This regional policy is based on a notion that distribution of knowledge is a fundamental driver for innovation. Furthermore, it is also based on the assumption that knowledge about the specific natural, cultural, economic and historical context within distinct regions is a prerequisite for regional development and innovation. In the 2000s, the regional institutions, both research institutes and university colleges, regained some momentum as central actors in what has been labelled the *new regional paradigm* (see Table 1.1). Whereas the old paradigm of regional policy centred on decision making by the central government, the new paradigm recognised regional specificities and complexities which called for a need to design and shape regional policies at the regional level. This has involved a place-based policy with focus on mixed, integrated and bottom-up approaches (Vanthillo & Verhetsel 2012). This implies that regional development and innovation warrant close collaboration between regional stakeholders and regional research institutes. In this respect the regional institutes may play the role as "brokers" between research and private/public sector, or they may operate as partners in common projects. In both cases they contribute due to their knowledge about the region and as an important part of the knowledge infrastructure in the specific region. Later in this chapter we introduce the term *participatory research*, where knowledge about both the regional partners, and the region as such, are important ingredients.

The establishment of regional research funds in 2010, as well as the Programme for Regional R&D and Innovation (VRI-programme) launched

Table 1.1 Old and new paradigms of regional policy

	Old paradigms	*New paradigms*
Objectives	Compensating temporarily for location disadvantages of lagging regions	Tapping underutilised potential in all regions for enhancing regional competitiveness
Unit of intervention	Administrative units	Functional economic areas
Strategies	Sectoral approach	Integrated development projects
Tools	Subsidies and state aids	Mix of soft and hard capital (capital stock, labour market, business environment, social capital and networks)
Actors	Central government	Different levels of government

Source: OECD 2010.

in 2007, have been important instruments in carrying out this regional policy in Norway. These tools were introduced to support and increase research efforts and subsequently encourage innovation, knowledge development and value creation within the regions. Regional research funds were established to support regionally prioritised efforts and strategies. However, they were also expected to enhance competence and develop relevant and competitive research communities in all regions. In spite of this regional policy, as much as 50% of the total public and private research and development (R&D) activity in Norway remains concentrated in the capital region of Oslo and Akershus.

In the 2000s, regional research institutes became increasingly affected by changes in regulations governing public tenders. The background for these regulations was a desire to improve public use of resources, secure equal treatment of market-based actors and to strengthen competition in these markets (NOU 2012, p. 2). For the regional research institutes, one implication has been increased competition from consulting firms offering evaluations, analyses and smaller studies for public principles. During the same period the competition to obtain financing from RCN has increased substantially, and now attracts an increased number of national and regional competitors. The basic grant to the research institutes is based on, among other things, the number of scientifically merited publications and the size of the academic staff. Due to demanding financial conditions in regional institutes, many researchers work with shorter assignments with little room for prioritising scientific publication, and hence most regional research institutes score lower than the national institutes on peer-reviewed publications. In smaller institutions, academic staff also often lack sufficient academic merit to pursue research activities of high quality resulting in scientific publications. This can be defined as a *catch-22* situation.

Recently, there has been a debate regarding the optimal size of research institutes in Norway.[2] There seems to be a consensus that larger research communities, which are more oriented towards scientific publications of high quality, are the way forward. To secure sustainable institutions, the lower limit for receiving a basic grant from RCN is defined to be 20 full-time equivalent researchers. On average, the regional institutes receive 12% of their income through the basic grant and other grants from RCN, with an additional 23% coming from competition-based research projects from RCN (contributory funding). In comparison, the total share for national institutes from RCN is 10 percentage points higher, including a higher basic grant.

From this, we argue that regional research institutes now need to adapt to a situation with increased competition in *all* markets; not only against national and international research institutes with better and more secure financial terms, but also with consulting firms and universities in need of external funding. At the same time, most of the regional institutes continue to define themselves as regional, with a clearly stated goal of contributing to various regional development processes, as originally intended. In practice, the most successful regional institutes have taken on roles as national institutes, maintaining a high academic level which makes them competitive in national and international research arenas.

Many regional institutes maintain that they have an improved relationship with the private sector, which is not affected by the strict regulations governing the system of public tenders. This relationship was reinforced by the establishment of the *triple helix* concept of research-industry-government relationships initiated in the late 1990s (Etzkowitz & Leydesdorff 1997). Triple helix became an influential policy concept that emphasised the potential for innovation and economic development by the hybridisation of elements from the three mentioned arenas (also exemplified in the VRI-programme (presented in Chapters 2, 3 and 12 in this book). As a result, some regional institutes have more emphasis on commercial innovation and development, and less research devoted to social and political development in the public sector. This kind of specialisation may be a good way to compensate for size, but many institutes have not managed to develop research communities of sufficient scientific merit to be competitive in national and international research arenas. One important question is how the original regional policy of supplying academic and research competence in a broad sense to the regions may be maintained in the future.

Applied regional research institutes, such as Agder Research, must successfully address a complex and often competing set of role expectations in order to secure a sustainable financial and professional business development. In this chapter we identify a typology with three roles for applied research; *contributory*, *commissioned* and *participatory*. These three roles represent different sets of stakeholders, normative expectation, competitors and collaborators, as well as demands on researcher training and expertise. Further complexity is added by increased national standardisation and regulation of the institute sector in addition to the specific characteristics of the set-up of the R&D sector in the Agder region and beyond. Shifts in the competitive situation imply that new business models must be developed in order to secure a sustainable practice for applied research. Based on this our main question is: *how can one develop a sustainable business model for an applied research institute, balancing the different and often conflicting institutional rationalities, demands and expectations?*

We present and analyse data from RCN describing the structure and dynamics of the Norwegian institute sector. The data identifies some factors that seem to support both academic and financial development in the research institutes, and based on an understanding of these dynamics we discuss the previous research question.

The Norwegian institute sector

The research institutes in the Norwegian institute sector were established at different times, with different stakeholders, user groups and policy areas in mind. The gradual and organic growth of the sector has led to considerable variations in size, type of institutes and academic specialisation.

This heterogeneity, in combination with a clear thematic and user-oriented specialisation, is characteristic of the institute sector in Norway. A common feature is that the institutes conduct R&D on a "not for profit" basis and that the organisations do not fit directly under an educational institution (e.g. a university). From this, the research institutes serve markets and develop knowledge for use in the private and public sector. The institutes are consequently inter-disciplinary and market-oriented, and most importantly, participants conduct applied research in Norway.

Structure

RCN is responsible for managing the Norwegian research institute sector. In 2014, they made a revision of the requirements for institutes to receive basic funding:

- Conduct research and dissemination of research in fields that are of interest for Norwegian industry, administration or society.
- Have academic and scientific expertise that is expressed through scientific publications in reputable publication channels.
- Have sufficient research activity so that real competence development happens in the organisation.
- Have multiple sources of income and participate in an open competition for national and international research funding.
- Be integrated in an appropriate division of labour in the Norwegian research system.
- Owners or individual companies may not be given preferential research results funded by basic funding.
- Must be organised and operated so that no dividend is paid.
- Must practise the principles of academic freedom.

The Norwegian research institutes are divided into five arenas: (1) technical-industrial, (2) social science, (3) regional, (4) environmental and (5) primary industry. Key figures are shown in Table 1.2.

Table 1.2 The Norwegian institute sector

Year 2013	*n*	*Revenue (*)*	*Operating profit (**)*	*Size (***)*	*Research staff (****)*
The technical-industrial	14	5,176.4	49.2	3,485	2,334
Social science	16	1,022.4	7.2	874	689
Regional	11	303.9	–3.3	283	249
Environment	8	1,077.4	–30.7	932	680
Primary industry	9	2,776.5	–5.6	2,402	1,113
Total	58	10,356.6	16.8	7,976	5,065

Note: (*) NOK mill., excluding revenue transferred to other (**) NOK mill. (***) Full-time equivalent FTE, and (****) FTEs.

Table 1.2 shows that the technical-industrial institutes are the largest group, with SINTEF and its 2,000 employees located in Trondheim as the largest institute. Agder Research is a social science institute, but is categorised into the group of regional institutes in this table.

Funding

The research institutes included in the basic funding system receive their funding from three main sources:

- *Contributory funding;* projects where the institute obtains support from national and international funding for their own activities, without contractual relations that are mutually burdening (without concession for support entered).
- *Commissioned research;* projects that the institute performs for consideration from an external principal(s), and where the contractual relationship is mutually burdened with the requirement specified in return from institution at the time of contract signing.
- *Basic funding;* free funding made available from RCN, or other funding agencies (without concession for support entered).

Table 1.3 shows the revenue streams of the institutes divided into the three main groups of funding sources. The table shows that the regional research institutes have a higher commissioned/contributory ratio than the social science institutes, while the technical-industrial institutes maintain the highest share of commissioned research. As we discuss later, the division between basic, contributory and commissioned funding has strong implications for the performance of the institutes.

Publications and research experience

One performance indicator emphasised by RCN is the research institutes' amount of publication points, one point roughly being the equivalent of one

Table 1.3 Funding sources in 2013

	n	*Total number of projects*	*Commissioned revenue*	*Contributory revenue*	*Basic funding*
The technical-industrial	14	1,0301	2,683.9	770.1	433.5
Social science	16	1,887	297.2	348.3	219.7
Regional	11	1,327	166.4	88.8	41.0
Environmental	8	3,142	381.6	354.1	166.9
Primary industry	9	3,795	383.3	841	269.1
Total	58	20,452	3,912.4	2,402.3	1,130.2

Note: In NOK mill. and excluding revenue transferred to others.

Table 1.4 Publications and research experience 2013

	n	*Publication (*)*	*Research experience (**)*	*Research experience development (***)*
The technical industrial	14	0.43	52%	7%
Social science	16	1.34	55%	8%
Regional	11	0.53	42%	9%
Environmental	8	0.67	54%	7%
Primary industry	9	0.61	76%	5%
Total	58			

Note: (*) Points per research position, (**) employees with a doctorate per research position, (***) percentage point growth of employees with doctorate 2009–2013.

journal article or one book chapter per research full-time employee (FTE). We see from the following table that the social science institutes are the most productive group with respect to this dimension. This table also shows that the formal competence level, measured as the share of employees with a doctorate, has increased by between 5% and 9% from 2009 until 2013. On average, in 2013, over half of the employees in the institute sector hold a doctorate.

Collaboration

The following table gives an indication of how much the institutes depend upon internal personnel resources in their R&D activities. On average, the institutes collaborate with others in about one tenth of their projects. Collaboration, measured by personnel in and out, is relatively modest on average, but also here with large variations between the institutes. At SINTEF as a whole, a quarter of its employees (500) have positions both at NTNU (Norwegian University of Science and Technology in Trondheim) and in SINTEF.[3] This indicator is important and, as we shall we see later,

Table 1.5 Collaboration 2013

	n	*Collaboration, personnel OUT (*)*	*Collaboration, personnel IN (**)*	*Collaboration projects (***)*
The technical-industrial	14	1.2%	1.3%	10.9%
Social science	16	2.4%	3.6%	12.0%
Regional	11	2.2%	3.6%	12.4%
Environmental	8	0.8%	1.3%	5.3%
Primary industry	9	1.3%	1.6%	12.8%
Total	58			

Note: (*) FTEs performed at other institutions in percentage of research FTE 2013. (**) FTEs performed at the institute of researchers employed at another institution in percentage of research FTE 2013 (***) Revenue transferred to other per research FTE 2013.

turns out to be essential in the understanding of why some institutes perform better than others when it comes to the degree of contributory funding and publication points.

Profitability

Table 1.6 shows that the institutes in practice are "not for profit" institutions. Collectively, the sector faces serious challenges and more than half of the institutes lost money in 2013 (median is a negative operating profit of NOK 100,000). In the following we will analyse these data more in detail, supported by data from RCN. We will try to identify the variables with the strongest explanatory power, in order to understand why some institutes are most productive in terms of publication points than others, as well as why some institutes are more profitable than others.

Analysis of the institute sector

Norwegian research institutes that receive basic funding from RCN must annually report information on a wide range of variables describing the activities of the institute. In our analyses, we utilise the data reported for 2013, due to the fact that these are the latest figures available. The variables selected for the conducted analyses are described below. We have also checked for other relevant variables and composites available in the reports from RCN. However, we only present the variables with explanatory power relating to our research question.

There are some methodological limitations to this approach. First, since we only analyse data from 2013, we cannot claim causality in our analysis, only correlation. Future studies of this topic should be longitudinal. Second, we recognise that there are important factors and variables that would explain the performance of the institutes that are not reported in the RCN reports. This includes the critical mass dimension, i.e. how large the research groups per research area are. This is recognised in the literature as an important dimension for developing more sustainable knowledge organisations (Horwitz, Heng & Quazi 2003; Johnsen 2014; Zack 2005).

Table 1.6 Profitability

	n	*Operating profit (*)*	*Descriptives*	
The technical-industrial	14	3.51	Mean	0.29
Social science	16	0.45	Standard error	1.39
Regional	11	–0.30	Median	–0.10
Environmental	8	–3.84	Mode	0.70
Primary industry	9	–0.62	Standard deviation	10.62
Total	58			

Note: (*) Mill. NOK on average 2013.

Table 1.7 Model and variables for analyses

Input variables	*Description (independent)*	*Performance measures*	*Description (dependent)*
Turnover	Departure of academic staff in % of academic FTEs 2013	*Total revenue*	NOK mill., excluding revenue transferred to other per research FTEs 2013
Project structure	Less than 0.1 mill. per FTE above 0.5 mill. per FTE above 2.0 mill. per FTE	*Publications*	Points per research position 2013
Funding structure	BASIC, (%), excluding revenue transferred to other of total revenue 2013	*Control variables*	No data available and not controlled for
	COMMISSIONED, (%), excluding revenue transferred to other of total revenue 2013 CONTRIBUTORY (%), excluding revenue transferred to other of total revenue 2013	*Work organisation*	Values Norms Strategy Culture Organisation Routines Structure Leadership Administration
Collaboration	Personnel OUT Personnel IN Project		
Size	Full-time equivalent FTE 2013		
Administration	% of FTEs		
Research experience	Employees with doctorate per researcher position 2013	*Critical mass*	Research FTE per administrative unit 2013 Research FTE per research area 2013

In addition, the competence, experience, history and strategic position of an institute within a particular research area are most likely very relevant variables, and RCN should maybe aspire to collect data relating to these dimensions in the future.

Third, a critical dimension not covered in these analyses is the impact of the work organisation itself. Factors such as organisational culture, leadership, administrative routines and structures, strategies and goals, participation and involvement at work, organisational design and more, are all important for understanding the performance of knowledge organisations. We believe that much of the unexplained variance in the regression analyses below is likely to be related to specific features of such work organisations.

Performance measure 1: publications

The following figure shows the regression plots for publications, operationalised as publication points per research position in 2013. The model with the most explanatory power in relation to this consists of three variables that all correlate positively with level of publication. These are: basic funding (in %), number of projects above NOK 2.0 mill per research FTE

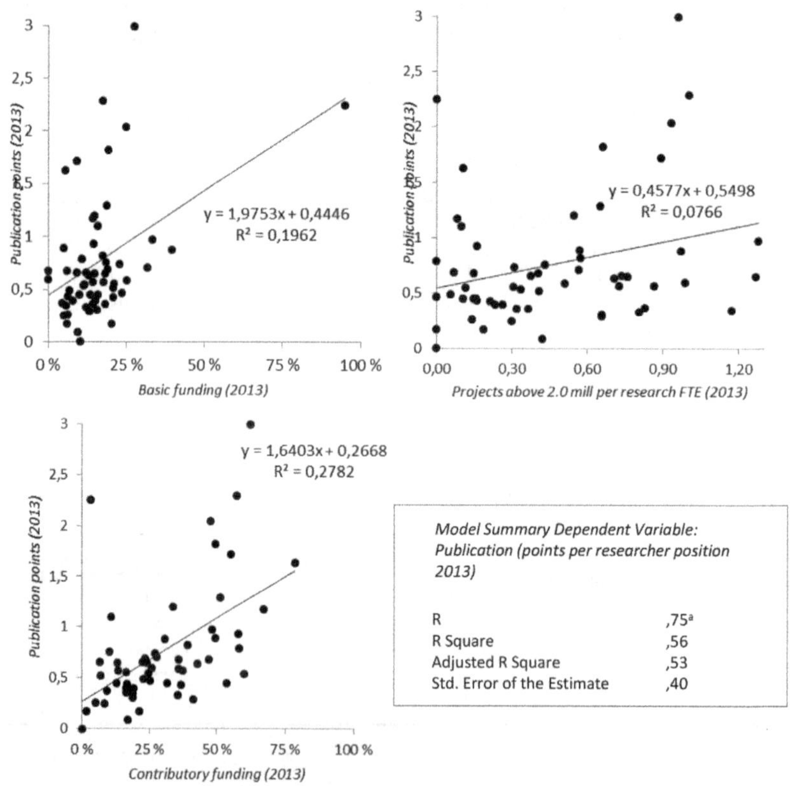

Model Summary Dependent Variable: Publication (points per researcher position 2013)

R	,75[a]
R Square	,56
Adjusted R Square	,53
Std. Error of the Estimate	,40

Figure 1.1 Regression plots for publication

Note: Predictors: (constant), funding structure (% contributory, excluding revenue transferred to other of total revenue 2013), funding structure (% basic, excluding revenue transferred to other of total revenue 2013), project structure (projects above 2.0 mill per research FTE 2013).

Sig.: Basic funding	.000
Project above 2.0 mill.	.059
Contributory funding	.000

and contributory funding (in %). The explanatory power of this model is approximately 56 %.

The single variable with the most explanatory power for publication points is, not surprisingly, contributory funding. This is most likely due to the fact that the main output from research projects often are academic publications. In the following regression analyses, we therefore identify the model with the most explanatory power for contributory funding.

Contributory funding

The model includes three variables: (1) research experience understood as employees with doctorate per researcher position, (2) academic publications

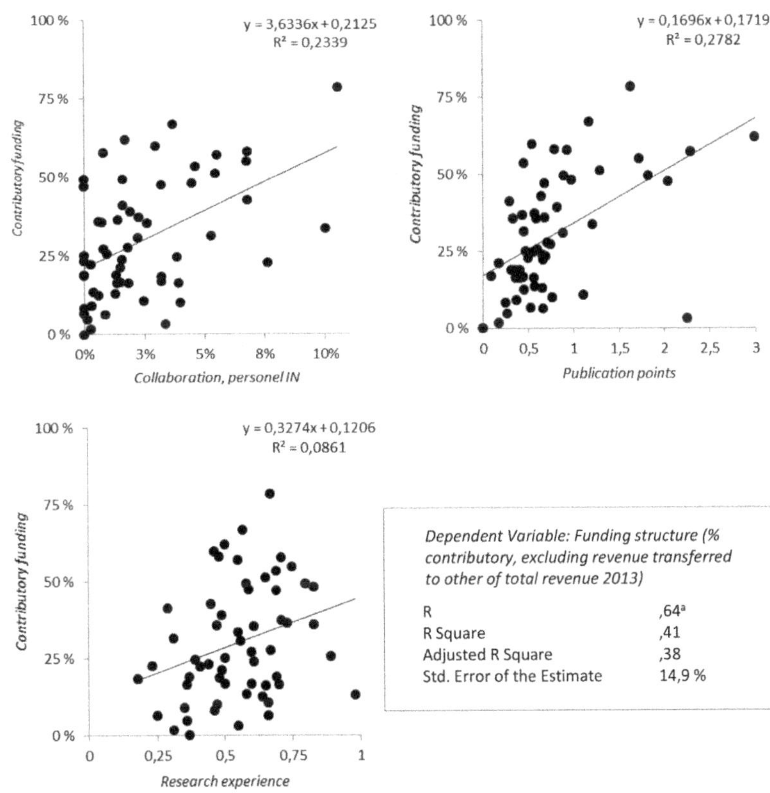

Dependent Variable: Funding structure (% contributory, excluding revenue transferred to other of total revenue 2013)

R	,64[a]
R Square	,41
Adjusted R Square	,38
Std. Error of the Estimate	14,9 %

Figure 1.2 Regression plots for contributory funding

Note: Predictors: (constant), research experience (employees with doctorate per researcher position 2013), collaboration, personnel IN (FTEs performed at the institute of researchers employed at another institution in % of research FTE 2013), publication (points per researcher position 2013).

Sig.: Collaboration IN .003
Publication .005
Research experience .088

and (3) collaboration with other institutions. The third variable is operationalised as Full-Time-Equivalents (FTEs) performed at the institute by researchers who have their main employment at another institution, measured in percent of the total research FTE at the institute. The model explains about 41% of the variance.

Collaboration

The finding that research experience and publication itself has a positive impact on the level of contributory funding in the institutes is not surprising. Institutes do not typically collaborate extensively. The regression model below shows the best fit model for explaining which institutions attracts personnel (collaboration in). It consists of two variables: (1) contributory funding and (2) collaboration out. The second variable, collaboration out, is a measure of the percentage of full-time employees at the research institute who also have employment at another institution. This explains about 31% of the variance in the model. In the following figure we explore the model showing the regression plots for commissioned funding.

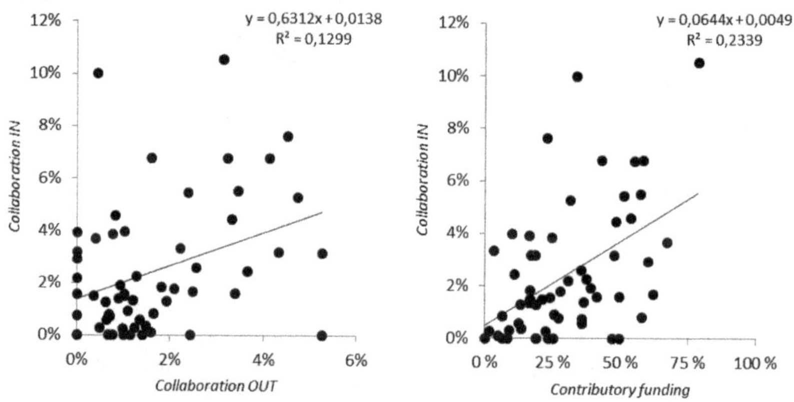

Dependent variable: collaboration, personnel IN (FTEs performed at the Institute of researchers employed at another institution in % of research FTE 2013)

R	,56ᵃ
R square	,31
Adjusted R square	,29
Std. error of the estimate	2,1 %

Figure 1.3 Regression plots for collaboration IN

Note: Predictors: (constant), funding structure (% contributory, excluding revenue transferred to other of total revenue 2013), collaboration, personel OUT (FTEs performed at other institution in % of research FTE 2013).

Sig.: Collaboration OUT .016
Contributory funding .000

Commissioned funding

The model consists of four variables, (1) contributory funding, (2) publication points, (3) small projects and (4) research experience. Three of the variables are negatively correlated with commissioned funding, namely contributory funding, publication points and research experience. The only variable positively correlated with commissioned funding is the number of small projects (less than NOK 100,000) per research FTE. The model as a whole explains 63% of the variance.

The earlier models tell the following story: Research institutes characterised by high levels of publication are those with large basic and contributory funding, preferably conducted through large projects. Furthermore, they are characterised by a high degree of research experience among employees (defined as a large percentage of employees with a doctorate). Interestingly, they also have the characteristic of being network organisations, measured by a large percentage of their own employees working for other institutions as well as having employees from other institutions working part time at the research institute.

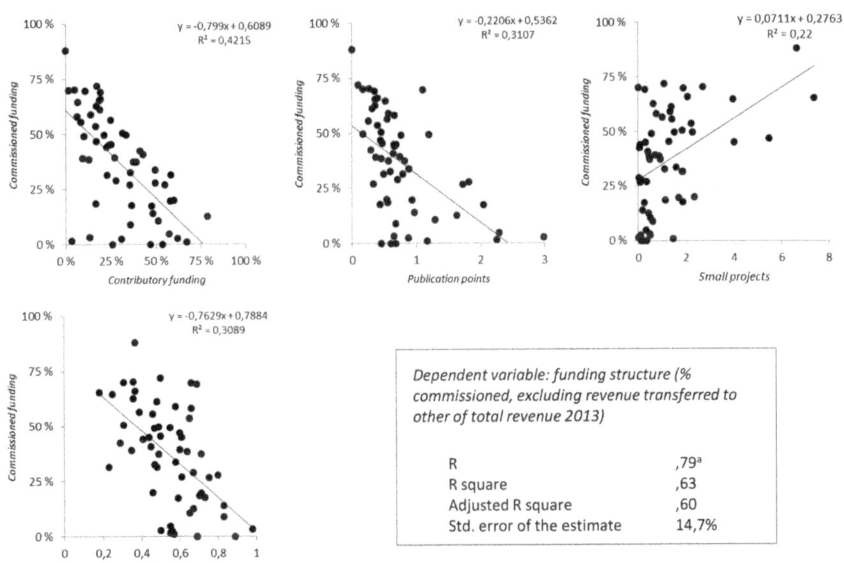

Figure 1.4 Regression plots for commissioned funding

Note: Predictors: (constant), research experience (employees with doctorate per researcher position 2013), publication (points per researcher position 2013), project structure (projects less than 0.1 mill per research FTE 2013), funding structure (% contributory, excluding revenue transferred to other of total revenue 2013).

Sig.: Contributory funding	.000
Publication points	.043
Small projects	.103
Research experience	.002

Our second performance measure in this analysis relates to the financial performance of the institutes. As presented earlier, over half of the research institutes lost money in 2013. Sustainable practice for applied research must imply that the institutes have a sound and solid financial status. In the following regression model we have identified the three variables that combined have the largest explanatory power relating to revenue.

Revenue is operationalised as total revenue per researcher in a full-time equivalent (FTE). The three variables are size (FTE in 2013), research experience (employees with doctorate per research position), and percentage of contributory funding. The model as a whole explains about 51% of the variation, and it is the variable size that explains most of the variation. Large institutions are more profitable measured by revenue. Research experience also correlates positively with revenue. However, the most interesting insight with this model is that contributory funding correlates negatively with revenue. It is not much, about 8%, but one could expect this to be a positive relationship, because contributory projects are often longer term and larger than commissioned projects.

Performance measure 2: total revenue

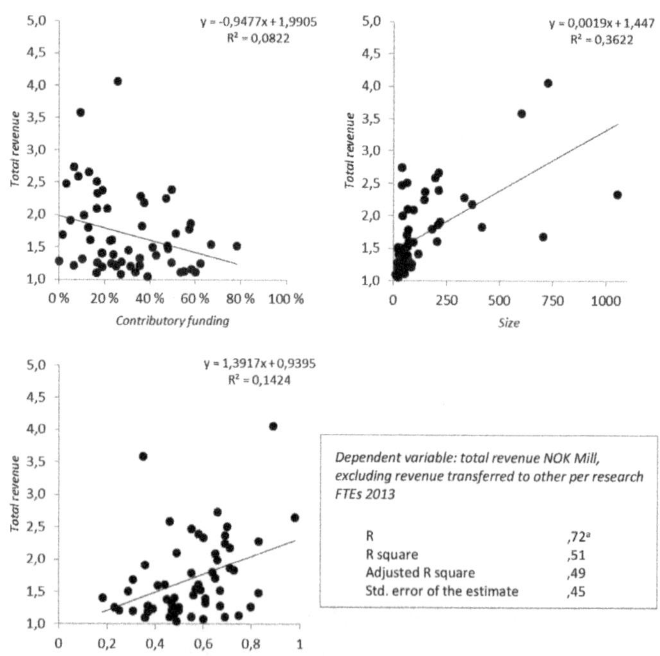

Figure 1.5 Regression plots for total revenue

Note: Predictors: (constant), research experience (employees with doctorate per researcher position 2013), size (full-time equivalent FTE 2013), funding structure (% contributory, excluding revenue transferred to other of total revenue 2013).

Sig.:	Contributory funding	.007
Size		.000
Research experience		.000

A path toward a sustainable business model for applied research

Findings

The data from RCN's Annual Institute Indicator Report shows that there are contradictions in the incentive structure for the research institutes. On the one hand, the institutes are expected to conduct research and disseminate research in fields that are of interest for Norwegian industry, administration or society (Meld.St.18 2012–2013). This will in its most direct form imply that research institutes conduct more commissioned work to solve particular challenges of various societal groups. On the other hand, research institutes are expected to have academic and scientific expertise, at the same time as they conduct high quality research, expressed through scientific publications in reputable publication channels.

In the data presented earlier, we have shown that: (1) contributory funding is strongly and positively correlated with publications, whereas (2) commissioned work consequently is strongly and negatively correlated with academic dissemination, in addition to most other factors showing an impact on publication levels (see subsequent figure). This can be seen as an unresolved cross-pressure in relation to the goals set by the government and RCN.

Our second finding is that different sets of variables explain the research institutes' financial status and the institutes' academic success respectively. The only common variable is research experience. Some of these connections are attempted illustrated in the following figure.

As previously shown, commissioned funding correlates negatively with all factors explaining scientific publications. From this, we argue that we have identified the first competing institutional demand that a sustainable business model for a research institute needs to address. The somewhat surprising negative relationship between contributory funding and financial status could be a result of the increased competition in the sector, where institutes having a large percentage of their projects in this category also use a substantial amount of resources on tenders and acquisitions to obtain these research projects.

The elements in the figures presented do not point to a single strategy that secures success within the field of applied research in regional institutes. As mentioned earlier, we also need to consider other important variables relating to the organisation and structure of the work organisation in order

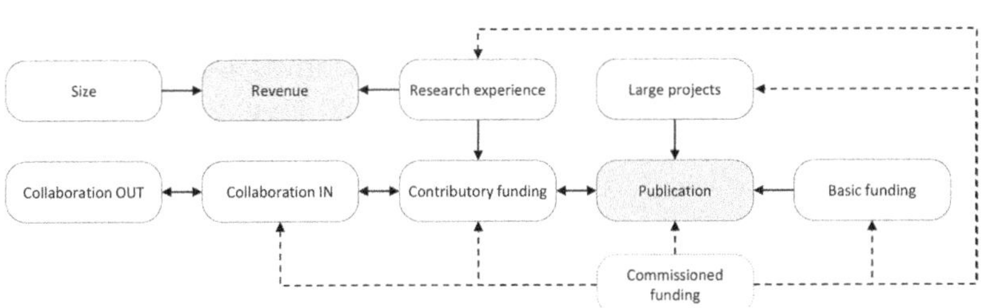

Figure 1.6 Sustainable circles model

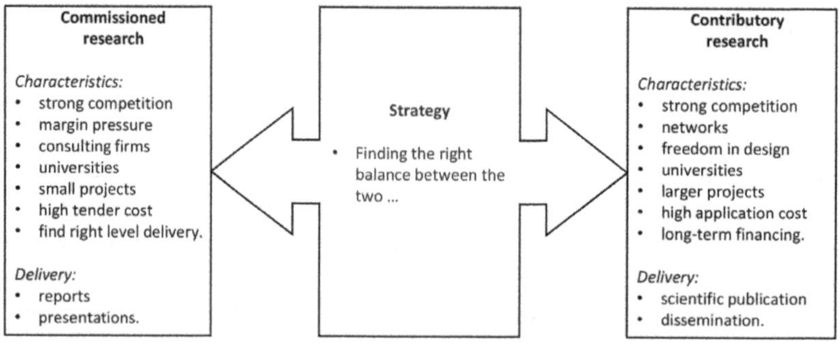

Figure 1.7 Balancing roles, funding and deliveries

to get a more complete picture (Johnsen 2014). From the data, however, we argue that there seems to be a contradiction between the performance measures, revenue and publications, and the type of funding, commissioned, basic and contributory. Looking at the instructions from RCN, there may also be a challenge in fulfilling the expected roles of both: (1) being relevant, measured by commissioned research and (2) producing research of high quality, measured by publications.

However, there might also be something wrong with us thinking of the roles of applied research as a dichotomy, where it is either commissioned or contributory. Is there a potential for expanding the scope of applied research and transcending this dichotomy? The question then becomes what a sustainable business model for applied research might contain. Can one regard this "stretch" as an asset, and hence a possibility, more than a challenge? How should one respond to these challenges?

Response to the challenges of balancing roles, funding and deliveries

Many Norwegian research institutes struggle with finding their way forward and defining the optimal balance between their various roles. One challenge is to find the right balance between commissioned and contributory research on the dimension of funding and deliveries. Another challenge is how to find the optimal balance between the various roles of these institutes: being regional, national or both, and how to respond to the different expectations. In addition, the definition of relevance changes over time and the research institutes need to develop accordingly to be competitive, also internationally. In this section we present some factors that could support the institutes' strategy in their objectives of being relevant to society, and at the same time delivering high quality research within certain fields.

It will be important to strengthen the areas with the strongest effects on the two performance variables, publications and revenues, and then find the balance between the two in order to transcend the possible dichotomy.

Furthermore, in the strategy development process, it will be crucial to design the proposed actions in such a manner that they reinforce both of the mentioned performance measures. The various initiatives need to push these measures in the right, and preferably in the same, direction.

We know, from the data, that the number and research of researchers' experience are the two variables showing a positive effect on the performance variable revenue. For the performance variable publications, the variables with the strongest positive effect are basic funding, large projects and contributory funding. Derived from this, not surprisingly, the data also show a positive effect of collaboration, publication points and research experience on contributory funding. Based on this, we argue that there is a need to grow, as well as strengthen collaboration and research experience in order to gain more contributory funding. This may in turn lead to more publication points and larger projects and subsequently have a positive effect on revenue and publications.

For the regional research institutes, obtaining sustainable size and high quality academic staff is a long-term process, due to elements like geography, traditions and a possible fragile financial status. Such a process needs to be well planned and part of a long-term strategy. We will now discuss some possible responses to address some of the future challenges for the institute sector in general, and the regional research institutes in particular. These elements are not either/or, and may overlap, but they need to be addressed in one way or another.

Develop research competence

New and increased demand for research competence is prevalent in society in general and in knowledge intensive industries in particular. This also counts for consulting firms that are in the process of giving their services a more scientific form. In order to differentiate themselves, research institutes need to recruit highly qualified researchers and at the same time develop significant research skills in their organisations. There are several paths to obtain this goal, by either educating already employed staff or recruiting employees already holding a doctorate. It will, however, also be necessary to recruit or have access to researchers with project experience and long publication lists, but for that to happen the institute must appear attractive. These issues are difficult to handle and are long-term processes including all of the organisation, its various networks, stakeholders and customers.

Focus on publications

Within each organisation there must be a culture for publishing at all levels, where young and more senior personnel take part in this effort. The number of publications needs to be a key performance indicator internally, according to the measures used by RCN. Senior researchers should be incentivised to support younger and more unexperienced researchers in their publication efforts. One can also implement rewards for publications, for example in the form of research time.

Focus on building strong research networks

The majority of Norwegian research institutes are relatively small, with limited areas of research. First, it is a matter of necessity to draw on other researchers and research communities due to capacity and competence. Second, it is a requirement in most large tenders and projects that several research communities, both national and international, are involved in the project. Strong academic research networks are becoming a competitive advantage for research institutes. Building strong research networks should be an essential part of the overall strategy.

Secure exchange of research personnel

Collaboration is one crucial variable in our data, and has a positive effect on contributory funding, which also has a positive effect on the performance measure publication. Exchange of personnel may contribute to organisations in several ways. It may increase the flexibility for the institute, both when it comes to capacity and competence in times where the project portfolio increases or shrinks within a relatively short time span, but also as valuable resources in tenders. This flexibility may also secure a more stable situation for the rest of the staff. The downside is the available time part-time personnel have to spend within the organisation due to other obligations. Also, if the institute lends out personnel, this may create an internal capacity challenge. Overall, however, exchange of personnel probably has a positive effect on the performance measures.

Participate in various arenas: public and private networks

More and more research is user-oriented. The implication of this trend is that networking is crucial to gain knowledge of existing and future needs, both in the private and public sector. Part of the assignment for the institutes is to be relevant to society. In order to fulfil this task, it is essential that they understand the driving forces for changes in various parts of the society around them. Researchers also need to gain knowledge on how user needs can best be met within the existing and predicted future development, and which framework this can be defined into. More knowledge is needed on impact assessment.

Utilise research competence in commissioned research

In order to differentiate themselves from consulting firms, research institutes must utilise their research competence in commissioned research. Many projects could gain from a scientific approach combined with an applied approach, and thereby give a higher value back to the customer. Research institutes should, however, concentrate efforts in the commissioned market in the areas where they have the greatest research competence. This may ensure further competence development, and at the same time secure relevance. On the other hand, it may be of great value for research projects that the institute has conducted larger commissioned projects within its main research areas. One can argue that it is difficult to design commissioned projects in a manner that makes them applicable for use in publications at a later stage. It may, however, be worthwhile allocating resources in making this a viable solution in order to gain publication points for the institute, especially on larger, long-term commissioned projects.

Secure sustainable financial development

Most of the Norwegian research institutes are "not for profit" organisations. This should not imply that they should be satisfied with financial results at the break-even level. The institutes need a sustainable financial situation in order to manage down turns in the market, as well as being able to take on larger, and often riskier, projects. It is furthermore of great importance that the research institutes are financially sound, and hence able to handle the increased use of "own contribution" into projects. This applies to national projects, but even more so in international projects. Furthermore, institutes need to be aware of the cost driving elements in their organisation, such as the tender cost to project size ratio, non-productive time and other cost elements. Here, the dilemma is short-term profit versus a more long-term strategic thinking, and where many institutes are forced into being too short sighted in their operations due to financial strain. This may lead to loss of future competitiveness and market opportunities.

Competitive advantage through regional relevance

In this chapter, we have aimed to account for the changes taking place in the traditional institute model. We have shown how many of the Norwegian research institutes currently struggle to live up to the standards set for the sector by the RCN. For the regional institutes, we have identified three sets of criteria that may be viewed as conflicting:

1 relevance, where maximising this criterion has, as we have seen, led to a weakened academic development;
2 high quality research, where maximising this criterion leads to lack of interaction with, and relevance for, practice;
3 economic, where both maximising relevance and maximising high quality research affect the institutes' economy.

In sum, we argue that it is critical for Norwegian research institutes to build robust research communities with big enough high quality research groups, high quality networks and a sustainable financial situation. With this in place, the institutes are more likely to increase their competitiveness in several markets.

An additional challenge for the regional institutes is that the new regime also challenges the original mandate of the institutes to bring and develop research competence, in a broad sense, to the regions in which they are situated. There are several research traditions that actively aim to transcend practice-theory dichotomies. These include various forms of action research, as well as many other forms of interactive, participatory oriented research traditions (Carr & Kemmis 1986; Flood 2001; Greenwood & Levin 2007; Gustavsen 2005; Levin 2002; Lewin 1951; Nielsen & Svensson 2006; Reason & Bradbury 2001a; Svensson & Nielsen 2006; Whyte 1991). They all have in common that they have the potential of fitting well into RCN's incentive scheme, even though we are aware of many other challenges this tradition poses (Johnsen & Normann 2004; Vasstrøm & Normann 2014).

The current challenge for the research institutes is that commissioned work and contributory work are often independent knowledge generating circles, where different researchers have specialised themselves in either circle. The potential of participatory modes of research lies in the ability to combine them into a mutually enriching knowledge-generating circle. Participatory research involves planning and conducting research *with* the people and stakeholders under study, so that both sides ideally benefit from the research process. In practice, this often implies temporary partnerships between researchers and stakeholders in the public, private and voluntary sector, organised around the task of studying and resolving issues of both theoretical and practical relevance. This also implies that the involved researchers often function as knowledge brokers between the different spheres of the private and public sector and academia, both within their regions and beyond.

One way forward for the regional institutes is to take advantage of their close connection to their region and regional stakeholders, and utilise this space in their positioning. This may create a competitive advantage and enable them to reposition themselves in several markets and research areas and hence, increase financial stability and profitability.

Notes

1 The information and data used in this article is taken from the following reports from The Research Council of Norway (RCN) 2009: Utredning om videre utforming av regionale forskningsfond. 2012: *Evaluering av de tolv regionale forskningsinstituttene*. 2014a: *Instituttsektoren – Forskningsrådets strategi 2014–2018*. 2014b: *Årsrapport 2013 Primærnæringsinstituttene Nøkkeltall, instituttpresentasjon og bruk av basisbevilgningen*. 2014c: *Regionalt arbeid.*

Forskningsrådets policy for 2014–2018. 2014d: *Utdyping av retningslinjenes grunnleggende krav til institutter for at de kan gis statlig basisfinansiering*. 2014e: *Årsrapport 2013 De samfunnsvitenskapelige instituttene Nøkkeltall, instituttpresentasjon og bruk av basisbevilgningen*. 2014f: *Årsrapport 2013 De teknisk-industrielle instituttene Nøkkeltall, instituttpresentasjon og bruk av basisbevilgningen*. 2014g: *Årsrapport 2013 Miljøinstituttene Nøkkeltall, instituttpresentasjon og bruk av basisbevilgningen*. These are available from: (www.rcn.no). The data in tables includes institutes that receive basic funding from (RCN) and with research as their primary activity, in addition to five institutes who do not receive basic funding, but are overseen by (RCN).

2 Damvad. (2012): Evaluering av basisfinansieringen til norske forskningsinstitutter som omfattes av retningslinjene for basisfinansiering. Oslo: see: www.damvad.no.

3 SINTEF. Retrieved 18 March 2015, from http://www.sintef.no/universitetssamarbeidet1/.

2 Why Norway has to develop its own innovation policy

Arne Isaksen

Two perspectives on innovation

This chapter discusses why Norwegian industry is seen as very competitive, as revealed by the Global Competitiveness Index, even when it scores low on international rankings on innovation performance. How can industry in a country with supposedly little innovation achieve global competitiveness?

The chapter examines the implicit and explicit understandings of innovation activity that underlie measurements of innovation performance in international rankings. The core of the argument is that international rankings do not really fit with how innovation activity takes place in much of Norwegian industry. The rankings, to a large extent, regard innovations as the result of science and research and development (R&D) activity, while our argument is that much of Norwegian industry innovates without, or with little use of, R&D. The chapter further argues that we make mistakes if we blindly trust international rankings and their implicit guidelines for innovation policy strategies. The Programme for Regional R&D and Innovation (VRI-programme) by The Research Council of Norway (RCN) builds on the regional innovation system approach. This programme is seen to be more adapted to "the Norwegian mode of innovation" than any policy tools building on the science based, linear innovation model, which is similar to the linear knowledge model that was presented in the introduction.

Underlying the chapter are two different, but complementary, views on how to achieve more research based innovation activity. The two approaches also influence how we view the role of applied research in innovation activity in Norwegian industry; from a very small role in the first approach, to a central role in the second approach

The first view argues that basic research in universities, colleges and research institutes can give rise to new products or services that are produced in new start-ups, or through licensing of patents. This is the approach found in the linear innovation model, which says that research results lead to inventions that are developed and tested in several steps, before new products are produced and launched on the market. The model dominated as the picture of how innovation activity took place in the 1950s and 1960s; to a large extent inspired by the report on *Science the Endless Frontier* from 1945 by Vannevar Bush, who was Director of the Office of Scientific Research and Development in the United States. The report underlined the vital importance of basic research and scientists as the source of new innovations. The chapter argues that main principles from the linear model still dominate the thinking behind international rankings of innovativeness and innovation policy in many countries.

Norwegian industry and society in 2016 is of course very different from the situation in the United States in 1945 with its dominant Fordist organised industry, at the time Vannevar Bush designed the principles for the linear innovation model. Norwegian industry is, to a far greater degree than typical Fordist industries, characterised by learning organisations. Norwegian and Swedish industry, thus, emerges in a European comparison with the greatest percentage of employees that learn new things at work, can use their own ideas and help solve problems. Such characteristics are reflected in flat structures where a lot of responsibility and decisions are moved to lower levels within organisations, and where learning and changes in some degree have become parts of daily work. Such organising provides good opportunities for continuous upgrading and development in companies when employees are well skilled, as is the case in Norwegian industry.

The learning organisation approach reflects a broader understanding of what innovations are, that is more than totally new products and services for the market. It also refers to a different, and far less elitist, understanding than in the linear model of how most innovations are created. The approach recognises other types of knowledge, such as applied knowledge at universities and research institutes than the one stemming from scientific basic research as important and essential for the development of innovations.

The approach fits the other main way to understand research based innovation. The starting point for innovation is then ongoing activities in industry, and not stand-alone basic research at universities and research institutes. The idea is that industry should employ more research based knowledge in innovation activity. This would contribute to the research based renewal of existing firms and industry, where universities and research institutes have an important role.

This approach is important as large parts of Norwegian industry innovate by the use of accumulated experience and knowledge. This contributes to frequent, mostly incremental improvements of products and services and more efficient production processes. Research based knowledge, however, is often required to achieve larger changes in products, services and production processes, such as when new technology should be incorporated into existing products or be used in production. Seen in this way, applied research in regionally located universities, university colleges and research institutes fits the need to improve innovation processes by much of Norwegian industry.

A science and experience based mode of innovation

The chapter is inspired by analyses of RCN's VRI-programme. This programme aims to strengthen research based innovation activity, and by that the competitiveness, of firms with little prior experience of this type of innovation activity. The chapter introduces the innovation mode concepts to analyse the VRI-programme and to characterise the Norwegian innovation model. Innovation modes denote the ways that firms organise and carry out innovation activity (Isaksen & Karlsen 2010; Jensen, Johnson, Lorenz & Lundvall 2007).

The basic distinction is between a science based and an experience based mode of innovation. The science based, Science, Technology, Innovation (STI-mode) sees R&D activity as the main input in innovation processes. Researchers at universities and research institutes are the main partners in innovation projects. Innovation activity in the experience based, Doing, Using, Interacting (DUI-mode) takes mainly place as incremental improvements by use of the combined skills of all employees in a firm. Main external partners are customers that, for example, expect higher quality or more adapted products or services.

The VRI-programme is distinguished by targeting DUI-firms in particular, and by being adapted to specific regional challenges. The programme is implemented by the counties in their regions. It has some dedicated competence brokers in each region, with missions to link firms with a specific innovation challenge, and researchers with relevant knowledge at universities and research institutes. The underlying aim is to teach more DUI-firms to carry out innovation projects with the help of external research capacity. The chapter argues that the VRI-programme is highly adapted to the innovation mode and innovation challenges in large parts of Norwegian industry.

Another starting point for the chapter is the fact that the STI-model, despite the VRI-programme, dominates general opinion in Norway (as well as in most countries) of how innovation takes place. Innovation and R&D are often equated in general debates. An influential commentator in the largest Norwegian newspaper for example, states that "Industry invests little in research. The share of the gross value added in firms used on *research and development (that is innovation)* in Denmark, Sweden and Finland is three–four times higher than in Norway".[1] The common misunderstanding in this phrase lays in the fact that R&D, as one of several input factors in innovation processes, is seen as the same as innovation, which is the result of the process, such as the launching of a new or improved product on the market. The goal of increasing the cost of R&D to reach 3% of gross value added in Norway reflects to some extent the same simple understanding; strengthened R&D activity will more or less automatically lead to more innovations.

The argument has been presented to several kinds of audience. Simply speaking, practitioners, such as regional policy makers and firm representatives, recognise and agree on the main message. The STI way of thinking, however, still underlies much of the public opinion and debate about how to develop the innovation capability and competitiveness of firms, and more generally industrial renewal. The chapter continues by discussing STI dominance in much of the reasoning about innovation policy.

The STI thinking dominates international rankings

The chapter argues that the STI approach influences much of the thinking internationally about how innovation processes occur. This leads, consciously or unconsciously, to the fact that much innovation policy also builds on the STI-model.

The STI view is seen, for example, in how innovation results are measured in international rankings. One example is the ranking of nations' innovation output by the European Union. Table 2.1 reveals that Norway is far behind the EU average in this ranking, while Sweden, and also Denmark and Finland, are seen as much more innovative. Norway is placed between the Czech Republic and Spain. Comparing for example the unemployment rates in these countries reveals that Norway has a lower rate than the Czech Republic, and particularly lower than Spain in which about one quarter of the labour force is unemployed. This fact should indicate that Norwegian industry in general has been more resilient, i.e. innovative, in the wake of the financial crisis from 2008, than Spanish industry.

The reason for Norway's low score in this EU ranking is largely found in the four indicators used to decide on countries' innovation output. Norway reveals a medium score on indicators 1, 2 and 4, i.e. number of patent applications per billion gross domestic product, number of workers in knowledge intensive activities in business industries over total employment and employment in fast growing firms in innovative sectors as a percentage of total employment in fast growing firms. Norway gets the last place with a good margin on indicator 3; the contribution of export of medium and high tech

Table 2.1 Ranking of innovation output; 35 countries

Rank	*Country*
1	Japan
2	Sweden
7	Denmark
8	Finland
12	EU-average
21	Czech Republic
22	Norway
23	Spain

Source: SWD (2013) 325 Final, European Commission.

Table 2.2 Innovation performance according to Innovation Union Scoreboard

Performance group	*Countries*
Innovation leader	5 countries: Switzerland, Sweden, Denmark, Germany, Finland
Innovation follower	11 countries
Moderate innovator	13 countries, including Norway
Modest innovator	5 countries

Source: Innovation Union Scoreboard 2014, European Commission (p. 28).

products and knowledge-intensive services to the trade balance. Oil and gas, fish and metals, which are important Norwegian exports, are classified as low tech products. These industries are integrated in Norwegian innovation systems in which much R&D activities take place in research institutions and at technology suppliers, and with much innovation activity along the value chains. The third indicator is more generally seen as an odd indicator for measuring innovation output. It envisages that low tech industries are not innovative at all.

Another ranking that has received some attention is the EU's Innovation Union Scoreboard. Our Nordic neighbour countries are seen as innovation leaders in this Scoreboard together with Switzerland and Germany. Norway comes in the third league as a moderate innovator (Table 2.2).

The Innovation Union Scoreboard builds on 25 indicators that are grouped into eight dimensions. One of these dimensions is excellent research systems, decided by three indicators: the number of international scientific co-publications per million inhabitants; the share of all scientific publications in Norway that is among the 10% most cited scientific publications worldwide; and the share of non-EU doctoral students among all PhD students in Norway. The inspiration for the STI-mode of innovation is clearly seen in these indicators; and measuring scientific publications and PhD students is far from measuring innovation performance.

Higher scores on competitiveness than on innovation performance

Norway scores higher on other international rankings that intend to measure competitiveness rather than innovation capability or performance. One example is the global competitiveness index by the World Economic Forum. Norway achieved place number 11 among about 150 countries in this ranking for 2014–2015. This is far above the Czech Republic (no. 37) and Spain (no. 35), which are ranked about similar to Norway in the two EU rankings on innovativeness presented in Tables 2.1 and 2.2.

The scores on the global competitiveness index are composed by 12 individual indicators. Two of these that are important for the subsequent discussion are highlighted in Table 2.3. The first one includes the

Table 2.3 Scores on the global competitiveness index 2013–2014

		Rank on two indicators	
	Total rank	*Institutions*	*Technological readiness*
Finland	2	2	11
Sweden	6	14	3
Norway	11	5	4
Denmark	15	16	6
Spain	35	73	27
Czech Republic	46	76	35

Source: The Global Competitiveness Report 2014–2015, World Economic Forum.

institutional framework, which consists of the legal and administrative framework, and aims to measure how the quality of national institutions affects competitiveness. The second indicator is technological readiness that includes the ability of a nation's industry to employ new technology, especially information and communications technology (ICT). Norway and the other Nordic countries have high scores on both indicators, in particular on the macro indicator of institutions.

Learning organisations

The two indicators, and the micro level indicator of technological readiness in particular, are at the core of the argument for why Norway is more innovative than measured by the STI inspired indicators. An important strength in Norwegian, and Nordic, industry in general, is the extent of learning organisations; indicated by the high scores on technological readiness in Table 2.3.

Learning organisations are characterised by the fact that learning and (incremental) innovation activity are integrated in the way firms organise their daily activity (Lam 2005; Lorenz & Valeyre 2006). Figure 2.1, based on results from a European survey of persons, demonstrates a high learning content in Norwegian firms in general. The y-axis shows the rate of persons in some selected countries answering that they learn new things at work, while the x-axis show the percentage who answer that they are able to apply their own ideas at work. Norway and the other Nordic countries are distinguished by a large share of people who, in their own opinion, both learn new things and can use their own ideas at work, while EU countries on average and large EU countries score significantly lower on both indicators.

The result demonstrated in Figure 2.1 is well-known in the literature; Norway and other Nordic countries have relatively many learning organisations, characterised by a diversity of work tasks, decentralisation of responsibility and decision making, possibilities of initiatives on the shop floor and integration of learning and improvement in work (Lorenz 2011).

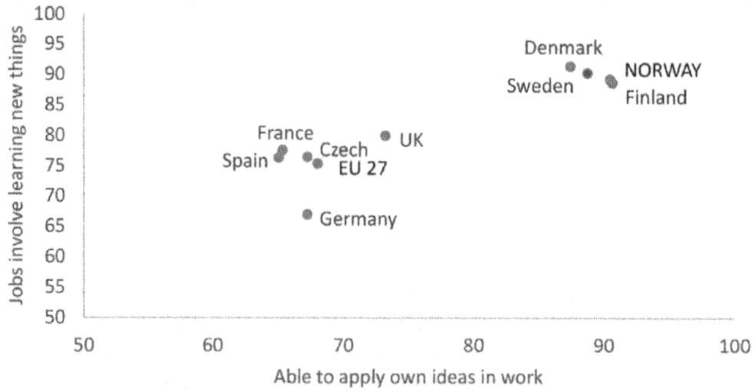

Figure 2.1 Aspects of the organisation of work in specific countries
Source: Own compilation based on the fifth European Working Condition Survey 2010.

Such a way of organising work makes it possible to utilise the competence, experience and initiative of a number of employees in upgrading of firms in many ways. When the labour force is in general highly skilled, as in Norway (OECD 2015), the characteristics demonstrated in Figure 2.1 can strengthen bottom-up innovation processes.

One illustration of the DUI innovation model is how the early pioneers in Denmark developed a functioning wind power technology by improving existing solutions by incremental innovations. Simmie (2012) contrasts this strategy with efforts in a NASA-led US public wind power research programme that aimed for breakthrough innovations. Such a strategy has led to many technological breakthroughs by US organisations, in particular in the ICT sector. In the wind power industry, however, the Danish actors' strategy is seen to succeed, while the US effort is described as mainly an expensive failure (Simmie 2012). The lesson may be that the DUI-model can lead to global leadership in some types of industries.

Another characteristic of relevance for explaining the relatively high competitiveness of Norwegian industry points to the notion of institutions. Figure 2.2 demonstrates that Norway, together with other Nordic countries, is regarded as a high-trust society. Nearly 80% of people in Denmark, Norway and Finland say that they have moderate or high trust in other people, while around 40% in the UK, Spain, Germany and on average in European countries, report moderate and high trust.

The extent of trust between people may be important for the innovation capability in a nation, due to the fact that innovation processes nearly always require co-operation and knowledge exchange between people; both among people inside organisations and between people in different organisations (Lundvall 2010). We also know that co-operation between persons that have different types of knowledge and different experiences is key to innovation; and mutual trust also triggers this kind of knowledge flow.

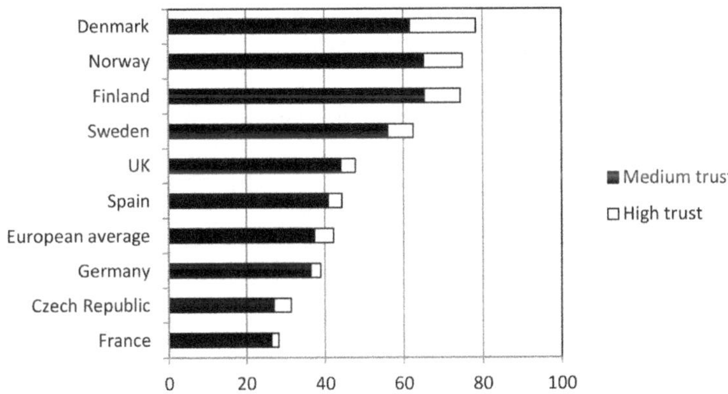

Figure 2.2 Extent of trust among people

Source: Own compilation based on the European Social Survey 2012.

Possible problems to achieve breakthrough innovations

We have so far argued that some of the strengths in the Norwegian mode of innovation are really not captured by the EU indicators on innovation performance, as they are inspired by the STI innovation model. The characteristics of the Norwegian model, such as broad participation, learning organisations and trustful relations, build on some specific historical, social and cultural factors, such as the fact that Norway is an egalitarian society with relatively small social differences.

This Norwegian model stimulates employee driven innovation through broad participation, and it encourages knowledge exchange and combinations of different types of knowledge through trustful co-operation. This model has the potential to achieve global leadership as in the Danish wind power industry and the Norwegian oil and gas equipment supplier industry. However, the model also has a drawback in a comparatively low R&D intensity in Norway (RCN 2014). The model mainly supports incremental innovations and then path extension; firms and industries improve their existing strongholds (Martin & Sunley 2006). Improvement of existing activity strengthens the productivity of firms, but the DUI-mode is often not sufficient when firms have to do things very differently than hitherto. Then research based knowledge, together with experience based knowledge, will be important to strengthen the innovation capability and competitiveness of firms and industries, which points to a third innovation mode.

The CCI innovation mode

Some studies point to the fact that firms that combine the STI- and the DUI-mode of innovation are often more innovative than those which focus on one of the innovation modes only: "It is the firm that combines a strong version of the STI-mode with a strong version of the DUI-mode that excels in product innovation" (Jensen et al. 2007, p. 685).

Combination of the strong parts of the STI and DUI modes is exactly the main idea with the third mode of innovation, denoted as the Complex and Combined Innovation mode (CCI) (Isaksen & Karlsen 2012b). When employing these concepts, the main task of the VRI-programme is to develop DUI-firms towards the CCI-mode by increasing the use of R&D based knowledge in DUI-firms. A core point in CCI-mode is that firms systematise their core competence by developing technology platforms. Firms codify parts of their tacit, experience-based knowledge. A weak point with the DUI innovation mode is the fact that much competence to be used in innovation activity is tacit and held by individuals, and firms therefore often have to start nearly at scratch in every new innovation project. The core of the CCI-mode is to make part of firms' core competence explicit (Nonaka, Toyama & Konno 2001). Externalisation contributes to the fact that knowledge is more easily spread and shared within firms, and it becomes more possible to link knowledge from different sources and develop new knowledge from such linking.

The CCI innovation mode can be illustrated by an example from the food industry in the county of Rogaland in south-western Norway (Isaksen & Nilsson 2013). Rogaland has traditions in agriculture and fishing and related production of food, and the county's main city of Stavanger was, for example, the centre of the canning industry in Norway in the early 1900s. The region now has a Norwegian Centre of Expertise (NCE) programme in the food industry, called NCE Culinology. The NCE is a national programme which aims to strengthen ongoing development and innovation activities in regional clusters with high capacities for growth and with international potential (http://www.nceclusters.no/om-nce/). The NCE Culinology programme includes both firms, private and public R&D organisations, education institutions and public agencies.

One part of the programme is occupied with studying the chemical and physical processes of cooking. Although this is quite a scientific task, the programme also uses the approach and experience of chefs. The chefs, however, co-operate with researchers, who apply scientific methods to document the relationship between taste and chemistry. This may take place when chefs prepare different types of tasty foods by use of their primarily experience-based knowledge. Researchers document, among other things by use of sensors, various chemical processes in the preparation of food as well as chemical characteristics of the dishes. Several R&D organisations in Rogaland have experience in this type of scientific documentation and analyses that has helped develop industrialised prepared food with, amongst other things, long durability. This co-operation between chefs and researchers demonstrates the linking of scientific and experience based knowledge that are in the core of the CCI-mode of innovation.

Norway has a DUI-mode of innovation

The STI versus the DUI innovation mode

The chapter has argued that the DUI-mode of innovation characterises the innovation activity in much of Norwegian industry. The DUI-mode dominates in firms that first of all innovate to solve challenges in their daily activity, or innovate to satisfy specific customer demands by use of the experience-based knowledge of employees. We will go on to discuss how the DUI-mode can be strengthened by policy tools.

The core of the argument is that specific innovation modes need different institutional support; that is, different backing from the knowledge infrastructure, the policy support system and so on. It is a well-established truth in innovation studies that no one-size-fits-all policy exists (Tödtling & Trippl 2005); for example, there are no policy tools that fit different modes of innovation equally well. This means, amongst other things, that policy prescriptions adapted to research and science based firms and industries, found in regions with good research universities, will not fit in regions and industries dominated by the DUI-mode of innovation.

Before discussing policy adapted to the DUI-mode of innovation, the conceptual background for such a discussion needs to be presented in more length than hitherto in the chapter. Innovation is defined broadly as new or significantly improved goods, services, production processes, organisational methods and marketing concepts, and innovative firms are those that introduce products and services on the market or implement new production processes (Fagerberg 2005). Innovation is thus defined as results. It is, however, vital to acknowledge that firms can achieve these results in different ways, through different innovation processes or different modes of innovation. Firms' innovation modes, however, affect what types of innovation firms develop (Jensen et al. 2007). The DUI-mode of innovation, for example, often leads to incrementally improved products and production processes.

The chapter has distinguished three different modes of innovation: STI, DUI and CCI. Firms may have elements of several innovation modes. However, one mode will often dominate in specific firms, industries and regions.

The STI-mode illustrates to a large extent the traditional way of seeing how innovations come about. The idea is that innovations mainly develop in research projects and are based on scientific knowledge. Innovations originate most often as ideas and concepts in the R&D departments of firms or in universities' research labs. The ideas enter a relay often consisting of research, documentation, development of prototypes, testing, industrialisation, marketing and launching. STI firms have products and technologies in which research and development is required in order to be in business.

The STI-mode of innovation and the corresponding STI-model of regional industrial development are inspired by perceptions of what are going on in large university regions, such as Silicon Valley in the US, and Cambridge in England (Saxenian 1994). The model proposes that regional and national innovation policy should support research, and often basic research, and that policy should back up spin-offs and venture capital in order to be able to commercialise results from the research activities.

The STI-model is important in some cases, as it can give rise to entirely new technologies and industries (Mazzucato 2013). However, the model is not really relevant outside big cities and university towns. The STI-mode illustrates *one* important element of innovation activity, but the mode can hide main strengths of the specific Norwegian way of innovating, which is more in line with the two other innovation modes.

The STI-mode is in many ways an elitist model, in which innovation activities are reserved for research intensive firms and higher educated personnel only. DUI supplement the STI-model (Jensen et al. 2007). The DUI-mode demonstrates that innovation activity can take place without long-term research activity. The DUI-model was also developed to describe how innovation takes place in, at least, the bulk of small and medium sized enterprises.

The DUI-mode is common in industries where firms do not base all their innovation activities on research and scientific knowledge, but rather on competence acquired through long experience with one specific type of activity. This includes firms that create new solutions in their daily activity, for example to solve practical problems in their own production, or adapt products, services or technologies to specific customer demands. The firms find solutions on such challenges mainly through trial and error, and by utilising experiences from what their employees have seen function previously, without necessarily knowing why a specific solution did work.

The oil and gas equipment supplier industry in the southern part of Norway (see Chapters 3 and 13 in this book for more description of this industry) have become world leaders in drilling equipment, anchoring and loading equipment and offshore cranes by, in large part, using the DUI-model (Isaksen & Karlsen 2012a). The core of their innovation process has consisted in solving demanding projects for customers, such as oil companies, by adapting and developing existing solutions and through trial and error. Several firms have lately become more systematic in their innovation activity, and are co-operating more with universities and R&D institutes. The firms have thus moved towards the third innovation model, the CCI-mode of innovation.

From the CCI-mode of innovation to CCI policy

The argument that the CCI-mode of innovation is most efficient when it comes to improving the innovation capacity and competitiveness of firms should have implications for the design and implementation of innovation policy. Innovation policy is, broadly speaking, policy that explicitly aims to promote the development, diffusion and efficient use of new products, services and processes (Lundvall & Borrás 1997).

Policy to strengthen the CCI-mode can have two starting points. It can supplement both the typical STI and DUI innovation policy with new elements. STI innovation policy is science driven policy, aimed first of all at increasing the R&D capacity of firms, their links to knowledge organisations and at supporting commercialisation of research results (Table 2.4). DUI innovation policy takes on board that innovation most often does not start in research, but sets off to solve practical problems in firms or to answer requirements from demanding customers. DUI policy then focuses on how to support organisational change and organisational learning, and support co-operation along value chains. Based on lessons about the CCI-mode, innovation policy should focus on building more commercialisation and industrialisation capacity of firms dominated by the STI-mode through, in particular, increased marked and process competence in these firms (Isaksen & Nilsson 2013). Policy should then help DUI-firms to move towards the CCI-mode by building more absorptive capacity of DUI-firms through increased formal competence in such firms.

In order to explain the need to complement the traditional STI innovation policy, the fact is that a one-sided focus on research and scientific activity can make it difficult for STI-firms to commercialise, or otherwise implement, research results. This may reflect a lack of knowledge in setting up production lines, in organising logistics, in marketing and so on. Karlsen, Isaksen and Spilling (2011) found a shortage of practical, experience based knowledge in a study of the marine biotechnology industry in Tromsø in northern Norway. The study started from the fact that several policy instruments have been implemented in Tromsø, to trigger the start and development of a marine biotechnology cluster in the region, however with seemingly rather small results with regard to number of employees and firms at the time of the study by Karlsen et al. (2011). One explanation of few new firms and jobs involves the fact that it may take 10–15 years from research results to the launching of a new product on the market in the biotechnology industry. Even when taken this information into account, the

Table 2.4 Innovation policy based on the STI and DUI innovation modes

STI policy (science driven)	*DUI policy (learning based)*
Aim: Increase firms' R&D capacity, and academic–industry co-operation	*Aim*: Foster organisational and inter-organisational learning and co-operation along value chains
Typical innovation policy: Supporting R&D-projects, R&D-infrastructure, and commercialisation of research	*Typical innovation policy*: Supporting on-the-job learning, organisational innovations, trust and network building

Source: Builds on Isaksen and Nilsson (2013).

results of the policy initiatives seem meagre in Tromsø. A relevant explanation is found by use of the innovation mode concepts. Tromsø is well equipped with relevant, research based knowledge at the university and at a division of the R&D institute Nofima. However, Tromsø has much less practical, experience based knowledge to set up and to operate a production line in the biotechnology industry, which is mainly due to little manufacturing tradition in the region.

Scientific knowledge is vital to carrying out innovation activity in marine biotechnology (and in other research intensive industries), but this knowledge has to be complemented by other types of knowledge in order to industrialise and commercialise research. This points to more general challenges in STI-firms, which are (1) to make such firms able to draw more on customers and other external actors beyond research organisations and (2) to make STI firms able to make more use of experience-based knowledge from different parts of the firms, in innovation projects. Both tasks demand internal capacity building, but the general aim is to create more learning organisations beyond the R&D departments in STI-firms.

DUI-firms, on the other hand, often have minimal in-house R&D activity. This characteristic lowers the ability of firms to produce innovations in-house, and it lowers firms' absorptive capacity. Firms may therefore strive to benefit from external knowledge, for example, at universities and research institutes. Innovation policy influenced by the STI innovation mode that aims to increase the research intensity of firms and increase university-industry co-operation is therefore inefficient in regions and industries dominated by the DUI-mode of innovation. DUI-firms simply often lack the necessary absorptive capacity to apply scientific knowledge (Cohen & Levinthal 1990). This fact provides one explanation for the apparently paradoxical fact that economies which consistently invest in research and development sometimes score low in terms of innovation output (Bitard, Edquist, Hommen & Rickne 2008). It resembles the "cathedral in the desert" phenomenon: a region may, for example, have some very good universities and research institutes which however have few local links and give few effects in terms of job increase because of low capacity to make use of their knowledge in the local industry.

Policies that target DUI-firms then needs to address the issue of the absorptive capacity of firms. One important part of such policy concerns to stimulate the recruitment of highly educated personnel in DUI-firms, which again requires relevant study programmes at regionally located universities. Although higher educated personnel can be recruited from anywhere, labour markets (in Norway) are still mainly regional and much recruiting takes place regionally, which justifies the need for relevant local education. A further way to improve the absorptive capacity of DUI-firms is through establishing closer links between industry and academia. Such links may enable more research-based innovation activity in DUI-firms even if firms do not recruit researchers. More research based innovation, however, requires long-term commitment from both parties. The entrepreneur or innovating DUI-firm most often possesses market and commercialisation competencies, and sometimes also extensive knowledge about the production process. Research based knowledge can be sourced on a more ad-hoc basis from external sources, primarily researchers and consultants.

Innovation policy should reflect mode of innovation

We have discussed why Norwegian industry is highly competitive, in spite of low scores in international rankings on innovation performance. The innovation mode approach represents relevant tools in interpreting this seeming paradox. The rankings see innovation through the STI lens, although much of Norwegian industry employs the DUI-mode of innovation. The next question includes what policy is most appropriate to raise the innovation activity and competitiveness of DUI dominated industry.

First of all, we acknowledge the general importance of the traditional STI innovation policy that focuses on raising the research intensity of industry, trigging academic spin-offs and so on. Nevertheless, we argue that this type of policy does not fit a large number of firms in countries like Norway, where the bulk of the firms do not follow the STI-mode of innovation. We rather argue that a main aim of innovation policy is to upgrade traditional DUI-firms in the direction of the CCI-mode of innovation, which means to make DUI-firms more able to absorb and use scientific knowledge. At the same time, firms should strive to become or remain learning organisations characterised by broad participation and decentralised decision making, which should not be underestimated as a vital, soft source of innovation.

The RCN's VRI-programme includes such activity, with its focus on connecting firms and researchers at universities and research institutes in specific innovation projects in firms. However, the VRI-programme should also focus on organisational development in firms so that external researchers can more easily contribute their competence. The argument is that the innovation activity in DUI-firms often is more or less invisible to outsiders. Incremental innovations are often part of "normal activities" in DUI-firms. Innovation can come from organised processes, as in lean-based development, but innovation processes can also be mainly ad-hoc in order to solve upcoming challenges. Therefore, researchers coming from outside can contribute to innovation activities inside DUI-firms, if the firms systematise their knowledge and organise specific innovation projects.

Finally, a central message is to be aware of and take the Norwegian characteristics into account when formulating innovation policy at national and regional level. Most countries base their policy on the STI-model (Lundvall, Vang, Joseph & Chaminade 2009), which includes putting much effort into raising nations' research capacity and to develop research based sectors like biotechnology and nanotechnology. This type of policy seems to be guided by information coming from the type of rankings of nations' innovation performance pointed to in this chapter, and the competition is strong in research based sectors, not least from China.

It is much more difficult for countries to quickly imitate the Norwegian (and Nordic) innovation mode with learning organisations. The Norwegian innovation mode constitutes a competitive advantage, in particular when it is complemented with policy tools to raise firms' capability to utilise applied research. The chapter therefore argues that policy makers and politicians should not blindly accept the international rankings and the policy advice that indirectly come from these rankings, but rather think about how a DUI and CCI based innovation policy that takes into account the inherited Norwegian strength can be developed.

Note

1 Joacim Lund, comments p. 3 in *Aftenposten*. 14 September 2015. My translation, italic added.

3 Knowledge transfer in different regional contexts

Nina Kyllingstad and Elisabet S. Hauge

Regional differences in types of knowledge

The aim of the chapter is to discuss the significance of knowledge exchange in different regional contexts related to the need for targeted regional policy. Earlier research has illustrated that knowledge sharing and knowledge transfer differ according to different regional settings; knowledge exchange between entrepreneurial firms is a less researched topic. Also, previous studies in this field have been quantitative data oriented, and not specified by sector (Aslesen & Isaksen 2014; Isaksen & Trippl 2014; Tödtling & Trippl 2005). The practice of this chapter enhances a more in-depth understanding of how knowledge exchange is taking place among entrepreneurial firms in the different regional contexts.

This chapter discusses knowledge exchange between firms and actors in different regional contexts, within an evolutionary economic geography perspective (EEG). We argue that different regional settings enhance different regional knowledge sharing and knowledge transfer processes. We aim to inspire in-depth insight on knowledge exchange by describing diversity related to different regional settings. According to EEG, certain characteristics within a business environment are crucial for firms' entrepreneurial and innovative practices, which is caused by historical and regional presumptions and factors. We find theory on regional innovation systems (RIS) helpful in order to approach the phenomenon studied. How firms and actors contribute to transfer and acquire knowledge, evolve networks for innovation and realise new innovations, is partly determined by the characteristics of the specific RIS and by its relation to the markets and production surroundings. We divide RIS into two main categories, namely organisationally thick RIS and organisationally thin RIS. However, the organisationally thick RIS can be further divided into thick and specialised RIS and thick and diversified RIS. Each of these structures enhances and promotes different ways of sharing knowledge. Based on these arguments, this chapter discusses how oil and gas subcontractors initiate knowledge sharing and transfer in different regional contexts.

Both policymakers, firms and individual actors, such as entrepreneurs, can benefit from evolving literature on the impact of regional context in regards to knowledge exchange. The consequences of today's practice in different regions can be helpful when creating future policies or business models, whether today's practice is something they wish to continue with, or that they would like to avoid. We live in a knowledge economy where knowledge flow between different actors is becoming increasingly important. It is therefore important to know the value of good knowledge exchange, in order to evolve both as a region, firm or entrepreneur.

Our focus has been on regional innovation systems and different types of knowledge exchange, identified within the entrepreneurial firms by extracting experiences from the regional firms interviewed. We avoid generalisation by highlighting how entrepreneurial firms in the different regions act and respond differently in knowledge development processes. We have found commonalities within the case-firms. It can be helpful for policy makers to be familiar with success stories as well as failures from entrepreneurial firms in different regions. This study supports research rejecting policy that provides "one size fits all" initiatives. The conclusion supports the evolution of more non-absolute policy initiatives.

The way we, as social science researchers, validate knowledge from the study firms is not with intentions to generalise, but rather to get an in-depth understanding of the phenomenon studied. This knowledge can add to the literature published on the significance of knowledge exchange in different regional contexts.

The chapter presents four cases studies conducted in the Norwegian regions Rogaland, Hordaland, Agder and Finnmark. Empirical data generation on knowledge exchange was conducted among small firms in the oil and gas industry sector. Before the data collection and date analysis was initiated, we had a presumption that knowledge exchange is related to RIS characteristics, by presuming that the more mature and thick a RIS is, the greater the frequency and quality of firms' knowledge exchange.

Comparing four Norwegian regions

The research question results from the chapter authors being involved in an ongoing VRI-programme project called "Path development in different regional settings: Regional policy approaches in the global economy". The VRI-programme (see Chapter 2: *Why Norway has to develop its own innovation policy* in this book) was initiated by The Research Council of Norway (RCN), and focuses on research and development at the regional level in Norway. This chapter relates to the policy frameworks and discourses in the regions. The project, which runs from 2014 to 2016, receives contributory funding from the RCN as well as other actors. Being involved within a large research group opened up opportunities to conduct interviews among oil and gas sub-suppliers in four Norwegian regions.

This chapter arose from an observation when analysing data generated in the VRI-programme project. By studying the interview guide used in the first informant interview within the overall VRI-programme project, we found that knowledge exchange among oil and gas subcontractors needed more coverage than the interviews could provide. The following fieldwork was therefore expanded to include questions regarding firm knowledge exchange. In addition, the information and feedback we received during the first interview gave us reason to believe that empirical data on the influence of regional context related to knowledge exchange is a key to understand firms' knowledge and production development.

The four cases

The four case regions in this study differ in regards to number of employees and their matureness in the oil and gas industry. The following table shows the number of business units and employees (exclusive of offshore employees), with county distribution in 2012 and relative distribution in 2003, 2007 and 2012.

Hordaland is one of the largest and most central regions in Norway. The number of employees and business units in the oil and gas industry is the second largest of the four study regions. Hordaland is also the home of the NCE Subsea cluster with over 100 member firms. The cluster competes internationally in operating, maintaining and modifying subsea equipment. Their expertise is grounded in hard work, innovation and collaboration between the industrial members, educational establishments and wide-ranging R&D communities. In addition to subsea, there are other important industries in Hordaland, e.g. the NCE media cluster, and there are also several R&D institutions and a strong educational environment in the region. The studied firms claimed that they co-operate, to a certain degree, within formal networks in the region e.g. NCE Subsea, even though they can likely co-operate within national or global networks. In recent years, a trend cultivating green technology, which stems both from incremental and radical innovations, seems to have evolved among regional oil and gas firms. Hordaland has characteristics of a thick and diversified RIS.

Table 3.1 Number of business units and employees

Region	*Number of business units*	*Number of petroleum employees*	*Percentage of the total 2003*	*Percentage of the total 2007*	*Percentage of the total 2012*
Rogaland	725	34,781	47.93	38.96	33.67
Hordaland	452	20,441	19.38	17.97	19.79
Agder	158	7,287	4.72	5.48	7.05
Finnmark	39	595	1.51	0.34	0.58

Source: Own modification after Vatne (2013, p. 18).

Rogaland is Norway's oil capital and has, out of the four regions, the longest history, the most employees and the most business units in the oil and gas industry. The region hosts the complete oil and gas value chain. Local industry has elements of both radical and incremental innovation. With a growing focus on high-tech, the incidence of radical innovations has also increased. The region is considered relatively large on a national scale and is, in addition to oil and gas, comprised of other industries. There is also a growing R&D and educational environment in the region. The recent focus on high-tech could indicate increased use of R&D, and therefore Rogaland might be a thick and diversified RIS. However, there is still not enough collaboration with the R&D institutions or the educational environment in the region to classify it as a thick and diversified RIS. Rogaland has characteristics of both thick diversified RIS and thick specialised RIS.

Agder is often described as Norway's "drilling bay". The GCE NODE cluster that consists of over 60 firms within the oil and gas supplier industry is located in this region. It encloses almost all oil and gas activity in the region. Even though there are numerous firms within the oil and gas industry, three companies are more important in terms of market shares and employed labour staff. These three major companies are National Oilwell Varco (NOV), Cameron and MHWirth and we describe them later as the locomotives of the industry at Agder. The oil and gas industry, mostly represented by the GCE NODE cluster, is very important for the Agder region, measured in number employees, turn over and export. A large amount of resources and capital is being used to develop both the cluster and the industry, making the region highly specialised. Agder is thereby classified as a thick specialised RIS.

Finnmark has the lowest number of employees and business units in the oil and gas industry and the industry is the youngest of the studied regions. The regional industry focus is to combine existing knowledge with new knowledge in order to develop both the industry and the region. Finnmark is a vast area, but the number of business units and employees is low and support functions in Finnmark, such as R&D, banking and finance is sparse. In order to work on projects that require R&D, the firms in Finnmark usually need to look outside the region to identify strategic business partners. In this study Finnmark is classified as a thin and diversified RIS.

Theoretical discussion

In order to conceptualise a study on knowledge exchange among entrepreneurial firms in different regional contexts, we have approached the study phenomenon by utilising theory on RIS and knowledge exchange. Theory on regional innovation systems (RIS) helps to frame and systematise regional differences among the four case studies. The regional innovation system is "made up by two subsystems embedded in a common regional socioeconomic and cultural setting". (Tödtling & Trippl 2005, p. 1205). External knowledge supplemented with internal knowledge is important in order to enhance innovative firms.

A RIS consists of two subsystems. The first is the business community that consists of companies, which may also be included in value chains and clusters (Isaksen & Asheim 2008). Regional clusters can be defined as a concentration of "interdependent" firms within the same or adjacent industrial sectors in a small geographical area (Rosenfeld 1997). The second system is the knowledge infrastructure of organisations such as universities, support service, technical colleges, research institutes, consultants and the like (Rosenfeld 1997). Depending on the facilitation of the two subsystems, the more ideal is the RIS. The first subsystem refers to customers, collaborators, contractors, competitors and industrial partners. The latter refers to institutions such as public research institutions, technology mediating organisations, educational institutions and the regional policy. All of these produce or spread knowledge and skills. To strengthen a RIS, "knowledge application and exploitation subsystem" and "knowledge generation and diffusion subsystem" must facilitate interaction with each other in order to create a flow of knowledge, resources and human capital (Tödtling & Trippl 2005). During the case description, we divided the regions in different types of regional innovation systems. We will further describe different RIS in more detail.

Regional innovation systems can, according to Isaksen and Trippl (2014), be divided into three types: organisationally thick and diversified RIS, organisationally thick and specialised RIS and organisationally thin RIS. Organisationally thick and diversified RIS can be found in larger and more centralised regions. The knowledge networks are mostly diverse and geographically open, and there are usually strong universities and a large amount of research facilities in the region. These trades can lead to spin-offs or further development of already existing firms by for example making use of local buzz (Bathelt, Malmberg & Maskell 2004). Nevertheless, because the case-firms are collaborating with the R&D institutions and the educational environment in the region, we have classified Hordaland as a thick diversified RIS.

The organisationally thick and specialised RIS is often characterised by having one or few clusters e.g. old industrial areas. In contrast to the thick and diversified RIS, the knowledge networks in the thick and specialised RIS are relatively closed. In addition, they are usually organised as inter-firm or inter-organisational. These RIS lack diversity, defined as supporting organisations and knowledge bases. However, clusters in these RIS might work very well. A limited access to external ties, to help create new knowledge, increases the risk of a negative lock-in situation (Martin & Sunley 2006). The clusters might have been successful in previous years but when problems arise, it might be too late to change the direction in which the RIS is heading. Both Rogaland and Agder are classified as a thick and specialised RIS, but Agder is the more evident example with its massive focus on the oil supplier industry and less on the rest of the region (see Table 3.2).

The organisationally thin RIS is characterised by low levels of firm clustering, and a few or no universities or R&D institutions. The innovation activity is mostly based on workers' experience. Also typical for this type

Table 3.2 Classification of the study regions

Organisationally thick and diversified RIS	*Organisationally thick and specialised RIS*	*Organisationally thin RIS*
Hordaland	Rogaland (and Agder)	Finnmark (and Agder)

of RIS is the presence of SME and/or branch plants. The presence of externally owned firms e.g. MNC, few universities and R&D institutions, and the general low number of actors, makes for little knowledge spill-over, and is rather headed towards conformity, which is negative for the regions innovation capabilities.

Static and dynamic knowledge flow and exchange

In addition to the RIS framework, it is also conducive to include a framework that captures various types of knowledge flow and knowledge exchange. Increased knowledge, innovation and learning are important to all firms in order to compete on a global scale. "Local buzz" is an interesting concept describing knowledge flow that is not formalised. It is defined as knowledge sharing and knowledge transfer at informal arenas and it happens when e.g. two workers, who possess relatively similar competence, meet at the same geographical location and exchange knowledge or experiences (Bathelt et al. 2004). Local buzz might create, with varying degree, consequences for a firm or a region, such as spin-offs. The term local buzz is mostly used in the cluster literature, but examples can also be found in regions without clusters, because local buzz is often characterised as unintended knowledge transfer (Schwartz & Tödtling 2011). Table 3.3 presents four types of knowledge exchange, where both the informal knowledge exchange e.g. local buzz and the formal knowledge exchange is represented.

The vertical dimension in Table 3.3 refers to the formality of the knowledge exchange. Formal collaboration is knowledge exchange formalised in one way or another e.g. buying a service from a R&D institute or signing a contract establishing joint development projects. Informal knowledge exchange happen unconsciously through local buzz (Bathelt et al. 2004), worker mobility, observation or as a result of groups of professionals developing knowledge in a community.

The horizontal dimension refers to the different types of knowledge exchange. The static knowledge exchange is "processed" information, which means that new knowledge is not produced during interaction between sender and receiver e.g. when a firm buys a finished report from a research institution. Another way of explaining the static knowledge exchange is to look at it as adoption of existing knowledge, because there is no knowledge production in the actual interaction between sender and receiver. The dynamic knowledge exchange consists of the co-production

Table 3.3 Type of external knowledge sources and type of knowledge exchange

Types of external knowledge sources	*Types of knowledge exchange*	
	Static	*Dynamic*
Formal collaboration	Sales relations: knowledge buy from KIBS, R&D institute, technology suppliers	Sparring relations: joint development projects between partners or long- term client-supplier relation
Informal knowledge flow	Knowledge spill-over: copying of methods and technology from other actors through observation or recruitment from others	Communities: autonomous groups of professionals who exchange and develop knowledge in a community

Source: Aslesen and Isaksen (2007), own modification.

of knowledge and collective learning between actors. The requirement for this type of knowledge exchange is a certain degree of common or shared knowledge between the actors, in order to keep the exchange stable and in progress. Whereas the static knowledge exchange can be viewed as clarified knowledge transfer, the dynamic knowledge exchange can be viewed as collective learning. Another way of explaining the dynamic knowledge is as creating new knowledge by being more interactive.

Concepts to analyse knowledge exchange

Next, we emphasise the concepts used to analyse knowledge exchange. According to Ellison (2001), Alfred Marshall claimed that knowledge is the most powerful engine of production. The importance of knowledge increases and knowledge development is an undisguisable factor of the knowledge economy, as well as a presumption for initiating innovation processes. Entrepreneurship, innovation processes and knowledge development is a social phenomenon (Holt 2008), which means that knowledge is dependent upon converging communication (Ellison 2001). There is a distinction between exploration and exploitation of knowledge (Landström 2005). Exploration includes search, discovery, novelty and innovation and involves creating variation in experience, risk-taking and experimentation. Exploitation is defined as refinement of existing knowledge, routines and implementation of knowledge. Exploitation involves efficiency and creates reliability in experience, as well as learning and tending to repeat successful past behaviour. According to Aslesen and Isaksen (2007) a firm's ability to learn, absorb and use knowledge inputs, and to interpret and put knowledge to use, is dependent on its internal knowledge bases and therefore its absorptive capacities (Cohen & Levinthal 1990).

Knowledge that human beings, firms and companies hold is important in itself, but knowledge exchange has become increasingly important when it comes to innovation (Powell & Grodal 2005). Innovation is a phenomenon on constant move.

The argument here is that innovation has come to be based increasingly on the interactions and knowledge flows between economic entities such as firms (customers, suppliers, competitors), research organisations (universities, other public and private research institutions) and public agencies (technology transfer centres, development agencies) (Asheim & Gertler 2005, p. 293).

One way to study knowledge exchange is to examine the interaction between producers and users, where users provide producers with knowledge in order to create the best possible and accurate solutions. To create this solution, the producers are also sharing their knowledge with the users. Another way to view knowledge exchange is the common aspects presented by Powell and Grodal (2005). The first aspect emphasises complementarity e.g. when firm A produces a component that firm B needs for their product development. The second aspect happens when a firm uses existing knowledge to create new knowledge that they would not otherwise come up with by themselves. Both aspects show the importance of knowledge exchange, whether the knowledge comes from external or internal sources.

For firms in organisational thick regions, the need for formal co-operation and networks is not as important as in organisationally thin regions (Jakobsen & Lorentzen 2015). It is claimed that these firms have easier access to R&D institutions, educational environments and other firms with different types of knowledge. They thrive on knowledge shared face-to-face and the local buzz in the region. The main difference between organisationally thick and diversified RIS and organisationally thick and specialised RIS is the amount of R&D institutions, a strong educational environment and to some degree the amount of clusters, as illustrated in Table 3.4.

Table 3.4 Expected knowledge exchange within the different RIS

	Categories of knowledge exchange			
Regional innovation systems (RIS)	*Formal static (services from R&D institutions or universities)*	*Informal static (local buzz and worker mobility)*	*Formal dynamic (joint development projects, client-supplier)*	*Informal dynamic (communities)*
Thick and diversified RIS	(X)	X	(X)	X
Thick and specialised RIS	(X)	X	X	
Thin RIS	X	(X)	X	

Methodological approach to study knowledge sharing and knowledge transfer

This study tries to develop knowledge on regional contexts and knowledge sharing, and knowledge transfer between companies, focusing on how it happens in a more qualitative research perspective. The study attempts to contribute to the development of empirical research, arguing that knowledge sharing and knowledge transfer is, in addition to historical presumptions, determined by different geographical settings. This is done by retelling individual business actors' experiences regarding how they acquire and use knowledge in innovation processes.

The fieldwork was consisted of 20 business interviews of entrepreneurial firms in four different regional settings. The entrepreneurial firms were found among micro and small oil and gas firms. Five oil and gas subcontractors in each of the regions were chosen for interviews. The businesses selected were relatively young, or had a relatively newly established entrance into the oil and gas sector. The study units had fewer than 30 employees. The 20 firms were also characterised by a dominance of local or national ownership. Decision-making authority for the corporate development strategy and innovation strategy was through local ownership located inside the business, and not tied to an external corporate management localised outside the region. In-depth qualitative interviews were conducted with key persons such as the firm entrepreneur, CEO, marketing manager or similar. Each interview followed a semi-structured guide, which focused on examples of knowledge exchange. Each interview lasted from 1 hour to 1 hour 30 minutes. The effort was dedicated to open questions that encouraged informants to retell their businesses stories and describe the firms' production ideas. The interviews were taped and transcribed verbatim in the aftermath of each interview.

Knowledge flow and regional context

This section presents the study results. The relationship between the four studied RIS and the knowledge flow in each of the regions is discussed. Findings from the research study attempt to highlight differences and similarities of knowledge flow in different regional contexts.

Hordaland

Hordaland has easier access to R&D institutions and educational environments, compared to the other three regions. In Hordaland, a RIS with many technologies but dominated by the subsea technology, we found evidence that formal static, formal dynamic and informal static knowledge exchange is the regional firms' practice. Hordaland hosts several R&D institutions and has a strong educational environment available in the region. Three of the studied firms had R&D institutions, or educational organisations involved in their product development by e.g. buying services from R&D institutions in the region. There were also several examples of a client-supplier sparring relationship. One of the informants illustrated this by claiming that "We have at least three other companies we work closely with and with whom we have joint studies with".

The amount of formal collaborations was a slight surprise because Hordaland constitutes a thick and diversified RIS. We did, however, find examples of local buzz and worker mobility during the interviews, which was less of a surprise. Even though we found several formal collaborations, they did not use the formal networks for this. The NCE Subsea cluster was mainly used as a marketing arena and somewhat for networking purposes, but not as an arena for co-operation or collaboration. The impression left was that the studied firms did not need the cluster in order to have vast and robust networks. The firms did however exploit the benefits of being a member of the NCE Subsea cluster. Or as one of the study informants told us, "We have joined the NCE Subsea cluster at oil conferences for a significant lower price than if we had to buy our own stand".

Rogaland

Rogaland has numerous firms in the oil and gas industry. The type of knowledge exchange prevailing in Rogaland is mainly formal dynamic knowledge exchange exemplified by the massive web of suppliers, and the informal static knowledge exchange exemplified by local buzz and worker mobility: "We have a big market and in addition a huge network".

When one of the interviewees was asked if they had formal networks or only knew a lot of people the response was: "It is probably the latter. It is probably only that".

The vast amount of actors in the oil and gas industry is, according to the informants, both an advantage and a challenge. An advantage with regards to the local buzz and the networks, and a challenge because there is a constant struggle to recruit and keep the most qualified employees. In addition, there is the economic aspect in regards to higher rent prices and salaries in such a competitive region. Rogaland exhibited both radical and incremental innovation. A couple of the studied firms are high-tech oriented, and are supported by both R&D partners and the public support system. Most of these however, are located outside of the region.

Agder

The Agder case-firms showed examples of both formal dynamic and informal static knowledge exchange. Even though there are some knowledge exchanging activities in the region, almost all of it happens within the cluster or between cluster member firms. This is the case with both client-supplier sparring relations and knowledge transfer through worker mobility. Innovation in Agder is often incremental and founded on workers' experience. Most of the interviewees from the Agder region explained that they have strong networks in Agder. Until now, the "drilling bay" has been successful in regards to market shares, number of business units in the oil and gas industry and the achievement of becoming a global centre of expertise (GCE). However, the theory on thick specialised RIS cautions against negative lock-in when external input is a rarity. What we see now is a downturn in the oil and gas industry that has led to massive lay-offs in Agder and most notably in the three big companies. How this will affect regional knowledge sharing and knowledge transfer is unknown. The case-firms in Agder were critical of the GCE NODE cluster because of their alleged focus on the three locomotives. Maybe the crisis can lead to a shift in the policy of the GCE NODE cluster, and contribute to strengthen entrepreneurship and SME policy. "At this moment, I would dare to say that we would exist better without NODE" and "We are not using it [NODE] to draw knowledge from it"(personal communications 28 November 2002).

The paradox here is that even though these locomotives make it difficult to co-operate within the GCE NODE cluster, most of the small oil and gas firms located in Agder operate as sub-suppliers to the three regional major companies.

Finnmark

The Finnmark case differs from the three other cases by being a relatively young petroleum region. Results from previous studies shows that organisational thin regions are more prone to creating innovation collaborations compared to organisationally thick regions. Decreasing region size leads to higher innovation collaboration (Jakobsen & Lorentzen 2015). This is because firms in organisational thin regions often have to go out of the region to find other firms, R&D institutions and educational environments they can co-operate with. In Finnmark, we found business intentions among the studied firms to co-operate with both inter-regional and intra-regional actors. However, they claimed that they have not co-operated as much as they would like to, but they see potential for high quality co-operation through e.g. the Arena project.

> Arena is a growing project. It is the first year we have received funding, but in that project, there is knowledge about the industry and networks. We have the opportunity to meet companies and individuals at certain arenas we would not have without those networks.
>
> (personal communication 2–3 March 2015)

The firms also commented that "You can deliver to more customers if we are a unit, one business cluster" (personal communication 2–3 March 2015).

They further observed that, "You are able to meet individuals and firms you would not encounter otherwise"(personal communication 2–3 March 2015).

The collaboration between different actors to strengthen the region is especially striking in Hammerfest, where the local industry and politicians are working together to create possibilities. Interviewees remarked that

"In addition, we get a pipeline directly to the politicians" (personal communication 2–3 March 2015).

The data analysis gave strong indication that Finnmark has a low degree of innovation. Innovation processes are mostly incremental, and originated from workers' experiences. One reason for low innovation activity can be found in the lack of R&D institutions and universities needed for scientific research and radical innovation. In regards to knowledge exchange, we found a few examples of formal dynamic knowledge sharing. Still, most knowledge exchange is a mixture of different local actors trying to improve Finnmark whichever way they can. An aspect worth mentioning regarding organisationally thin RIS and knowledge sharing and knowledge transfer, is the branch plants in Finnmark. Several MNCs have offices in Finnmark. It is likely that these firms exchange knowledge with actors outside the region because of their ownership, but because of our entrepreneurial focus we did not interview these firms.

Table 3.5 Summary of types of external knowledge sources and types of knowledge exchange developed in the four regions studied

Types of external knowledge sources	*Types of knowledge exchange*	
	Static	*Dynamic*
Formal collaboration	Sales relations: Organisationally thick and diversified region: Hordaland and the collaboration with R&D institutions and universities	Sparring relations: Organisationally thick and diversified regions: Hordaland with web of suppliers Organisationally thick and specialised region: Rogaland with web of suppliers and Agder dependent on a few big clients
Informal knowledge flow	Organisationally thick and diversified regions: Hordaland with local buzz and worker mobility Organisationally thick and specialised regions: Rogaland with local buzz and worker mobility and Agder with worker mobility	Autonomous groups of professionals who exchange and develop knowledge in a community

Source: Aslesen and Isaksen (2007), own modification.

By combining the information provided throughout the interviews and the information in Table 3.1, we divided the regions into three different RIS: organisationally thick and diversified RIS, organisationally thick and specialised RIS and organisationally thin RIS. There are no absolutes when dividing the different regions into different RIS. Not all firms within a region are necessarily complete matches with characteristics belonging to a given RIS and some might say that Norway and the four regions are too small to be characterised as RIS. Furthermore, we aimed to combine theory of RIS and of knowledge exchange. By doing this, we intended to find evidence whether some RIS have certain ways of sharing or transferring knowledge that is more prevalent than other ways. In the following table, we combine the four regions, the three RIS types and the four ways of sharing knowledge.

Regional differences in knowledge transfer

The overarching goal of the book is to discuss how to practise theory and theorise practice. This chapter cultivates a hypothesis claiming that different regional contexts create/enhance different regional practices for knowledge exchange between firms and other agents. Therefore, we have collected and analysed qualitative data with a focus on describing knowledge exchange practice. Such an in-depth understanding is useful for policy makers, in order to design improved policy practices for knowledge development initiatives.

The position we take, as applied social science researchers in a regional knowledge system, is a confirming or enforcing role. Throughout the chapter, we are not criticising the different ways of exchanging knowledge, but rather enhancing a more in-depth understanding on how knowledge exchange is taking place among entrepreneurial firms in the different regional context. During the study we have not been attached to the interviewees, thus we are at a non-involved level of study unit involvement. The empirical data is subjective opinions from significant persons in entrepreneurial firms who have been challenged to describe how their knowledge exchange is taking place with other actors in the region. Ergo, the level of analysis is a social level.

This study might contribute to a better understanding of the complexity of implications thin and thick organisational regions have on co-operation that strengthens innovation by using qualitative data and sector specified research units.

The four regions share and transfer knowledge differently. The organisationally thick and diversified Hordaland region made use of local buzz, a vast private network, collaboration with R&D institutions and the educational environment, as well as collaborations with their web of suppliers. The need for formal arrangements like clusters, in order to innovate, within or outside of the region was not very high. What we found in this region was standard contracts with a client, an R&D institution or a university that they had dealt with or spoken with beforehand.

The case-firms in Rogaland, like the case-firms in Hordaland, made use of the local buzz and worker mobility to share and transfer knowledge. They also highlighted the huge number of suppliers that they can co-operate with. The number of employees and business units within the oil and gas industry can explain the reason for these findings in Rogaland and not in Agder. The case-firms in Rogaland did not have the same collaboration with R&D institutions or educational environments as in Hordaland. There is an increasing degree of collaboration with such institutions, but not enough to be a determining characteristic of the region Rogaland.

All the firms interviewed in Agder were members of the GCE NODE cluster. However, most of them claimed that NODE was less positive for them and figured more as a hindrance. The smaller regional firms claim that their experience is that the three major companies get most of the cluster initiatives attention. Therefore, co-operation within the oil and gas cluster is the main motivation for knowledge exchange, and vice versa. The few examples of knowledge exchange identified during the study came from client-supplier collaboration and worker mobility. Both the mechanisms often happen between GCE NODE members, but are not managed by the cluster management.

The Finnmark RIS differed compared to the other study regions. It was challenging to identify specific regional knowledge exchange. The firms have intentions to co-operate to enhance knowledge exchange. Therefore, one Arena project has been established, and we also found and upcoming milieu of business incubators. However, the regional oil and gas industry is still premature. The coast outside Finnmark is the new national investment project within the petroleum sector. It is therefore reasonable to argue that the need for innovation initiatives will increase. Focus on knowledge exchange will become an important strategy for regional innovation. The lack of knowledge exchange in Finnmark is demonstrated by the lack of boxes in Table 3.5 in which to place the region.

The knowledge generated in this project shows how firms in four diverse regional contexts exchange knowledge. The experiences learned from the case studies are important contributions for target innovation policy initiatives. This knowledge is especially important for businesses and industry milieus in financial hardship and crisis.

Our chapter helps describe the context of different Norwegian regions. Through highly qualitative interviews, we have come to know the four regions Hordaland, Rogaland, Finnmark and Agder very well. The regions differ in both size and number of employees as well as in maturity of the industry we were analysing, i.e. the oil and gas industry. We sought out to explore how entrepreneurial firms exchange knowledge in different regional settings. We aimed to analyse how different regional contexts have importance and significance for knowledge exchange between firms. In addition, we sought to find how our results can make a difference with regards to the policy framework and discourses in the region. By studying firms within the oil and gas industry in different regions in Norway, we purpose to discuss knowledge exchange at the regional level.

4 Collective knowing

James Karlsen and Miren Larrea

Comparing territorial development in the Basque Country and Norway

In this chapter we discusss *collective knowing*. How can we construct collective knowing? The cases we refer to are from the province of Gipuzkoa in the Basque Country (Spain) and the Agder region in Norway. We use lessons learned from the first case, which is a 6-year action research project (a participatory approach to research), to discuss the Agder case.

Construction of collective knowing takes time. It is constructed in a continuous dialogue between actors who meet regularly. It can be a conflictual process that should not be avoided, but handled carefully and with wisdom. Through the process, a shared vision can be constructed, and actions taken to change the situation for the actors in the region.

The dominant discourse over the last 20 years, within the regional development and regional innovation literature, is that knowledge is the most important resource, and learning the most important process. The argument was first launched by Lundvall and Johnson (1994) and has since that time been repeated over 3,500 times.[1]

Knowledge is important. Knowledge construction has often been interpreted as the construction of theoretical knowledge within epistemic communities. We widen this concept by defining the construction of collective knowing as another approach to knowledge construction. We interpret learning as a knowledge building activity. We question the belief that there is an automatic transformation from theoretical knowledge, interpreted, to regional development. This is an overly simplified understanding of the complexity of the relationship. Theoretical knowledge is necessary, but not sufficient, in regional development. Collective knowing is needed in order to transform theoretical understanding of regional development into regional development in practice. We define collective knowing as shared understanding that regional development actors create through dialogue in action (Karlsen & Larrea 2014). In the construction process, regional development actors, including social science researchers, need to interact, build trust relationships and a shared vision, i.e. to create social capital. Social science research has a role to play in the construction of collective knowing.

The chapter argues that construction of collective knowing is a different mode of knowledge construction from creation of theoretical knowledge. The latter has been named Mode 1 knowledge production by Gibbons et al. (1994); see also Chapter 2. In the construction of collective knowing, action and regional development are the main aims, while in Mode 1 the focus is on the construction of theories and concepts that can enlighten our understanding.

The book focuses on the role of research in relation to the public sector and businesses, and presents a variety of approaches to such relationships. We focus on interactive and action research, and help understand how these can contribute to a more fruitful relationship of researchers with actors. The introduction presents the idea that key to the discussion of the book is the meaning of knowledge, what knowledge is developed through applied social sciences and what we mean by talking about the region as a knowledge system.

This book is about regional knowledge systems. Our contribution to the discussion that the book raises, is to present the concept of collective knowing. Collective knowing is not the same as explicit, analytical knowledge, or theoretical knowledge within epistemic communities, rather it is a construction of understanding that happens within a social environment.

We elaborate our argument by connecting it to two cases we have been working with in recent years. The first case is Gipuzkoa Sarean, a regional development project in the Basque Country (Spain), and the second is SINPRO, a cluster development project from the Agder region, Norway.

Gipuzkoa Sarean is an action research project that started in 2009 when the government of the Provincial Council of Gipuzkoa (a regional government) decided to work with researchers to generate social capital in the territory that would help increase the competitiveness of the region. In 2011 there was a change in government, and the project kept its methodological approach, but the goal was redefined, with the construction of a new pattern of relationship between the regional government and eleven county developing agencies in the region. The case focuses on one of the stages of the development of this new pattern of relationship.

SINPRO is a cluster project established in spring 2013 by 21 firms. The aim of the cluster project is to increase the absorptive capacity (Cohen & Levinthal 1990) of the firms through establishing arenas for collaboration between the firms, and between the firms and research institutions, both in the Agder region and outside the region. The majority of the firms are manufacturing firms which sell their products in national and international markets. They are not competitors, because they belong to different value chains, but they have acknowledged that in order to stay competitive they have to collaborate with each other and with research institutions. We discuss the phases from the establishment to their situation in mid-2015.

The two cases are connected, because there has been a learning process shared by the facilitators of both processes (the authors). One of the cases has been used as a background to reflect on the other. Both cases connect with one of the aims of the book, in terms of sharing studies that deliberately aim at influencing regional policy, as in both cases researchers worked in interactive processes with policy makers and decision makers that co-generated potential solutions for the problems faced by their organisations.

Finally, the chapter presents a discussion where lessons learned are shared, to help researchers and practitioners involved in similar processes reflect on their own experiences. The lessons learned are complementary to the model that is presented in the introduction for analysing a regional knowledge system, as it helps connect some of the dimensions of knowledge presented in Table I.4 in the introduction chapter, to practical implementation problems met in development processes. The lessons learned about the management of conflict and the generation of trust are connected to the analytical categories proposed in terms of power, beliefs and position.

Two cluster projects

First we present the cases we are discussing (see subsequent Table 4.1). There are many differences. They developed in different contexts, (Basque Country in Spain and Norway), Gipuzkoa Sarean has been an ongoing action research project for 6 years, while SINPRO is a relatively new project where we have been invited into specific events into the process. Gipuzkoa Sarean mainly involves policy actors, while SINPRO mainly involves firms. Table 4.1 illustrates some of the structural characteristics of the cases.

It is possible to learn from differences (Ennals & Gustavsen 1999). Inspired by Ennals (2014) we try to learn from differences using the case of Gipuzkoa Sarean as a background to reflect on SINPRO. That is why the discussion mainly addresses SINPRO's challenges. In order to present the cases, thick descriptions of the processes are used (Geertz 1973).

Gipuzkoa Sarean: a new approach to territorial development

Gipuzkoa Sarean is an action research process that was initiated in 2009 by the provincial government of Gipuzkoa, and continued when this chapter was written in 2015. To reflect on collective knowing, we focus on the stage from May 2011 to May 2013. In this period the authors worked together with the government of the province, with the goal of developing a new approach to territorial development that would later be proposed to territorial actors in the socio-economic field (prioritising county development agencies as intermediary agents working with firms, universities and technology centres). The government wanted to reformulate the way the previous governments had been relating to territorial actors. They worded the change mainly in terms of a more participatory

Table 4.1 Descriptions of structural characteristics of the two projects

	Gipuzkoa Sarean, Basque Country	*SINPRO, Norway*
Who initiated the project when?	Political actor, the provincial council of Gipuzkoa in 2009	Manufacturing firms in the Lindesnes region in 2013 and in spring 2014 the cluster organisation SINPRO was formally established
Organisation of the project	Politicians in the provincial council of Gipuzkoa and representatives of 11 county development agencies in the province of Gipuzkoa	Manufacturing firms from the Lindesnes region and University of Agder
Main problem	Develop a new participatory approach to territorial development in Gipuzkoa	Create a shared vision for collaboration among the firms and implement it
What was the process of developing research questions?	Done in a dialogical and participatory approach with the actors; knowledge was constructed together with the participants	Done in a dialogical and participatory approach with the actors; knowledge was constructed together with the participants
Deliberation on role of researchers	Action research (participatory approach)	Interactive research (participatory approach)
Type and intensity of interaction between researchers and participants	Regular meetings every week (22 in total) with representatives of the government and eight workshops with all members of government in the period analysed in the case	Regular meetings with the board and the manager and two seminars with firms and regional actors
Results from the project	Establishment of a new Directorate for Territorial Development and a new mode of collaboration with county agencies in Gipuzkoa	Construction of a shared vision, establishment of arenas for collaboration and an application to Innovation Norway
Research outcome and how was this research debited in the research community?	Book about Gipuzkoa Sarean, book chapters, journal articles	A project report from the foresight process and an article in the research magazine *Teft* at University of Agder

approach that would give voice to actors who had not had opportunity to participate in the policy process previously. County representatives together with small firms and trade unions were mentioned.

The challenge for researchers was to facilitate the construction of this proposal, and the implicit research question was how a new approach to territorial development could be constructed for the province of Gipuzkoa.

Action research had already been used in the previous stage of the project, and when it was proposed by researchers the government decided it was adequate for their purposes. The work plan until the proposal was ready consisted of 22 meetings and 8 workshops with different members from the government and the research team. One of the authors participated in all of them, with the responsibility of facilitating the process.

The outcome of the process in terms of policy learning was a proposal of a new model for territorial development that was made into a 10-page document, and the creation of a Directorate for Territorial Development with the mandate of working on the implementation of such proposal. The academic outputs can be seen in Karlsen and Larrea (2014).

When asked why they had decided in 2011 to work with social science researchers in the development of their proposal for a new model for territorial development, the policy maker in charge of the project at that time said:

> At that time we could say what we wanted to achieve from a political perspective, and how we wanted it to be done, but considering what society, habits and power relations we have, how could we make it happen? We thought that there was no other path than research and learning. That is precisely why we found Gipuzkoa Sarean could be useful.
>
> (Iñaki Errazkin in the project document *Gipuzkoa Sarean* 2015, p. 44)

The decision to work with researchers was made after a 3-month process of dialogue between policy makers and researchers. The quote is from 2015, more than three years later, when the rationale for this decision was made explicit by the policy maker in a very clear manner. The discourse had not been so explicit in the initial moments of the period.

The construction of shared vision

The first step was to construct a shared understanding of what territorial development meant. At a workshop, one of the researchers shared his definitions and frameworks of territorial development with most of the deputies (ministers) and directors of the government. In his first speech the researcher presented theoretical knowledge on territorial development. Then, participants discussed what the concept meant for the government. That was the beginning of the transformation of such knowledge into collective knowing. After two workshops and several meetings, there was an agreement to define territorial development as follows: "Territorial development: the process of mobilisation and participation of different actors (public and private) in which they discuss and agree on the strategies that can guide individual as well as collective behaviour" (*Gipuzkoa Sarean* 2015 document "Proposal for a New Approach to Territorial Development in Gipuzkoa").

This process was not without conflict. Participants wanted to know who the actors mentioned in the definition were. The government wanted to integrate county representatives in the project, and there were county development agencies in the 11 counties they wanted to work with. Not all government members agreed that these were the best actors for a new approach to territorial development, as they were at the core of the old model. One of the critical decisions made by the government was to work with the existing county development agencies.

The researcher who had shared the concept of territorial development was not local, and participated in the project periodically. Some months later he was invited to a new workshop. When he heard how politicians had integrated the concept in their decision making processes, he said: "I shared a concept with them and now it has become a guideline for action" (personal communication in Gipuzkoa Sarean workshop on 23 September 2013).

The concept was being transformed from theory into practice, which is at the core of the construction of collective knowing.

Once practice had slowly started to emerge, the government felt the need to have the adequate structure to take reflections into practice and integrate the county development agencies in Gipuzkoa Sarean. In May 2013 the new Directorate for Territorial Development was created, with three people working in it and the main mandate of taking the new approach to territorial development into practice by constructing a new pattern of relationship with territorial actors, prioritising county development agencies. The structural dimension of social capital had been reinforced. The new Directorate is a tangible result, closely linked to regional development. Its creation was neither a direct result of the knowledge shared by researchers nor the result of recommendations given by researchers. It was the result of a collective capability developed by researchers and policy makers together, which was rooted in trust, shared vision and the construction of spaces for dialogue.

SINPRO: construction of a shared vision

SINPRO is a cluster project at Agder established in spring 2013. The first aim of the foresight process was the construction of a shared vision for SINPRO. The second aim was to secure proper co-operation on ownership and management level in the member firms, so that time and human resources could be allocated for participation and collaboration. The third aim was that the collaboration would make a difference for the collaborating firms in 5 years' time.

The idea of collaboration among manufacturing firms in the Lindesnes region at Agder was created in 2013 among five of the leading firms in the region. In 2014 the cluster organisation SINPRO was established with 21 firms as members. One of SINPRO's first strategic actions was to initiate a foresight process, with the aim of creating a shared vision for the new cluster organisation.

The foresight process was organised by one of the authors, in collaboration with the manager of SINPRO and the board. The members of the board were the firms that initiated the idea of a cluster development project, i.e. the core firms. In addition to three meetings with the board before the foresight seminar, three interviews were done with firms that were not so central in the process, but were of interest as follower firms in the development process of the cluster organisation. The main events were the two foresight workshops, one in August and a follow-up seminar in September 2014. There was broad participation in the workshops. The participants were from the firms in the region (16), administration in SINPRO (2), the municipalities in the region (2), different regional development actors (4) and knowledge institutions (12, one dean and one administrative staff from Faculty of Technology, nine master students from master in Innovation and Knowledge, School of Business, University of Agder, and one administrative staff from SINTEF, Raufoss).

Two reports were written based on material from the workshops and strategic document. Their main argument was developed in collaboration with the manager and the board of SINPRO after the workshops. The following citations and Table 4.2 are from the strategic document *Report from the Foresight Process* (SINPRO 2020, 2014). Most of the 21 member firms of SINPRO are small and medium sized manufacturing firms. Many of them compete on the global market, and are thus exposed to global competition, but they are not competitors in the same markets.

Through the foresight process, it became clear that there was a general opinion among the participants that collaboration is necessary for the firms to stay competitive in the future, because market conditions and the technology are changing. During the first workshop the following vision was constructed by the participants: "We create and share knowledge".

This is a radical vision for a group of manufacturing firms that are producing concrete manufacturing products. In the SWOT analysis created by the participants, one weakness was that they did not have much experience from collaboration with each other or with knowledge institutions. Despite this, the vision was accepted without much discussion among the participants of what it actually meant in terms of change of behaviour.

Four arenas for collaboration were defined: *Automatisation*, *Energy management*, *Lean and Competence* and *R&D*. Lean is a management philosophy derived mostly from the Toyota Production System. There was a proposal to hold regular breakfast meetings with information sharing and invited speakers.

The arena application process

After the foresight process the Arena was created around the end of 2014. These were spaces for firms to meet, facilitated by SINPRO. The social science researcher's work with the foresight process was over. In order to observe how the firms were collaborating in the forums he signified his

Table 4.2 SWOT analysis from the foresight process

Strengths	*Weaknesses*
Differentiated business structure where firms are not competitors Some companies are globally oriented and world leaders in their niches, while others have a strong national position Strong technology orientation and good manufacturing expertise Flat organisational structure and short decision lines Physical proximity between firms Mandal is an attractive city to live in	Little tradition of collaboration between businesses and educational and research institutions Can be challenging for outsiders to understand the social norms in the region Few jobs in tertiary industries Recruitment Satisfied with the current situation Poor infrastructure Much commuting out of the region
Opportunities	*Threats*
New technology Outsourcing Climate focus and renewable energy Increase cooperation between enterprises and educational and research institutions Cluster partnership Deliveries to the oil industry New technology Outsourcing Climate focus and renewable energy Increased collaboration between firms and educational and research institutions Cluster Deliveries to the oil industry Building of a new highway Inward commuting	New technology Competition from low cost countries Outsourcing The level of cost of in Norway Competition for skilled labour

Source: Report from the foresight process.

interest in participating in the Lean forum. He was not invited into this forum but was asked if he knew a researcher from University of Agder with knowledge about Lean who might be interested in participating in the Lean arena. They were looking for researchers in the technological field.

In February 2015 the same researcher (an author of this chapter), together with a colleague, was asked by the board to contribute to the writing of an application to Innovation Norway for financial support of SINPRO. Innovation Norway is financing different cluster development programmes such as Arena, Norwegian Centres of Expertise and Global Centres of Expertise.

In this process, social science researchers built on the knowledge from the foresight process, and during meetings and email exchange with the manager of SINPRO and the board the application was finished in late April 2015. It became evident that the board wanted collaboration with research organisations. There was not so much talk about "quick wins". The argument from the board was that industry in the region had stayed competitive because of their capability to create incremental process and product innovations, but that this strategy had its limitations. As one member of the board said: "We are about to reach this limit now. In order to stay competitive in the future we need to collaborate with other firms in the region and we need to engage with research institutions in this process" (personal communication, B. Reiersen, 3 February 2015).

He argued that the innovations they need to create in the future are more expensive to develop so they need to distribute the cost among several firms, and innovation is more complex and knowledge intensive so they need to involve researchers.

Though the initial step in SINPRO was the integration of researchers in the technological field, positive steps have also been taken related to social science researchers, but at a more strategic level.

What is collective knowing?

Knowledge is not enough to generate regional development. It is the development of collective knowing, and not knowledge, that can be interpreted as contributing to regional development.

A critical concept to understanding collective knowing is the agora. The agora is the public space in which "science meets the public" and in which the public "speaks back to science". It is the domain (in fact, many domains) in which contextualisation occurs and in which socially robust knowledge is continually subjected to testing while becoming more robust in the process. Neither state nor market, neither exclusively private nor exclusively public, the agora is a space in which societal and scientific problems are framed and defined and where what will ultimately be accepted as a "solution" is negotiated (Nowotny, Scott & Gibbons 2001).

In the agora, theoretical concepts are contested and made actionable. Dialogue is a means to create changes in language and behaviour. Collective knowing is a dynamic capability (Teece, Pisano & Shuen 1997), a learned pattern of collective action, where the actors in the agora systematically modify their actions over time through the learning process in the agora (Karlsen & Larrea 2014). Collective knowing can only develop over time between actors that regularly meet and interact with each other. It is a dynamic capability for knowledge in action. This is pursued through dialogue between different actors (Karlsen & Larrea 2014). Through dialogue, theoretical concepts, discourses and real life situations connect to create a mutual foundation for action and change (Gustavsen 1992; Johnsen 2001), in a given situation in territory.

Our approach to collective knowing is inspired by Nahapiet and Goshal (1998), who propose three dimensions of social capital: the structural, the relational and the cognitive. The extent to which knowledge can be transformed into collective knowing is linked to the generation of the conditions related to the three dimensions.

The *structural* dimension is the impersonal configuration of linkages between actors. The *relational* dimension describes the kinds of personal relationships people have developed through a history of interactions. Among the key factors in this dimension are trust and trustworthiness, norms and sanctions, obligations and expectations and identity and identification. The last dimension is the *cognitive*, which is referred to as shared representations, interpretations and systems of meaning among actors.

Agoras and conflict

Agoras are naturally spaces for conflict. This means that our understanding of how collective knowing is developed is linked to our understanding of how conflict can be managed. Agoras are spaces where regional complexity takes place (Johnsen & Normann 2004; Karlsen 2010). This means that there are different actors with different interests in the agora, who do not necessarily have the same opinion about the main problems in the territory nor the possible solutions to such problems. No actor has the position in the agora to instruct the rest on what will be done. This means that negotiation and collaboration are necessary. Dialogue is the process through which negotiation and collaboration are constructed, and the conflict is solved.

When conflict is solved we talk about consensus. Consensus does not mean that everybody agrees, but that there is agreement enough to initiate some action (Koppenjan 2007). Usually such action leads the agora to new conflicting situations, so that complexity is faced in cyclical processes of conflict, consensus and action.

Conflict can be implicit or explicit. It is difficult to solve conflict unless it is made explicit, but this can have negative consequences. That is why it is important that conditions to solve conflict are created while making conflict explicit (Karlsen & Larrea 2012).

Agoras, and collective knowing developed in them, contribute to territorial development. The academic community has a challenge in understanding how this happens. Still, agoras and collective knowing are not part of the mainstream language in regional development and innovation literature.

The concept in Regional Innovation Systems (RIS) literature that best connects with this approach to collective knowing is policy learning. Policy learning is social learning in communities or networks (Bennett & Howlett 1992) that develops in the process of defining policy. Our proposal for territorial development is linked to the role social science researchers can play in policy networks, where policy learning happens and collective knowing can be constructed. Both cases are policy networks where policy learning is the main process.

We interpret social innovation, following Moulaert and Nussbaumer (2005), as innovation in patterns of relationship, and propose that the role of researchers in policy networks is to construct social innovation. This process of construction requires a position of the researcher who is not an outsider, observing and analysing regional development. The researcher is also a territorial actor who influences the process.

This is the case in both cases, where the authors have participated. Still the cases have differences in the language used to name the type of research developed and the role played by researchers. Gipuzkoa Sarean has been named by the participants in the process as *action research* whereas the process in SINPRO is called *interactive research*.

We define action research as a research strategy for change in real time where the three elements of research, action and participation are connected and combined in the same process (Greenwood & Levin 2007). The definition of interactive research is inspired in the following: "The many kinds of communicative action that innovation researchers perform in interaction with policy makers and other key actors within a regional innovation system, can from a methodological point of view be considered a form of interactive research" (Pålshaugen 2014, p. 230).

We do not intend to discuss in-depth the difference between action research and interactive research. Any kind of interaction from a speech, via construction of a report, to participation in dialogues with actors can accordingly to the aforementioned definition count as interactive research. In this sense any research that involves interaction with actors within a regional innovation system is defined as interactive research, including action research. There are many approaches to research in policy learning processes, but they do not always share the same ontological or epistemological propositions. The authors represent the connection between the two approaches.

Following the foresight process, SINPRO has formulated ambitious common aims. If the lessons learnt in Gipuzkoa Sarean make any sense, behind their explicit agreement there could be differences in interests and interpretations that need to be made explicit and worked on, in order to take the goal into concrete applications.

The SWOT analysis from the foresight process indicates that the firms do not have much experience from collaboration with each other, and even less with knowledge institutions. Since the collaboration is relatively new, conflicts have not been made explicit, but there is potential for conflict between firms when they are prioritising areas for actions.

Another potential conflict can be between knowledge institutions, especially universities, which are searching for long-term research projects and the firms' needs and interest in quick wins.

Gipuzkoa Sarean also faced the challenge of evolving from the abstract idea of a new pattern of relationship in the territory to the practical development of the new relationship. One of the lessons was that it is easy to agree on big principles, but practice did not develop until the different and conflicting perspectives in the group were slowly made explicit and managed. This did not mean that that they declined common aims. Having different interests and interpretations of the process is the usual situation, and a shared understanding of such differences needs to be built in order to advance.

Making conflict explicit can be difficult. People feel tempted to take a conflict-avoiding attitude. It is important that the value the participants see in collaboration is greater than the cost of making their differences explicit.

Creating arenas for collaboration requires more than technological knowledge

Technology is one of the strengths of the firms in the SINPRO cluster. In order to stay competitive, they want to invest in new technology. The firms are technology-oriented. Even Lean, which is a learning tool for reducing cost, is defined by the firms as technological knowledge, not as an organisational learning process where social science researchers could have a role to play.

Learning, reflection and action, which are a part of the researcher's vocabulary, are not yet a part of the discourse in SINPRO. Knowledge for the firms is technological knowledge, but they do not define what this means. It is neither theoretical knowledge developed by researchers, nor collective knowing. It might be that the firms expect a concrete answer to a concrete technological challenge, or that they see that they have to co-generate the answer together with technological researchers.

When reflecting on this structural dimension of social capital in order to understand the construction of collective knowing, we have gone back to the experience of Gipuzkoa Sarean in order to see if there were lessons learnt that could help reflect on this.

One of the differences is that there was recognition of policy as a social process, and thus a natural understanding that social science researchers should have access to the different spaces where reflection was going on with territorial actors. This does not mean that researchers were in every space, but every space was discussed in terms of design and learning by policy makers and researchers. The second feature was that these meetings were part of the management routines of policy makers. They had integrated researchers in their routines as outsiders to the government, but not to the project. The process was based on team work between policy makers and researchers.

Conflict must be made explicit and managed in order to have collaborative processes going. Social science researchers can be relevant in facilitating such processes, but in order to do so effectively they must have a role that gives them the whole picture of the process and access to opening dialogue with different types of stakeholders in the process.

Lack of collaboration indicates that the firms will need time to build trust in each other, even if they are not competitors. They will also need to build trust in working with researchers. Firms and researchers have their own "language", and included in that "language" is what they take for granted. An indicator of this "language", seen from the firm's part, is in the expression in the SWOT analysis: "difficulties to understand the norms in the region". Researchers' "language" can also be technical and difficult to understand. Therefore, one of the first challenges in building trust is to try to accept the others' language, and try to see if a co-generated and shared language can be constructed.

The experience from SINPRO so far shows that trust can be built by a process approach. Researchers were invited to participate in developing an application for funding. This role might seem initially more instrumental than the role played by researchers in Gipuzkoa Sarean. A similar pattern was found when we compared the initial stages of Gipuzkoa Sarean. This indicates that researchers can play a relevant role in facilitating development processes that require social change, as the generation of collaboration in a cluster. The role played by researchers in the initial stages can be very instrumental. It is through the construction of trust that researchers can play a more critical role in the construction of shared vision in the whole process. Although the contribution by researchers to SINPRO at present is mainly instrumental, it is still part of trust building that firms acknowledge that different types of researchers contribute with different types of knowledge.

Constructing collective knowing is not a quick win game

In our discussion of the foresight process, there was a discussion about quick wins, while in the writing of the application to Innovation Norway this was less evident. There had been a change in the cognitive framework among the firms about the contribution from research, as the manager of SINPRO argued in a discussion. The manager and the board had constructed collective knowing about this issue different from other member firms of SINPRO. Quick wins belongs to what March (1991) called exploitation, which generally encompasses activities such as refinement, choice, production, efficiency, selection, implementation and execution of current knowledge in firms. However, March (1991) argued that, in order to survive in the long run, firms also need to explore new possibilities. Firms need both to exploit and explore at the same time, but due to internal and external tensions and pressure, it is not easy to do both.

Construction of collective knowing takes time, resources and management awareness. These resources could alternatively be used for exploitation. In SINPRO this is manifested between the core firms and the follower firms. The core firms, in the board, see the need for exploration activities, while not all the follower firms see the same need for the exploration activities. This can slow down the process of creating collective knowing among the firms, but also create the possibility of making the conflict explicit between exploration and exploitation. SINPRO has just started on the journey of constructing collective knowing. If Innovation Norway grants the application, SINPRO will have the economic resources to continue on the journey of constructing collective knowing.

Construction of collective knowing is a context-sensitive process, and cannot be transferred, because it is a part of the context in which the action took place. What can be transferred is the verbal description of the process and the concepts and frameworks such as collective knowing. This implies that every time it is decided to start a new regional development process, the actors have to go through the different stages of discussing a shared vision, establish arenas for concrete collaboration and then collaborate. Social science researchers who have been trained for example as action researchers, and have participated in such processes, have developed knowledge that can contribute to such processes.

It is not easy to work in such processes; either you are representing a firm, an agency or you are a researcher. Seen from the researcher's perspective, often the other participants expect that the researcher knows the answer to the challenge, or has knowledge that can solve the challenge quickly. However, there is no recipe or quick fix if the participants want real change. Real change implies change in behaviour, and this might also imply cognitive change. This can be much harder than expected for participants; it involves practice, and practice is connected to action and change of behaviour (Freire 1996, 2008a, 2008b). It is not a matter of getting the knowledge from those who have it; i.e. as a linear knowledge transfer, it is a more radical change: "It's a matter of changing our inner beliefs, confronting our fears and changing the status of different actors in a process" (Karlsen & Larrea 2014, p. 151).

Learning in agoras for territorial development, either as a cluster development project, or a mode of relationship as in Gipuzkoa, is connected to action and consequently to change in behaviour. Gipuzkoa Sarean has gone through that phase, and SINPRO has just started. If the firms in SINPRO really want achieve their shared vision, they have some hard years of intense discussions ahead, and they must also be willing to use their own money in that process and not only rely on public funding. They can try to avoid making conflict explicit, but then they will probably only achieve quick wins and not their shared vision.

How to develop collective knowing

Our main conclusion is that there is a long journey from what we call solution-oriented research to collective knowing (Karlsen & Larrea 2014). Territorial development is linked to knowledge, knowing, learning and related concepts, but there is a significant difference between having knowledge as a resource, and having collective knowing which is only observable in practice.

Researchers, as well as other actors involved in territorial development, can be relatively quick in reaching solutions to practical problems. These can take the form of definitions, like that of territorial development in the case of Gipuzkoa Sarean, a vision statement as in the case of SINPRO and applications for public money or policy recommendations, as social science researchers often produce in reports and articles. These are relevant. They are needed in the process as collective knowing is developed by the continuous transformation of such stocks of knowledge. These stocks of knowledge, though relevant, are not enough for territorial development. Still, researchers use most of their time in the production of such definitions, statements and recommendations and very little in the transformation of these into practice for the development of collective knowing. Researchers seldom engage in the process of creating collective knowing. Many researchers argue that industry and university should collaborate more, but few really enter the agora and try to collaborate on a long term basis. Therefore concepts, such as Mode 2 knowledge production (Gibbons et al. 1994), or the third mission of university, remain a black box.

There are probably many reasons behind this. We focus on assumptions about what social science research is. The generation of knowledge as a resource is widely acknowledged as a scientific endeavour. The production of reports, chapters and articles is the horizon for most research in the field of regional development. The processes of constructing trust, shared vision with territorial actors and new spaces where collective knowing can develop, are not in this category. There is little recognition in the academic environment of such processes as part of science.

This is a challenge for regional development. Scientific production in the field could increase its impact in terms of actual development if the mechanisms for doing it were integrated into research processes. This is the main contribution approaches such as action research and interactive research can bring into regional innovation literature.

We end with a plea for the co-existence of different research approaches in the field of regional development. There are possibilities to learn from each other and the combined efforts, far from undermining any of the approaches, would show a potential path for mutual reinforcement.

Note

1 Source: Google Scholar, downloaded 25 May 2015.

Part II

Understanding regional practice

The chapters in this part of the book take the perspective that knowledge is developed in a process. Research knowledge is part of a social knowledge development process. We could say more technically that all the chapters are within the interpretist tradition of philosophy, emphasising the epistemological challenges facing science.

The chapters share the view that knowledge does not exist prior to the researchers' producing it, but emerges in a collaborative process between researcher and "researched". All chapters also take the everyday life perspective as a starting point. Also, the chapters in this part are all critical to dominant ways of framing a topic, whether the research concerns environmental planning, music education, integration of immigrants, or when the whole social development discourse is involved.

The chapters suggest how research can contribute to (1) giving voice to marginalised perspectives and (2) to a more diversified political space. The researchers believe that this is possible not only by criticising "the system" from the outside, but by introducing (different versions of) an alternative dynamic between the research community and the regional field of practice.

In Chapter 5: Opening or reproducing understandings the point of departure is an Action Research project related to environmental planning. The chapter argues that the role of social science research is to understand the tensions in, and the oppositional critique between, different meaning and knowledge systems, but also to interact with, challenge and facilitate communicative processes. Research in this case is about "deliberate contextual knowledge" and the chapter discusses a Pragmatic, a Dialogical and a Critical-Utopian model for how Action Research can intervene in such a situation.

In Chapter 6: Social integration of refugees the case is integration of refugee women in the labour markets in the Agder region. By using institutional ethnography, it is demonstrated that the applied social science researcher should both be applied, by answering questions that different actors find relevant and important, but also attempt to bring in knowledge that is not represented nor necessarily considered relevant. The argument is that researchers should be more than allies for people representing organisations and institutions that already have a lot of power, and that if we manage this we prevent other and better ways of doing things from being obstructed, or even from coming into being.

In Chapter 7: Comparative reflection the case is integration of female immigrants from Africa in Norway. The chapter discusses how to exploit researchers' experiences from fieldwork in "far-away places", i.e. economic activity in Tanzania and rights to property in Mozambique, in studies of integration in a Northern context. The example granted is a project called "Job Opportunity project" (Jobbsjansen) which is about immigrant women's ways into paid labour. The chapter argues that ethnographic studies contribute to diversity by allowing us to move beyond stereotypes, and that such an approach is possible in applied research. It only requires that the researcher possesses/holds ethnographical experience and is able to apply such skills in situations where time is of the essence.

In Chapter 8: Phenomenology of music students the case is music education. The author takes a phenomenological perspective in order to understand what happens besides music production and performing when students develop into artists and musicians. This case illustrates that becoming a musician is broader than practise and performing. A key term is *projecting*, and the case demonstrates how education is something that develops in a social, lifeworld situation. It links this to the institutional setup for music education, where music practise and performing is considered as being the only aim of a musician.

In Chapter 9: Power and knowledge the argument is that social science research has other roles to play than the ones it is normally given, as either relevant or useless. The chapter presents two alternative ways of influencing society, beyond funders and policy-makers. Either you deliberately construct counter-hegemonic discourses through the research process or you target the structuring of political space and tease out powerful agents inviting to debate about limited topics within the hegemonic story. The chapter demonstrates these two alternatives by revealing how an ethnographic study of female economic activity in Zanzibar may institute a rival project to the Eurocentric development discourse.

5 Opening or reproducing understandings

Mikaela Vasstrøm

Action research in a planning process

Action research aims to understand and develop existing knowledge systems in a particular situation, through generating dialogue between actors for processes of learning and change. In situations marked by conflict and contested agendas, involved knowledge systems can be oppositional, and unwilling to establish arenas for dialogue. This chapter questions how an action researcher interacts with different layers of institutions and actors that represent distinct (and conflictual) paradigmatic knowledge systems, in an environmental planning process in Southern Norway: research involvement at different arenas in the planning process of *Heiplanen*.

The planning process was "wicked" in the sense that it did not have any objective solutions at hand, it mobilised and influenced several interests, and it involved several institutional levels representing a variety of knowledge and value claims. In such a situation the action researcher is faced with a dual challenge of opening a social dialogue space or field: to encourage critical internal reflections in a given knowledge system, and to incite transverse learning across oppositional knowledge and practice systems. The chapter considers how a critical theoretical foundation can serve to support a critical reflexive role in action research methodologies. Learning and collaboration across institutional levels requires each participant to critically reflect on their perception of knowledge and values as a necessary remedy to recognise the legitimacy of other perspectives. The role of the critical action researcher is thus not only to facilitate dialogue, but to challenge established value perceptions and worldviews with the participants at each "institutional level".

The case presented here is about the action researcher role in wicked situations where oppositional knowledge claims are used to strengthen and reproduce existing interest claims (Brunner & Steelman 2005). The case illustrates the role of the action researcher in the emerging openings and closures of dialogue and knowledge development between municipal authorities and citizens on the one hand, and regional-state nature protection authorities on the other. This chapter addresses the question: *how can the action research role contribute to open new understandings across regional institutional planning perspectives and local community perspectives in the regional planning process of Heiplanen?*

I start by introducing the contextual field of environmental planning and society-nature relations and the particular regional case of Heiplanen. Second, different ramifications of action research approaches and roles are explored. Special attention is given to the critical theoretical contributions to action research, and their implication for the action research role, particularly understanding the tensions between the planning institutions and local communities. I do that by exploring and challenging the regional institutional planning actors *and* the local communities' perspective of nature planning, participation, and knowledge *during an ongoing* planning process. The research ambition was in this sense to open, rather than reproduce, different knowledge and meaning systems, enabling new mutual understandings.

A case of environmental planning in Norway

The Heiplanen case

Heiplanen was a regional planning process from 2009 to 2012 in southern Norway that involved 18 municipalities within 5 counties and concerned approximately 12,000 km^2. The plan was commissioned from the Ministry of Environment in 2007. The purpose of the plan was (1) to secure potential wild reindeer habitats, and (2) to explore perspectives for rural development. The planning authority was placed at the political level of the county and municipality, but all decisions had to be grounded on natural science knowledge. The natural science knowledge was provided by the wild reindeer centre as a map of potential wild reindeer habitats and by the environmental officials at the county governor office.

Three municipalities in Setesdal were central to Heiplanen; they had some of the most essential wild reindeer habitats in the region, their entire municipal area was included in the planning area and they had a 40-year-long history of nature protection conflicts with national authorities (Falleth & Hovik 2008). Setesdal is a narrow 200 km long valley situated in the southern mountain area of Norway. The three most northern municipalities Bykle, Valle, and Bygland are large mountainous areas (app. 4,500 km^2), but sparsely populated (app. 3,500 inhabitants). The nearest city is Kristiansand (app. 85,000 inhabitants) situated on the coast with a distance of 1–3 hours' drive respectively. These rural municipalities, like similar peripheral rural areas in Scandinavia and Europe, face socio-economic challenges related to workplace development and a declining number of citizens. Rural development is an important issue in the municipality, understood as a broad, diverse, and long-term process (Normann & Vasstrøm 2012).

This particular case of regional nature protection planning in three municipalities reflects the challenges related to knowledge, steering, interests and values. The case represents the complexity of having several levels of vertical government involved, as well as a wide range of horizontal actors representing different interests and worldviews in an ongoing conflictual process. There is thus a "dissonance" in nature planning in general, and in Setesdal in particular, that could be explored and understood through a critically-inspired action research approach. Further, it provides the possibility of exploring alternative perspectives on nature planning with local communities and of understanding the resonance of these among the planning authorities in the present planning process. The case created the possibility of critically exploring how a regional nature planning process approaches participation, how the "local community level" of citizens and authorities perceive and challenge this approach, and if and how the development of common understandings can improve the planning policies and practices. These aspects will be reflected in relation to the role of an action researcher, and will open some theoretical reflections about different ramifications of action research, the research role, and its relevance and potential in critical social science.

Research roles and planning process evolvement

The richness and complexity of the Heiplanen process cannot be described in the format of this chapter. The purpose of this description is rather to

Table 5.1 Phases in the process

Time	*Case process*	*Description*
2004–2007	Pre-planning process	The pre-planning process was the research and policy process that led to the commissioning of nine regional wild reindeer planning areas and the particular planning programme of Heiplanen.
2008–2011	Formal regional planning process	The formal planning process underlies the entire Heiplanen process. It represents the operationalisation of Heiplanen by the formal planning authorities at the regional and municipal level.
2009–2010	Informal planning process	The informal planning process represents a researcher-initiated parallel process with the municipalities and citizens in Setesdal. It is labelled informal because it did not have any formal authority in the Heiplanen process, but was accepted as an additional process by the planning authorities. It explored the everyday life oriented understanding of nature and society based on Critical Utopian Action Research inspired participatory processes.
2010–2011	Semi-formal planning process	The semi-formal process emerged as an outcome of the communication between the informal and formal planning arenas. It is labelled semi-formal because it did not constitute a formal planning arena in itself, but each participant represented different formal planning authority roles in the process.
2011–2012	Post-planning process	The post-planning process was the final hearing and approval of the plan outcome.

describe how the research interactions and roles simultaneously evolved with the involved planning actors during the process. Table 5.1 attempts to systematise the planning phases of the Heiplanen process as a contextual overview for the research role descriptions.

The pre-planning phase was assessed through search in policy documents and research reports that influenced and formed the national commission of Heiplanen. Further, research reports and chapters concerning nature protection and environmental planning in Norway (and especially in the Heiplanen area/Setesdal) were scrutinised. These findings gave a broader contextual framework, and nuanced the societal discourses and interest conflicts at play in nature protection planning.

The researcher entered the formal planning arena on the first public regional meeting in October 2009. The meeting was hosted by the responsible county governments and attended by most municipal mayors and planners from the 18 municipalities. During this meeting I approached the regional planner responsible for the process to ask if I could participate as an observer during the planning process. I explained that my primary concern was to understand the tensions in the planning process, and the potential for opening broader local participation in the plan. He considered my perspective relevant, not least in the light of the conflictual atmosphere already present between the municipalities and the regional planning authorities (county government and county governor).

During the next months I was invited to participate on the formal planning meetings between the regional planning authorities and the municipalities in Setesdal. These meetings and my role as a participant observer provided an opportunity to learn about the tensions and conflicts at play between the regional and municipal point of perspective. It also provided a space for me to critically question the purpose rationality of the plan and the espoused role of local participation in the process. This critical research role in return created the opportunity for municipal authorities to reflect on how local participation could be improved.

I proposed to facilitate (in collaboration with the three Setesdal municipalities) citizen workshops as a way of deliberating a different perspective on nature protection and use, related to the lived life in the area. I emphasised that such a process would not necessarily change the formal plan or reduce existing conflicts. I argued that it could contribute to generate a different perspective about nature protection and use in the local communities that could lead to local change or actions. Further, it could broaden the understanding of nature use among the formal Heiplanen actors and perhaps facilitate or encourage the county governor to consider a more direct dialogue with the municipalities.

The idea of organising Future Creating Workshops (FCW) (Nielsen & Nielsen 2006a, 2006b) was presented to the political and administrative leaders in the three municipalities as an attempt to open a citizen or community perspective in the Heiplanen process. This approach was gradually accepted. Some actors were sceptical about the "purposelessness" of the process, the risk of opening citizen participation, and that it would not yield direct strategic action in Heiplanen. However, due to the level of conflict with the county governor, it was also seen as a potential to frame the discourse about protection and use in a new way.

The informal planning process and its formal continuation

During the first part of 2010 the researcher and municipal planners worked together to organise the community workshops. This entailed iterative meetings with discussions about the different conflictual aspects of Heiplanen in relation to the Setesdal and community past nature protection experiences, their current rural development challenges, and their problematic relation to the county governor. They considered processual elements about the workshops regarding who to invite, how to mobilise citizens, how to "frame" the participatory arena, how to participate as citizens, and how to communicate the linkage with Heiplanen. The participatory role of the municipality as an authority was thoroughly discussed. In the practical organisation, Idébanken (an NGO who has worked with future creating workshops, sustainability transitions and municipal change) was engaged as process facilitator along with the researcher.

The FCW was named "The good life for humans and wild reindeer in Setesdal – now and in the future". The title and the opening of the workshop thus emphasised that the idea was to open up perspectives from the citizens about life in Setesdal and relations to the nature of the area. It was in this sense not an arena for negotiation of particular interest groups. Rather, it was an arena or "free space" that did not have a given purpose, but was aimed at developing meaningful deliberations in a social setting. The FCW was thus an attempt to create a different outlook for local participation in planning that was not based on interest negotiation between "qualified stakeholders", but deliberations of citizens' everyday life perspectives in relation to their common concern of nature and society.

The workshops were attended by 20–25 persons in each municipality over two days. The workshops were divided into three main phases: the critical phase, the utopian phase, and the reality making phase. In this way, the process first considered the current situation in a critical perspective: "We are not satisfied with . . ." Second, the critique was reversed by asking, "If we could decide . . ." And last, the participants selected what thematic focus they wanted to work on realising during a group work session. During these workshops, the researcher (in collaboration with Idébanken) facilitated the process, systematised the proposals, and documented the contextual outcome. After the three workshops, the researcher synthesised the experiences and perspectives from the entire informal process in a report. The report was sent to the local authorities and citizens involved in Setesdal – the county government, the county governor, and the project leader of Heiplanen – and to people involved with the regional wild reindeer planning in the Ministry of Environment.

The researcher was invited to present these findings at formal regional Heiplanen meetings: a board meeting, and a work meeting for the administrative municipal staff. The role of the researcher was to give a critical "research" perspective on the Heiplanen process in relation to other similar nature protection planning conflicts in Norway and Europe. The theme was the dichotomies of protection and use, and local-national steering governance. At the same time, this was an opportunity to enact a critical utopian action research role that could mediate the local community perspectives to an institutional setting. My intention was that the communication of the diverse and life related perspectives of nature protection and use could open a different kind of dialogue between the municipalities and the county governor. Not only as a means to ease conflict between the actors, but as an approach to develop new inter-subjective understandings about how to approach nature protection and use in a long-term perspective.

This intention and ambition might have been naïve. The county governor representatives did consider the local community perspectives interesting. However, related to the "objective" and "hard" ecological facts about the wild reindeer habitat and the planning purpose to set boundaries on a map, the local perspectives were considered as tokens of "subjective" opinions and "unplannable" dreams. In this sense, the deliberation of local community, or life oriented, perspectives on nature and society were neutralised and naturalised with references to natural scientific science and the purpose of the plan.

After these presentations, the municipalities decided that they would not continue to work with the local citizen fora, but rather focus their capacity on strategic positioning in the formal Heiplanen process. For me as a researcher this was a difficult process, because I had hoped to continue the citizen process as an alternative to Heiplanen. After much reflection and discussion with colleagues, I decided to continue to follow the formal planning process as a participant observer, and to critically enquire into the understandings of nature and knowledge prevalent with the regional planning actors and county governor representatives.

The research role was in this sense more classic qualitative in methods (participant observation and semi-structured interviews), at the same time as it included a change oriented dialogue perspective. My role was thus to enact further reflections inspired by theoretical perspectives and related to understandings expressed by the local community perspectives. The questions and comments were for instance mounted on understandings of legitimacy and purpose of participation, or the type and role of knowledge in the planning process. The research role during this period became engaged as a critical reflection partner between the municipal level, the county government, the county governor, and, not least, the project leader of Heiplanen. These dialogues opened the opportunity to discuss and reflect on the challenges of local participation from the municipal perspective and in relation to the purpose of the formal planning process. This iterative reflection between researcher and project leader created a collaborative research arena that also influenced the formal planning process development, and in particular the emergence of the semi-formal planning process that will be described in the next section.

In the autumn of 2010, I was invited to participate on the study trip for all the Heiplanen actors (county governor representatives, county government planners, municipal planners, mayors, and the project leader) and in return write a documentation report. The study trip visited one regional park and one national park in England to learn about their way of planning, managing and steering nature protection and use issues (and conflicts). The visit to these parks created a reflective mirror for the Heiplanen participants. The English participatory steering methods and nature perspectives presented by the rangers revealed that they worked very closely with local communities. These experiences and the continuous critical dialogue between the researcher and the county governor representative opened a new space for self-reflections about nature and knowledge understandings.

Shortly after the study trip I invited three county governor representatives involved in Heiplanen to a focus group interview to discuss and reflect on the role of local participation, their own role, and the role of different types of knowledge in Heiplanen. The interviews and focus group also opened an arena where the researcher could reflect on theoretical perspectives and experiences from the local meetings in the municipalities with the county governor representatives. The different interviews also served to discuss aspects of planning with the formal institutional actors.

The semi-formal planning process

In the first part of 2011, the municipality and county governor representative finally agreed to create a dialogue arena in the formal planning process. Five dialogue meetings were held between the parties.

> We all heard what you [the researcher] said a year ago – but we had never thought that it would be possible to meet in this way. I have never seen this type of negotiation before . . . but there has also been maturation with many small processes that have opened the way for this type of meeting.
>
> (project leader at meeting, 21 February 2011)

The researcher was present as a participatory observer at all the dialogue meetings. The researcher's role was to listen to the discussions and negotiations to understand the different perspectives, but also to reflect and comment on the development of the conversation with general theoretical perspectives on planning and representing different understandings of the planning matter that had been expressed in other arenas and especially the local community perspectives. The main task of the researcher was in this sense to create room for reflection about the development of the process during these meetings and to explore how the communication evolved, what the main controversies were, and where the main turning points in understanding arose.

During these meetings the final plan document was crafted as a collaborative effort between municipalities and the county governor representatives.

After the finalising of the plan document, the researcher carried out evaluative group interviews with the Setesdal municipalities (administration and politicians) to explore how they perceived the Heiplanen process and outcome, the most important events, the role of local involvement in the "informal phase", and the role of the researcher. Single evaluative interviews were also made with the project leader of Heiplanen, the county government official, and the county governor. These single interviews were also concerned with documenting how they perceived the development of the Heiplanen process, the most important events, the importance of the local involvement, and the role of the researcher in the process. "It was a plan nobody wanted – and nobody understood what it was . . . These areas [of the plan] have been negotiated directly across the table between municipalities and county governor – something that I have not experienced in 20 years" (project leader, 23 May, 2011).

All the formal planning actors considered that the engagement of the researcher had contributed to the development of the process. The municipalities concurred that the presence of an independent research perspective during the process had not only contributed to increased awareness of their relations. It had also contributed with a more diverse local perspective on the regional planning. In this sense, the engagement and collaboration between the researcher and the municipalities had been important to understanding their own role in the process and subsequent development towards increased dialogue with the regional actors. This point was also reflected by the county governor representative. They considered my role and engagement at different planning "levels" had been difficult to understand in the initiation of the process, but had contributed to reflecting and discussing aspects of the planning process on a more general level. My engagement had in this sense contributed to facilitating the development of dialogue between the actors, because it has been possible to question the process, practice, and different understandings from a more distanced perspective. This consideration was also accentuated by the project leader and county government. They pointed to the engagement at both the local and regional level which facilitated the ability and legitimacy of presenting different concerns of the planning process and the questioning of conflictual issues in the regional planning arena.

Different roles for action research

Contextual setting: regional planning in contested nature society relations

Sustainability is one of the most pressing concerns in our modern society, and now influences general discussions about societal development and planning (Elling 2008; Meadowcroft 1999; Nielsen, Elling & Jellsoe 2010). Current environmental planning or nature protection endeavours can be interpreted as an institutional answer to cope with the societal sustainability challenges (Cowell & Owens 2011). The challenge in environmental planning should address the question, "Who should define what values and rationalities should have a say in the definition of what and how to balance these interests?"

Environmental policies have since their emergence in the 1960s been a policy area with strong national state responsibility (Reitan 2004), and the planning and management processes orchestrated by state agencies (Dietz, Ostrom & Stern 2003; Sandström, Hovik, & Falleth 2008). Such a "top-down" steering approach gives the environmental authorities mandate to define a planning purpose in relation to national policies and based on the prevailing natural scientific knowledge. This type of environmental government is influenced by an understanding of the state as a superior and omnipotent actor that must act to avoid the risk of the *tragedy of the commons* (Björkell 2008; Nelson, Howden, & Smith 2008; Ostrom 1990;). Further, it demonstrates an epistemological understanding of natural science as objective knowledge provider within a rational planning approach (Brunner & Steelman 2005; Innes & Booher 2010).

Norwegian environmental policies have, since their appearance on the political agenda, been centralised at the state level, and later to regional state agencies; the environmental agency of the county governor (Hovik & Reitan 2004; Sandström et al. 2008). The nature view of these authorities has been strongly influenced by urban-recreational values of pristine and untouched nature, and by natural scientific positivistic knowledge ideals. At the same time, Norwegian rural development policies have considered nature as a vital and necessary resource for rural settlements. These differences in perceptions and conceptions illustrate the three-dimensional conflict of nature-society relations in Norway: the protection-use dimension, the nature-culture dimension, and the local-national steering dimension (Daugstad, Svarstad, & Vistad 2006).

During the 1980s and 1990s the legitimacy, efficiency, and outcome of expert-oriented, top-down nature policies and government have been increasingly challenged (Dietz et al. 2003; Hajer 2003; Ostrom 1990) and criticised for ignoring the relationship between the socio-cultural and ecological dimensions of nature and landscapes (Berkes & Folke 1998; Folke 2006). It has been argued that the implementation of nature protection policies mobilises many different perspectives of interests and values (Zachrisson 2009), and not least knowledge and legitimacy (Björkell 2008; Grönholm 2009). The participatory rationale in environmental planning has spread in Norway, as well as on the international arena, as a way of increasing legitimacy, reducing conflict, and improving efficiency of policy implementation (Engelen, Keulartz, & Leistra 2008; Stringer et al. 2006).

However, participation has a wide scale of justification: it can be used as a legitimising ingredient in a ready recipe, or as a democratic process of deliberating values, interests, and knowledge (Arnstein 1969; Cooke & Kothari 2001). Despite the presence of a local participation ethos, nature protection and environmental planning remains a contested practice and creates conflicts in local communities (Arnesen & Riseth 2008; Björkell 2008; Daugstad et al. 2006; Grönholm 2009). The participatory endeavour is criticised for being a token of coerced legitimisation of national policies (Daugstad 2011). Participation based on an instrumental and legitimising rationality creates an ethical and democratic deficit and participation fatigue (Elling 2008; Hansen 2007; Nielsen & Nielsen 2007). Rational instrumental participation limits the planning arena to concern the actors (experts or stakeholders) that are considered relevant from the planning system perspective, i.e. that can serve to fulfil the purpose of the plan. This neglects deliberations about how social, economic, and cultural values and interests should be balanced with ecological concerns from a "non-scientific" or life-world perspective (Vasstrøm 2014). The introduction of a participatory perspective in nature protection planning therefore calls for a critical questioning of how the underlying rationale and arguments of participation influences the premises of the process and outcome (Elling 2008; Hansen 2007; Nielsen & Nielsen 2007).

The question is what the current local participation approaches based on legitimacy, efficiency, and effectiveness do not answer. The problem cannot be reduced to a matter of creating a better structural fit of nature protection policies to local community agendas. That would simply reduce the complex problematic to a matter of national policy legitimisation and reproduction of the existing conflicts. The role of critical social science research must be to understand the tensions in environmental planning, and the oppositional critique between different meaning and knowledge systems. If these tensions are to be opened, and not just understood, there is also a need to interact, challenge and facilitate communicative processes across these rationalities.

Regional policy making, planning and development processes are complex in scope and organisation. Research in general, and engaged or action research in particular, has a role to play in such situations to communicate generic knowledge, deliberate contextual knowledge, and co-create new knowledge with relevant stakeholders (Johnsen, Knudsen, & Normann 2014; Pålshaugen 2014). Action research covers a broad range of engaged research approaches that aim to develop and change a particular situation in participation with relevant institutions and actors (Greenwood & Levin 1998;

Pålshaugen 2007). The engagement of an action researcher occurs in the juncture between existing knowledge systems and rationalities held by a diversity of actors and institutions at different scales (Johnsen et al. 2014; Svensson & Nielsen 2006). The action research role is thus on the one hand challenged with a normative concern of facilitating contextual learning for societal change (Gustavsen 2007; Pålshaugen 2014), on the other hand it contains a critical challenge of reflecting and disputing domination of hegemonic discourses and established interests (Nielsen & Nielsen 2006b). My case shows how the research role can be enacted in "wicked" situations where there are interest conflicts and oppositional (paradigmatic) knowledge claims.

The term "wicked planning" was originally coined by Rittel and Webber (1973) to emphasise that the process of planning does not have an objective problem definition, purpose, or solution. Societal planning is a process of considering and negotiating different, often contrasting or oppositional, interests, values, and knowledge perspectives of the situation between interdependent actors. Such a process involves a multitude of institutions, (political) actors, stakeholders, and other non-profit organisations and associations, and thus also brings about tensions of power relations in steering and governance processes. Environmental planning can be seen as particular example of wicked processes (Lachapelle & McCool 2005). An environmental planning process is, in theory, concerned with creating arenas for deliberation about ecological, social, cultural and economic aspects of sustainability (or nature protection) between institutions, stakeholders, and affected communities (Cowell & Owens 2011). The balancing of nature and society interests and values in a particular materiality concerns the negotiation between diversified and complex societal policies and claims, and (natural scientific) knowledge about how these are perceived to influence and effect the environment and landscape. The planning of nature-society relations in this sense mobilises a variety of (layman and scientific) knowledge systems that perceive the planning and development process from different paradigmatic perspectives (Brunner & Steelman 2005; Elling 2008). These rationality negotiations and knowledge disputes are known to raise strong steering conflicts between local and national authorities and stakeholders, which have fostered a sense of legitimacy crisis in national environmental policy making (Elling 2008; Engelen et al. 2008; Sandström et al. 2008).

The primary challenges in this legitimacy crisis and conflictual planning processes are concerned with questions of who should participate and whose knowledge counts. These challenges have been explored from many different theoretical perspectives related to steering rationalities (Elling 2008; Meadowcroft 2007), (institutional) management systems (Berkes 2007; Dietz et al. 2003), and the role of social learning (Steyaert et al. 2007, Berkes 2009). What is however, less discussed is how an engaged research role can influence these conflicting and wicked planning situations.

Theoretical foundations in the action research role

The concept of action research covers a diversity of research approaches and performances in relation to both theoretical and practical aspects (Pålshaugen 2007; Reason and Bradbury 2001b; Svensson & Nielsen 2006). It entails different perspectives and arguments concerning the role of the research and the researcher in relation to the grade of involvement, the knowledge making process, and relation to the larger societal and academic context. However, these different perspectives share some common ontological perspectives.

A founding assumption in action research is that our social reality is "unfinished"; that is social structures, norms, and understandings are dynamic and changeable. There might be seemingly frozen realities, but these can be challenged through development of new conceptual understandings and thereby generate alternative horizons. Action research can be seen as a co-generative learning process that iteratively reflects on a variety of knowledge and experience, and thereby creates new perspectives and knowledge to change a situation (Greenwood & Levin 1998). The action research role is to explore existing reality, create new understandings, and open new horizons for change. This is a reflective process of challenging our existing perceptions (and theories) with practical experiments (practice), as well as desired realities (imagination and hope) (Nielsen & Nielsen 2006b). The boundaries of the "situation" and the scope of change are perceived differently in the distinct action research traditions; some are concerned with organisational or regional "systems", while considering a larger societal context. The dimensions of change therefore differ substantially, ranging from "organisational improvement" to societal transformation.

A second common trait of action research is its democratic core. This aims to combine research with engagement of "people" in order to generate a knowledge creation process that empowers the participants to change their reality (Reason & Bradbury 2001b). In this way, action research is a critique of knowledge creation as an authoritative process that delivers undisputable truths. Rather, knowledge is constructed by the participation of a variety of understandings about the world in a continuous and dynamic process that leads to some sort of desired development (Gustavsen 2007; Nielsen & Nielsen 2006b).

A third common aspect is the normative role of the researcher. The researcher is not a neutral value-free observer, but participates as a normative partner by encouraging (collaborative) critical reflection on existing and future realities as a way of changing discourses. The aspect of knowledge production and the understanding of dialogue and change differentiate the distinct ramifications of action research. The following sections will shortly describe the pragmatic (or socio-technical) approach, the dialogue tradition, and, last, the critical utopian action research approach.

The pragmatic approach

The pragmatic (or socio-technical) action research emphasises the development of relevant knowledge with relevant stakeholders for improving a specific (problematic) situation (Greenwood & Levin 1998). The co-generative learning model takes the point of departure from the problem perspective of the participants, where insiders (the problem "owners") and outsiders (the researchers) develop relevant knowledge through mutual reflection and learning. The pragmatic understanding of dialogue and change was inspired by the pragmatic philosophy of John Dewey and his perspective of theoretical and practical knowledge in societal development and planning. The dialogue and action is perceived as a continuum; what we say is what we do. The dialogue can, in other words, develop new perceptions and understandings, and through this create social change (Pålshaugen 2004). The arena for dialogue is aimed at fostering new understandings between knowledge claims from different relevant stakeholders, as means to "solve the problem" or improve the situation.

The pragmatic approach can prove problematic in wicked situations, like environmental planning, because the definition of the problem itself may be a matter of conflict. In such situations there are several powerful discourses at play, striving to dominate the very understanding of the problem situation: and thereby the perceived solutions. There is, in other words, a critical and democratic aspect that requires attention as to define who are the relevant stakeholders, who is affected, what contrasting powers are at play, and who is not included in the model. Otherwise the action research role can end up as a legitimiser and facilitator of changes that benefit the established powerful interests without considering its societal impact (Svensson & Nielsen 2006).

The dialogue tradition

The Habermasian perspectives of democratic dialogue arenas, and communicative action through mutual understandings, have strongly influenced societal ideas of steering and planning (Amdam 2005; Elling 2008; Flyvbjerg 1998a), as well as contributing to re-orient the socio-technical or pragmatic school of action research towards the democratic dialogue tradition (Nielsen & Nielsen 2006b; Toulmin & Gustavsen 1996). This discourse-oriented approach emphasises the importance of constructing democratic arenas for dialogues for organisational change. Communicative arenas are seen as means to allow different pre-conceptions and rationalities to reach reciprocal or mutual understanding, and in this way change the existing patterns of communication and understanding. Communicative arenas can in other words reorganise discourses through democratic process in an organisation (Pålshaugen 2004).

The role of the action researcher is mainly process-oriented and focused on the facilitation of communicative processes, while the generation of the contextual knowledge is a matter for the participants (Gustavsen 2007). This communicative orientation is aligned with the Habermasian perspective that considers the facilitation of the communicative process as essential for how the dialogue develops, while the substance of the dialogue should not be in focus for the researcher (Flyvbjerg 1998a; Nielsen & Nielsen 2005). The development of generic knowledge is concerned with the methodological or processual knowledge dimension, the theories of dialogue, and the communicative action procedure. The development of contextual (or societal) knowledge is considered situated and imbedded in a local frame of interpretation (Toulmin & Gustavsen 1996). The verification and quality of the research dimension becomes a question of diffusion of local learning to a larger environment (Gustavsen 2007; Toulmin & Gustavsen 1996).

The focus on communicative processes is an important aspect of the democratic core of the action research role. However, this communication process is also influenced by local context as well as societal discourses. In order to facilitate communicative action through dialogue, the researcher is therefore also required to reflect on how the local context is related to broader (and dominating) societal structures, interests, and values. Research, as action research, must also fulfil objectives of contributing to a more generic knowledge horizon and emancipatory societal critique (Nielsen & Nielsen 2006b).

Critical utopian action research

Critical utopian action research is an approach that attempts to link the analytical, emancipatory, and dialectic aspects of critical theory with participatory research process in a particular situation. The core of critical theory is to explore and understand societal phenomena by challenging established or dominating cultural-political presumptions about "reality". It aims to interpret structures of social phenomena in a historic and cultural context in order to shed light on how existing power structures and dominating discourses influence and reproduce these phenomena (Willig 2007). The ambition of knowledge generation is to develop an emancipatory perspective in a theoretical and empirical perspective, and to unfold the dialectic tension in society (and in humans) between *what is* and *what could be* (Alvesson & Sköldberg 2009; Elling 2008; Nielsen & Nielsen 2006b). Critical theory defines itself as a contrast to traditional theory. Science is not perceived as a neutral "truth", but as constructed knowledge perspectives that are embedded in existing societal structures and vice versa influencing or reproducing political and societal discourses (Alvesson & Sköldberg 2009; Kincheloe & McLaren 2005). The cognitive emancipatory interest is concerned with the *collective* aspects of how we want to organise, create, and collaborate towards a more genuine democratic society liberated from dominating power structures. These collective emancipatory aspects are complemented by an individual perspective of emancipation, where the "human" as such is brought to the centre of attention for developing perspectives of how *we want to live* as humans independent of the ties of society, and in a collective whole as a society (Nielsen & Nielsen 2006a). In a sustainability perspective, such phenomenological approaches to understanding how citizens perceive and reflect on potential development paths are important in challenging the existing course of society.

Critical theory is, in other words, not concerned with "correlations" between phenomena, but with the structures behind these phenomena. The task of the researcher is to reveal the relations between the apparent "fixed" (reified) social structures and the larger contextual frame by which they are influenced. The creation of knowledge should in this sense not only be directed at criticising dominant structures, but also to critically engage in opening the dominating discourses that work as discursive closures for deliberating new courses for development on a democratic arena (Alvesson & Sköldberg 2009; Deetz 1992). The researcher must therefore explore the immanent critique of the studied phenomena or the emergent "inside" learning of the situation. The immanent critique is also relevant in an action research perspective, where it can be extended not only as a theoretical-analytical perspective, but also as a practical dialogical learning endeavour for change (Eikeland 2007). The immanent critique can in this sense be perceived as a potential methodological approach to explore or open the critical perspectives of (the silent) societal actors and as such "reload" the theoretical critique. In his treatise for critical theory, Willig (2007) argues that critical theory is in need of being empirically revitalised and points to a more critical-oriented participatory methodological approach that can explore the critical vocabularies of the public as practical negations of society This can be seen as an argument for critical-oriented action research that does not only facilitate change, but a change that is critical to the established societal structures by engaging in an immanent critical interpretation *with* the participants.

Critical Utopian Action Research (CUAR) bridges the abstract academic and distanced critical theoretical perspective with the empirical reality and engaged research role. The critical theoretical emancipatory perspective is coupled with the empirical reality as a process that must also be "lived out" at individual, as well as collective level to create a better society. The role of research is thus to encourage participants to engage in critical and dialectic reflections about their own situation and future perspectives, and in relation to a more common societal horizon. Such encouragement necessitates that the researcher is able to emancipate from existing social and academic constructions of the phenomena, to develop understandings with the participants beyond the existing limitations.

The generation of knowledge from such research processes can serve to create changes in a particular context, but it should also reflect more generic learnings that can point to critical aspects in a broader societal context. It reflects the endeavour to open "general" societal theories and discourses through "local" human actions and learning. Vice versa, it seeks to reflect common societal and theoretical concerns in the particular action research process with the participants. Emancipation is in this regard not only a meta-theoretical concept of macro level changes, but a human everyday-related process of iterative reflection and change of individual and collective horizons. Immanent critique and participatory reflections in a particular case can in this sense point to more general dialectic tensions and emancipatory concerns in society and from there generate theoretical contributions. The emancipatory perspective, in this sense, bridges the critical dialectic *theoretical* perspectives with the *practical* contextual change perspectives of action research.

The emancipatory and dialectic perspective in CUAR implies developing a critique of the current situation grounded in an everyday life perspective (Nielsen & Nielsen 2006a) or from a phenomenological perspective of reality. This is an approach that transcends the existing "system" perspective and opens an everyday life-oriented "utopian horizon". The everyday life perspective is (in contrast to a sector, "system", or organisation that only represents a fragment of the life-meaning) able to create a utopian horizon with a common human dimension and thus also seeks to problematise the ambiguities and difficulties such change may endure. CUAR, in this sense, is an approach that engages people as citizens in a collective social learning sphere, to conduct their own critical interpretation of a situation as a basis for developing everyday life-oriented utopian horizons.

It is, however, not easy to change perspectives in an everyday life situation that is filled with routines and challenges, or even contested interests and dominating discourses. The creation of "free spaces" as experiential rooms for reflection and learning is therefore an important methodological concern. CUAR applies a critical perspective in deliberative arenas that allows research participants to create an emancipatory room or "free space" from the existing restrictions. The critical theoretical core of dialectics is, in this sense, used as a practical method to create an opportunity for the participants to interpret their situation through a critical lens. Social imagination is used as an "encouragement structure" in the action research process to facilitate the creation process of alternative horizons in a dialectic relation with the critique of the current situation. The theoretical concept of dialectics and emancipation is, in this way, reflected in the practical approaches of CUAR to allow the participants to interpret, imagine, and create changes towards a more emancipatory future. This duality between the common and the particular, and the critical and utopian, is a core foundation in the research approach of CUAR (Nielsen & Nielsen 2006a, 2006b).

The role of the CUAR researcher is thus multi-facetted. The researcher seeks to be a representative of a common dimension, on the theoretical analytical level, in the contextual discussions. The researcher, so to speak, encourages the reflections on the common normative and societal dimensions in the social and individual learning process on the local arena. The researcher facilitates the expression of plural values and human ambiguity, as a process of gaining improved understanding but not necessarily consensus. The researcher is a critical researcher on the (meta) theoretical level, but in a reflective process with the particular situation. In the analytical work (embedded in the action research) the researcher reciprocally seeks to extract the common perspectives and immanent critique in the particular situations that can add to a better understanding of society and its democratic challenges. According to Nielsen and Nielsen (2010) this reciprocal opening and reflection between the common/universal and the local/contextual knowledge perspectives is the very core of the democratic dimension, and thus the primary task of (action) research.

Table 5.2 is an attempt to summarise the different action research orientations described in this section in relation some of the key aspects of a research process. The purpose of the table is to illustrate that different action research approaches might serve different purposes dependent on the context. However, it also illustrates some of the disputes within action research related to theory of knowledge, the role of the researcher, and the nature of action.

Table 5.2 A simplified matrix of the action research orientations in relation to empirical reality and knowledge generation

Orientation/ Perspectives	*Pragmatic*	*Dialogue*	*Critical-Utopian*
Case/"Situation"	Problem situation	Organisation or region	Everyday life and broader societal context
Participants	Stakeholders	Stakeholders and organisational actors	Citizens (and experts as citizens)
Action/Change	"Solutions"	Organisational improvement	Transformative Democratic
Communication and learning	Contextual	Contextual in substance, common in process	Social and Exemplary
Role of researcher	Reflective outsider Expert	Process facilitator	Critical reflective participant
(Theory of) knowledge	Local adaptive	Local theory Common process	Reflective local – common

The contributions of a critical utopian action research role in an environmental planning process

There are different knowledge systems at play in environmental planning processes. These systems are based on distinct ontological and epistemological foundations. The point made in this chapter is not that one type of knowledge is more legitimate or valuable than others. Rather, the argument is that each type of knowledge system has different contributions to make in a planning process. The role of the action researcher is to facilitate a space where these knowledge systems can deliberate on more equal terms. This case illustrates that, in order to create such spaces, the action researcher has to employ a critical role to challenge the "taken for granted truths" among the environmental planning actors, and the superior position of natural scientific knowledge in the current planning rationality.

In this case the researcher facilitated co-generation of knowledge at different levels. The action researcher disturbed the regional planning purpose rationality and natural science knowledge premise, by introducing a community life oriented perspective. At the community level the researcher encouraged the opening of a free-space arena to deliberate critical-utopian perspectives of the situation. This allowed the local communities to challenge the existing planning system logic that otherwise dominated the formal planning process, and to develop other themes of relevance related to their life situation in the area. The researcher in this sense facilitated a "reversed participation" process (Nielsen & Nielsen 2007), where citizens in a social arena were encouraged to generate new knowledge and substantially different contributions to the nature protection perspective.

At the institutional level my role as a critical action researcher facilitated a discussion of how different kinds of knowledges have different ontological and epistemological foundations. Further, it served to develop recognition of how these types of knowledge can contribute with different substantial understandings in a planning process. This critical reflective role served to encourage the semi-formal dialogue processes between the municipalities and the county governor. The research role in this sense contributed to opening a more egalitarian dialogue, and budding knowledge co-generation, between the municipal community perspectives and the county governor nature protection position.

The role of research and the research role are decisive in complex environmental planning situations, where there are no simple truths or given solutions. If environmental planning is a search to reach more sustainable trajectories, then the planning arena should be able to address nature as something more than ecological or economic interests, or simple categorisations of protection and use. It requires a planning arena that can address nature as a common matter of concern between bureaucrats, scientists, politicians, and citizens. This implies the ability to address nature and society relations through a variety of knowledge and value perspectives, as well as an acceptance of their equally legitimate orientation. It requires that the public in planning are allowed to challenge and broaden the initially set purposes of the planning institutions and the expert perspectives on the subject matter, even though these might be radically different. This argument is not only furthered because such deliberations constitute a prerequisite for a democratic planning arena. Also because they generate the potential for developing new and different approaches to nature-society relations that may be more sustainable than what currently exists.

6 Social integration of refugees

May-Linda Magnussen and Ingunn Kvamme

Doing institutional ethnography

How can researchers use institutional ethnography (IE) (Smith 2005) to produce knowledge that is useful for social change "from below"? In this chapter we discuss this question, using the case of an ongoing pilot study exploring refugee women's process of getting a job in a small municipality in the Agder region in Norway. We argue that the broad and long-term relevance of applied social science research relies on researchers critically investigating the knowledge that applied research projects starts out in, and is based upon. We further argue that the importance of this research also depends on researchers knowing ways of bringing new knowledge into the research process. The applied social science researcher should, at the same time as exploring research questions that different actors find relevant and important, contribute to opening other relevant research questions and bring knowledge that is not represented nor necessarily considered relevant into the process. It may even be considered unwanted. Even if this may complicate rather than simplify the understanding of social reality, we think that this way of doing research increases the potential for bringing social change. If we as applied researchers do not bring critical perspectives on knowledge production and power into the research that we do, what makes us different from consultants highly skilled in research methods? How can we become more than allies for people representing organisations and institutions that already have a lot of power when it comes to defining social reality?

Defining the need for a certain kind of knowledge and deciding on how to produce it

Invisibility, silence and lack of knowledge "from below"

The research we use as a case here was initiated by a team of sociologists and development researchers from Agder Research and the University of Agder, and initially funded by these two organisations. This research team recognised that even if the amount of refugees coming to Agder was steadily increasing, and statistics indicate that there are challenges integrating these new citizens, and especially women from certain countries, into the labour markets in the region, these challenges are remarkably quiet in public debate and in different regional plans and strategies. We found this situation troubling, seeing it as a sign of low political and public interest and possibly also of limited knowledge on questions that are important both to the region and not least to the people who are unemployed.[1] The regional silence surrounding the question "integration of female refugees into the labour market" stood in sharp contrast to the regional public concern, debate and research on questions concerning ethnic majority women living in Agder and their high tendency to work part time. It also stood in sharp contrast to the concern that surrounds integration of immigrant women into the labour market at the national level.

Initiating discussions with the regional branch of The Directorate of Integration and Diversity (IMDi Sør) and looking into national quantitative studies on the area of immigrants and labour market integration, we learned that much Norwegian "integration work" does not work as well as it ought to. We also learned that Agder is the region in Norway that employs the lowest share of their immigrant population. Not least, we learned that a considerably lower share of women than men attending the so-called introduction programme, where most immigrants learn the Norwegian language and also about Norwegian society, get jobs directly after finishing the programme. Part of the problem, the way representatives from IMDi Sør saw it, was that considerable research studying the integration work of different public actors studied the relevant social processes from a system point of view. The ones most affected and the public employees working closest with them in an employment process, were to a large degree not informants in the research these "practitioners" met in their daily work. Further, Norwegian anthropologist Marianne Rugkåsa argues that considerable existing research implicitly or explicitly explains the lack of integration among immigrants with individual or social group characteristics among the immigrants themselves (Rugkåsa 2012), saying little about how a *social process* involving a lot of different actors can be improved.

Acknowledging the importance of work affiliation, the challenges of getting a job often facing refugees and also the overall differences in societal power between the ethnic majority in Norway and different ethnic minority groups, we considered the lack of knowledge about "integration work" from the standpoint of refugees and other immigrants alarming. Further, recognising local and regional differences in labour markets and other local and regional conditions and also the importance and relative autonomy of, and considerable variations between, Norwegian municipalities' integration work, we also considered the lack of *local and regional* research on integration work alarming. In other words, we can say that the lack of knowledge "from below" not only entails a lack of knowledge from the ones integration policies are supposed to help and the public employees doing much of the integration work. It also entails a lack of knowledge from the local and regional level. In addition, IMDi Sør confirmed that systematic interaction between researchers and so-called practitioners in the field of labour market integration of immigrants was close to non-existent in the Agder region.

This early dialogue strengthened our belief in the need for regional research, and also for systematic interaction between researchers and practitioners on issues concerning integration of immigrants into the labour market and also into society at large. We organised a resource group consisting of people from both private, public and civil sectors in the region, and some of these representatives were in close contact with unemployed immigrant women. In our initial meetings, these representatives confirmed what we perceived as a need for a certain kind of knowledge. That means that in our case, an initiative from researchers proceeded to other regional actors co-defining research needs and questions that are important for regional development, even though they are *not* discussed much in regional media, or defined as key challenges with need for knowledge in different regional plans and strategies.

A fundamental epistemological point in IE, the sociological "method of investigation" which inspires our research, is that all knowledge is produced by people standing somewhere in society with different chances of making their experiences and perspectives visible and of getting support for them (Smith 1999, 2005). The Canadian sociologist Dorothy Smith argues that much sociology too uncritically starts out with both sociological and lay concepts, adopting them instead of exploring them as people's actual practice. As a result, we often end up replacing people and people's doings with seemingly self-explanatory concepts, making *them* the de-facto actors of our research (Smith 2005). This impedes the discovery of social action and the connections between different forms of social action, leaving us to render their probability with theory instead of showing them empirically. This way of doing research contributes to producing a deep divide, and a too arbitrary relationship between research and reality around us, Smith says. Instead of exploring and understanding, we actually generate a layer of theoretical concepts that subjugates and displaces the actual what happens "out there", beyond the text, and which involves real people (Smith 1999, 2005). Doing this, we often simultaneously end up reproducing and even strengthening the power of social actors who already exercise a lot of power. This problem may be more critical than ever, seeing that the degree of conceptualisation of social phenomena is so high.

From this point of view, the mentioned regional plans and strategies are not neutral reflections of challenges and needs of a region, and what is more; "regions" cannot act. In IE, attributing agency to a region ultimately entails concealing the power of the actual people who have contributed in the production of these plans and strategies. All knowledge is someone's knowledge, and knowledge that they were capable of defining as valid and relevant and feed into a knowledge development process. Further, some standpoints will often not even be represented in such processes. The dialogue with our resource group gave us good reason to believe that the invisibility and silence surrounding challenges and knowledge needs concerning integration of immigrants into the labour market did not mean that these questions were not important or that regional actors had the knowledge they needed to maintain status quo or make necessary changes. Instead, it probably had to do with immigrants and people working closely with them in the process of getting a job having a limited voice, or no voice at all, in the processes of defining regional challenges and knowledge demands.

Parallel to acknowledging the invisibility of immigrant women's experiences concerning employment in national and regional research, and in regional public debate, plans and strategies, we became aware of the growing number of female immigrants entering Norway based on their husbands' guarantee to provide for them economically. These women's experiences and perspectives have even lower visibility. This acknowledgement, coupled with the research team's experience with ethnographic research, made us decide to design two research projects, both starting out in the standpoint of immigrant women. Our resource group informed us that a municipality in the Agder region was starting the "Job Opportunity" project mentioned in Chapter 7 at the time when we were initiating our research. This project would probably involve women whose husbands had guaranteed their provision. Two researchers in the team chose to study what happened in and connected to this project. In dialogue with the resource group, the writers of this chapter chose to study Afghan women who had come to Agder as refugees and their process of getting a job. Women migrating from Afghanistan have among the lowest employment rates in Norway today and our resource group confirmed that the same applied for the Agder region. So, both the relevance of our research questions and the more detailed design of our studies were matters involving both researchers and representatives from the regional field of practice.

The authors of this chapter started out interviewing Afghan women in a large municipality in the region, but quite quickly ended up interviewing women in a much smaller municipality. Some of the women we initially interviewed told us that while women from their country of origin in this large municipality often did not have jobs, Afghan women in the nearby, small municipality were often employed. Our resource group confirmed that this municipality was known for "doing a good job" when it came to integrating women who come to the municipality as refugees into the labour market. Having limited time and a need for further local, regional and national funding later in the process, studying what could be considered best practice in a field that *nationally* receives a lot of attention, seemed like a good choice. Our inspiration from IE played a role in this decision. The ontological and epistemological bedrock of IE is that "the social", or what we often call society, is and must be studied as the co-ordination of people's consciousness and activities (Smith 2005). For us, this means that even if we wanted to start our exploration of the process of getting a job from the standpoint of immigrant women, our research gaze would even from the beginning be directed towards what is happening in social relations these women engage in. Also, other social processes than those most directly tied to getting a job would probably become relevant for our study. Having quite high ambitions when it came to understanding the complexity of the process of getting a job, while at the same time having limited funding, the choice of starting off in a small-scale society made our research goals seem more realistic.

Critically exploring central concepts

It is important to identifying *who* has been involved in producing a certain kind of knowledge, and whose knowledge has been defined as knowledge and at the same time not take established sociological theory as a starting point. This is essential not only for critically studying the production of a certain kind of knowledge, but also for bringing new knowledge into the process (Smith 2005). In our study, the concept of integration made its appearance early on. In the social sciences, the term integration is supposed to say something about the relations between individuals and society, or between social arenas and society as a whole. In Norwegian public and political debate, however, "integration" has become almost exclusively related to certain ethnic minorities. Generally, Norwegian public policies are to a large degree designed to facilitate paid labour for both men and women, and this principle has been strengthened from the early 1990s onwards. Paid labour is considered even more important for the minority population than for the majority. This is due to the belief that paid labour, besides the economic benefits it produces, is the best way of "integrating" into society at large. This is particularly so for minority women. If they do not have a job, they are often labelled "unintegrated", while the same does not apply to majority women. We may therefore go further than saying that paid labour is considered of primary importance for integration in Norwegian society today. For immigrants, paid labour *is* integration (Rugkåsa 2012). Of course, social integration can include many other ways of participating in society. These are, however, given little visibility by the way "integration" is defined in Norway today.

Doing IE, one never starts out by uncritically adopting concepts. Instead, it is always people's doings in social relations. If concepts are relevant, they will always be investigated as actual doings. Smith's notion of "doings" is, however, a generous one, and she includes both physical, linguistic, mental and emotional activities in it. In order to direct and keep research focused on people's doings in generating and analysing data, she advocates a specific understanding of the concept of work. In IE, "work" is used as a general term for the previously mentioned *intentional* activities – activities that enter into the social organising of people's everyday lives. In order to identify people's work, the dialogue between researcher and informant should produce what Smith calls "work knowledge". This knowledge includes "a person's experience of and in their own work, what they do, how they do it, including what they think and feel" (Smith 2005, p. 151). It also includes the implicit and explicit co-ordination of a person's work with the work of others. According to Smith, people are "knowers"; they know their own work and also the co-ordination of their work with the work of people they interact with. However, this knowledge may not be articulated and if so cannot count as "experience", the way Smith sees it. The dialogue between informant and the skilled researcher may, however, produce this experience. Also, from one person's standpoint, one can only see so much. The researcher has the possibility of identifying factors that shape what happens in multiple so-called local sites without necessarily being visible at these sites.

Our broad, initial research question was, in IE-language, to identify work being done in social relations our informants were a part of now or earlier, and which contributed or had contributed positively to the process of getting a job. We knew the process we wanted to study and we knew who we wanted to start out with, but not which other actors would be made relevant for us or whose work we would end up focusing on in the end. In contrast to qualitative studies on what we may call people's life worlds, an institutional ethnographic study moves into and follows the social relations that are made relevant by the initial informants, but without leaving these informants' standpoints behind. It can and should also enter what is conventionally called "the system-level", and the goal of IE is ultimately to show how what happens "locally", and is visible to the people who are engaging in social relations there, is "hooked up with" things going on in relations that are not necessarily visible from the individual's point of view. Going about this way, "the system(s)" is not made into something existing outside human action in social relations. Instead, we can trace when and how it/they shape(s) what happens in the local relations we started our investigation in, and at the same time identify both constraints on, and possibilities for, action.

Moving our research activities to the small municipality, we started out with a group interview with female refugees, and proceeded with a number of individual interviews. Despite having the same country of origin, the informants had different ethnic and educational backgrounds. While some had lived in the municipality for many years, others were newcomers. Their health, physically and mentally, also varied. Instead of dwelling on such characteristics, we very early on directed our data production towards identifying the social relations that our informants thought were important in the process of getting a job. All of the women mentioned the importance of the people working in the municipal refugee service, defining their work as important in what looked like a long and complex employment process. This, and the fact that we realised that due to language barriers, doing a detailed study of the "integrating work" of the refugee women themselves would call for participant observation as a method, caused us to move on to an exploration of the work of the two people employed in this public service at that time. Doing participant observation would simply be too costly at this point in the project. By doing interviews in only one municipality, we found it difficult to highlight women studied for anonymity reasons. We quite quickly discovered that the employees in the refugee service had close, "active" and long-term relations to many of the refugees we interviewed, and actually co-ordinated local, regional and even national work involving them. This made the choice of studying their work seem like a good next step. Even though these employees come closer to seeing the process of getting a job from the refugee women's point of view than most other actors, their accounts can of course never substitute those of the women themselves, and we aim to generate more data directly from the point of view of refugee women further on in the research process.

The importance of time, place and actual people

Studying the work of the employees in the municipal refugee service, we did not start out in, or even look at, organisational maps, legislation or other kinds of documents saying something about what the refugee service was supposed to do. Rather, we started out with detailed questions about the work that they did, and in which relations they did it, and we did not narrow it down to the work that at first sight might be most closely connected to "integrating the women into the labour market". The process of unfolding this work to a large part involved making our informants translate concepts into "work". People working in organisations tend to tell about their work in an institutional language, and with concepts which actually "swallow" a lot of it, rendering it invisible, Smith says (Smith 2005). For example, our informants often talked about "following up" the female refugees.[2] What this actually means, in detailed work of different kinds. For example: talking with the women and other social actors, arranging meetings and paying for expenses, came as a result of patient probing. The employees in the refugee service were not used to articulating their work in such detail, and they confirmed that participating in the research was a process of discovery and learning for them as well as for us.

Going about the way that we did, it quickly became visible to us that the employees in the studied refugee service did a great deal of work, and that much of it mattered in the process of employing the Afghan women we focused upon. Their work is physical, mental and emotional, and involves both talking and writing. Among many other things, they provide people with housing and arrange introduction programmes for adults and kindergarten, school and day care facilities for children and also leisure activities for children and youths. They do practical work in the category of helping newcomers shop for groceries and showing them how to pay bills, and their work also involves granting money for different expenses. They talk to the refugees about their daily problems and their needs, and this work involves both emotional and reflexive work. Several Afghan women we talked to said that the people in the refugee service are "kind", and that they see and feel that they care for them and want what is best for them. Their compassion and understanding seem to build trust and to give them authority in discussing and planning the women's process of getting a job and other important life choices. The people in the refugee service we studied also do quite a bit of work involving texts. They both read texts, write texts (for example e-mails, budgets or CVs for the refugees and texts for the municipality council) and fill in forms (for example reporting to The Directorate of Integration and Diversity [IMDi] on different issues). According to Smith, the use of institutional texts can show us how large institutions shape everyday life, and we will study such texts further on in our research.[3]

The people working in the refugee service also talk to the refugees about "work" that they need to do in order to be employed later on and in order to increase life quality. This kind of work can for example concern one's health and education. We have already mentioned that our informants in the local refugee service probably come closer to seeing the world from the perspective of the refugee women than most other social actors directly or indirectly in contact with them. In fact, we found that they communicate the circumstances and experiences of the refugee women in many of the institutional relations they do their work in. We can say that the people in the refugee service bring the experience of the women into these relations, not mainly by using texts (for example case files), but by talking. Further, people employed in other local and regional organisations co-ordinating their work with the work of people in the studied refugee service, often *trust* the knowledge and judgment of the employees in the refugee service concerning the refugees' situation. We know this since we moved on to interview these actors as well.

What this means is that the female refugees we took as our starting point to some degree get a *trusted voice* in these relations, in spite of not always being meeting those involved face-to-face, and in spite of speaking a limited amount of Norwegian. At the same time, "Norwegian society", the way the people in the refugee service see it, also gets a voice in the dialog between the people in the refugee service and the refugee women. For example, they may say that even though wearing a hijab is allowed in Norwegian work life, the women probably have a better chance of getting a job without it. They do what we might call negotiating work; negotiating on behalf of the women in a multitude of institutional relations, but also negotiating with the women on what to do in the local community and in the larger society, in order to be employed and integrated more generally.

Mapping the work of the people in the refugee service, in a generous IE manner, and already from the outset being oriented towards social relations they did it in, made visible to us the enormous, complex and huge variety of work that is being done to improve the living conditions of the refugee women and to "integrate" them into the labour market and beyond. We have described only a very limited amount of it here. We have reason to believe that the refugee service employees do a particularly broad range of work compared to other "street level bureaucrats". They are supposed to help refugees with "the things they need and that no one else is supposed to do". We also say this because they are supposed to do work others may be obliged to do, but which will be done later or demand more work, be less effective, if someone else does it. Not even in granting money do they have very detailed guidelines. Instead, they pay for things that matter (for example for public transport tickets and for glasses) and that nobody else is supposed to pay for, or which will be paid for later and/or demand more work if someone else is paying. While many other public organisations have a relatively specific and narrow mandate concerning their work with the refugees (for example, some do work helping them get a job, some with improving their health), this seems not so much to be the case for the people in "our" refugee service. The impact of the refugee service employees working in this manner, which probably involves getting a relatively broad knowledge about their "users", needs to be studied further. This also goes for what seems to be considerable pragmatism, user orientation, trust and room for judgment for the individual employee.

Our orientation towards co-ordinated work also showed that the people in the studied refugee service not only bring the experiences of the refugee women into numerous social relations by talking about these, but also by pulling the women themselves into the relations that they need to engage in. Early in their work with the refugee women, the refugee service employees define most pressing needs. They will then do part of the needed work themselves. However, they also "activate" relations between the refugee women and people working in other parts of what can be called a substantial local welfare apparatus, contributing towards making important integrating work happen here as well. These relations may involve other public actors, but also private and civil society actors. Also, the relations extend beyond the local, into regional and national levels. The refugee women, the refugee service employees act as both an entry to, and as navigators, activators and co-ordinators of, a web of integrating work done by a broad diversity of societal actors. We see this as a key to understand the work of "our" municipality.

In a complex society like Norway, it is common knowledge and regularly mentioned in the media that "navigating the system", for instance when being sick, involves a lot of work and can be fatiguing. One can then only imagine how overpowering this navigating work can be for a newly arrived immigrant, maybe having health problems, not always knowing whether one is allowed to stay on a permanent basis and speaking little or no Norwegian. The people in the refugee service in the municipality we have studied do quite a bit of this navigating work for their refugee inhabitants, especially when they are newcomers. While some employees working with refugees and other inhabitants do this work even if they are not supposed to do it or are rewarded for it (Guribye & Hidle 2013), the people working in the refugee service under study are actually supposed to do this often invisible and also quite unrewarded job. They can do "the work that works" because of the broad and relatively open mandate that we have mentioned earlier and because of the lack of short-term and simple measuring of the "success" of their work. This can at least partly be accorded to the fact that the studied refugee service is not organised as a part of the local NAV-office, like most other refugee services in the Agder region are. The mentioned trust and the pragmatism that seem to characterise the work of both refugee service employees and others they co-operate with, probably also matters, and we believe that the small size of the municipality also enables these public employees to do a good job in the eyes of the refugees. On one hand, it probably feels good to have a relatively high degree of freedom doing what one has experienced as necessary and effective when it comes to helping people. This freedom probably contributes to giving the people in the refugee service a lot of work, and they were actually quite astonished by the map (of the work they did) we made during our research. While having to say "I know this is what you need, but it is not my job" can be hard for a welfare state employee, it at the same time demarcates their work. From the refugees' point of view, however, we believe it is best to meet people who take responsibility, see the whole picture and collaborate with others in doing "the work that works".

Focusing on integrating work may make questions of time, place and the actual people involved seem irrelevant. Dorothy Smith wants us to focus more on people's practices and how they come about, more than on the people themselves (Smith 2005). The people involved in doing the integrating work, the place it is being done in and also the time spent, however, seem to be important for the quality of the integrating work we have studied. Concerning space and time, several refugee women mention that the refugee service office is in the town hall, and that their door is "always open". When it comes to time, the employees in the refugee service spend a lot of time working with their "users" when they are newcomers, and they also make sure that other actors do a lot of the initial work needed as quickly as possible. Over time, both the refugee service employees and the refugees contribute towards gradually decreasing their interaction. The time dimension is also relevant for explaining why the people in the refugee service do work or grant money that other public organisations are obliged to do or grant. In their own words, they "fill the gaps" in the refugee women's process towards getting a job: with "work" or with money. They want the women to "come out of their homes and be active in the community" in some way or the other. If the refugee women for example have to wait for a couple of months for a NAV course designed to qualify them for work, the employees in the refugee service will often arrange for so-called work practise during this period, and pay the refugees directly instead of sending them to the local NAV office, asking for an income from them. Experience has taught them that periods of spending more time at home are often counterproductive in the process of getting a job.

In the studied municipality, time, persons and place also matter because many of the same persons do and co-ordinate their integrating work over time. We believe this to be crucial to, even if it does not guarantee, the quality of the work being done. In such long-term relations, understanding and trust have better chances of being built, needs have a better chance of being identified and understood and the possibility of understanding relatively more of the big picture is better. This in turn gives the employees in the refugee service more room for doing good work. We know that some local NAV offices in Norway regularly assess each other's work in relation to specific clients (in Norway called "users") without ever meeting these clients/users in person, but merely by going through the case files of other offices. This suggests that "producers" and "receivers" of a public service knowing each other may "pollute" what is going on there, making the producer "too kind" and contributing towards passivity on behalf of the user and unfairness compared to other users. This may be so. The people working in the refugee service we have studied make decisions that, also in the eyes of the refugee women, make them not only "kind", but also "strict". One of the employees told about an episode where one woman asked them for more money, but was turned down. "She got a bit angry with me, but when she comes home she will cool down. And after all, she knows that I have done a lot to help her over the years, and that I want what's best for her," she said. Their long-term relation helped the refugee service employee endure the short-term discomfort of doing what she intended to be best for the person she was helping.

Applied research and politics

How does the knowledge produced in the case presented in this chapter differ from the knowledge we probably would have generated not being inspired by institutional ethnography? What difference does this difference make? Not being inspired by IE, we probably would have proceeded the way we have done in many of our previous research projects; focusing relatively more on the informants and less on what happens in the social processes they engage in. Most probably, we would have paid most of our attention to their everyday lives and discussed their different degrees of labour market integration up against social markers such as gender, class and ethnic group. Such markers or categories are undoubtedly important in studies concerning social inequality, and we ourselves used such categories to identify our entry point informants. Dorothy Smith, however, warns against objectifying them; writing in ways that assign them existence independently of peoples' doings, and in ways in which peoples' doings only illustrate the workings of the categories (Smith 2005).

While it is important to understand the background and the situation of refugees if we want to understand their social integration, it might be even more important to study what happens in refugees' interaction with other actors in the society they have settled in, especially if one wants to contribute to increasing this integration. One reason for this is that the consequences of refugees' traumas, gender or lacking education on "labour market integration" clearly depend on how they are met in their local communities. To put it simply: if people working in municipal refugee services and other parts of the local welfare apparatus work in a manner that responds to the broad range of needs of refugees, and at the same time co-ordinate their work with the work of other relevant actors, this will decrease the influence of these backgrounds and situations on their chances of getting a job. When we interviewed female refugees in another municipality in the Agder region, they partly blamed the low degree of paid labour among refugee women from certain countries on the often used category of "culture". However, women from these countries relatively often have paid labour in the municipality. Being absorbed in categories may conceal the potential for action that is actually there.

By starting with the standpoint of refugees and studying "labour market integration" as a process involving a multitude of social actors in different institutional relations, exploring the content of concepts, being relatively less "caught" in institutional discourses than we would otherwise be, and not being limited to studying the work of only one institution or organisation at a time, puts us as researchers in a position where we are able to understand more about what is happening, and relatively quickly as well. We also got an understanding of this process starting out with what ought to be the most important point of view: that of those who are supposed to be "integrated into the labour market". In the introduction to this chapter, we advertised IE as a method of inquiry facilitating social change, benefiting what we may call groups with relatively little power. It is precisely the improved understanding of what is actually going on. The standpoint the understanding of this process starts out in, that opens up these possibilities. Proceeding this way, we have a better chance of identifying room for improvement and improvement that matters to those who need it the most. Also, even if the integrating work in the municipality we have put our main focus on up until now actually *does* seem to be doing much right, further research will undoubtedly reveal potential for improvement here.

In addition, the integrating work in this municipality can act as an example for others. Our initial interviews in a nearby, and much bigger, municipality indicate that no one does the holistic, co-ordina*ted* and co-ordina*ting* integrating work of the people of the refugee service described in this chapter. Seeing that this is so important in our first case, we will direct our research gaze towards this point in our further research. Understanding that integration work will vary from place to place is one reason why we argue for the need for local and regional applied research on the subject of integration of immigrants. Still, even if studying new municipalities will and should produce new maps of social relations, there is always something to learn from the maps made in other municipalities. Doing IE in other municipalities, we will also gradually improve our chances of identifying so-called extra-local relations; relations in which work, often involving texts, influences what happens in multiple local sites at different points in time. As of now, we only see glimpses of local consequences of what happens in such relations. For example, as we mentioned earlier, it seems to us that the autonomy of the employees in the studied refugee service when it comes to doing their work is at least partly due to them not being a part of the local NAV office.

Studying "labour market integration of refugees" as a process involving a multitude of social actors in different institutional relations also puts more of the responsibility for integrating work on people others than the refugees themselves; people who have more knowledge of the different "systems" and the local community, and who also have more power. Moving research scope, from social categorisation of immigrants to locally based descriptions of the work and social relations of the Norwegian integration policy system and other actors, may also make integration policy makers more aware of the accountability of the systemic part of integration and the possibilities for improving "the system(s)". We want to generate new knowledge: knowledge produced in a new manner, and from standpoints that are to a large degree excluded in existing research. Even if this knowledge will probably contribute towards improving the social integration of immigrants, it can still be knowledge that for various reasons is not wanted. This remains to be seen.

What *has* happened in the aftermath of our study in the municipality is that the refugee service has been allocated more money, and has been able to hire more personnel. "I am going to show your map of all of our work to my superiors here in the municipality administration," said the leader of the refugee service when we left after an interview. Also, at the same time as we were drawing this map, we as researchers suddenly found ourselves "inside" it, being pulled into the processes of employing local refugee women. The people in the refugee service knew which women we were interviewing, that we met with some of them repeatedly. Therefore, one of the people working in the refugee service at one time asked us if we could talk to Zahra about the importance of higher education the next time we met her. We were told that Zahra wanted to start working in a grocery store because the family needed more money at the time. However, she was doing very well at school and the people in the refugee service thought that in the long run, it would be the best for her and her family if she got a university education. She, however, decided to work at the grocery store to make money so that they could move into a more suitable house. After a few months, however, her husband got a job and she went back to school, aiming for a university degree.

In the end, why is lack of exploration in applied research a problem? This kind of research to a large degree feeds into policies, and knowledge generated by researchers often has particular authority. Our ways of understanding, talking and writing "the social" have real consequences. What happens when research that does not explore enough, understand enough and is not critical enough, enters into the field of public measures and policies? Public money and effort are spent on measures that may not "work", at least not as well as they should. More seriously, other and better ways of doings things are obstructed or never even come into being. As applied researchers, we are in a position where both bad/failed policies and the role of agile research in it are visible. From this standpoint, we do not only criticise those commissioning research, but also ourselves.

In this chapter, we have argued that even if applied research is often funded by political or commercial actors, there is still potential for researchers to generate knowledge. We argue that borders between applied and basic research may be more blurred than strictly separate. When research is being applied by both national and regional policy makers, it may thus have real and significant consequences in common people's daily lives, as mentioned earlier. However, through scientific methods, the knowledge and experiences of so-called common people may also go the other way around and influence policy makers. The challenge of researchers doing applied research is to make sure that we have both the critical awareness and methods that open up knowledge based on common people's experiences: and not least the experiences of marginalised groups. Comte's hierarchical division of knowledge might serve to legitimate a social hierarchy in which people's social status and position depend upon the category of knowledge they possess. Hence, actively opposing the hierarchical divisions of knowledge within research may contribute to social change.

Notes

1 In addition, the lack of discussion on integration issues probably also has to do with the majority population's fear of over-generalising groups who already have many challenges. Immigration and integration are highly contested issues, and when discussing societal challenges concerning integration one also runs the risk of being used by anti-immigration actors. In our mind, however, the ability to manoeuvre in this terrain is also a question of the competence or knowledge of persons engaging in the debate, but we are not able to go further into this here.
2 "Å følge opp" in Norwegian.
3 According to Smith, co-ordination of work in large institutions is to a large degree possible because replicable texts are being read, "activated" and often acted upon by a large number of people. If we see that texts make something happen in social relations, that they *do* something to what is going on, the ethnographic exploration of people's doings should include these texts (Smith 2005).

7 Comparative reflection

Hanne Haaland and Hege Wallevik

Ethnographic research and comparative reflection

In this chapter we discuss how ethnographic research emphasising comparative reflection can contribute to the field of integration of immigrants in Norway. The case we refer to is an ongoing research project on immigrant women's ways into paid labour, in a municipality in Southern Norway. This project results from discussions between researchers and practitioners in the region. The chapter argues that in a globalised and changing world, with increased mobility between the Global South and the North, experiences from the field of development studies can and should be brought into studies of integration in a Norwegian context.

This chapter discusses the relevance of researchers' experiences from doing long-term fieldwork in the Global South when engaging in the field of integration of immigrants in Norway. Working in societies that are not one's own, and where language, cultural practices, norms and codes are unfamiliar, requires time, patience and a strong interest in understanding what is taking place, why it is taking place and how. Building knowledge in such situations requires an interaction between the researcher and the informants which goes beyond the usual 20 interviews. There is also a need to employ a methodology of participant observation in order to see what people do in particular situations and how they interact with and respond to other actors. As development researchers with a strong background in the field of anthropology, we argue that such experience with ethnographic research is of great value to understanding processes of integration of immigrants in Norway. We have both carried out long-term fieldwork in Africa, namely Mozambique and Tanzania, in rural and urban areas alike (Haaland 2008; Wallevik 2012). Our research had a community or neighbourhood focus, and was actor-centred. The phenomena explored in our research, economic activity and rights to property, were approached with an aim of understanding from within and from below, and overall we argued for an anthropological approach when engaging with development. Here we advance the argument, and acknowledge the importance of fieldwork experience when engaging with the field of integration in Norway.

In our present project we have also aimed at achieving an insider's understanding of the women participating in a project called the "Job Opportunity Project" (JOP) or "Jobbsjansen". We have aimed to generate knowledge on how our informants live and organise their daily lives in Norway, how they relate to the public welfare system (PWS) and how they manage their trans-local lives, a situation that leads to an engagement in both the country of residence and the country of origin. In short, we have aimed to gain an understanding of women's lifeworlds. This means aiming at a *holistic approach*, where data are contextualised in relation to local epistemology and ontology, and also a *cultural relativist perspective* (Howell 2011). However, ethnographic research within the discipline of anthropology also requires something else. According to Howell, the overall aim of anthropology is "comparison of human sociality and meaning-making with an overall ambition of generalisation" (Howell 2011, p. 168, our translation). Hylland-Eriksen (2004) adds that comparison is about contrasting, and that it builds on the ethnographic encounter itself, namely that of cultural translation, as learning about "the other" also involves a learning about "self". The insights that come from long-term fieldwork thus enable a comparative reflection where the mirror is turned, and where we are put in a position to reflect upon ourselves. Such a gaze enables a reflection on the PWS that both we as Norwegian citizens, as well as the immigrant women, interact with. More generally such insights can tell us much about how our own society works, for example issues related to social organisation.

This understanding was the starting point for a discussion among researchers from development studies and sociology at University of Agder and Agder Research, eventually also involving representatives from the practice field (i.e. municipalities and Directorate of Integration and Diversity, IMDi). The result was an applied research project on how immigrant women enter paid work. We discuss the benefits of researchers' experiences from fieldwork in "far-away places" when understanding immigrant women and their efforts to find paid labour, through a case study from a municipality in Southern Norway.

The Job Opportunity Project in Lyngdal

Our case study of immigrant women trying to find work through JOP reflects the overall priority and aim of the integration process in Norway: to provide opportunities for employment. It is generally assumed that the best way to become a part of Norwegian society is through paid work. This of course comes after finding people a place to live and providing them with a basic introduction to Norwegian society. Nonetheless, the general idea is that once settled, with a permit to stay, people must find work. "Arbeidslinja", to get people integrated into the workforce and thus enrolled into the taxpaying system, has a strong position in Norwegian integration politics. Thus, there is a need to learn the language and understand the Norwegian society and welfare system in order to prepare for working life. Consequently, there are several public measures put in place, including adult education (hereafter referred to as AE).

The project came about as a result of discussions among researchers and practitioners. The background for the meetings was general frustration on both sides with how the existing systems handled immigrant women and their way into paid work. As researchers, we were particularly interested in understanding the problem from women's point of view. Based on recommendations from IMDi we chose a small community in Southern Norway as our case study; Lyngdal Municipality.

Lyngdal is a small town with approximately 8,000 inhabitants. About 10.5% of the population have an immigrant background (immigrants or Norwegians born of immigrant parents).[1] This number does not only include refugees, but also work migrants (mainly men) and people (mainly women) seeking family reunion. In general, finding work for immigrants can be difficult in Norway. It is even harder in a small community where work life is not as differentiated as in cities with a larger population. The municipality of Lyngdal has had an active approach to attracting and welcoming all newcomers in order to stimulate population growth, particularly through the project "Lyngdal for All". Lyngdal was awarded money from the Ministry of Local Government and Modernisation for a 3-year project (2012–2014), where 25% of the costs were to be covered by the Municipality itself. "Lyngdal for All" did not exclusively focus on foreign immigrants; rather the idea was to welcome all new settlers to the area, regardless of nationality (key informant 2014).

When we started our project on immigrant women and work, Lyngdal had recently been awarded funds from IMDi to participate in JOP, a programme focusing on immigrant women who have no employment and who are not covered by other welfare programmes. The overall aim of the programme is to facilitate a way into paid labour.

In JOP, women would attend AE, get job training financed by the project and, equally important; get language training with particular emphasis on the language required for particular jobs. When we started our fieldwork, our initial focus was on immigrant women and their perceptions of getting into paid work. However, because the JOP participants also interact with people in the welfare system we acknowledged the need to understand the system and talk to representatives of the PWS. Consequently, the project leader in the JOP project in NAV Lyngdal, and the AE were included as part of the study. By including representatives of the PWS that interacted with our informants, we gained insight into how they dealt with the diversity of the job applicants and their different backgrounds, through a system of categorisations.

Considering this was an applied research project, we were of course unable to carry out long-term traditional fieldwork in Lyngdal. Rather, we ended up coming and going about once a week, meeting the participants and representatives from JOP, NAV Lyngdal (the work and welfare department) and AE over a period of months. In our work we included the core values of doing participant observation and applying a cultural relativist approach, together with an aim of a holistic understanding. This gave a particular focus on the participants of JOP, and a gaze that allowed for an exploration beyond the pre-defined.

When we started our work in Lyngdal in February 2014, the project was in its initial phase and only a few participants had entered the project. NAV Lyngdal is the project owner, and a new project manager had been employed in the fall of 2013 to be in charge of the funds granted to the project by IMDi. After an initial presentation of our project in a forum for local politicians[2] and with the reference group for JOP in Lyngdal, we were introduced to the programme participants. Our first meeting with some of the project participants was a group meeting, four immigrant women and ourselves. All of them had lived in Norway for some time, from 3 to 6 years. In the initial meeting we spent much time on making a proper introduction of ourselves as researchers, emphasising our experiences with doing ethnographic field work in contexts not our own, and hence also our experiences with being in a situation where one is not familiar with the language, nor with cultural practices and codes. We emphasised our experiences of being "outsiders" and having worked our way into a different culture ourselves. This communicated competence in cross-cultural understanding and thus translation. We also talked about our work experience and our private life, presenting ourselves as social individuals as well as researchers.

All of our informants were enrolled in the same project, but were meeting each other for the first time in our initial meeting. During this first interaction, we heard short versions of the women's life histories; that is, a description of their family situation, their previous work and life situation in their home country, their migration experience and their current situation in Norway. They told us about their aspirations and goals for their life in Norway, particularly with regards to getting paid work. The women came from Asia, Africa and Europe, the youngest was 19 and the oldest in her fifties. Discussions revealed very diverse experiences linked to the different circumstances, but yet also common experiences of migration, crisis and resettlement.

Considering our ethnographic approach focusing on participant observation, we met project informants in many different situations. As part of the JOP project the participants attend classes in AE every week. We would meet them in the classroom and in breaks in between the classes. We also invited participants home, in order to meet in a more informal setting. This particular meeting was nearly five months into the project. It became a turning point, in the sense that our informants spoke even more openly than before about their experiences in Norway; about their meeting with the education and work system and their everyday lives.

In the following discussion we describe some of the project participants in order to highlight some themes recurring in our interaction. We have changed some of the characteristics of our informants to ensure their anonymity. Through these cases, we also discuss our points about the gaze of the researcher, knowledge production and how comparative reflection is enabled through this type of approach and methodology. Towards the end we return to the overall argument of why comparative reflection and seeing beyond "what meets the eye" are of importance when dealing with integration issues.

The gaze of the researcher and the importance of comparative reflection

Case 1: a question of definition – to be resourceful or not?

Armita, a woman in her fifties comes from a country in the Middle East, and arrived together with her daughter in Norway as a refugee 3 years ago. When we met Armita her son was also in the process of seeking asylum in Norway, a situation which left her worried. Armita holds a university degree in natural science, and told us in our initial meeting that her aim was to teach natural science to children in Norway. Her limited language skills had so far stopped her from achieving this. Her participation in the JOP was supposed to help her overcome the language barriers. After having been part of the JOP for almost a year she is currently working as an assistant in school, but still paid through the JOP. She does not know when she will find regular, paid work. Armita is very engaged in the political situation of her home country, a country where no open opposition is allowed. Several of her close relatives have lost their lives as part of a political struggle, which is why Armita is now living in Norway. She follows the political situation in her home country closely through social media, and constantly talks about her home country, expressing sorrow and longing. She is politically active through social media, and expresses no desire to settle in Norway on a long-term basis.

Armita is one of the women with the highest academic education amongst our informants, and she has broad working experiences from her home country. As such, she is quite resourceful, both in terms of formal education and in terms of political participation. However, in Norway she is in a situation where she is perceived as a difficult case, and amongst the JOP supervisors she was talked about as one of the least resourceful participants. How can a highly educated woman become one seen as less resourceful? Our argument here is that it is in the meeting between an actor and a system, here between Armita and the PWS, such a categorisation can emerge. Once categorised, Armita becomes a difficult case. Due to the interaction between the representatives of the PWS, the narrative of Armita as difficult sticks to her, a narrative which leaves her with limited opportunities for negotiating her position within the system and also in Lyngdal.

In the PWS, immigrants are talked about as "resourceful" and "less resourceful", a categorisation which reflects their level of Norwegian language skills, but also how easily employable they are considered to be. In this system of categorisation, Armita is put among the least resourceful despite her high education and her work experience. She is defined as being at the margins in the public project of integration, because her main focus is not directed towards in Norway and settling down in Lyngdal but remains with the political sphere of her home country.

The JOP staff and staff at the AE consider her political involvement in her home country to be hindering her progress and integration. Had her political engagement been towards Norwegian society, it would most likely have been different, as Armita would have been considered an active citizen. However, in the current situation, her political involvement is considered more as disengagement with Norwegian society, also implying a lack of interest in learning the Norwegian language. The result seems to be a vicious circle. The more she engages with her home country, the less she learns about Norwegian language and society, which again makes her a difficult case regarding employment and thus also not easy to integrate. Can this be understood differently?

Armita argues that she has not settled in Lyngdal permanently. Unless she finds a relevant job she will not consider staying in Lyngdal. Without a job and also a permanent place to stay, she also finds it difficult to socialise in Lyngdal. She talks about moving to Oslo if her daughter moves for further university studies. She spends time with her family and a few more friends from her home country, in addition to the social networks she has gained through the JOP. Much of her social interaction takes place with people from her home area and on social media, which allows her to keep in touch with people in her country of origin or in diaspora. The important point is how the representatives of the PWS find her way of "being on the outside" as a constraint on successful integration. For Armita, on the other hand, it is a way of coping. Her strong interaction with her home environment can equally be understood as a reflection of sense of belonging and a way of planning for the future. Armita is quite open about her desire to go back to her home area if or once the political situation allows for it. "I miss my country" and "I want to go home", she says repeatedly in our conversations. Armita is an example of the many immigrant men and women who live trans-local lives. She reminds us how many refugees may want to seek to rebuild their lives but not necessarily be tied to Norway on a permanent basis. This is an important insight which increasingly needs to be accepted when discussing integration politics and policy in Norway.

Remittances are an important topic in Norwegian development research. With reference to immigrants and remittances, we know that people in diaspora send money back to family in their home country. They maintain a financial involvement in their areas of origin. However, we pay less attention to how immigrants nurture social relationships with people in their home area. Political involvement is one way of nurturing social relationships and networks, as well as contributing to society. The fact that her political engagement is perceived as hindering Armita's integration and defining her as less resourceful is problematic. Such a categorisation, made by representatives of the PWS, leaves Armita less room for manoeuvre and negotiation of her identity. It may even lead to increased involvement outside of Lyngdal. The case of Armita is not unique. She is a clear example of how categorisations made by the PWS put restraints on individual manoeuvring and thus potentially also the range of possibilities for immigrants. This leads us to our next case.

Case 2: a question of being "realistic" – or getting people through the system?

Emebet, a young woman in her early twenties, came to Norway 3 years ago. Emebet's past is filled with war conflicts, violence and abuse. Despite her young age she has a long experience as carer for a sick relative. Emebet spent years in a refugee camp before she came alone to Norway. Although she now has been granted asylum, and is in many ways safe and secure, she told us many stories of loneliness and "being all on her own with no one to rely on". She knows that Norway will be her place of residence and that this is where she needs to settle, but she finds it difficult. Given her young age, Emebet can be considered as someone who can make a fresh start. She dreams of becoming a lawyer and potentially a judge. However, Emebet has experienced that in the meeting with the JOP and the PWS her dreams have been replaced with an educational path of becoming a health worker. This path is considered to be more realistic by those helping Emebet with her education and process towards finding work. The argument used is twofold, referring to both Embet's own experiences and to how Norwegians will embrace Embet in working life, referring to her "perfect face for working in health care, as she has a beautiful smile which will easily get her in touch with people".

How can we possibly understand the apparent mismatch between Emebet's ambitions and the efforts to guide her into health work? The first thing that springs to mind is that Norway now and in the future needs health workers. As Emebet is young and holds experience with caring, such an educational path seems promising and doable. Reflecting upon her experiences as a young refugee, we can move beyond the focus on her experience as a carer, but rather see how her dream about being a judge can result from her experiences of war and violence, and create an inner drive to work with the law and a system of justice. Such an inner motivation is useful for a longer educational path. Heading for law studies rather than health services will of course be more expensive and time-consuming. It presupposes a willingness to invest in Emebet's future beyond 2 years of secondary school with a focus on health subjects. Moreover, it presupposes a willingness to imagine Emebet's future life outside Lyngdal. Emebet is very clear on how lonely she feels in Lyngdal, and how she struggles with her social life in the area. Emebet is, through her life experiences, much older than her fellow Norwegian students. These experiences, in addition to her limited language skills, help to explain the lack of a network of friends from her age group so far.

The example of Emebet raises the following question: In our integration efforts, where work participation is perceived as an indicator of success, do we fail to acknowledge work life in a long term perspective, i.e. that people need to remain interested and motivated to endure a long working life? Are we so concerned with integration through employment on a short-term basis that we fail to acknowledge people's aspirations and motivations, and hence also the importance of ensuring a certain quality of life? We return to this discussion in our third case, as well as in the concluding remarks.

Case 3: work as integration or work as exclusion?

Miljana, a woman in her fifties, comes from a Central European country and came to Norway seeking family reunion with her husband. He arrived in Lyngdal as a work immigrant many years ago. Their country of origin was war-torn in the early 1990s, a war which completely changed the life of Miljana. She describes how she lived a comfortable life in her hometown, having her own house and her own job running her own small business. All of a sudden it changed: neighbours became enemies, former friends turned on each other and life was never the same again. Miljana has grown up children; one of them lives in Norway. Unlike Armita, Miljana's plan is to permanently settle in Lyngdal, and after 2 years here she is working very hard to rebuild her life, as it once was. When we first met her, she was a participant in the first JOP group. She was very optimistic and motivated about finding a job and entering the Norwegian job market. "I have to learn Norwegian to find work, I have to find work," she would keep repeating, like a mantra.

For her, the motivation for finding work was closely tied to her desire to rebuild her life as it once was, which involved owning her own house and having a secure income and a social environment. When we met Miljana, she and her husband had recently bought a house as part of their larger plan to permanently settle in Lyngdal. They now needed more than just one source of income to be able to pay their bank loan. Together with the project leader in JPO, Miljana had decided that a job in the sales industry (e.g. hardware) could be an opportunity for her, as she had previous experience and skills from this sector. It took some time for such an opportunity to materialise. Therefore, when some months into our fieldwork Miljana got the opportunity to work for a cleaning agency as part of work training, she embraced it. Shortly after, she got a job offer from the very same agency and accepted the job. Consequently, she is now "ticked off" as a participant who has successfully completed the JOP programme and secured paid work. This gave an opening for a new participant to join the JOP programme.

When we met Miljana 5 months later she invited us home to her house for lunch. We had the opportunity to discuss her experience with the JOP project and her encounter with Norwegian society and the integration process, including her social life as well as working life. Over coffee she told us how she and her husband had friends in Lyngdal, but all of them foreigners, mostly from her home country. "You are the first Norwegians that have visited my house," she said, somewhat sadly. During our conversation we learned that Miljana had now successfully entered working life and thus seemingly also achieved the goal of integration through work (arbeidslinja). We also learnt how she worked at irregular and often inconvenient hours. Miljana has a temporary position which involves going to work in the early morning. She returns home a few hours later, and goes back to work in the afternoon, at the same time as her husband comes home from his job. She comes home late at night. In other words, there is not much time for social interaction, neither with her family nor with anyone else. In her work she meets other immigrants, many of them poor Norwegian speakers. She complained to us about not being able to practise the Norwegian language with anyone. As a consequence, she felt that she had lost some of the Norwegian skills that she had gained through the JOP. She felt that her working hours were unfavourable. She did not find that she had any of the security that she had hoped to get through accessing a job.

The motivated and enthusiastic woman that we had met a few months earlier was replaced by a very discouraged woman. She was frustrated about many things and she referred to the Norwegian culture, codes of behaviour and system as "not normal"; the lack of any social interaction with ethnic Norwegians ("*Always talking on the street, but not being invited in; it is not normal*"), the requirements for language skills for working in an old people's home ("*How much Norwegian do we really need to know to serve the old people food? I don't understand this, it is not normal*"). Most of all she reported that the only job offers she could get were for less than 50% positions, where work hours implied that she had no social life and could not continue with any Norwegian classes ("*I don't understand how Norway can say that people can come here and work and then there is no job for us, no opportunity, I don't understand the system: it is not normal*").

Reflecting upon Miljana's experiences, there are two noteworthy factors. The first concerns the general assumption that integration is best achieved through entering the labour market. This idea is based on the following argument: Having a job will provide people with an arena for socialising, it will allow them to practise the Norwegian language, and will generally provide a stepping stone towards inclusion into Norwegian society. Miljana's case illustrates how the opposite may happen. Inclusion in working life can ironically lead to exclusion from social interaction and social participation in society. Miljana is very disappointed with her work experience so far. It has not provided her with the economic safety she wanted, because she has not found a full time job, and it has not given her a social network and a feeling of integration. Miljana's case can of course be seen from two different points of view. When Miljana accepted the job with the cleaning company, the JOP leader had a success story to report in terms of the project. For Miljana, however, her entrance into the cleaning industry actually implies a reduction of her opportunities. As a job holder she is no longer entitled to AE classes, which means reduced opportunities to improve her language skills. Her job environment is not favourable for language practise, and the social integration she longed for seems to be out of reach.

The second point which can be made from the case of Miljana concerns the social environment. Miljana tells us that she longs for good neighbours and social interaction. The social environment is something Miljana has talked about from our initial encounter; how she misses everyday interaction with a larger social community. She also stressed the significance of meeting other women at the JOP and at the AE classes. Whenever Miljana had expressed her concerns about a dynamic social milieu, the JOP leader and other representatives of the welfare system had reminded her that the situation would improve once a job was secured. Even the women themselves would say this when discussing with each other, internalising the argument. However, when discussing the ideas of a social environment, it is important to understand how our expectations as ethnic Norwegians, and the expectations of immigrants, to some extent seem to differ. For Miljana, the idea of a social environment goes beyond the notion of having someone to talk to at work, or knowing the people in the house next door. When she talks about neighbourhood or community, she wants reciprocal social relationships with more interaction and commitment.

Miljana's longing for a good neighbourhood provides a typical example where comparative reflection has something to offer when trying to understand our own society, and our informants' perspective on their integration into Norwegian society. One may argue that social relations are reciprocal in all societies, including our own. We do not argue against this. Rather, we want to highlight how reciprocity is found in particular forms and acted out differently, depending on whom we interact with and in which cultural context we are situated. In a Norwegian context, ideas of reciprocity often reflect a more general focus on individualism, meaning that one should not be indebted in one's relationships to another. Thin lines seem to be drawn between private relations (family) and work relations. Miljana, who comes from another cultural context, wishes for a different reciprocity where the core ideal is one of continuous interdependence and obligations. Taking such a perspective into account provides a better understanding of why Miljana's expectations about the social are neither met through her work participation, nor in her local neighbourhood. Moreover, it provides us with an increased understanding of the "self" as argued by Hylland-Eriksen (2004), an understanding of how social life is organised in Norway and more importantly, understood by new citizens.

Acknowledging the need to go beyond "what meets the eye"

Ethnography should be seen as both practice and product, where the "insider's point of view" is emphasised. Instead of imposing categories upon the subjects, ethnographic research allows us as researchers to enter into the life worlds of people and see things from their perspective. It is this first-hand interpretation, often referred to as emic, which allows categories to emerge from the ethnographic encounter. Because the ethnographer is concerned with more than mere descriptions of everyday lives, they will aim at interpretations and representations which also involve more analytical and distanced descriptions, called etic descriptions. The more distanced second-hand interpretations give room for reflexivity and comparison, and the ability to see the ethnography produced in relation to overarching theoretical debates. This mix of emic and etic descriptions very much corresponds to a methodology of both participation and observation.

When employing participant observation, there are two broad categories of data, namely the verbal statements of members of the society and their observed behaviour (Holy and Stuchlick 1983). To be a participant observer means living together with the subjects, and somehow trying to be a part of the social and moral universe of the research subjects, to adjust to their situations and take part in daily life and social events. This participation enables collection of data on social interaction. By employing such an approach, researchers often find that what people say they do does not always concur with what they do. Such divergence informs us about notions and attitudes that exist within a given society.

Here we are at the core of ethnographic research; acknowledging that different aspects of a lifeworld are intimately connected implies a holistic perspective and also a cultural relativistic approach, meaning that the researchers gaze must always seek an understanding from *within*. Through observation and participation in everyday activities, spending time with people in everyday situations, we can embrace and encounter lived experience, accessing tacit as well as embodied knowledge that people may not always be able to express, but which they will know through carrying out or participating in certain activities.

Trying to grasp tacit and embodied knowledge through participation observation reminds us about the close links between phenomenology and participant observation. The aim of phenomenology is to account for the total horizon of our lived experience in a comprehensive way, through describing things or phenomena that are inherent parts of this experience (Primoziz 2001). Phenomenology involves a shift from standing on the outside to trying to situate oneself in the field of enquiry. Jackson's thinking on practical mimesis, or "thinking with one's feet" (Jackson

1996) refers to the way one can gain insights through taking part as others do. Doing this kind of research demands willingness and openness on the part of both researcher and of the participants. Trust has to be built, and the researcher needs to have a good command of the language and the social context. It demands both patience and vigilance, and is therefore often quite time consuming. We argue that such an approach should increasingly be used in more applied research, and more specifically so in studies of integration in a Norwegian context, in order to create a better understanding of what works and what does not work when it comes to integration policies.

Needless to say, long-term fieldwork is not possible in an applied research project, due to high costs and often limited time available. However, acknowledging an anthropological approach implies an interest in going beyond "what meets the eye", or what is already pre-defined. Ethnography brings about a different focus and knowledge; both in the way data are produced and in the way data are interpreted and reported. The ethnographic approach is possible also within a limited timeframe, but requires that the researcher has ethnographical experience and is able to apply such skills in situations where time is of the essence. Howell (2011) argues that even though such an exercise is difficult, it may be possible if one has the experience of doing "traditional" anthropological fieldwork.

Through the examples from the case study in Lyngdal, we have not only introduced the individual histories of three new citizens in Lyngdal and their aspirations for their future life here. Their particular experiences also generate knowledge on how the PWS employees interact with new citizens, its core ideals for integration and its system of categorisations. Through these examples, we have seen how certain ideals seem to dominate when considering who is resourceful or not, or how immigrants' opportunities are negotiated with reference to short-term perspectives on employability and assumed personal suitability. The examples also tell us something about the organisation of Norwegian society, in terms of social interaction and ideas of interaction between work life and social life. By listening to our immigrant women and their experiences, we become painfully aware of the difference between "getting a job", and getting access to social relations and society at large. Whilst Norwegian policy makers and representatives of the PWS continue to base their policies on the assumption that work is the main way of integration into society, our cases illustrate how this is not necessarily the case. Ironically, getting access to work can also mean a reduced or non-existing social life, which again may create situations of loneliness and sensation of exclusion. Thus, a situation where people are placed in jobs where they may feel isolated or with limited opportunities is perhaps not a sustainable long-term solution. If the general belief is that work life will provide immigrants with a platform for socialising and hence also social integration, there is a need to rethink the strategies of, for example, Emebet's educational path. Providing Emebet with work in a sector in which she does not want to be may leave her in a situation like Miljana's. Miljana's life in Norway is not as an integrated citizen but rather more like that of Armita's, who mainly interacts with her fellow countrymen, mostly speaks her own language and hardly takes part in Norwegian society. The difference between the two is that while Armita's dream is to go back to her home country, Miljana dreams of a permanent life in Norway and to be fully participating in Norwegian society. The latter requires, in Miljana's view, more than raising a salary and paying taxes. It involves a social life and a possibility to negotiate and maneouvre in Norwegian society, which she finds difficult in her current employment.

Rugkåsa (2012) argues that the integration process based on "arbeidslinja" reflects a process of civilisation: that the overall aim of Norwegian policies is to turn immigrant women into blueprints of ourselves. The dominant view amongst representatives of the PWS is that differences are regarded difficult and "cultural". Rugkåsa (2012) refers to such things as clothing as an obstacle for women when trying to find a job. Armita's political engagement in her own country would also serve as an example of an activity reflecting difficulties to be overcome, as this is perceived as disengagement with the Norwegian society from Armita's side. If her engagement had only been in local politics the case would be different. This might indicate that PWS employees in Norway tend to categorise and conceptualise all citizens according to the Norwegian way of "being in the world". Through a focus on immigrant women and their lived lives, we have a chance of rethinking through comparative reflection. Insights into other life worlds may challenge a perception of a predefined "Norwegian way of life" as being *the* only meaningful way of life. Perhaps it could also spur a discussion on integration into a plural society involving ethnic Norwegians as well.

Moving beyond predefined solutions to integration

We began this chapter by pointing to how experiences from field work in development studies can and should be brought into the studies of integration in Norway. Our core argument has been that experiences from doing long-term ethnographic work in "far away" places, and the competence in cultural translation this gives, must be seen as a resource when exploring a new field of research such as integration. There are two main arguments for this: the first concerns how an ethnographic approach with a basis in phenomenology and participatory observation as a core methodology enables us to move beyond stereotypes and taken for granted understandings of actors and situations. In the Norwegian field of integration, where emotions and facts are often mashed together to serve political argumentation, moving beyond established narratives and stereotypes is certainly called for. Development researchers should increasingly contribute to the production of knowledge, along with anthropologists and sociologists researching the integration field. The second argument concerns the idea of comparative reflection, which comes as a result of the experience of understanding "the other" from within and thus dealing with cultural translation. Learning about "the other" also implies learning about "self", because comparison can make us reflect on our own way of thinking and doing. Instead of looking for a way to confirm assumptions, comparison enables amazement and surprise, and perhaps reflections on alternative approaches to how to organise society. This enables humility, a rethinking of approaches, moving beyond predefined solutions to integration and questioning the very meaning of integration and the role we as researchers or practitioners play in it.

Consequently, a perception of the variety of lived life, i.e. 'cultures', as constraining a process of integration, would be impossible. Instead of seeing culture as a barrier to integration, comparison enables an understanding of the diversity of cultures as foundational for integration into a plural society.

Notes

1 Lyngdals Avis, 4 December 2013.
2 Listerrådet is the regional council for co-operation between the municipalities of Kvinesdal, Lyngdal, Farsund, Flekkefjord and Hægbostad.

8 Phenomenology of music students

Elisabet S. Hauge

A phenomenological study of music education

For centuries music has been important in people's daily lives. Music has been created and performed on big and small stages for generations. During the 17th century music became a profession for musicians such as Mozart, Haydn and Beethoven. All three of them were employed composers who performed live music for a privileged audience. With the development of new technology, high quality music became a public domain through recorded music, a development that started in the 1890s. The early recording industry was characterised as a voice without a face. Music became a product that was possible to buy, and buyers could listen to their favourite songs again and again. To make a living, the artists were dependent on the record companies. The record industry became the growth of a mass medium (Gronow 1983) opening huge global business opportunities for musicians such as Billie Holliday and Bing Crosby in the 1930s and1940s, Frank Sinatra, Nina Simone, Elvis Presley and the Beatles in the 1950s and 1960s and David Bowie and Abba in the 1970s. By their characteristic voice, melodies and styles, these artists managed to leave footprints in the music business. The artists were joined by a huge number of other more or less known musicians. In 1981 the TV channel MTV was launched. The TV channels vision was to present music videos guided by popular DJs. Michael Jackson's music video *Thriller* from 1982 was revolutionary. MTV has later on stated that "*MTV did not create Michael Jackson, he made us*". MTV's approach to youths was the key to its success (Hujic 1996). MTV became an enormous world-wide mass medium that opened a new music markets and introduced new business models for music production and performance.

In the 1990s a new technology disturbed the music economy. ICT actors started to grab market shares from the recording music industry by sharing music on the internet for free. A new mass media competed on recorded music that had been a cornerstone in musicians' income. This situation had a positive and negative impact on all the actors in the music industry value chain. The possibility to create economic value was harmed in the process. Both small and big record companies experienced economic decline and bankruptcy. Distribution of music economy through the internet grew fast, and helped or pushed artists to emancipate themselves from record labels. New technology opened up new potential added value that goes beyond the classical ways of selling music. As a result of the digital revolution, artists had to become less dependent on traditional players in the music industry. It is impossible for most artists to earn a living by selling recorded music. Money making nowadays is through concerts and live performance, merchandising and branding, and rights management and music licencing, and streaming has become a useful tool to gain attention and to promote concerts.

Due to the introduction of new music business models, young musicians are in need of renewed and timely knowledge and competence. To succeed in the music markets, it is not enough to "only" be a talented musician. The modern business logic in popular music is more based on a "do-it-yourself" business logic. Becoming entrepreneurial is one strategy to adjust to the movements in the world-wide music economy, and to make a living out of music talent and performance. Many upcoming and young musicians do therefore attempt to enhance their entrepreneurial skills.

This chapter is one example of how philosophy of science can be made explicit in applied research. The objective is to present a phenomenological description of how, for children and young people, different contexts evolve into opportunities that merge musical talent and entrepreneurship. Through a regional education and training system, they are supposed to set up a world-wide space for themselves, in a world constituted by adult rules and norms of existence. Children and youths act, interact, absorb, interpret and project opportunities that iteratively guide and affect their upcoming musical careers. The paradox is that, for most musicians, money making does not seem to be the driving force for starting the entrepreneurial processes. The process of young musicians becoming entrepreneurial is rather a result of their existence and engagement in a complex world set up by crossing everyday spaces. Engaging in the music business is constantly on the move, and influences how upcoming artistic creativity evolves. At the same time, the new generation of creative and entrepreneurial musicians contributes to moving the music business. In this process education and training are important, and often crucial, for musicians developing the skills and qualities necessary to become professional musicians. This is a hermeneutic process of designing and redesigning a lifestyle. This chapter examines a regional perspective on the relationship between education and training systems and entrepreneurial musicians. Therefore, I ask the research question: *how do arts community schools (ACS), Vågsbygd high school (VHS), the University of Agder (UoA) and The Competence Centre for Music in Southern Norway (SØRF) contribute to promote talented youth's artistic and entrepreneurial successes?*

Music education at Agder

The motivation behind the research question is a curiosity that came in the wake of doing fieldwork for PhD studies among Norwegian metal musicians. During the PhD I became aware that many self-employed musicians lack entrepreneurial skills. Informants claimed that the school system does not offer satisfying entrepreneurship training and education. To get more information about the observed situation, I invited the principals from the three public schools and the manager of SØRF to a workshop. At the workshop we discussed how their music students learn to become self-employed musicians. The four actors representing each of their regional music education and training organisations had never met before, which was a situation that fostered a discussion that raised many new and complex research questions about how music students develop entrepreneurial skills. This coincidence paved the way for a joint brainstorm regarding how to improve education and training for youths who want to succeed as self-employed musicians. Even though both VHS and UoA offer entrepreneurship subjects such as young entrepreneurship programmes, none of the educational institutions have entrepreneurship as a compulsory subject for music students. In line with national guidelines for education, entrepreneurship training and education is not a core purpose in secondary music education or university fine art education. To equip students with good self-employed skills, this focus was claimed to be important for future education and training programmes. Additionally, the educational institutions highlighted that they have an important role in the young musician's career. Therefore, the four actors liked the idea of systematising knowledge on how young musicians become entrepreneurial. Based on this common interest, a proposal for a pilot study was worked out for Regional Research Fund Agder. The proposal aim was to expand the knowledge base of how young musicians obtain and learn skills to become entrepreneurial. The proposal was fully granted. The study was managed by Agder Research AS.

In the study of entrepreneurship among young musicians, a phenomenological approach to philosophy was a research platform for studying the complexity of entrepreneurship learning, and for describing the temporal dimension of becoming. A phenomenological approach in applied research is explorative by nature, meaning that *a phenomenological research method* is dominated by the production of qualitative oriented data. For this purpose, data from a case study that aimed at expanding the understanding of how eight young musicians participate and acquire knowledge within a regional educational and training system, was produced. The informants were interviewed using a semi-structured questionnaire, with a focus on the young musicians' understanding of future entrepreneurial opportunities. Each education and training institution in the pilot project was represented by two informants.

The highly qualitative conducted fieldwork was followed by *a phenomenological analysis* of entrepreneurial opportunities described by the young musicians. In this work I had a special focus on Heidegger's two concepts; the concept of place and the concept of projecting when analysing the process of musicians in education becoming entrepreneurial. Place should not be thought of as a geographical location, but rather as an arena consisting of (human and non-human) beings, norms, values, rules, potentialities and possibilities. In short, place consists of the platforms where beings act and live their life. I interpret Heidegger's concept of *projecting* as a description of an activity where beings accumulate understanding that carries them into the future where they evaluate and calculate according to their resources, understood possibilities and companions. The activity is always temporal, because our possibilities are under constant change as time moves on.

The study results were presented in a working paper at the fifth Nordic geographers' meeting, June 11–14, 2013, in Reykjavík, Iceland. The study's main finding was that schools and the university promote and produce highly qualified people in terms of becoming refined musicians, not entrepreneurs. Youths entrepreneurial skills evolve in isolation from the formal education and training system.

The school system

The following description of the regional music education and training system is based on how the institutions portray themselves at their web homepages, and how they introduced themselves in the pilot. Figure 8.1 illustrates the regional music education and training system in Agder, which is mostly localised in the city of Kristiansand.

The Education Act describes art community schools as statutory public art education, offered to all children and youths from 7 to 19 years old, and who want to learn and practise art. The intention is to promote high quality, enrich diversity and ensure both variety and talent. The art school is part of the municipal cultural sectors. In addition to instrument

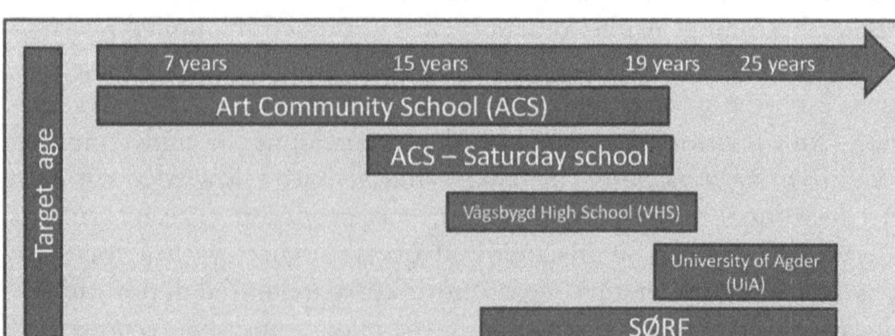

Figure 8.1 The music education and training system in the Agder region

learning and singing courses, the art community schools often organise student concerts and performances. Education is offered in groups and in one to one tuition. In specific municipalities, such as Kristiansand, the most talented students are also offered additional hours of music practice and performance.

When teens start high school they might choose between general education and different forms of vocational education. Students who choose general education might also choose between different study programmes. One high school in the Agder region offers a music programme. Students entering this programme normally spend 3 years at school, where they receive music lectures in addition to general subjects. A diploma confirming completed education, and passed exams, gives admission to start university education.

The UoA hosts the Faculty of Fine Art. Rhythmic music is one of the faculty's focus areas and is also one of the university's two signature studies. At this faculty, performance programmes in classical and popular music are offered both at bachelors and master's level, as well as bachelor programmes in music education, drama education, art and crafts and music. Shorter programmes and courses are also offered as selective modules in the university's teacher education programmes. A deliberate emphasis on music technology provides many interesting interdisciplinary connections between technology and music, which is related to music performance, production and mediation, studio technology and multimedia production.

SØRF is a member association and a non-profit organisation whose aim is to facilitate and improve commercial skills for musicians in the counties of Agder and Telemark. The service office is located in Kristiansand. SØRF contributes to development and visibility of the cultural business sector, and promotes co-operation between music genres and other cultural milieus such as film, literature and art. Members of SØRF might achieve support to solve challenges such as business establishment, finance, concert arrangements, business courses, tour support and so on.

Musicians' talent and entrepreneurial experience

The research question introduces two concepts that have to be clarified: talent and entrepreneurship. The concept of talent is blurred, and difficult to frame and measure. The concept is understood and framed differently from person to person, and between different scientific perspectives. This can be the reason why many musicians and students are concerned about "how much talent they have". Talented musicians are often regarded as people who possess a mysterious gift that makes them different from the rest of the population. The concept of talent is relational in its logic, because more than one person must have an idea that the musician is in possession of a talent that can be traded in economic terms. Talent is broadly understood as potentiality through actual qualifications (Kingsbury 2001). Without target training, talent is not released into a professional approximation to music business. The author Malcom Gladwell (2008) claims that talent might be a congenital qualification. But, claims Gladwell, the difference becomes visible by the time the talented young unfinished musician becomes 8 years old. The best students start to practise music more than their friends and classmates. The talent becomes a phenomenon of fine practise and a matter of persistent hard training. Not only is musical talent relational, but the social relations are characterised by the descriptions that certain inter-linked persons are also involved in the process. Talent is a highly cultural symbol constituted in the crossroad between political and musical practice (Kingsbury 2001).

An entrepreneur can be defined as "individuals who create new business opportunities by founding a venture and focusing on the development of independent new ventures that are not sheltered by sponsoring organisations (such as spin-offs)" (Clarke & Holt 2010, p. 318). Approaching the concept of talent by a process view highlights that entrepreneurship is studied as a dynamic process. The researched individuals are not studied as beings, but rather as human beings of becoming. Here the research focus is on youths who are in the process of becoming entrepreneurial. By approaching entrepreneurship with a process-oriented view, I assume that entrepreneurship is a movement in time. The movement is driven by individuals who act and respond according to how they grasp the world of entrepreneurial opportunities, which refers to situations that can introduce "future" goods and services (Shane & Venkataraman 2000). It is important to note that intermediate talents do not necessarily end up as entrepreneurs. The targeted research focus attempts to reveal the entrepreneurial opportunities such as described in entrepreneurship theory on opportunity recognition (Ardichvili, Cardozo & Ray 2003; Gaglio & Katz 2001; Hills, Lumpkin & Singh 1997; Shane 2000). This perspective implies cultivating the evolution of entrepreneurial ideas.

Developing the skills to become entrepreneur

When music students enter the ASCs they get an opportunity to practise music in rehearsal rooms at least once a week. Students are offered one to one tuition for 45 minutes once a week, and may also be offered education in groups. This way of exercising music promotes students' awareness of the importance of having good practising routines. ACS is a place to learn how to handle music instruments and singing voice, and to practise music interaction. At ACS children and youths meet friends who also have a music interest. New friendships are established. Some of the ASC music students also supplement ASC by participating in marching bands or music band units. Often music bands initiatives are bottom-up processes resulting in music friends meeting in more organised structures such as ACT. The students also applaud the ACS focus on concert experiences by arranging monthly public concerts at the school concert hall. At ACS, music students become familiar with a practice of conceptualising music performances as projects. Project thinking or conceptualising includes regarding the musician's project tasks and performing as time limited, including a start and end of different goals, tasks, inputs, efforts and outcomes.

One to one tuition follows a traditional education strategy; the lecturer teaches and the student receives. It is the teacher who decides the education content, like what pieces of music to play, how to play them and when to progress to more challenging compositions. When performing concerts, students often interplay with their teacher. This gives the student a feeling of delivering a professional performance. Close contact between the student and the master ensure that the most talented students are offered additional training at Saturday school. In the early stages of life, parents influence their children's talent development and interests in music performance. Parents who are familiar with music activity and performance seem to particularly appeal to and provoke music interests and joy. Still, most students at ACS end up as happy amateur musicians.

Experiencing place to project a future as an entrepreneurial musician

For many musicians born in Agder, VHS is the first entrance into a formal music education system. Since the school is a high school, the institution's duty is to offer the students 3-year schooling, where those who pass the exams and the professional education end up with formal admission to university education. At high school, students may choose to specialise in study directions. At VHS music specialisation is organised both as theoretical and practical education. Music training and education for young people enters a phase where music as subject and music as practice become more rigorous and expand young people's ideas about music as a profession. Norms and practice of how to be a musician are a part of students' learning, whether teaching is given by school teachers or obtained as silent knowhow within the groups of students that the young musicians hang out with.

In order to be capable of creating artistic and creative projects, musicians need to be concerned with credibility within the music industry and milieu. Other people must believe in the ideas and the music that the musicians perform. In the music industry, this kind of respect is called "cred", short for credibility. To "have cred" implies that a talented musician is able to design and redesign artistic creativity. Having cred can be seen as a parameter of how respected one is as a talented, competent and creative musician. To become credible, trustworthiness must be constantly renewed in order to open up new beginnings within ongoing creative processes. Big names within the music industry might help support smaller and upcoming artists by honouring them with their own cred. Image and identity is part of the artistic and business game, and often decisive for the musician's credibility among their listeners.

Being within attractive networks and with popular band partners is a sign of having cred. It is important to be asked and invited to participate in other musicians' artistic projects. Learning, handling and using all the music milieus codes, that being a musician demand, increases the attractiveness. The VHS students confirmed that important learning from school is about how to be a musician. Norms for music behaviour are in focus. The students, consciously or not, continually evaluate their own and other music students' credibility. Questions such as how talented they are, how often they practise, with whom they perform, how many concerts they play, what's their gig history, do they compose and what pieces of music they play become endless discussions among the music students. Their own music potentiality becomes a subject of constant self-evaluation. At the same time the students, consciously or not, observe their classmates to see how they respond to and react to new everyday practices of how to become and be a musician. The world of becoming a musician is related to new and more challenging and upcoming projects, such as school assignments and music gigs at or outside school. At a young age, the informants also claimed that by having a "media strategy" they attempt to professionalise their "music business".

Music students rate loyalty as a highly respected personal characteristic. Classmates and music colleagues are to be treated with respect. Within the music industry, supporting colleagues by doing favours for each other is very usual. Most musicians are dependent on a barter economy to be able to fulfil music projects. Favours may be activities such as being support musicians at gigs, concerts and in studio productions. But the economy also expands its importance and crosses into other cultural business sectors such as design, art, venue, film and videogame companies as the musicians becomes more familiar with doing entrepreneurial activities. At this stage, students normally have not established their own enterprise, but start to think about their music activities as a profession. Therefore, commercial activities are based on a gift economy. For small jobs, students are rewarded with a small gift such as a present, a gift card or a small symbolic amount of money. Money earned is saved with the intention to invest in new and better instruments. As students become more familiar with everyday life practice, ideas of projected futures that include entrepreneurship might be born.

The learning process regarding how to become a musician continues at the UoA. At the university, students are in a situation where education becomes more significant, providing a more refined visualised idea about choice of working professional to achieve more in-depth knowledge about music theory and practice, which might be a source of projecting alternative job opportunities.

When studying at a university, many youths have to move out of their parents' home and into the student city. This was also the situation for the two students interviewed, representing university students. They had left their childhood home to start a university degree in music teaching and practice. During their stay in Kristiansand both of them lived in small bedsit units, being responsible for feeding themselves and paying rent and buying school books, which is also normal for most Norwegian students. This is a situation where money income becomes important. They are considered as young grown ups. Besides credits and scholarships, many music students supplement the economy with part time jobs, preferably doing music gigs and work as music teachers. Working with gigs is often students' first introduction to an entrepreneurial lifestyle. The oldest students claimed that entrepreneurial experience often comes as a result of invoicing. When bills are to be sent, the musicians need a VAT number, which implies that they have to establish a company.

When firms are established, the students need to increase their business competence. They come into a situation where they ask for new and often unfamiliar knowledge about how to run a business. Such knowledge was discussed minimally in UoA's music education programmes. The learning objectives related to performance programmes in classical and popular music are offered on both the bachelor's and master level and are to stimulate music performance skills, music production creativity, innovative and traditional forms of expression, composing, techniques and music educators. Courses in entrepreneurship are not an integrated part of these studies. After identifying a demand for entrepreneurial training among students, the faculty has initiated time-limited entrepreneurship courses with a limited number of credits. As an extensive response the faculty established a master in music management in 2010. Music management is designed as an interdisciplinary and comprehensive master's programme, where the students develop the necessary skills and knowledge to understand and work within today's international music industry, either as entrepreneurs or as employees. The master was taken out of the UoA education offers in 2015, and entrepreneurship education was sorted into different electives organised in other education programmes. Still, music management is not integrated in music composing and performance education.

Even though the university does not seem to put emphasis on the music business in performance programmes in classical and popular music, the students interviewed underlined how the university becomes important in the regional music milieu and business; when starting a university education, students get access to other students in the same situation of being a performing musician, who have established a one-man company. Students learn business skills from each other, and they participate at seminars organised by the Norwegian music union and SØRF. Many students also use family members and entrepreneurial friends outside the university as business mentors.

SØRF's target is to promote musicians that become economic units who are able to make a living out of music composing and performance. SØRF offers an alternative community for musicians who focus on the music business. The association is a network where musicians are offered support such as counselling, information on cultural business support programmes and scholarships, participation at courses and seminars and identifying smart partnerships for doing business. The two informants representing SØRF confirmed that through SØRF they got help in understanding the music business and industry. Most entrepreneurial processes, from establishing a firm to developing business activities, are covered by SØRF. One important service is the competence in business contracts offered by SØRF.

This was a short presentation about how students and users of different training and education music institutions' experience their attendance at the institutions. During the interviews it was obvious that older informants at VHS, UoA and SØRF had more or less started a process where they become entrepreneurial on behalf of the music. This process was not driven by the regional education and training system. Strengthening students' entrepreneurial competence is therefore an important strategy for promoting future commercial success.

Data provide strong evidence that as soon as the students come into a situation where they have to send a bill, they are suddenly in need of holding a VAT number. On a general basis, most emphasis for the youths is on how to become the best musician in the sense of being able to control musical qualifications. The aspect of where to do business and perform music has to expand to become entrepreneurial. Becoming entrepreneurial is also about the ability to project situations that might end up in commercialising music performance. The narratives retold illustrate how place and projecting influence musicians' entrepreneurial processes. The regional education and training system promotes firstly musicians of high quality. Entrepreneurial qualifications are not in focus. Entrepreneurial knowhow is a competence that accumulates as a result of young musicians for different reasons organising their musical activities such as gigs, teaching and studio activities in economic terms.

Projecting entrepreneurship

The research question wording, where the query word is "how", intends to open up exploratory explanations in terms of depth descriptions of how young people approach entrepreneurial processes within a regional education system. Entrepreneurial processes are driven by people who face a broad horizon of opportunities when acting within a complex world. Musicians often enter an entrepreneurial lifestyle with other intentions than money making. Those who attempt to live a life where composing and performing music is their main occupation often choose an entrepreneurial strategy to be able to do so. Using a phenomenological approach to study how musicians become entrepreneurial might help shed light on multiple aspects of entrepreneurial processes. In order to investigate such processes in the music industry, I have tried to strengthen my study by using a philosophical framework to evolve understanding and knowledge of how musicians gain education experience and respond to potential opportunities, and the relations between people and their way of interacting in a complex world. Research method and data analysis is therefore based in a phenomenological oriented epistemology found in Heidegger's *Being and Time* (1996). In knowledge development and applied studies regarding young musicians in regional education systems, there are mainly three ways of utilising phenomenology in research: (1) as a philosophy of science of how to understand existence, (2) as a research method to study existence and (3) as a tool to analyse existence in order to contribute to theory development.

Phenomenology might serve as a powerful tool for exploring and enriching received theoretical constructs such as the evolution of opportunities, by investigating how entrepreneurs actually interpret and enact them. Heidegger describes phenomenology as the philosophical study of the nature of a being, and the science of how beings understand and interpret reality, which is a reality that changes as the eyes that observe and interpret face a continuously renewed reality. The reality of entrepreneurial opportunities is on a constant move, and the eyes that observe and interpret are introduced into a constant renewed reality.

Personally, I like Heidegger's understanding and conceptualisation of the way life develops in *Being and Time* (1996), as we face the many crossroads where beings make choices regarding how to act implied by simply being-in-the-world. As soon as we ask "*What is being?*" he claims, we have some understanding of the "is" without being able to determine conceptually what the "is" means. Part 1 of *Being and Time* provides an analysis of the being of the being. We are not talking about a physical body of flesh and blood. Instead, Heidegger (1996) argues that the "essence" of Being lies in its existence. According to Dreyfus (1991) the best way to understand what Heidegger means by Being is to think of the term "human being", which can refer to a way of being characteristic of all people or to a specific person: a human being. The only way to determine the content of the "is" is to ask questions about being. Ergo; the question of the meaning of being has to be formulated. The search for new knowledge becomes an investigation, as the revealing determination of what the question aims at. Rather than trying to confirm or disconfirm existing theories, the aim of phenomenological research is to develop "bottom-up" interpretive theories that are inextricably "grounded" in the lived world. The research goal is to give a thematic description of experience. Heidegger's concept of place and projecting might be useful categories to provide a thematic description of educational institutions influence on how musical pupils and students understand the evolvement of opportunities to become entrepreneurial. Such a description provides useful knowledge to stimulate and boost regional music business entrepreneurship through targeted education and training.

How beings observe and interpret is influenced by their surroundings (place) and resources. As time passes, reality changes and new ways of living life appear. As humans we all have different experiences, implying that the past exerts an influence on beings' future interpretations and acts. Since phenomenology deals with our understanding of being, it must be hermeneutic (Dreyfus 1991). In an ideal world, understanding will constantly continue growing and can never be complete. Therefore, beings' projecting is constantly adjusted to changing realities.

Place and being-in

Place is the platform where the rules and norms of how to cope in the world are learned by beings. Place expands and shrinks, depending on the relations with other human and tools that beings activate. When place changes, so do also the possibilities for achieving an entrepreneurial lifestyle. Heidegger's famous hammer might have a different function and significance for e.g. a carpenter and a doctor. The bodily utilisation of place is the basis for beings' relations, existence and the formation of their identity. Identity can be describe as "what people are supposed to have, but also what they are building in some kind of bricolage as an individual response to the demands of a complex society" (Frykman & Gilje 2003, p. 9). The concept thus corresponds to Heidegger's concept of "the nature of being". The music business is built on the basis of a certain identity, an identity that seems to have allowed the different music styles and movement to grow. To understand a musician's identity, it is necessary to understand the places they act within, or as Heidegger expresses it:

> Place is always the definite "over there" and the "there" of a useful thing belonging there. Actual belonging there corresponds to the useful character of what is at hand, that is, to its relevant belonging to a totality of useful things.
>
> (Heidegger 1996, p. 95)

To understand what Heidegger means by his often-quoted concept of being-in-the-world, you must first understand the concept of being. Beings do not find themselves in a purely ontic world, or in a purely ontological world, but in both: at the same time. It is a unified phenomenon. What does *being-in* mean? Initially, the expression "being-in" is supplemented with the phrase "the-world", and there is an inclination to understand this being-in as "being-in-something". This term is used to describe the kind of being of a being which is "in" something else, as water is "in" the glass or the dress "in" the closet. By this "in" we mean the relation of being that two beings extended "in" space have to each other with regard to their location in that space. "Water and glass, dress and closet, are both 'in' space 'at' a location in the same way" (Heidegger 1996, p. 50), as the same way as informants are "in" the world of music education and training.

When opportunities are revealed by beings, belonging is an essential and relevant factor of the process. Relations needed to explore entrepreneurial opportunities are intelligible only when beings find themselves in a disclosed world (Heidegger 1996, p. 168). It is necessary not only to know the world, but also to make use of the possibilities that the world offers. In practice, this means in addition to knowing how to compose and perform music, the musician also has to know what doors to knock on to get a gig or record contract. In other words, they must understand the game to be able to control and to use the keys (that place offers) in order to play the "game". The big question then is how to play the game to realise opportunities into real commercial concepts. Realising musical ideas into marketable concepts has to be done authentically! To be visible and credible in the public eye, the musicians' life project must stand out as different as and more ingenious than the musical projects of his or her life competitors, who also fight to attract market attention. According to my informants, it is legitimate to be inspired by other musicians or bands, but copying these sources of inspiration is considered a mortal sin. The answers are again found in their being – their existence. When the world is experienced, learned and manifested in the musicians' acts, they hope to become more capable of acting and simply coping in the world. How to cope in the world is found in the being of a being: 'A world must be disclosed to it [being]. The world is disclosed with the factual existence of Da-sein, if indeed Da-sein essentially exists as being in the world' (Heidegger 1996, p. 333).

It is in the world that the beings find their potential to constitute their being. The world exists as a consequence of being, and being exists as a consequence of the world. The music industry is made up by musicians (and other actors), and musicians are a result of the music industry. Musicians and the music industry are two phenomena that cannot be separated: "being-in-the-world belongs essentially to Da-sein, its being towards the world is essentially taking care" (Heidegger 1996, p. 53), and "being-in designates a constitution of being of Da-sein, and is an existential" Heidegger claims (1996, p. 50).

Space, which is discovered in circumspect being-in-the-world as the spatiality of a totality of useful things, belongs to beings themselves as their place. In a primordial sense, space is a product of beings' existence. Space can therefore only be understood by going back to the world where beings make their experiences. Space does not become accessible only by depriving the surrounding world of its worldliness. Spatiality can be discovered in general only on the basis of the world in such a way that space, after all, also constitutes the world in accordance with the essential spatiality of Da-sein itself with regard to its fundamental constitution of being-in-the-world. In this chapter, being-in-the-world is related to being a music student in the education and training system in the Agder region. To develop authentic universes in economic terms, being-in is a basic condition, although the musician happily says that he removes himself from the world in order to compose music.

Projecting

Perhaps the most radical feature of Heidegger's theory is the intrinsic role of movement in his theorising. Movement, however, is not physical. Movement is characterised by the incessant *projection* of understanding upon the world. Understanding in itself has the existential structure, which we call project. In a mind-set inspired by Heidegger, existentials are a potential for acting and the following results. As time, as previously mentioned, has a crucial role in existence and existential, it is not possible to presume what the outcome of the actualisation of potentials will be. Heidegger stresses that the being is always already ahead of itself. It is through projection of understanding upon the world that Da-sein understands itself. Projection accompanies all being's ways of behaving. Existing implies that a being has already projected itself upon definite possibilities of its existence; and in these existential projects it has also projected pre-ontologically somethings like existence and being.

The character of understanding constitutes in-the-world, with regard to disclosing its potentiality of being. Projecting is the existential constitution of being in realm of potentiality of being. Projecting always concerns the complete disclosure of being-in-the-world. Like understanding, being projects its being upon possibilities. This being towards possibilities that understand is itself a potentiality for being, because of the way these disclosed possibilities come back to being. In interpretation, understanding appropriates what it has understood in an understanding way. By interpretation, understanding does not become something different, but rather itself. Interpretation is existentially based on understanding, and not the other way around: "In the projecting of understanding, beings are disclosed in their possibility" (Heidegger 1996, p. 141).

Projecting constitutes how musicians' being-in-the-world enacts beings' potentials, and is linked to the process of sense making. Sense, for Heidegger, as opposed to Husserl, is the structure of the general background that can never be fully objectified, but can only be gradually and incompletely revealed by circular hermeneutic inquiry. Sense, which relates to Heidegger's concept of meaning, is always filled in, in some specific way, in some specific situation. As a concept, "meaning includes the formal existential framework of what necessarily belongs to what interpretation that understands articulates", and further meaning "must be understood as the formal, existential framework of the disclosedness belonging to understanding" (Heidegger 1996, p. 142). Sense is the formal structure of the background practices, in terms of which ontologists can make sense of the understanding of being itself.

Projecting is authentic, and underlines the evaluative phenomenon of authentic actualisation of potentials. The same can be applied to recognition;

without projecting (or recognition) entrepreneurial possibilities, there cannot be an actualisation of an entrepreneurial opportunity. Both projection and recognition demand a source of energy represented by beings, so that potentials can be realised. The driving force behind entrepreneurial processes is found in the existence of being, underlining the descriptive phenomenon of the authentic: those who are able to turn potentials into actions, and involve other beings in their movement, might be considered to be good entrepreneurs (if, of course, the commercialisation process is considered to be good), and those who do not manage to project for entrepreneurship might be said to be bad entrepreneurs (if entrepreneurial at all).

The need to change the education system

The students interviewed claim that the regional education and training system does not satisfy their need for more entrepreneurial knowhow among music students. The study of the regional music education and training system gives strong indications that entrepreneurship is not part of the young people's music education. The students projecting activity while attending classes at ACS, VHS and UoA is all about becoming a high qualified musician, and not an entrepreneur. Entrepreneurial training and education is left to SØRF. If the students at ACS, VHS and UoA are not introduced to SØRF, they will probably be less familiar with merging entrepreneurship and music. At least it is reasonable to believe that merging entrepreneurship and music has the potential to increase a change of focus in favour of more entrepreneurial courses in the traditional education system.

When music education comes to an end, music students seem to change reality and face a new reality of being a ground up. Their stay at each institution naturally focuses on what is going on at the institution. If the institution's main aim is to become a good musician, this is also the informants' main aim. Integrating the institutions better may contribute to help young people to develop entrepreneurial skills and opportunities.

Even though entrepreneurial knowledge is not a compulsory subject at ACS, VHS and UoA, one should not assume that the students do not demonstrate entrepreneurship, although the education institutions focus is on creating highly qualified musicians. Perhaps the most important contribution is that educational institutions offer a venue – an environment in which to grow as a musician. Key card becomes an important tool to gain entry. Having a key card gives young people access to a rehearsal where they can both compose and perform music. At the same time the school becomes a place where they can meet like-minded people who are interested in music as a possible career path. This meeting venue also houses exchanging entrepreneurial knowledge between the young musicians; of knowledge, which can be crucial to their eventual entrepreneurial future. Entrepreneurial processes are driven by people who face a broad horizon of opportunities when acting within a complex world, and any act has an uncertain outcome.

The students' stories recount a lack of focus when it comes to merging music and entrepreneurship in the regional formal education system. This is a barrier for participating in a future world-wide music economy. Music education is about becoming good and talented musicians, not entrepreneurs. The lifestyle designed and redesigned at ACS, VHS and UoA is about becoming credible musicians with advanced music qualifications. We have to change what is going on in training and education to make room for entrepreneurship training.

In an ideal world, understanding will constantly continue growing and can never be complete. Education and training will not produce fulfilled musicians, we can only produce better musicians, and entrepreneurship might be a strategy to promote more artistic success stories. For this to happen, the educational system probably has to change, by putting more effort into initiatives that promote young people's entrepreneurial skills.

9 Power and knowledge

Jørn Cruickshank and Hege Wallevik

Research and power

This chapter discusses the role of the researcher in the process of constructing knowledge. We discuss how research can contribute to practice, other than by providing knowledge within already framed conceptions of the problem at hand. The case we will refer to is a PhD project focusing on women, income and social change in Zanzibar. The chapter argues that, by redefining the hegemonic understanding of the relation between knowledge production and power, researchers can regard themselves as change agents, even if they do not provide "relevant" research to policy-makers. There are different ways to define your role as an academic than either being relevant or critical, and being aware of this may contribute to making social science matter more than it does at present. We propose two alternative role-definitions: the researcher as (1) an actor who constructs another meaning during the research process, and (2) the researcher who strategically addresses the way the problem at hand is framed by powerful actors. The first role resembles the phenomenological approach where the purpose of research is enriching the evolvement of opportunities. The latter enables an opening up of the debate that again allows marginalised interest more influence. We present the two alternatives under the headings "constructing another meaning" and

Table 9.1 The funder and the researcher

	Relevant	*Irrelevant*		
	Problem-solving	*Critical/ deconstructivist*	*Constructing another meaning*	*Altering the structuring logic*
Funder/ policy-maker	FRAMING			
Researcher		FRAMING (long run)	FRAMING (short and long run)	FRAMING (short and long run)
	Simplify	Diversify		

"altering the structuring logic" towards the end of this chapter. Table 9.1 places these two approaches into an illustration of how we in this chapter understand the interplay between funder and researcher.

Table 9.1 illustrates several dimensions in the following discussions. First, it indicates how knowledge can, from the perspective of a funder, be regarded as either "relevant" or "irrelevant". Second, to the left in the figure the drive in the research process is simplification, whereas in the three roles for the researcher to the right the aim is at diversifying and bringing in alternative conceptualisations. Third, it is only in the three critical approaches to the right that the research community frames the field. Finally, even if the critical/deconstructivist approach might contribute to more diversity in the long run, this chapter suggests two alternative ways of intervening in the field immediately, even if the researcher does not attempt to be relevant to funders. These are the two approaches to the right in the table.

We prepare the background for the two alternative ways of being a researcher, first by discussing more generally the relation between power and knowledge, and thereafter a description of the case, and how it links to the activities at Agder Research. We then elaborate on why we regard the relation between power and knowledge as problematic in the case of the discourse on development. This is done first in the section on ethnocentric development, where we claim that it is a problem that the Western cultural experience frames what development is, and what kind of knowledge is relevant in defining development. We describe the two ways that most academics approach powerful actors in the development debate, by (1) producing relevant knowledge or (2) criticising the hegemonic conceptualisation of development. Finally, we remind the reader of a space for researchers who are frustrated that social science does not matter (enough).

Power and knowledge

The relation between knowledge and power is not straightforward, and is a much debated topic, also in the development discourse (Arowosegbe 2014; Escobar 1995). Francis Bacon famously stated that "knowledge is power" (Flyvbjerg 2002, p. 354); i.e. the more knowledge we gain about reality, the more power we have to control it. Policy-makers that adopt the philosophy of positivism tend to think that knowledge producers "first observe, and then go on to describe, a world that has already been made: that has already settled into final forms of which we can give a full and objective account" (Ingold 2011, p. 2). In such a non-constructivist approach, knowledge is sought in order to learn more about your subject, about causes and effects, and some findings are then truer than others. There is a

> belief that the knowledge produced in such an exercise is neutral, value-free, and objective, which can be tested by any scientific method and be replicated in any geography regardless of its peculiarity.
>
> (Tripathy & Mohapatra 2011, p. 94)

Researchers furthermore do problem-solving and there is a sharp division between the formation of political opinions and the professional competence of experts.

At Agder Research we repeatedly experience funders intervening when our research breaks with, or interferes with, values and ideologies that powerful agents take for granted. This setting forces applied researchers into one out of two possible positions: (1) we solve problems within the frames of the dominant way of thinking, or (2) we position ourselves outside by criticising or producing a kind of knowledge that there is no demand for. In the latter case the research risks being "irrelevant". "We cannot use this" is a well-known phrase among bureaucrats. Our question is: how can we escape this dilemma? To do away with one tempting answer, we do not think that the only solution is for critical researchers to find ways to become more useful. We instead suggest two different ways to deal with this.

Knowledge is power, but it is also the case that "power is knowledge"; that power gets to determine what counts as knowledge, and what kind of interpretation should dominate (Flyvbjerg 1998a). Doing research, one may come to learn that the hegemonic understanding of your topic is simplifying, and thus represses alternative narratives. We suggest that one strategy would then be to attempt to change the discourse "from within", not by bringing knowledge about the world to policy-makers, but through a process within which researcher and the researched co-produce knowledge. This way research could alter and prevent hegemonic dominance through the way knowledge is produced, by ensuring that people's everyday interpretations are incorporated into discourse (Jones 1995). A second, related strategy, is for applied researchers to be reflexive about their role in a discursive play about, in our case, development, not by "giving voice" to others (Murdoch & Pratt 1993), but by addressing the structuring logic that governs the debate on development. We believe that it is possible to work strategically against the simplification of the debate attempted by the dominant discourse by complicating, introducing agonisms and thereby instituting a rivalry project that prevents the development discourse from maintaining hegemony.

Both alternatives demand that applied researchers define their role as something more than what funders regard them from project to project. It is about being targeted and being pro-active, in addition to complying with the demand from funders. As demonstrated in the next section, the case that we present is not just a project, but an attempt to be strategic.

The case

The case presented in this chapter builds on PhD research funded. The research questions and the overall approach was thus in the hands of the researcher, and as such not an applied research project from the start. However, the PhD project was developed under, and was one of several projects, in a Strategic Institute Programme (SIP) at Agder Research, a programme which was closely linked to the international portfolio of projects within the NORAD framework agreement that Agder Research had at the time. Here we focused on local government, civil society and private sector development in so-called developing countries where the theory-practice encounter was highlighted. In addition to this emphasis on the theory-practice dialogue, Agder Research also took part in an academic council for development studies in the region which included resource persons from development studies at UoA and from organisations such as Strømme Foundation (one of the largest NGOs in Southern Norway) and the UN Association in Kristiansand. Here discussions evolved around the role of research in development practice and thus the theme, the problem statement and the overall approach of the PhD project developed in close contact with the practice field.

The PhD research, also presented in Chapter 7, was motivated by an interest in Zanzibari women's lives, how they pursued their economic affairs and influenced changes. The folloing figure illustrates the hegemonic and an alternative storyline linking women, income and change.

To the right is the hegemonic story; the narrative of the economically independent female change agent, once economically empowered becoming a change agent for development. The circle to the left in the figure reflects how a study on economic activity among women in Zanzibar Town may be approached differently. Seen through the lens of an ideal of interdependence,

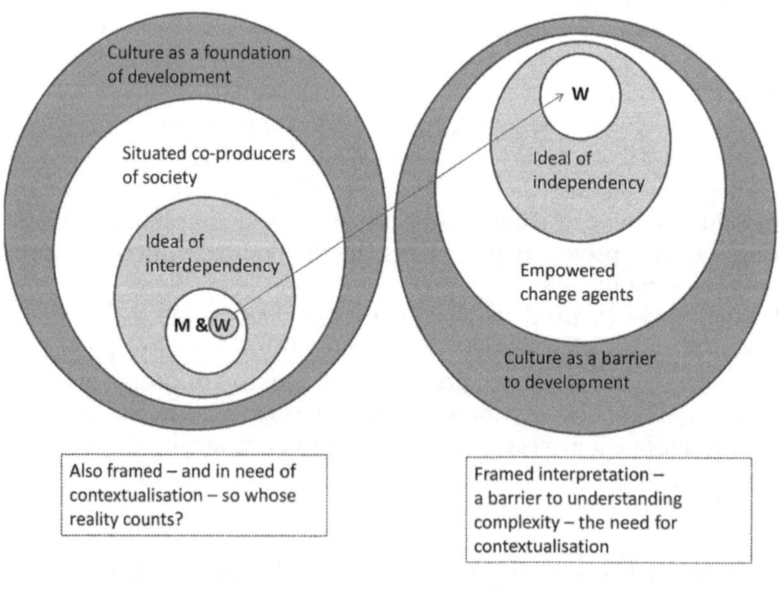

Figure 9.1 The hegemonic and an alternative storyline linking women, income and change

Source: Wallevik 2013.

seeing both men and women as situated co-producers of society, produces a different narrative. We will come back to these two narratives later.

The overall aim was to produce knowledge that could intervene with hegemonic understandings and engage in discussions of predefined links between women, income and social change with a knowledge production based more in lived lives in the South. This again could enrich discussions across the theory-practice divide, and thus strengthen the knowledge base at Agder Research on such encounters.

Ethnocentric development

Why is the earlier dilemma, being forced to either comply or risk being irrelevant, a problem? The problem is not limited to the way development is framed or to the mere content of hegemonic discourses. In general, we believe that it is always important to prevent a simplification of political space, which excludes not only diverging and alternative narratives but also prevents everyday life experience of many people's admittance in collective action. In a deliberative democracy we should avoid any tendency to narrow the scope of politics (Flyvbjerg 1998b; Mouffe 2005), and academia has a role to play in facilitating an ongoing debate in which we accept that the social is always structured by elusive and ephemeral discourses, and that such elusiveness should not be done away with (Bond 2011; Hillier 2003; Mouffe 1999; Pløger 2004).

The previous Table 9.1 illustrates our point, where we suggest that when funders seek knowledge for the purpose of solving pre-defined problems, the dynamic between powerful agents and researcher contributes to a simplification of the field. In either of the three cases where the researcher has a critical perspective on hegemonic understandings, we claim that this will contribute to diversification.

Attempts to simplify political space are highly visible in current development debates, where theoretical interpretations linked to neo-liberal understandings have gained status (Edelman & Haugerud 2005; Nustad 2003).[1] The development discourse strives to establish the Western cultural experience as the universal model to which development in the South should conform. There is an overall framing of the discourse on development, as many scholars have pointed out:

> From the eighteenth century to the present, Enlightenment thinkers have provided a pattern for intellectuals throughout the world who wish to make their societies rational, scientific, secular and therefore modern. And through Europe's dominance of the world – made possible through colonization, economic productivity, the deployment of military might and state building – the Enlightenment model has become dominant throughout the world.
>
> (Arowosegbe 2014, p. 310)

We are facing a normative belief that there is one superior way of understanding and organising society, and that this way thus should be exported. Development is at the same time being de-politicised, as in the case of total hegemony for this discourse, truths about non-Western cultures generated beyond the universalised model are either non-existing or irrational. In the utopic situation of total hegemony for this discourse it is not possible to articulate non-Western experiences without using the language generated in the Eurocentric order. We are of course not there and will never be.

However, Crewe and Harrison (1998) have demonstrated how much development theory and practice is ethnocentric, and built on knowledge generated from generalised, "universal" perspectives. They discuss the perceived dichotomy on "tradition" versus "modernity" in development practice and argue that developers talk and write much about "traditional ways of life" as a hindrance to development. Rational motivation is assumed to direct people towards maximising gain, while "traditional culture" relies on something far less reasonable. "Traditionalism is partly attributed to economic or ecological conditions, but is often conceived of as being linked to a psychological or cultural disposition that is in some sense backward and prevents people from embracing modernity" (Crewe & Harrison 1998, in Edelman & Haugerud 2005, p. 232).

Almost 20 years later the idea of "traditions holding people back" is still persistent across the development industry.[2]

Research in the field of development necessarily involves some kind of interaction with development practice. Within more practical development issues, we are often confronted with very categorical discussions on women and their role in societal change in the South. Realising that there is a need for a generalised knowledge in this field, the underlying assumptions which prevail when discussing women in general, and the links between women, economic activities and change specifically, are surprisingly general. Despite all the research undertaken on these issues, women are often portrayed in generalised ways, as detached from society and culture. Moreover, the processes underlying changes in women's economic activities are approached in an almost deterministic manner.

One example is found in the narrative of the independent income-earning woman. The main idea in this narrative, which was coined during the early 1990s, is that once women become financially independent, they become empowered agents of change. This storyline or narrative underlies much development thinking on women and income generation.[3] The story of the economically empowered woman is one among many storylines presented and acted upon in the field of gender and development.

In this way "culture" is reduced to a fixed set of ideas about how things are in a particular place, which also conveniently explains undesired outcomes of planned interventions. For researchers within the field of development, and especially commissioned research, it is of course commonplace to produce knowledge within these frames (Green 1995),[4] but according to Foucault (1980) there is no "truth", only a regime of "truth" i.e. discourses that society accepts and which are allowed to function as the "truth". The "truth" is centred on the sciences and institutions that produce it, and this is why Tripathy and Mohapatra (2011, p. 112) even claim that the relation between knowledge and development goes both ways, because "[D] development knowledge was the base on which stood development power".

This means that the relevance of research that feeds into the development discourse is not necessarily dependent on what philosophy of science it is based on, whether it is positivistic, constructivist, hermeneutic, phenomenological or critical, but rather the degree to which results are meaningful in the context of the dominant discourse. As development studies is a field marked by theory, models, institutions and policy, much research is concerned with large random samples basing data collection and analysis on quantitative approaches. However, also research based within qualitative research traditions, if conducted in consent with the overall hegemonic perspective, is acknowledged, unlike much of the research focussing on particular places and cases, presenting alternatives to the established "truth". It is, in other words, the logic in the dominant discourse that decides what kind of knowledge and truth that is produced. The challenge then is breaking with the dominant force that energises the making of development, which is why many voices urge academia to counter the hegemony or expand the debate.

How researchers face hegemony

Because development studies aim at producing knowledge with relevance for practice and policies, it is important that research also stimulates debate (Whitehead, Cornwall & Harrison 2008). Thus researchers continue arguing that the main objective should be to "write back" at the hegemonic discourse, and always be critical towards streamlined and generalised knowledge. Findings negating the hegemonic discourse should also be stimulated (Roe 1991, 1995). We will provide some examples of such critiques. Elisabet S. Hauge argues that there is "a huge lack of focus when it comes to merging music and entrepreneurship in the regional formal education system." (See Chapter 8: *Phenomenology of music students*, in this book.) Whitehead, Cornwall and Harrison (2008) have examined a number of myths that have come to be embedded in development policy and practice. They argue that:

> development needs its own myths to guide and motivate action, but mistaking these stories of change that inspire intervention for actual, given realities of development work is to miss the point.
>
> (Whitehead et al. 2008, p. 4)

We should not mistake such stories for general or universal truths, acting upon these irrespective of context. We should be aware that the storyline on the female change agent depends on certain linkages made between women, income and change.

Since the 1990s, a body of work has appeared which attacks the "development discourse" in one way or another, with the aim of deconstructing it (Escobar 1995; Ferguson 1990; Hobart 1993).[5] According to Edelman and Haugerud (2005):

> the alternatives-to-development or "alternative development" [position entails] "the abandonment of the whole epistemological and political field of post war development" whereas others focus on development alternatives (alternatives *in* rather than *to* development) and favour reforms within the existing development apparatus.
>
> (Edelman & Haugerud 2005, p. 2)

The argument is that the developing world itself must be seen as constantly being produced and reproduced, and that research should also inform the debate about this construction process. This may enable a fruitful debate which could deliberate development from the constraints inherent in dominant discourses. The same applies to the "gender and development" discourse (Abu-Lughod 2006; Mohanty 2003; Mohanty, Russo & Torres 1991; Whitehead, Cornwall & Harrison 2007, 2008).

Criticism of hegemonic discourses over the years has also come from other directions:

> Western intellectual traditions tend to be privileged over all others, as though no edifying account of human social life could be rendered by using African, Islamic, Indian, Chinese or Polynesian traditions of thought. . . . detailed descriptions of lived reality are seen as a way of resisting the estranging effects of conceptual models and systematic explanation which, when pushed too far, disqualify and efface the very life one wants to understand.
>
> (Jackson 2005, p. 2)

The actual lived lives of people should be emphasised in order to challenge or negate hegemonic discourses. There is a large body of anthropological literature on the multitude of lived realities worldwide, emphasising lived experiences within particular life worlds as a standpoint for an alternative voice. The ethnography on women and their economic affairs used as an example in the earlier figure was a result of such a positioning in the development field.

The dominant discourse assumes that given their capability as carers, women themselves, their children, households and whole communities will benefit, and development will occur. Given women's capability as good providers and carers this story allows for the idea that women, once they are given a gentle push, will become good "change agents" for development. It is in this context that ideas of micro-finance (MF) have to be understood. Targeting women with micro-credit ensures access to capital and enables them to become economically independent. Through entrepreneurial activity women are believed to have a better life. The problem is just that women are set outside their context, and they are seen through the lens of an ideal of independence which provides developers with the legitimacy that there is a need for intervention.

It is, however, possible to construct another meaning that acknowledges multiple realities and sees the importance of knowledge based on lived experience, as illustrated on the left of Figure 9.1. Here, women are not taken out of their context but are rather seen as embedded in relationships. Women are engaged in economic activities with a kind of embodied knowledge about an economic system different from the neoclassical economic man, which is guiding their engagement in economic affairs. Overall, in this approach economic rationality is emphasised as culturally based and no intervention is needed for them to be understood as "change agents for development". Paying attention to the way women actively produce and reproduce their society through their everyday lives, it becomes evident that women are already important "change agents" in their societies.

With this perspective in mind, we will suggest two ways of doing applied research that explicitly attempt to influence development beyond the framing of the hegemonic discourse.

Alternative roles of researchers

Constructing another meaning

How relevant is knowledge based on lived experience for development debates? It may be questioning, enriching or complementing the hegemonic discourse, but then what? What difference does it make? One may argue that the complexity of lived lives will slowly penetrate the hegemonic discourse and with time the discourse also absorbs more complicating narratives. In spite of multiple attempts to "write back" at the hegemonic discourse and criticism of streamlined and generalised knowledge, thick descriptions of women's daily life are slow to filter into the development discourse. We still seem to struggle with the overall idea of a hegemonic discourse versus an alternative one. Returning to the overall theme for this book on applied social sciences, the question is how to go beyond the dichotomy.

An alternative perspective on applied social science research would be to see it as part of meaning construction in itself, a way to construct an alternative truth. We then need to think that applied research can attach to social reality directly. This is in line with an anti-positivistic position that rejects the linear knowledge development model. In this perspective, research is seen as a social construction among stakeholders. It takes as a starting point that one cannot have knowledge of an outer objective world. It is a phenomenology that "cannot be reduced to the maxim 'look and describe what you see', but is, instead, comparable to the formula 'look and tell me why you see what you see'" (Stoller 2009, p. 712).

How we understand reality is a consequence of the society in which we live and is relative to the context. There is no such thing as "truths", separated from human constructions of it. What kind of approach does such a focus imply? Following a constructivist epistemology, we acknowledge how we as researchers influence development and how data are co-produced with the subjects. Knowledge is not external to the discourse, but something that is co-produced in the development process, during which "what is taken to be valid knowledge and facts are actively 'produced' rather than merely objectively existing" (Healey, de Magalhaes & Madanipour 1999, p. 125).

Research plays a role in the social sense making, and is part of the local/regional/national language game. Development is then a result of different actors "making sense together". Doing research in another context we should therefore be aware of our double role. We both gain insight into the lifeworld of the people we study, but we also participate in a process where knowledge is produced. If we return to the earlier figure with such an understanding, our point here is not just that researchers should nuance the dominant understanding, but that we in the process construct the world.

Research does not only describe the world; it also enacts it. How? Zanzibar is a predominantly Muslim society. Muslim women, in particular, are often portrayed as oppressed by religious codes and the unbalanced relationship with men. These images have incredible power "because of the deadening effect they have on our capacity to appreciate the complexity and diversity of Muslim women's lives: as human beings" (Abu-Lughod 2006, p. 1). Abu-Lughod further argues that such simple images enable many of us to imagine that these women need rescuing:

> If one constructs some women as being in need of pity or saving, one implies that one not only wants to save them from something but wants to save them for something: a different kind of world and set of arrangements.
>
> (Abu-Lughod 2006, p. 5)

Generalising about Muslim women also means categorising Muslim women who do not feel oppressed, who do not need "pity" or "rescue" or "empowerment". If we narrate that women should be rescued from something, saved for something else through a process of empowerment, this not only does not necessarily reflect the actual experience of women, but also performs a particular way of thinking and doing empowerment. We will elaborate.

In the context of this book about the relation between knowledge and power our point is that women's self-perception has implications for their economic choices, and in this process women play upon different discourses of what a woman in Zanzibar Town can and cannot do. The way women are portrayed by researchers is of course part of one such available discourse, from which women may slowly start to adopt for instance the ideal of independence, both as objects of research, or indirectly from being confronted with results from such research. More concretely, according to the grand narrative of neoliberalism and of MF, women need economic independence in order to become change agents. Credit facilitates a road to independence. This idea rests on one type of economic rationality, presupposing sometimes a change which will alter much more than a change of the economic activity performed by individuals, but also their positioning in society and ideas about identity. Our point is that such a framing also "produces" women in need, because when we see women in this way they are also enacted as women in need. Going through the exercise of taking credit, with the financial, education and economic rationale underpinning it, might also produce women who think about themselves and talk about themselves in different ways than before.

There is however room for manoeuvring where social scientists may choose not to reproduce the hegemonic discourse. Turning back to the left side of the figure we need to acknowledge that understanding women and men as co-producers of society and seeing their economic activities and everyday practices through a lens of inter-dependency is also a framing that involves the ideas of the researcher. Throughout the research process the researcher in our case experienced that women in Zanzibar were listening to interpretations, and that talks about life ended up shaping of mutual understanding. In these discussions, concepts and categories were filled with Zanzibari meaning. However, these interactions also entailed a sharing of views on different issues where the researcher's experiences of life became the subject of talk and comparison with Zanzibari women's lives. Through such talks women often ended up reconfirming their ideas. They sometimes collectively laughed at what they saw as *Wazungu* (Europeans' or Westerners') ideas of independence, as ideas were evaluated according to their way of thinking and doing. This experience enabled reflections on how it must feel to be evaluated through someone else's eyes, perceived as in need of change; from traditional to modern, from oppressed to liberated, from basing one's life on ideals of inter-dependence to becoming one favouring independence.

Throughout the PhD project and in the aftermath, the research produced knowledge that has been communicated into the field of practice. An unintended consequence of this particular PhD project focusing on women, income and social change in Zanzibar was that a decade later when Agder Research started to build up a portfolio of projects on integration of immigrants with a focus on women and work, the knowledge built up through work in the Global South now had a renewed relevance. Including knowledge from development research into integration research where the ideas of comparative reflection was explored and emphasised in theory-practice encounter within the region.

Altering the structuring logic

Seeking influence outside and beyond the hegemonic discourse, as is suggested earlier, is not the only possible strategy. Researchers could also attempt to intervene with the dominant discourse itself and thus change it "from within". This way we could attempt to get inside the discourse, instead of criticising or deconstructing it from the outside. The structuring logic of the debate on development emphasises some versions of the truth, but it may also prevent "another meaning" from informing policies. Could it be that critics or those who produce alternative "truths" underestimate the weight of the underlying structuring logic that people within the hegemonic discourse act according to? If that is the case, how can we target this underlying force more effectively? We then need an increased awareness of the discursive landscape that applied researchers enter into, for instance by putting to work some analytical tools from discourse theory.

Two different logics can be said to dominate the political space: a logic of equivalence built on antagonisms of real conflict between enemies (the excluded "Other") and a logic of difference built on agonisms in a constructive debate between adversaries (Andersen 2003; Laclau 2005; Laclau & Mouffe 2001; Winther & Svendsen 2012). The logic of equivalence simplifies political space by dividing it into two: for instance; development versus traditionalism or interdependence versus independence. By contrast, the logic of difference expands and complicates the political space. Laclau and Mouffe (2001, p. 129) remind us that "just as the logic of difference never manages to constitute a fully sutured space, neither does the logic of equivalence ever achieve this". However, a hegemonic project will attempt to establish antagonism, to construct an equivalent chain that will inevitably weaken the differences produced within the logic of difference.

The point here is that the fight is not necessarily between different perspectives on, for instance, what kind of economic activity should be supported, or whether the ideal of independency is relevant. It might as well be the structuring of political space that is the problem. In our case, the strength of the development discourse lies in the way the different elements of the discourse are chained to each other, providing together the resilience of the overall logic. Confronting this understanding is commonplace, but constructing an alternative discourse does not necessarily complicate political space, because an alternative discourse is already inherent to the development discourse; where it for example is labelled "traditional practices" and talked about as "barriers to development" (Harrison 1998). The logic of equivalence where political space is divided in two, development versus traditionalism, dominates, and the effective strategy is then to introduce complexity so that the political space is instead dominated by the logic of difference. One way to do this is to introduce agonisms.

In Figure 9.1 we could focus on the internal linkages between the elements to the left; the cultural base of economic rationality, women as situated co-producers of society, the ideal of interdependency and the complementarity of women and men. However, this only contributes to the simplification of the debate, the division of political space into two. Instead, we could more strategically articulate the several agonisms i.e. different approaches to a common topic, inherent in the debate about development. This way the dominant discourse is not rejected as such; but its advocates are instead invited to respond. Intervening in the framing of the debate by introducing agonisms, researchers could for instance focus in on the role of MF in our efforts to fight poverty.

Rankin's argument is that we have to see MF contextualised as part of neo-liberal thinking, where women are given a role as entrepreneurs with the task of taking care of their own and their children's well-being. Rankin questions the burden put on women in this. Targeting women with MF on the basis of their roles as caretakers puts a heavy responsibility on women. Such ideas also include an understanding of women's agency, understood as their ability to act as rational, economic actors in line with the idea that they should take care of their own lives (Rankin 2002, 2003). The ethnography from Zanzibar reveals that relationships of inter-dependency are prioritised in order to secure the flows of resources within and between households.

The "trick" of agonisms is to join with the dominating logic, but also to turn the arguments against themselves. We could for instance ask why MF does not work. Researchers then need to go a bit political, for instance confronting developers with that, if micro-credit loans are intended to secure not only women but the whole household, other policies may be just as efficient. If the embodied knowing guides Zanzibari women's way into economic activities, this means that changing perceptions of economic affairs takes much more than attending a workshop, which again will make women embrace a new economic rationality. What becomes evident are the many challenges contained in MF's attempt to educate women through brief workshops into a new way of thinking, behaving or relating, into changed perceptions and meanings, and thus finally making different choices.

Another question could be why some women do not take up credit through MF projects. A common interpretation is linked to gender inequality and the perception that men decide against it. Thus, in the story of the economically independent woman, men have somehow come to be seen as the ones women have to free themselves from. However, paying attention to the way women perceive the male-female relationship as complementary can enable a discussion on how to bring men back into the development arena as more than a constraining factor vis-à-vis women (Cornwall 2009). If women's economic activities are interwoven in relationships of inter-dependence, we have to see these as socially and morally embedded. The reproduction of the idea of complementarity of genders is based on a belief that men and women contribute with distinctly different qualities necessary for a relationship.[6] This is not to say that women are subordinate to men;

they are simply seen as different from men, and this difference can be celebrated (Larsen 2008).

It follows that the idea of being an "independent woman" is not highly valued in Zanzibar. What matters is to belong to a house, to be taken care of and appreciated, be it by a husband, a boyfriend, family or friends. This does not mean that Zanzibari women are not preoccupied with finding ways to feel economically secure and that such predictability is of importance, but there is a need to acknowledge that this does not have to depend on an idea of independence. In a Zanzibari understanding, securing a house and those belonging to it presupposes involvement in relationships of inter-dependence, and these relationships also enable women's engagement in economic activities.

Accepting that research enters into a play for development, the next question is how to manoeuvre in this terrain. We have demonstrated that one strategy is not to confront the hegemonic discourse directly, but instead take a more pragmatic approach where the dominating truths are taken seriously, but that their contested nature is brought forward. What is needed is a way to provoke reaction, and that is best done by adapting products of the hegemonic discourse in order to use it for your own strategic interest. This will direct the critique from the outside and place it within the discourse itself, where the similarities between dominating and alternative discourses are emphasised. Relating to topics that are already core to the dominant discourse, such as micro-credit, and emphasising similarities, might make it impossible for powerful actors to argue against their own arguments. This is how the introduction of agonisms might open up the hegemonic discourse and expand the debate by complicating political space. The aim must be that alternative conceptualisations of the different topics manage to make the whole concept of development vulnerable.

Going beyond the inherent power in research

The common expectation for applied research is for it to produce relevant knowledge for policy-makers. It is in other words "power" that decides whether knowledge is valid. In this chapter we have taken the concept of development to demonstrate this point. If development is about helping the poor or empowering marginalised groups in the non-Western world, then the influence of applied research is greater if it helps developers to do this job. We argue against an uncritical acceptance of this limited role allocated to research. We believe that it makes it difficult for social scientists to nuance development practice or to prevent development becoming a means by which the West effects domination over the Third World. Academics are, however, not bound to channel knowledge through powerful agents in order for it to count, and we urge an increased awareness of the many other ways that knowledge production touch upon the processes that construct reality.

The chapter reminds us that development does not only result from foreign or domestic policy initiatives, such as micro-credit, but it also emerges from the researchers and the researched making sense together. Focusing on this important role for applied social sciences in contributing to democratic and sustainable development might be just as rewarding as attempting to become relevant for powerful actors. Alternatively, we suggest that researchers understand their role as actors in a discursive play. The inherent force in the very way that the debate about development is structured should not be underestimated. Hegemony is a result of successful attempts to simplify what the debate is about. If political space is being simplified and allowing only for two alternative positions for example development or traditionalism, we would advise researchers not to confirm the dichotomy, but to attempt to complicate this picture by instituting several agonisms around which the debate can evolve. This will inevitably make the hegemonic discourse vulnerable, especially when core assumptions in the development discourse are being questioned.

This chapter has not provided concrete examples of how applied researchers could expand their room for manoeuvring in a context where they also need funding for their activities, and where results therefore are bound to feed into a practical agenda. We believe that being aware of alternative ways to make knowledge count may open up new perspectives on how to perform research within the frames of the dominant discourse, but also that it might stimulate attempts to find funding in institutions and actors that are not closely linked to the Eurocentric development discourse.

The power of research and its ability to influence development should not be reduced to a question of relevance. Our view is that research is also a practice that contributes to the making of development, regardless of whether it forms the basis of policy or not. Doing research on development, we are not bound to adopt hegemonic perspectives, and we should not underestimate the direct effect of our framing on the people we make sense together with. The way we do research influences development directly, through the way women may alter or maintain their self-perception through the dialogue with research communities. It should not be underestimated either, how knowledge is disseminated in academia and beyond the context that each researcher intervenes with. This way, we can say that applied researchers have other means of influence than through powerful agents, and that constructing another meaning, or even altering the structure of the debate, is one way of escaping the dilemma of being relevant or powerless.

Notes

1 Foucault discusses the new form of governmentality where subjects are disciplined in a new manner, as self-entrepreneurs contributing to well-functioning competitive markets. Western governments are thus now dominated by neoliberalism or neoliberal governmentality. There are many researchers who argue against this neoliberal project and link this particularly to women and their economic activities (see Rankin 2002, 2003; Roy 2010 for further references).

2 Crewe and Harrisson argue, however, that "development workers, expatriate or national, sometimes explicitly state that they should not interfere with the 'traditions' of a culture. In some agencies this is particularly the case when it comes to gender relations . . . the idea that culture is worth protecting when gender is involved is inconsistent when set beside other social transformations brought about by development" (Edelman & Haugerud 2005, p. 234).
3 Søndergaard defines a storyline as a naturalised and given cultural story which is often also used as a frame for interpretations of one's own and other's actions (Søndergård 2000, p. 77 [our translation]).
4 See Nustad (2003) for a discussion of this link in Norwegian development thinking and policy.
5 See for example Escobar (1995), Ferguson (1990) and Hobart (1993). However, Escobar (1997), who has drawn a sharp line between "anthropology of development" and "development anthropology" also calls attention to work which transcends the two, referring to Gardner and Lewis (1996). See also Long (2001).
6 The argument of seeing different aspects of women's lives as interlinked and of relevance to their economic choices is never-ending. I only highlight the aspects which are results of my fieldwork. Other aspects of women's lives also influencen their choices. Of great relevance to a Zanzibari context would be the links with the spiritual aspects of Zanzibari lifeworld. See Larsen (2008) for in-depth descriptions of how spirits and humans meet in a Zanzibari lifeworld.

Part III

Explaining regional practice

Part III of the book presents studies that are aimed at explaining regional practice. Common to these studies is that they have a proactive ambition to be able to say something about causes, and important and decisive dimensions for social development.

In Chapter 10: Network ties between universities and cultural and creative industries argue that collaboration between university and industry is hard to achieve. The case here is how the regional university at Agder could help support the cultural industry. The project investigated the collaboration between university and industry, and found that it was dependent on competence and willingness to co-operate. Thus institutional barriers seem to be at work.

In Chapter 11: The usefulness of applied research the discussion is about the interdependence between researcher and practice. The case is a network of women leaders, and the researcher was invited into the project in order to support this initiative. The evaluation of the process was seen as part of the learning in and development of the process.

In Chapter 12: Regional knowledge infrastructure looks into how the VRI-programme has contributed to developing an institutional infrastructure for innovation in the Agder region.

In Chapter 13: The Mittelstand the case is an analysis for a large set of data from different mid-size companies, in order to find if there is a special feature of mid-size often family owned companies, the so-called Mittelstand. The argument is that these companies have different development dynamics than larger corporations.

10 Network ties between universities and cultural and creative industries

Barbara Zyzak, Rómulo Pinheiro and Elisabet S. Hauge

The role of the university in regional development

This chapter discusses what characterises the relationship between the university and specific external actors, like the local creative sector. The case study is the University of Agder (UoA) in the context of its surrounding region (Southern Norway). The main thesis is that, despite the willingness of actors from both sectors to collaborate with one another, the lack of mutual knowledge and an institutionalised framework for co-operation, leadership/strategy included, creates major structural and cultural barriers, thus making this collaboration a sub-optimal one.

The main objective is to investigate how network arrangements between the local university and cultural and creative industries (C&CIs) in Southern Norway can be characterised. It explores different ways through which the university interacts with C&CIs and the factors that influence the co-operation between them, by using the network theory perspective. The discussion focuses on the types of networks and its main characteristics for network success, and their implications to regional development. We adopt a case study research design, and resort to semi-structured interviews with representatives from both local creative industries across six distinct branches, as well as senior academic administrators. Our findings suggest that network arrangements between academia and C&CIs in Southern Norway are sub-optimal, and that a number of key conditions need to be in place in order to enhance the level of engagement between actors across the two sectors.

Co-operation between university and cultural and creative industries

The role of universities in economic development has recently received ample attention (Boschma & Frenken 2009; Comunian, Faggian & Jewell 2011; Pinheiro, Benneworth & Jones 2012). Various approaches have been explored by scholars from different perspectives (economic, geographic, sectoral). Many researchers have also investigated co-operation between university and different kinds of industries.

The rise of the knowledge economy has catapulted universities to the forefront of policy debates, at national and regional levels, as regards localised innovation systems (Lester & Sotarauta 2007) aimed at fostering local competitive advantages (Asheim, Coenen, Moodysson & Vang 2007; OECD 2005). More recently, and in Europe, smart specialisation has emerged as a critical policy area, both at the national and the regional level (McCann & Ortega-Argilés 2013; Thissen, van Oort, Diodato & Ruijs 2013). Regions and localities are looking at areas where they have considerable endogenous assets and around which sustainable competitive advantages can be developed. Creative industries are one such area.

There is a growing interest in the role of C&CIs in processes of national, regional and local economic development (Andersen, Hansen, Isaksen & Raunio 2010; Asheim 2009; Chapain, Clifton & Comunian 2012; Pinheiro & Hauge 2014), partly motivated by the attention of policy and academic circles, associated with the rise of a creative class (Asheim 2009; Florida 2003; Florida, Mellander & Stolarick 2008; McGuigan 2009). Few studies have looked at the types of relationships and formal and informal networks between the institutions responsible for forming the creative class, i.e. universities and other types of higher education institutions (HEIs) and the various C&CI branches. The few exceptions include enquiries on the transfer and commercialisation of creative knowledge assets (Hearn, Cunningham & Ordoñez 2004), as well as policy proposals focusing on the critical role that universities and other knowledge producers have in the context of strengthening the R&D base of C&CIs (Cunningham, Cutler, Hearn, Ryan & Keane 2004). This knowledge is particularly salient at the regional level, since local HEIs are now, more than in the past, expected to directly contribute to processes of regional economic development and innovation (Goddard & Vallance 2013; Harding, Scott, Laske & Burtscher 2007; Lester & Sotarauta 2007; Pinheiro 2013; Pinheiro, Benneworth & Jones 2012).

The chapter's main contribution to the overall theme of the book is to enrich knowledge on the critical role of HEIs in regional economic development, with a special focus on the co-operation between the local university and C&CIs located in one region. The chapter addresses a knowledge gap between the university and various arms of the creative sector in Agder region. The initial project took advantage of dedicated funding from both the VRI-programme at Agder, as well as the RIS Centre based in Agder. The chapter shows how applied research is integrated with stakeholders and practitioners in a local/regional setting, and how knowledge development is a mutual concern, dependent on ongoing dialogue.

The case C&CIs and case university selected for this study represent the Agder region that is also being investigated by other researchers in this book. In our chapter, we view 'knowledge systems' (KS) as consisting of network ties between private/semi-public actors and an organisation that perform or sometimes struggle with a number of functions (including research, education, innovation and development) that link knowledge and practical actions. We try to focus on initiated relationships from a network perspective that somehow are less or more developed (formal vs. informal). We also try to investigate main network characteristics that actors share, and then we categorise the relationships into three types of networks: co-operative (short term horizon), co-ordinative (medium-term horizon) and collaborative (long-term horizon).

We address the knowledge gap identified earlier by investigating the network co-operation between one case university and various arms of the creative sector in Southern Norway. The research question addressed in the chapter is: *what characterises the relationship between the university and the local creative sector in Southern Norway from the perspective of network theory?*

The project

The project was initiated by three researchers at Agder Research (AR) (innovation group) with an interest in both higher education and creative industries. Two of the researchers involved had written doctoral theses within the area, thus making them competent to undertake such enquiries. What is more, the research team took advantage of its direct involvement with a research network/standing group focusing on C&CIs based at the Regional Studies Association. As part of that, the researchers attended two international conferences and one seminar (at Kings College and Copenhagen University), presenting preliminary findings, with participants from all over the world. The problem, as presented by stakeholders, lies in the importance of creative industries to regional and national economic development, and the critical role of higher education in providing skills and competencies in the region. A major element, as identified earlier in the literature and corroborated by stakeholders, lies in the often disconnected words of academia and industry, despite the existence of mutual informal networks amongst the two sectors. The research questions were developed in accordance to the objectives of the study, the pre-understanding of the topic by the research team and via consultation with other colleagues within and outside AR. Given the attention paid to multimethods as a means of fostering data triangulation and enhancing validity, the team decided to adopt a combination of desktop research and qualitative interviews with the actors involved, so as to gather first-hand accounts regarding the types of relations and bottlenecks.

Causality is chosen as an argumentative strategy in this chapter. Our research is case oriented, and it is stimulated by an interest to explore interrelationship between cases: a university and C&CIs located in a region. The goal is to identify which combination of conditions characterise the relationships between university and C&CIs, and what type of network they represent. The outcome reveals that the selected cases are characterised by a set of similar (but not identical) features, and they represent two of three types of networks. Hence, the discussion concentrates on the obstacles to enhance better collaboration between actors in the region. Our research suggests that university-C&CI relations in Southern Norway are both underexplored and underdeveloped, despite the recognition by both actors that there is strategic value in collaborating more closely.

Case region

Southern Norway is a leading export oriented region in energy intensive raw materials (aluminium, nickel and siliceous), offshore oil and gas equipment and hydroelectric power (as discussed in Chapter 13 in this book). The region is known for hosting music festivals. The latter have doubled every decade since the 1960s, which testifies to the growing interest in cultural activities across the region (Hjemdahl, Hauge & Lind 2007). In addition, there is an increasing interest in C&CIs across the region's two main counties, which together account for about 290,000 inhabitants (about 6% of Norway's population), mostly located throughout coastal areas and between the two largest urban areas, the cities of Kristiansand and Arendal, the capitals of West and East Ager Counties, respectively. Between 2000 and 2009, the number of C&CI firms across the two main counties more than doubled, from 202 to 406 (+101%) in East Agder and from 289 to 738 (+ 155%) in West Agder. The annual growth of C&CIs industries in Southern Norway was much higher during this period than the national average (79% versus 12%, respectively) (Espelien & Gran 2011).

The importance of C&CIs in Southern Norway has been recently acknowledged. One of the five priority areas in the current *Regional Development Plan Agder 2020* is *regional culture*.[1] The ambition, by 2020, is to achieve the diversity and creativity in terms of new jobs in the culture-based industries and innovative cultural initiatives. The main policy measures are concentrated on the development of a comprehensive cultural strategy that emphasises broad involvement and volunteerism. Regional authorities are also planning to establish a joint centre for 'experience industries' (cultural industries, businesses, public institutions and academia) as well as some cultural and sport venues that meet local, regional and international needs. The region is well-known for hosting a variety of music festivals, mostly in the summer time, where it also attracts a considerable number of tourists, mostly from other parts of Norway.

Case university

Located in Southern Norway, UoA was originally established as a university college in 1994,and became a fully-fledged university in 2007. In 2014, it enrolled 11,000 students (59% female) and employed 1,000 employees across its seven sub-units.[2] Since its inception in the mid-1990s, the university has actively engaged with regional actors across the public and private sectors and has contributed towards its broader socio-economic development. Earlier studies suggest that actors within UoA are actively engaged with external actors across the public and private sectors, but that substantial variations exist across sub-units and fields of specialisation (see Chapter 17 in this book). One of the major limitations pertains to the fact that the case university has a strong vocational and teaching profile, with less capacity in the realms of knowledge production, particularly of the basic (Mode 1) type. Another limitation is that regional industry is less knowledge intensive than in other parts of the country, with innovation patterns characterised by strong interactions with users and learning by doing, rather than traditional R&D (science and technology) driven.

The three different types of networks in this chapter are investigated in the form of a qualitative case study. The latter is an ideal research method to explain a phenomenon that is embedded in a specific context. The data collection and analysis adopts a mixed-method approach (Bryman 2008), based on desktop research and face-to-face interviews with key actors across both sectors. A total of 18 in-depth semi-structured interviews were conducted during January and February 2013, with: (a) representatives from local private and semi-public creative industries (N=10) across the following branches: music/arts, gaming, design, ICT, film and multimedia branches and (b) key university actors, senior academic administrators (N=8). The interview material was transcribed verbatim and data themes were developed and patterns recognised, with the use of data categories (Miles, Huberman & Saldaña 2014), which were then linked to the theoretical concepts used in the study.

Whilst investigating the types of network arrangements between various university actors/C&CIs, it is important to bear in mind that these do not operate in isolation. The actors in networks interact with other organisations outside the network in order to meet their individual and collective goals. The primary focus of this study is to investigate the factors that determine the level and type of co-operation between the local C&CIs and the case university, and hypothesise on how the degree or level co-operation might affect (enhance or constrain) future regional development trajectories and competitive advantages.

The key concepts used in this research study are identified and described in the following Table 10.1. Table 10.2 shows the main characteristics used for 3Cs, while Figure 10.1 highlights the description and measurement of the factors (independent variables) that are presumed to be 'necessary conditions' to identify a specific type of network in the empirical part of this study. All the variables are the independent variables and are relevant for all the three types of networks (co-operative, co-ordinative and collaborative).

Table 10.1 Operationalisation of the key 3Cs concepts

Factors (independent variables)	*Definition*	*Indicators*
Social relations	The nature of relations between regional actors	Formal/informal ties
Communication	The ways in which regional actors (universities) communicate with each other	Direct/indirect/no contact
Purpose/Strategic interests	Primary aim or goal for co-operation	Short/long-term
Knowledge and information sharing	The extent to which regional actors share knowledge and information	Confidential/ project related/ none
Resources dependency	Level of dependency amongst actors	Resource exchange
Autonomy and accountability	The responsibility of individual actors during co-operation	Own agency/ project/network
Power and influence	Individual actors' position in the network	Actors with certain resources Core/periphery Inclusion/exclusion

Source: Based on Keast and Mandell (2013).

Network theory

Literature on organisational and social networks across the various branches of social sciences is constantly developing. Due to this, there is still some confusion regarding network theorising, despite the fact that the primary focus of the analysis is on either the actor or network level, or both. A basic assumption in the literature is that collaborations through network structures often lead to innovative responses on how to solve a particular problem, or how to accomplish a specific goal that would otherwise be difficult for individual organisations or actors. While studying network formation, it is important to differentiate between two relatively distinct concepts; 'networking' and 'network'. The former process is less formal, and occurs when different actors make personal connections through face-to-face meetings, or remotely as well as, e.g. via e-mail or phone. The latter term ('network') is used to refer to more formalised ties between actors, including more institutionalised networks. Existing literature highlights that networks share a number of common characteristics in the context of network structure (e.g. network size, age or actors) and/ or network context (e.g. resources or rules). Thus, in this study we use network theory to identify the formal and informal ties between actors.

The focus is on the dyadic relations between university and C&CIs. We are not interested in complex relationships of those actors with others, or ties between C&CIs and ties between university faculties. Network theory is very broad and over the years, different network typologies have been developed. In this chapter we adopt three of the most commonly used types of networks (3Cs) – *co-ordinative*, *co-operative* and *collaborative* – in order to investigate co-operative patterns between C&CIs and the case university in the context of regional development and innovation. The proposed model for network investigation in this study corresponds well with the empirical part, as well as the main objective.

In the case of *co-operative* networks, ties between actors are relatively infrequent and loose. This type of network arrangement is often set up when it is deemed necessary to adjust individual goals. The low intensity of relations and the fact that only general information and expertise are shared results in low levels of trust or social capital between the actors involved. One of the basic characteristics differentiating *co-ordinative* networks from co-operative is the degree of involved risk and the strength of relations amongst actors. In the case of co-ordinative network arrangements, actors remain rather independent, but are nonetheless keen to make changes in the context of service delivery without losing their individual autonomy. The establishment of relations with other organisations is a key requirement in order to deliver more effective individual services. Finally, as for *collaborative*

Table 10.2 The main characteristics of 3Cs

Network characteristics (3Cs)	*Co-operative*	*Co-ordinative*	*Collaborative*
Relations	Short-term (often informal and largely voluntary) (Unstable relations)	Medium-term (based on prior relations)	Long-term (stable relations)
Communication	Infrequent	Structured	Thick
Purpose	Autonomous/ independent	Semi-independent	Interdependent
Knowledge and information sharing	Guarded/known Low levels of intensity and risk	Project related	Tacit/confidential
Resources dependency	Remain own	Shared resources around project	Pooled, collective resources
Accountability	To own agency	To own agency and project	To the network first
Power	Self	Directed	Shared

Source: Adapted from Keast and Mandell 2013; Mandell and Keast 2007.

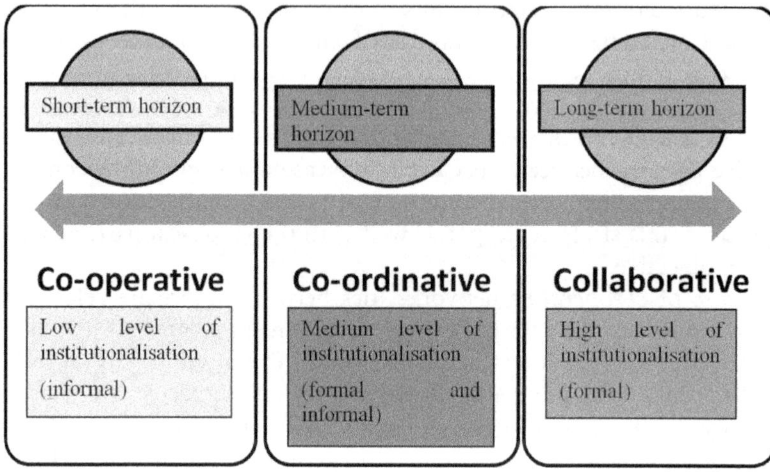

Figure 10.1 3Cs: time horizon vs. institutionalisation
Source: Authors.

network arrangements, these are by far the most developed and innovative ways to deliver services and solve so called 'wicked' and complex problems. This type of network is often established under a crisis situation, or when other modes of functioning have all but collapsed, thus making it the riskiest arrangement among all three types of networks.

Collaborative networks are usually discussed in the public arena as an alternative way to deliver services (Huxham, Vangen, Huxham & Eden 2000), but also in other domains as economic development (Agranoff 1998). What is more, the individual (strategic) interests of the actors involved are not at the forefront. Instead the focus is on joint and innovative solutions that require breaking down of old rules and standard operational procedures (cf. Oliver 1991) result in new, innovative ways of working and organising. Hence, the primary focus of collaborative partnerships is the network itself, rather than the gains by the individual actors involved.

Norwegian approach towards C&CIs

Historically, the Nordic countries have chosen different paths in their efforts to improve and identify C&CIs. In contrast to Sweden and Denmark, there has not been any major public debate on policy initiative focused on the C&CIs in Norway. The Norwegian policy approach towards C&CIs was centred on the interaction between culture (arts) and commerce (business). In 2011, and for the first time ever, a mapping of Norwegian C&CIs was presented, in tandem with a definition of the sector: 'Cultural industries are industries that produce more or less commercialised cultural expressions through esthetical means such as symbols, signs, pictures, colors, moves, different sounds and stories' (Espelien & Gran 2011, p. 10).

A recent investigation has identified that, in the Norwegian national context, C&CIs are located at the intersection of multiple policy layers and distinct government agencies, each with their own logic and strategic rationale. This, in turn, has meant that the local (national) translation of the (global) concept of C&CIs was permeated by key contextual dimensions such as path dependencies or historical trajectories and endogenous characteristics, including dynamics at the sub-national (regional) level as well. Notwithstanding this, the previously mentioned enquiry has also revealed that the 'Norwegian policy trends tend to follow European policy-making trends, for example when it comes to designing and implementing initiatives by using C&CIs as a strategic tool to promote economic, cultural and social development' (Pinheiro & Hauge 2014, p. 90).

Between 2000 and 2009, the number of professionals employed by Norway's C&CIs grew by 50%, accounting for 4% of the domestic labour force in 2009 (Espelien & Gran 2011). This amounts to a total of 75,000 creative professionals located across 27,000 firms, of which about a third are active within publishing media. At the sub-national level (Southern Norway), there is a broad recognition amongst regional policy circles of the strategic importance attributed to C&CIs when it comes to triggering processes of innovation and economic growth, including the sector's role in the development of new local, national and global markets. Our previous study revealed significant variations in the profile and orientation of the various C&CIs branches across Southern Norway.

Analysis and interpretation of key findings

Our analysis reveals that two out of the three basic types of networks (Figure 10.1) are rather prevalent in Southern Norway, namely, co-operative and co-ordinative. None of the identified case networks (see Table 10.2) were found to encompass all the basic characteristics associated with collaborative networks. By and large, the types of network arrangements identified in the case are characterised by rather unstable social relations between actors, characterised by a short-term orientation and infrequent communications. From the side of C&CIs, network activities are very often related to companies' operational and strategic needs, for instance when the company can get economic benefits from research projects or teaching (e.g. the cases of news and media and game industries). Formal co-operation was found to occur mainly through joint projects involving specific key actors, i.e. students' traineeships or thesis writing (bachelor/master/PhD) at a C&CI (e.g. news and social media, game industry and performance arts and entertainment). In addition to that, some entrepreneurs (C&CI staff) hold guest lectures for students at the university (e.g. at ICT, information systems and economics departments). Informal co-operation is characterised by individual contacts of students or academic staff with staff at C&CIs.

Such informal contacts are often the first steps for further, more formal types of co-operation involving individuals from both sectors. Both formal and informal co-operation were found to be rather short-term oriented and mostly project-based (specific goal/end time). None of the sampled C&CIs possess a strategy for close and long-term co-operation with the university. Notwithstanding, most C&CIs consider themselves as a relevant potential partner for the university, largely because they are a future workplace for students (Hauge, Pinheiro & Zyzak 2013).

Even though networking between actors is more informal, and co-operation is short-term orientated, there were nonetheless several C&CIs actors (especially performance arts and entertainment) that stressed that the university is an important arena for them, because both actors have a social responsibility in the region. According to one interviewee linked to the performance and entertainment branch: 'it is important for the C&CI – a regional institution that he/she represents – to co-operate with the University of Agder – regional university." In addition to indirect ways of communication between actors (i.e. through students), direct information and knowledge sharing occurs mainly during the different seminars, conferences and meeting arenas. The data show that this often occurs within

Table 10.3 Case networks

University departmental network(s)	*Cooperation with regional CCIs – types of branches*	*Type of relations (formal vs. informal)*
ICT	Two partners from news and social media Two partners from game industry Co-operation with regional cluster	Formal, with informal elements
Information Systems	Two partners from news and social media Co-operation with regional cluster	Formal
Nordic and Media Studies	One partner from performance arts and entertainment	Formal
Music – Music Education	No regional partners, only national and international	Informal
Visual Arts and Drama	One partner from news and social media Three partners from performance arts and entertainment	Formal
Economics	Co-operation with regional cluster	Formal, with informal elements
Education	None	None

Source: Authors.

the following networks: Nordic and media studies; visual arts and drama and ICT (see Table 10.3 for more details). The longer and more structured co-operation occurs when network actors possess external incentives to work on joint research projects, as it was the case at the departments of ICT (*The Marieke project*) and visual arts and drama (*The Art in context project*).

Diversity of interests and/or purposes amongst the actors involved was found to be a barrier for long-term co-operation and/or co-operation as a whole. Several respondents indicated that their companies are 'born' to co-operate at the national or international level, so they try to find or establish a network with actors outside the region. Moreover, academic staff emphasised that some employees at the smaller C&CIs lack the adequate professional skills and competences (e.g. in terms of educational levels) and that they 'talk different languages'. As for the staff at the C&CIs, many stated that network creation, particularly within a long-term time horizon, is time consuming and requires economic and human resources that are thought to be rather scarce (lack of capacity from the C&CI side). Thus, conflict of interests was found to be a major barrier for the establishment of collaborative networks, with the actors involved neither wanting to lose control over the network nor possessing the considerable (human and financial) resources required for it to succeed.

A more in-depth look at differences between the profiles of the actors involved, and in the case of the university, six out of the seven academic departments sampled fulfilled the criteria for either one of the two types of networks (expect the collaborative type of network as a whole). Only in the case of the educational department has co-operation with local C&CIs failed to materialise. As for the differences amongst the six networked departments, half of them – ICT, Nordic and media studies and visual arts and drama – have, as of time of writing, developed co-ordinative type networks with regional C&CIs, with some elements of collaborative network features as well e.g. more stable and long-term relations (the case of Nordic and media studies and a firm from the performance arts and entertainment). This type of network will most probably develop (near future) into a 'collaborative type', given the relatively high degree of dependence amongst the actors involved, especially to commitments in the critical area of human resources (students, academics, creative and cultural staff). Hence, these types of networks are examples of successful regional co-operation with the potential for having a positive impact on regional development. The remaining three departments and their partners fulfil the criteria for *co-ordinative network*, characterised by a medium degree of institutionalisation and mid-term time horizon (Table 10.3). This, however, does not necessarily mean that their potential regional development impact is of less significance in the long run, particularly if they turn out to evolve (near future) into more sophisticated (institutionalised) forms of collaboration. However, these networks require nurturing (strategic attention and resources) by the actors involved, including leadership structures across both sectors. One way of doing that would be e.g. to more strategically align (tighter coupling) the aforementioned network arrangements (objectives) with the long-term strategic objectives of the sub-units involved, as well as those (vision) of their respective organisations, in the light of future challenges facing either sector. From a regional standpoint, collaborative networks (the most sophisticated type) have the potential to foster path extension and path creation, which can help overcome possible 'lock-in effects' (e.g. reliance on past/current industries/clusters), and enhance the development of long-term (sustainable) regional competitive advantages as a result of industry diversification and specialisation (path extension) and potential (positive) spill-over effects, in the form of new industries/clusters emerging (path creation).

University's attitude towards co-operation with business

In the Nordic countries (and beyond), universities are increasingly pressurised to contribute directly to regional economic development and innovation, amongst other aspects by engaging more closely with collaborative partnerships with regional partners like industry. In this chapter we focus on one particular manifestation of this phenomenon, network creation and development involving university and C&CIs actors. Our empirical findings suggest that the types of collaborative arrangements differ from context to context, in the light of the characteristics of the academic units as well as the respective C&CI branches. That said, and in spite of slight variations, the majority of network collaborations were found to be rather unstable, and based on short-term projects rather than mutual beneficial strategic engagement. The university (central and unit levels) has not identified C&CIs as key strategic partners, at the same time as it seems to have failed in reaching out to university actors in a more systematic and comprehensive manner. Interestingly, while the bulk of the literature on university-industry collaborations seem to focus on the importance attributed to the co-generation and transfer of knowledge (for a recent review of the existing literature see (Perkmann et al. 2012). Our data suggest that this type of activity is still relatively marginalised as far as Southern Norway is concerned. Instead, informal arrangements, more often than not involving students and graduates, were found to be an effective means for collaborating (build social capital or trust), albeit not sufficient when it comes to more strategic, long-term endeavours aimed at enhancing the competitiveness of the regional C&CI branch (and the region as a whole) on the one hand, and the (teaching and research) profiles of the case university on the other. So, our overall conclusion is that university-C&CI relations in Southern Norway are both underexplored and underdeveloped, despite the recognition by both actors that there is strategic value in collaborating more closely with one another. We acknowledge that our study has limitations as far as methods, sampling and theory are concerned and, thus, going forward, we would invite researchers both, from within as well as outside the region, to provide additional insights on the conditions under which university-industry collaborations (within and beyond C&CIs) in (Southern) Norway occur; and, the extent through which key lessons can be learnt from comparing local efforts and dynamics with those from other local, regional, national and international (e.g. Nordic) contexts.

AR is partly owned by UoA but it is an independent organisation. Researchers from UoA and AR often collaborate with one another along selected areas. Therefore, AR is a knowledgeable and independent broker that, knowing the situation facing region industry and UoA, is capable of not only providing new knowledge that is useful for strategy and policy but also, equally important, bringing together key actors from both the higher education and the cultural sector.

This case sheds light on the current situation insofar as the state of academia and external relations in a Norwegian region at a time where universities, in Norway and elsewhere, are increasingly expected to play an active role in processes of socio-economic development and strategic engagement with key actors. The case also reveals the limitations associated with the absence of a systematic approach towards industry collaborations, which is in part a result of the lack of strategic attention given within UoA as well as the low interest by UoA academics from 'creative' fields in reaching out to industry. This is rather surprising, because UoA claims to have a strong developmental role in the region, acting as a catalyst and engine for the development of new industries and clusters. It is also worth noting that peripheral regions like Southern Norway are at a disadvantage, not least because creative professionals, including graduates from creative fields, tend to move away into more cosmopolitan and creative environments, often located in and around larger urban (and more liberal) settings. Finally, this case demonstrates the value of combining traditional approaches towards the production of knowledge within the social sciences with more applied methodologies, so as to gain a better understanding of the phenomenon under investigation.

Notes

1 *Regional Development Plan Agder 2020*. Can be obtained from: www.vaf.no
2 Social sciences, health and sports sciences, humanities and education, fine arts, engineering sciences, business and law and teaching education unit.

11 The usefulness of applied research

Christine Svarstad and Ellen K. Nyhus

A commissioned study to support the female network

The purpose of this chapter is to describe the research process and report results of a project designed to increase our knowledge of work conditions for women working in two industrial clusters in the oil and gas industry in Norway. In order to retain and increase the share of female employees and leaders, the cluster's female network project, NEW (NODE EYDE Women), initiated a research project to produce knowledge about female employees and leaders working in the cluster member companies, and to acquire information about their situation and any needs for improvement. The project and its results are described later in this chapter. In particular, the interaction between researchers and stakeholders of the project, as well as the use of the results of the project, are reported.

The chapter also serves as an example of construction of regional knowledge. The purpose of the project was to map female representation in the oil/gas sector in Agder, and to produce knowledge about factors that may promote or hinder females' careers in these sectors. This is especially interesting in a regional perspective, because Agder has a low percentage of women in the work force. It has also been a knowledge foundation to strengthen some of the already ongoing initiatives such as NEW Faces and NEW Mentor, established with the purpose of recruiting more women to these sectors and developing good female leaders.

In our study we found that being part of a network, flexible work hours, a higher number of working hours, working in a company that facilitates family life and a work culture with tolerance for diverging opinions are positively associated with work satisfaction. These are findings contradictory to the assumptions of female full-time employees in Agder.

This is an example of one of Agder Research's commissioned projects. It is characterised by co-operation and knowledge exchange between stakeholders and researchers to secure legitimacy and relevance. The strengths and weaknesses of such an approach are discussed. The project serves as a good example of how applied research can be useful in organisational and regional development.

Gender issues in the process and oil and gas industry in Agder

The NODE Cluster consisted of 57 member companies at the time this project took place, and constituted a strong global cluster. In 2012, the cluster employed 6,778 people, of whom 4,292 worked in Kristiansand, 970 in the rest of Vest-Agder, 943 in Arendal and 573 in the rest of Aust-Agder. This corresponded to 4.8% of all employment in Agder in 2012. NODE accounted for a value added contribution of NOK 9.32 billion to the Agder region and more than 9% of Agder's CDP is related to NODE through the value chain (Bøgh Homen & Fjose 2014). This makes NODE a key contributor to value added in Southern Norway and it makes NODE an important employer.

The EYDE Cluster is a competence cluster which consisted of nine member companies in 2011. It gathers members from key process industry enterprises and related suppliers, located in the Southern Norwegian region. The members produce specialised products for the world market, and export around 90% of their production. The annual revenues are NOK 10 billion, and in 2014 the number of employees was about 2,750.

The background for the project "NEW Facts"

As often is the case in manufacturing and petroleum related industries, the ratio of female employees is relatively low. The cluster managements of both NODE and EYDE wished for a higher ratio of females at all levels of the various member organisations, and in 2010 a strategic project to enhance women in hard-hat companies in the southern parts of Norway was established. The project was called NEW (short for NODE EYDE WOMEN) and its primary purposes were to recruit and retain female workers as well as improving females' career opportunities. NEW's vision is broad, as the network aspires to develop the whole region in which it is embedded, by focusing on women's conditions, experience and competence.

In order to succeed with its missions, NEW recognised the need for more knowledge about female employees in the NODE and EYDE member organisations and their experience and perspectives. In order to acquire this information, NEW teamed up with Agder Research and the Centre for Gender and Equality at the University of Agder (UoA) and initiated the research project "New Facts". The project was funded by VRI-programme at Agder, the Competence Development Fund of Southern Norway and the Centre for Gender and Equality at UoA.

The purpose of the project was to map female representation in the oil/gas sector in Agder, and to produce knowledge about factors that may promote or hinder females' careers in these sectors.

The development of research questions

From the outset, the NEW representatives who participated in the project group emphasised their wish for a high degree of involvement throughout the entire research process. They consistently communicated that they wanted ownership of the project. A working group, consisting of eight women from NEW, three researchers from Agder Research and one person from the Centre for Gender and Equality, was formed at the beginning of the project. This working group took part in all parts of the project and the NEW representatives played an important part because they had experience and field-knowledge from what we may call a female point of view. Their insight was an important complement to the researchers' more generic competence in research methods and equality issues. They contributed to the quality of the project by ensuring relevance.

The working group collaborated in formulating the research questions. An area of special interest was the distribution of women in scientific, administrative and leader positions. Hence, the first research question was to get an overview of the number and ratio of female employees, and also the types of positions they held.

The second research question addressed the characteristics of the female workers. NEW wanted knowledge and numbers to "turn claims into facts". In particular, they wanted to do a quantitative study of the female workers and managers in the cluster member companies, to find out more about them. They wanted to collect information about age, education level, place of birth, place of residence, distance from workplace, household composition and how the workers perceived their workplace. In relation to their situation at work, questions about satisfaction, job motivation, responsibility, salary, overtime, travel, possibilities to change jobs and attitudes towards Agder as a region to work and live in, were to be asked. The project work group had lots of input regarding which questions to include in the survey and how to formulate these question in order to fit the average work day for the respondents. This was a critical input for the research team, as their knowledge about the sector was limited. The suggestions from the NEW members were then supplemented and modified, based on suggestions from the researchers in the team.

The initial plan was to distribute a questionnaire to the female employees only, because this is NEW's main target group. The researchers, on the other hand, argued in favour of including male respondents in the sample, because this would allow for comparisons of the situations and opinions of males and female employees respectively. After putting this suggestion to the NEW board, it was decided to include men in the sample. In a way, this changed the research questions, so that it was not just the situation of the women that was investigated, but the situation of the female employees compared to that of the males.

Research methods

It was decided to have two rounds of data collection. The first was a mapping of the number of women in different positions in the two clusters. A short survey was distributed to all HR managers in the member organisations of the two clusters (n=64). They were asked about the total number of women working in their company, and the number of female skilled workers and managers.

The second round of data collection was done among all employees in the two clusters' membership organisations. The work group co-designed the survey questions and response options in co-operation as previously described. The involvement of the representatives of NEW in this part of the research process ensured quality and relevance. The survey (a web-based questionnaire) was distributed to all employees, which means that more than 11,000 employees were asked to fill it in.

A total of 1603 respondents answered the survey: 645 women and 957 men. Of the respondents, 124 female and 337 male respondents worked in the process industry and 467 female and 540 male respondents worked in the oil/gas industry. The data was analysed using different statistical techniques. First, frequency data were used to describe the sample (reported in Magnussen & Svarstad 2012a), while multivariate analyses were used to analyse more complex relationships between variables (reported in Magnussen & Svarstad 2012b).

Results

The NEW representatives were invited for a presentation and discussion of the preliminary findings. These workshops were very useful for both the NEW members and the researchers. The NEW members got early knowledge about the findings, and could give the researchers information and feedback that was useful for interpretation of the findings and decisions about further analyses. This information exchange was essential in order to make the report relevant and useful for the principals. The project work group had two meetings after the data collection; the first to present the preliminary findings and to discuss them, and the second to present the final results. Due to practicalities it was difficult to meet more often, and much of the correspondence between the researchers and NEW team about the result was therefore also done electronically. Although the discussions in the meetings resulted in direction and input for the research team, the email correspondence was related to more detailed discussions about the survey and the findings.

Some of the results from the surveys are highlighted in the following. The complete reports of findings can be found in the two reports by Magnussen and Svarstad (2012a and b).[1]

Web-survey among human resource (HR) managers

The interviews of HR managers took place in December 2011. Of the HR managers interviewed, eight of nine HR managers in the process industry and 35 of 55 HR managers in the oil/gas industry responded.

Table 11.1 is based on the responses from the HR managers, and shows the ratio of women of all personnel in fixed positions, as well as the relative distribution of these in different types of positions. The results show that there were 2,227 employees in fixed positons in the eight EYDE organisations, of which 17% (384) were women. In the NODE cluster, in the 35 organisations that replied to the survey, there were about 12,264 employees in fixed positions, of whom 18% were women. The total number of employees reported from the NODE cluster is too high, which means that some HR managers probably also included employees working within other units of their company than in those situated in the Agder region. This bias must be taken into consideration when interpreting the results.

Assuming that the data from the NODE-businesses are representative, it seems like there is a much higher ratio of the female workers working in administrative positions in the oil and gas sector than in the process sector, while it seems somewhat easier for women to get leadership positions at the corporate level in the process industry than in the oil and gas industry.

Table 11.1 Distribution of positions of female workers in the EYDE and NODE organisations

Cluster	*N of fixed employees*	*N of women (ratio of all employees)*	*N of females in skilled worker positions (ratio of female employees)*	*N of females in admin positions (ratio of female employees)*	*N of female leaders at lowest level (førstelinje) (ratio of female employees)*	*N of middle manager (ratio of female employees)*	*N of females working in corporate management team (ratio of female employees)*	*N of female top leaders (ratio of female employees)*
EYDE (8 of 9 companies)	2,227	384 (17%)	230 (60%)	82 (21%)	18 (5%)	14 (4%)	7 (2%)	2 (0.5%)
NODE (35 of 57 companies)	12,264	2,178 (18%)	577 (26%)	1,511 (69%)	89 (4%)	58 (3%)	6 (0.3%)	3 (0.1%)

Note: Overview of data submitted from the HM managers in the EYDE and NODE clusters. The response rate from NODE was relatively low, and the data may therefore not be representative for the whole cluster.

Study of female and male employees

A link to a web-survey was distributed to all female and male employees (via the HR managers) in the two clusters. This means that the survey was sent to more than 11,000 employees. Of these, 1,603 employees answered the questionnaire (1,368 completely). The response rate is rather low, and the sample is therefore unlikely to be representative of the population of employees in the two clusters. The response rate is lowest in the NODE cluster. The characteristics of the sample or respondents were as follows:

- 645 women, of whom 124 worked in the process industry and 467 in the oil/gas sector, while 31 worked in both industries. Of the women respondents, 119 reported that they were managers.
- 957 men, of whom 337 worked in the process industry and 540 in the oil/gas sector, while 59 worked in both industries. Of the male respondents, 336 reported that they were managers.

Although the knowledge of the distributions in the full population the sample comes from is not accurate, it seems like female and male managers are overrepresented in the sample. In addition, male employees are underrepresented, and female NEW members are overrepresented. As the questionnaire was only available in Norwegian, it is also likely that foreign workers are underrepresented and that the results are most relevant for the Norwegian workers. If we look at the answers to the question about where the respondents grew up, over 90% say they grew up some place in Norway, and 64% of the women and 72% of the men grew up in Southern Norway. This means that the results cannot be used to draw conclusions about the whole population of employees, but it may be possible to compare some of the groups represented in the sample.

The findings indicate a clear difference between the women working in the two clusters and the average of female workers in the Agder region. A much higher ratio of the women working in the two clusters work full-time, and many also overtime. They have higher education than is usual for women in this region.

Some findings indicate that the female respondents, more often than the males, have challenges with juggling their private and professional lives. The female respondents are younger than the male respondents, and this is reflected in the respondents' household composition. More women than males report having children living in their household, so more of the female workers have care responsibilities. In addition, 85% of the women living with a partner say that their partner works full-time either as an employee or manager, while only 58% of the males say the same. Twenty-six per cent of the males have partners working part-time or with leave of absence from work, and only 3% of women say the same. This means that, compared to their male colleagues, a higher ratio of the females working in the hard-hat industries in our study raise children, but a smaller ratio of the females have a spouse/partner that works less than full-time. A large part of the women still report that they manage work and family life in a good way.

More women than men report that they think there are challenges related to gender equality, and that they would welcome measures to increase equality. Many of the women who responded to the survey reported that they would like more challenging work and more responsibilities. Hence, the survey uncovered potential for an increase in the ratio of female managers.

Most of the respondents report high satisfaction with their work. Multivariate analysis of factors that contribute to higher work satisfaction showed that being a female increases the likelihood of higher work satisfaction. In addition, being part of a network, flexible work hours, a higher number of working hours, working in a company that facilitates family life and a work culture with tolerance for diverging opinions are positively associated with work satisfaction, while worries about the welfare of children and difficulties with juggling work life and private life have negative associations.

The project results are summarised in two reports: *NEW Facts Forsprojekt* (Magnussen & Svarstad 2012a) and *NEW Facts Hovedprosjekt* (Magnussen & Svarstad 2012b). In addition, two workshops were held with participants from NEW to discuss some of the findings and thematic areas from the reports. A summary of the results can found at the webpage of NEW, where interested readers also can find links to the full reports.

The results of the survey have been published in a chapter in a book about equality, knowledge and innovation in Agder (Magnussen & Svarstad 2013). Results have also been presented at various conferences (e.g. New-Gathering 19 September 2015).

Impact of the findings in the project

When NEW Facts was initiated, NEW already ran four projects: NEW Faces, NEW Communication, NEW Mentor and NEW Arena. After the results of New Facts were known, NEW initiated the project "NEW Leader" as a response to the findings of a low share of female leaders in the cluster member companies. This project focused on recruiting more female top leaders. So far, only one workshop has been held, and the initiative has not been prolonged. Although it is difficult to establish a direct link between the research findings and any development of the ongoing NEW projects, it is likely that the research project has also had some effect on these projects.

NEW Faces is a project that aims to enhance recruitment of women into hard-hat jobs. In this project, female employees from the process and oil/gas industry visit the 10th grade in schools in Agder and talk about their jobs. The idea is to give students female role models, and it is important to try to influence the students' choices before they choose their specialisation in high school. NEW Faces has also hosted two large gatherings to discuss the understanding of recruitment and recruiting strategies. NEW Faces is an investment in long-term recruitment to increase the share of female workers in the sector.

NEW Mentor is a project with the purpose of developing good leaders of both genders. Through the programme, employees with a talent for leadership are recruited to take part in a development programme. In addition, existing leaders get support and training. This programme is run by NEW, but with external counselling in conducting mentorship. The mentors are top leaders from industries in NODE or EYDE. The mentors and protégés are linked across cluster and gender, i.e a protégé from EYDE is connected with a mentor from NODE and a female protégé is linked with a male mentor and vice versa. The cross linkage between mentor and protégé has apparently proven to be a success. NEW Mentor is open for male employees, since the relationships created across clusters is positive for leadership development regardless of gender.

NEW Arena is a collective name for all the social activities initiated by NEW, for example, excursion, company visits and family days. These activities are open to all female employees in the two clusters.

NEW Communication is a group established to support the other NEW projects with communicating their activities. They edit the NEW Facebook page, maintain the NEW webpage and publish a regular NEW newsletter. They also enhance the visibility of women working in hard-hat companies. NEW Communication was involved in creating the communication strategy for the publication of NEW Facts. NEW wanted to use NEW Facts to put gender diversity issues on the agenda, and accentuate that women in these industries differed from the assumptions of this having to be over-worked women in a time-squeeze who did not thrive in their jobs. To the contrary, these women worked more, did not relate to a time- squeeze and thrived more than their male colleagues.

NEW now wants to do a new mapping of the situation in the two clusters, in order to get updated information. This time, there will be a special focus on regional differences within the sectors. The leaders of NEW have experienced that it is easier to get support for projects that will enhance women's situation when they have the results from the research project to show. Hence, collecting data about the gender equality situations in the sectors is important, in order to secure a continuing focus on the challenges and support for measures intended to reduce gender imbalance.

Strengths and weaknesses of commissioned research

There are some advantages and challenges related to commissioned research that we have experienced in this project. Challenges are usually related to available resources, which may prevent the researchers from conducting research in the way they would like based on scientific criteria. On the other hand, the researchers often get insights relating to practice that they would not get if they were not co-operating tightly with the principal.

The research team always aim to make the most of the available data material collected, in order to make a contribution to the stakeholders as well as to science. In commissioned research this is not always possible to achieve. Scientific contributions require a large theoretical basis and use of theoretical models, and this type of theoretical work is often not possible within the tight budgets that often characterise commissioned research. Literature reviews and the development of research questions and hypotheses are time consuming activities and therefore costly. This often leads to a more descriptive approach, because the aim of the research for the principal is often to create a basis for decision making rather than a scientific contribution.

In many ways, commissioned research is twofold. Commissioned research is often based on a request from a stakeholder who has a "problem" they need help to solve. This often requires a concrete and practical response in regards to findings, measures and recommendations to the stakeholder. This practical approach goes on the expense of the scientific contribution; on the other side a scientific approach could go on the expense of the promised delivery.

There is also a potential mismatch between stakeholders' and what researchers' wish to utilise data and material from the process. While the stakeholder wants a report to refer to, the researcher wants scientific publications. Because the format of a scientific publication is extensive and often not compatible to answering the assigned task, this is not something the researcher can stress.

In this project, we had a limited amount of time, which influenced the project and left little time for critical reflection afterwards. There are some aspects of the project that should have been reflected upon more critically. All the representatives from the industries were leaders, and not considered as representative for "regular" employees. We designed our survey based on input from these representatives, and it is reasonable to believe that this leader perspective has affected both results and continuation of the project. In addition to limited time, we also had a limited amount of financial resources. We therefore decided to send our survey out only in the Norwegian language. That means that our results are not representative for English speaking employees in these industries.

Being researcher close to stakeholders

This chapter contributes to the overall theme of this book exemplifying how a commissioned project can be done with a high degree of involvement from stakeholders. The project was characterised by co-operation and knowledge exchange between stakeholders and researchers, to secure legitimacy and relevance. In our case the stakeholder was the project group, consisting of eight women from these industries. They were engaged in the project and wanted to learn as much as possible about their fellow co-workers. In many ways our relation was characterised by a mutual interdependency. This was based on the project groups' important insight about the oil and gas industry that we as researchers did not have. By involving our project group, we got access to detailed information about life as a woman working in the oil and gas industry in two ways. First of all, the project group participated in creating our questionnaire and we needed their input to formulate suitable and relevant questions. Second, our project group provided background information to help us understand our findings (we presented our preliminary findings and they helped us interpret/understand them). The involvement of the project group was also important in providing valuable feedback on where we should take our statistical analyses next.

There are also examples of how we, as researchers, strengthened the project with our perspectives. For example, the initial plan was to distribute a questionnaire to the female employees only, because this is NEW's main target group. As researchers, we argued in favour of including male respondents in the sample, because this would allow for comparisons of the situations and opinions of males and female employees respectively. After putting this suggestion to the NEW board, it was decided to include men in the sample. In a way, this changed the research questions so that it was not just the situation of the women that were investigated, but the situation of the female employees compared to that of the males.

NEW's primary purpose is to recruit and retain female workers, as well as improving females' career opportunities and NEW facts played an important role in providing the information/regional knowledge and numbers to reach these goals.

Note

1 http://www.nodeeydewomen.no/media/91684/new-facts-kartlegging.pdf. http://www.nodeeydewomen.no/media/91681/new-facts-hovedprosjekt.pdf.

12 Regional knowledge infrastructure

Sissel Strickert

Developing knowledge infrastructure in the region

In this chapter, I discuss the long-term effect of the Programme for Regional R&D and Innovation (VRI-programme) in the Agder region. The programme is also presented in Chapters 2 and 3 in this book, and referred to in other chapters. It has been discussed in several academic texts, i.e. Johnsen and Ennals (2012) and Johnsen, Knudsen and Normann (2014). The programme was initiated in the mid-2000s, following the discussions on globalisation during the 1990s. In practical terms, these discussions led in Norway (as in many other European countries) to new perspectives on regional development, with emphasis on regional advantages. The idea behind this is that regions have their own characteristics, and contribute to development differently. There is local knowledge that will be better utilised by means developed locally, compared to general policy tools developed at a national level. In theoretical terms the turn towards regionalisation was an answer to the ongoing discourse on globalisation at the start of the millennium, as outlined in the chapters in the first part of this book.

The VRI-programme has since 2007 been The Research Council of Norway's (RCN) main support mechanism for regional innovation in Norwegian regions. Regional development throughout the 1990s was characterised by interaction and settlements between work life organisations, and the focus was on creating mutual understanding for organisational development. This chapter looks into how the 10-year VRI-programme has contributed to developing an institutional knowledge infrastructure for innovation in the Agder region: the infrastructure to develop, absorb, diffuse and challenge knowledge. RCN and the two counties in the Agder region each fund 50% of the VRI-programme at Agder. The programme has four focus areas, which are: Energy and Technology, ICT, Cultural and Creative Industries (C&CI) and Emerging Industries. It was Agder Research (AR) that got the assignment as the leading research institute in the VRI programme at Agder. With the VRI-programme in the portfolio, it is interesting to understand how knowledge is generated and used by AR.

This chapter outlines three main lines of contribution related to applied social science:

- How was knowledge developed?
- What knowledge infrastructure was established?
- What was the role of researchers in the interplay between research and practice?

My own engagement in this programme started as a result of a decision in the programme board. It was a deliberate choice to put AR in the position of managing the programme. "It was our intention to strengthen and develop Agder Research when we decided to place the function of project management of the VRI-programme at Agder to be located within Agder Research" (Kirsten Borge, regional officer and president of VRI board at Agder, at the board-meeting on November 27, 2015).

This decision has been important for how the VRI-programme has evolved, and for why it has been able to promote stronger co-operation between research and practice in the Agder region. For the last 6 years, I have been project manager of this long-term industrial development programme.

The argument in this chapter places itself somewhere in-between the argument found in Chapter 4: *Collective knowing* and on the other hand the arguments in Chapter 10: *Network ties between universities and cultural and creative industries* and Chapter 17: *Universities' external relations*. In Chapter 4, the argument is that developing knowledge with stakeholders in a region is a long-term process of mutual trust building. My case is in line with this argument. In Chapters 10 and 17, however, the lack of institutional support for external engagement by the university, is discussed. My case illustrates that institutional development is important in order to support mutual knowledge building and learning. It also shows a positive case of how this is done with the strategic support from the regional counties and the research institute.

Action learning

I use the term "Action Learning", coined by Revans (1980) as a theoretical reference to the process I will describe. Action Learning is a wide concept, but at its core it can be understood as an approach that is in a certain opposition to the idea of having a predefined strategy for change. The core idea of Action Learning is that knowledge is accumulating (learning) as the activity unfolds (action). "Action learning is optimistic, humanistic, engaging, but also pragmatic and sceptical, suspicious of canonical ideas (and the experts who trade in them) and distrustful of speculative knowledge untested in action" (Pedler, Burgoyne & Brook 2005, p. 62).

I try to explain how the VRI-programme has initiated this kind of learning through its activity, and thereby has been a tool for building knowledge infrastructure between industry and R&D institutions using experimental methods of co-operation and interaction. It opens up potentials not easily revealed by ordinary public funding instruments (Gustavsen 2005).

The point made by Bjørn Gustavsen (1992, 2007) is that dialogical development of mutual learning requires some structure. It requires that people actually meet, that they solve problems together and that there are organised arenas for dialogue. This is in line with what Karlsen and Larrea (2014) call *developing collective knowing*. Subsequently, there is an institutional and organisational dimension to mutual learning. Thus, the knowledge infrastructure might be understood:

1 physical surroundings like institutions, universities, agencies, libraries
2 traditions, experience, tacit knowledge and regional advantages
3 change towards digitalisation in gathering of data, access to data and possibilities to process data though internet technology.

I show how the VRI programme has contributed to developing learning through its activity (action) by supporting institutional development in the region, including both establishing research groups at AR and networks among industry. I do this by describing the co-existence of research and industry in the VRI-programme and the actors within these knowledge infrastructures. I illustrate this and concentrate the discussion on C&CI at Agder.

The development of the VRI-programme at Agder

During the 10-year period from 2000 to 2010, several events in Agder marked a shift towards the region itself as an active regional development actor. The University of Agder started working with the idea of establishing a Technology Transfer Office (TTO) (see Chapter 17: *Universities' external relations* in this book). Several institutions were established in Agder based on the public sector selling its shares in a regional electricity company. As one of Norway's largest water power producing regions, the sale of majority holding in the company gave enormous revenues. From these revenues, the two competence funds *Cultiva* and *Sørlandets kompetansefond* were established in the early 2000s. Later, another fund, *Aust-Agder utviklings- og kompetansefond*, was established. Among politicians and regional authority in Agder there was consensus around two main issues: the aim of developing the regional college so that it would gain university status, and the building of a highway between Grimstad and Kristiansand, two central cities in Agder's urban area. In 2007 the University of Agder was established. Two years later, the highway connecting central parts of Agder was opened.

VS 2010 and the VRI-programme were established in a period when strengthening the regional level, as mentioned earlier, was a leading trend within policy development. At the same time, the Agder region had an ambition to strengthen its regional position in Norway and desired to make use of regional development tools. The combination of these two drivers explains the strong emphasis on the VRI programme in the region. This was further confirmed when in 2010, the county authorities in Aust-Agder and Vest-Agder developed a common plan for development, Regional Development Plan Agder 2020. The same year The Regional Research Fund of Agder (RFF) was established.

At the national level, efforts have been made to enable the regional authority level to develop existing knowledge institutions and establish new ones. In 2007 when RCN initiated the 10-year VRI-programme, the idea was to give the regions both resources and time to develop. The VRI programme is based on the idea that this kind of knowledge and competence development is a long-term process.

Every third year applicants, counties together with R&D institutions in the region, can apply for funds for a period of 3 years. The RCN had previous experience in several programmes which intended to create value in the private sector, based on a variety of collaborative initiatives with university industry links. The special feature of VRI was that it should last for 10 years and aim at long-term development of capability to innovate in the region. RCN and the county authorities of the Agder counties, together with regional funds, are responsible for the funding of the project, while the private sector and the University of Agder contribute in kind. RCN covers a maximum of 50% of the resources in the project. The programme at Agder is now in its last year.

Altogether all major R&D financial institutions situated in the Agder region have participated in the VRI-programme for most of the 10-year period. AR has been responsible for managing the project and contract institution with the RCN, together with the University of Agder and the incubator Innoventus Sør (formerly named Coventure). Since 2011, Teknova, an applied technological institute, has also taken part. Each partner in the consortium is responsible for its own thematic area: ICT, C&CI, Energy and Technology and Emerging Industries. There has been continued participation both from financial participants, consortium and personnel.

The VRI-programme works at three different levels, all related to building regional knowledge infrastructure. The programme is a tool for regional steering and operationalisation of regional policy and is also a coupling-agent, gathering business activities with R&D in order to create value. Finally, the programme has aimed at competence building; developing individual and team competence, social relations, mobility between the knowledge institutions and capacity for learning. I will next present one of the thematic projects in the programme, C&CI.

Case: cultural and creative industry, a desired development

In 2007, the VRI-programme was in its beginnings and there were discussions on letting C&CI be part of the effort within the VRI-programme. At the time the scientific community, as well as the industry itself, in the region, was fragmented and there was no established R&D community to support and develop. C&CI was not a part of the R&D community's universe of understanding or focus. With its single units, small enterprises and the low degree of co-operation that characterised the sector, many questioned the potential for developing in this sector. Exceptions were that this was a case of traditional co-operation between travel agents and infrastructural travel co-operation within transport and accommodation.

Today, the C&CI cluster organisation USUS organises more than a hundred small- and medium-size companies within the travel and experience industry. All are situated in Agder and Telemark. The main goal is to achieve re-purchase from consumer customers/visitors to the Agder region (Sørlandet). The cluster is organised around competence building activities, building and developing relations with R&D. For 5 years, from 2010 to 2015, the cluster USUS has had status as an Arena project through the cluster developing programme in Innovation Norway. Today the R&D community in the region has strengthened, and has developed national recognition and international relations. The travel and experience industry has matured in regards to R&D co-operation. Innovation and knowledge development are now part of their vocabulary. This was not the case in 2007.

VRI-programme as a coupling-agent

Over recent decades there has been a transformation of how knowledge is generated, shared, distributed and disputed. Knowledge institutions like universities, government agencies and libraries have begun to adjust, and are opening up initiatives with access to open data. Internet technologies make way for new business models, new ways to co-operate and co-create. New ways of communicating, both human to human and through communication technology, are made possible through the internet. All this affects how we establish knowledge. The VRI programme was built on the idea that by following a company and industry over a long period of time, the researchers would together with the company develop unique knowledge. By accumulating knowledge this way, the researchers have the possibility to work closely inside both the industry, and from time to time going into the academic work to structure, reflect and produce new scientific knowledge accordingly; thus both academic and practice establish knowledge.

The VRI-programme supports business activities with clear R&D ambitions. It helps develop this ambition from its birth in a defined industry, through the challenge of collaboration and onto the road to research maturity.

A precondition is that more than one company is involved, and that there is established co-operation with R&D institutions.

When the VRI-programme started, there was no established R&D community to support and develop the industry. The common understanding of entrepreneurial activity, value-creation and return on investment in the cultural R&D community was close to non-existent. See also Chapter 10 and Chapter 17 in this book. Both the culture, travel and experience industry have matured over the last years in regards to R&D co-operation supported by the focus on culture industry by AR.

This was made possible by the mutual strategy from the region (see the introduction from the president of the VRI board at Agder) and the internal strategy of AR. The counties in the region allocated resources to form the USUS network. AR built a group of researchers dedicated to the topics of C&CI. However, coupling these two strategies and initiatives required building trust. It was a process of developing trust and mutual understanding over time (Hjemdahl 2011). The VRI-programme became the platform for this trust building process.

Developing knowledge

The VRI-programme has several objectives, the most obvious being value creation and innovation through coupling and collaboration between industry and research institutions. There is also huge potential for scientific development in establishing knowledge on innovation processes in organisations, clusters and more systemic views of innovation. The VRI-programme has supported researchers to participate in practice, and to go in and out of the traditional role of the researcher. The researchers hold a combination of different roles as programme managers in the VRI-programme. The developing of new knowledge takes place in different arenas, with different ways of communication and development processes. Thus, the co-operation between theory and practice that this supports, builds knowledge infrastructure.

The knowledge infrastructure for C&CI and the Experience economy is a diverse landscape consisting of small- and medium-size enterprises and diverse transdisciplinary field workers. There are diverse institutions and agencies with bureaucrats, public policy support systems and policy instruments. This involves institutions like the university and institute sector with diverse scientific approaches, consisting of knowledge workers, transdisciplinary scientific fields, theoretical developers and discourses. In between there are actors working closely with the industry, producing scientific material and at the same time acting as an integral part of the industries' development. They are an active part of development through participation and the mere dispute of knowledge. These actors are trusted to become an integral part of industrial development, invited into the boardrooms, strategic decision making and playing a part in developing practice in the field. These actors are trained in scientific methods and theoretical modes of thinking. These actors work as translators between the worlds of practice and science, and sometimes this leads to the development of new ideas and co-operation and interaction. Thus there has been a *scientification* of the sector.

The role of the researcher as a knowledge broker between practice and scientific knowledge is a delicate balance between being raised in the language of research but also being operational in the world of practice. Building trust is essential in this role in order to participate close enough to being part of industrial development. Barriers might be communication and "tribal" scientific language, understanding of value creation and return on investment among others. Hjemdahl (2011) gives an example of mis-communication leading to distrust between industry and research society based on challenges in communication: New knowledge is derived from the industry's ability to absorb scientific knowledge, and applied scientific knowledge is depended on trust in relation to the field of practice. Trust is a mutual phenomenon that opens for knowledge development both in the field of practice and the field of scientific knowledge.

Building a regional knowledge infrastructure

The county authority secured an extended role as regional development actor with administrative reform in the late 2000s. At the same time, it was clear that an expected change in the geographical sectioning of Norwegian regions was not going to be followed though. Over the last 10 years, regions in Norway have established a new role for funding research and development. The county authorities have had to develop a research and development strategy. The VRI-programme was launched as RCN's most important initiative towards regional innovation and development, and with the aim of supporting collaboration and coupling of players in industry and knowledge institutions, as well as interacting with public policy instruments.

Even though the VRI-programme built on ideas of regional development, over this 10-year period the programme has gone through changes. There have been three periods in the VRI-programme: phase 1: 2007–2010, phase 2: 2011–2013 and phase 3: 2014–2017. These can be characterised as different phases in a development process. Again, I use C&CI as a case.

During the 2007–2010 period there was a fragmentation in the culture and experience industry. From 2007, AR has had the responsibility for development activities in the culture and experience industry. The same researcher has had this responsibility over the years, with a 1-year exception. The first activity by the VRI-programme was to couple the industry with the R&D community.

During the period 2011–2013, more co-operation emerged in the culture and experience industry. In 2010, the industry organisation USUS was granted Arena status for the next 3 years, with an option to apply for prolonged status for another 2 years. In these years, VRI-programme funding was used strategically to gather information, mapping awareness and knowledge of different aspects on re-purchase depending on seasonal variety. VRI-programme was used as a means to achieve knowledge development among the Arena USUS member companies, and cluster management aimed at lifting the sector into further co-operation and interaction with innovation research. The USUS organisation is associated with a PhD candidate doing research on this development of how the public and visitors experience industry (see Chapter 14: *Getting China-ready* in this book). Regional research funds allocated funding for the development of the culture and experience industry. At this time, however, only a few RCN programmes were directed at cultural industries, and there was still no strongly developed understanding of relevance and importance of service innovation in the cultural industry.

In the present 2014–2017 period we have seen divergence and maturity in this industry. The initial 3 years of Arena status were prolonged by another 2 years, until 2015. In 2014 the USUS organisation applied for NCE status. The application failed, but the cluster board and administrative organisation are eager to follow up at the next announcement. Parallel to this, the researchers at AR, together with businesses, have stared becoming recognised and have been able to receive national research funding.

Based on the case have presented here, I argue that the VRI-programme has had the long-term effect of establishing a regional knowledge infrastructure. As is seen in the case of cultural and creative industry, this development has taken time. Researchers have engaged together with the industry in developing a mutual understanding of the challenges, and at the same time have been able to develop their research perspectives. In this case we can see a pattern where research competence and development of an industry go hand in hand. In addition, strong links have been created between the two and to public policy and strategies. This is what I understand as contributing to the creation of a knowledge infrastructure in the region.

Table 12.1 Development of the VRI-programme project for cultural and creative industry at Agder

Level / phase	*2007–2010*	*2011–2013*	*2014–2017*
Regional steering	Fragmented and non-existing	Co-operation and funding	Distributed responsibility
Coupling-agent	Fragmented; individual researchers working with their own projects	Co-operating closely with USUS and individual companies	Divergence and maturity; receiving research recognition
Companies	Worked individually	Co-operation through USUS	Increased R&D activity and network on innovation

The researcher as contributing to knowledge infrastructure

Collaboration and coupling of players in industry and knowledge institutions, interacting with public instruments, is the working method of the VRI-programme. This makes VRI an important tool, both financially and operationally, for innovation and development of knowledge-bearing institutions regionally. In light of the expectations, set in the VRI-programme's regional footprint, the VRI-programme has been a good starting point for looking into the creation and development of regional knowledge infrastructure.

The concept of knowledge is central to promote understanding of how to understand, generate, share, dispute and diffuse knowledge. The editors introduce this book by exploring the concept of knowledge: "What knowledge is developed through applied social sciences?" they rhetorically ask; is there a specific knowledge established by applied research, as opposed to other knowledge creation? In my case I have investigated and described how combining different roles establishing knowledge both within and outside academia has contributed to knowledge development in practice.

We have to widen our concept of knowledge and our understanding of how knowledge generation can take place, and with what value knowledge can be generated. Seen from an applied researcher's point of view, there has been knowledge creation manifested in the increased co-operation and R&D activity in the sector. By accumulating knowledge, the researcher has the possibility to work closely inside both the industry, and from time to time going into academic work to structure, reflect and produce new scientific knowledge accordingly. I argue for the importance of combining academic and practice established knowledge.

The VRI-programme has several objectives, the most obvious being value creation and innovation through coupling and collaboration between industry and research institutions. There is also huge potential for scientific development on establishing knowledge on innovation processes in organisations, clusters and more systemic views of innovation. The main actors are researchers by profession, but at the same time go in and out of the traditional role of the researcher. This interaction process has initiated Action Learning. The researchers inhabit different roles when acting as programme manager in the VRI-programme. Establishing of knowledge takes place in different arenas, with different ways of communication and development processes. Altogether this contributes to the regional knowledge infrastructure.

13 The Mittelstand

Michael Ricke, Kristin Wallevik and Geir Jørgensen

Understanding the firms in the region

As a result of the global financial crisis from 2008, there has been a renewed focus on the factors underpinning the resilience of regions (Simmie & Martin 2010) to withstand economic and technological shocks of both the acute and chronic variety. This has inspired many regions to revisit the structure and drivers that typify and invigorate them, in an effort to better understand, anticipate and influence their most important dynamics (Davies 2011; Fingelton, Garretsen & Martin 2012). This includes a clearer idea of who the actors were, how they relate to one another and how these elements add up to a whole.

On one end of this aggregation spectrum, the region is seen as greater than the sum of its parts: the result of interactions between black-box firms and the external trends and forces acting upon them. On the other end of the spectrum, firms are seen solely as one-off actors composed of bounded knowledge, rules, norms and procedures and uniquely-organised, self-motivated agents who generate independent outcomes in the search to exploit new market opportunities. The region is simply an agglomeration of its individual parts.

Between these two extremes, there is a need for grounded, theoretical and practical research to be done. While much of the focus of recent research on Southern Norway (Sørlandet or Agder) has been regional or industrial in nature, there has been a call to reintroduce the firm into the discussion. This chapter will discuss how this was done through the work of two projects carried out by Agder Research: *Crisis, Adaptation and Growth–A Regional Analysis of Southern Norway* (2013) and *The Mechanical Industry in Agder: Status, Challenges and Proposals for Action* (2014).

We highlight the initial shift in theoretical focus: the introduction of the Mittelstand concept allowed Agder Research to develop a better understanding of who the actors are, and to better contextualise the grounded research. Building on this, and working in concert with regional institutions and with direct input from the firms under study, Agder Research was able to add to the understanding of these firms and industries in the region, present a deeper understanding of one of the key industries under threat and make relevant proposals its firms could act upon.

The concept of Mittelstand

Background

The origins of this research can be found in the industrial nature of Southern Norway and the results achieved there, before and in the wake of the recent global financial shocks. Many OECD countries have experienced downsizing of traditional industries, and in the past few years, they have become vulnerable, because they have allowed their industrial base to deteriorate and to become dependent upon a small collection of large service-providers. As a consequence, there is now greater focus on how a competitive and sustainable production of goods can be maintained or rejuvenated in the most developed countries and regions.

Norway is a small, open economy, where a large export sector is necessary to generate the hard currency needed to underwrite its reliance on imports. Long-term economic development is dependent upon Norwegian firms that can compete internationally and generate import-earnings in the face of effective international firms. Competitive production solely based on the exploitation of Norwegian natural (raw) resources will not be enough to secure long-term balanced economic development in Norway. Competitiveness further up the value chain in processed industrial goods is also necessary.

The sustainability issue for traditional industries is especially significant for the Agder region because it has a higher portion of this type of industry than the national average in Norway. In Agder 28.5% of the region's collective business income in public corporations comes from industry, compared to 12.8% for the country as a whole. The dominant industrial branches in Southern Norway measured by employment are: the production of machinery and equipment, metals, wood processing and products, computer and electronics and means of transportation. Industry in Agder is internationally oriented and Southern Norway is the foremost export region for processed goods in Norway. Agder is the leading county for this type of export. Export of processed goods from East and West Agder measured in real terms, corrected using the Consumer Price Index, has grown by 9.258 billion kroner; an increase of 60% in 15 years.

Change of perspective: who are they really?

In recent scholarly and business literature, Norway has been viewed as somewhat of an exception to the normal workings of international economics. The oft-cited low research and development investment levels, and the consequent interpretation of this data to imply low innovation, are well-documented. The continued existence and even flourishing of heavy industries in one of the world's highest labour cost markets, defying expectations that they would be early victims of globalisation and inevitable migrants to lower cost markets, generates ad hoc explanations rooted in a snapshot in time that may be neither sustainable nor reproducible. The "Norwegian paradox" summarises the perception that something else is going on in the Norwegian economy that is unique on a fundamental level (OECD 2007b).

As a part of the *Crisis, Adaptation and Growth* research, we took a step back from the general thrust of recent theory-building and asked three basic questions:

1 What are the core characteristics that describe the industrial producers of Southern Norway?
2 Are these characteristics uniform between firms and across branches?
3 Is there a construct that helps to understand and explain these characteristics?

These questions were explored in detail in the report, and were the primary focus of the data collection. The desire was to develop a generalised model that provided a solid foundation for uncovering key characteristics, and which provided a tool for systematically analysing firms in the region. The goal was to lead to a more robust capability to synthesise relevant policy recommendations for private and public sector actors. The model that best fits the traits and observations uncovered in the course of this research derives from broad, but not necessarily deep, existing research on Mittelstand firms in German and from Hermann Simon's (1992, 1996, 2009) research on what he calls "Hidden Champions".

The Mittelstand firm

The creation of the Mittelstand has been an important and formative economic and socio-cultural factor, consciously chosen in the wake of World War 2 for the development of the modern Germany. These firms receive much of the credit for how well Germany has grown, prospered and come through the recent global finance crisis and recession. This success is rooted in cultural dimensions that draw on Germany's craft traditions connected to how firms are led and managed, how they produce and market their products and how they develop their people over time. The overall aim with the development of Mittelstand firms has always been inextricably tied to social equality and social well-being.

Mittelstand companies are a subset of small- and medium-sized enterprises (SMEs) that possess features that differentiate them. These differences have long been an accepted part of the German legal, business, training and social environment, dating back to the beginning of modern craft corporatism in the 1890s. As a model it has evolved, but it has typically been analysed along two criteria: its quantitative attributes and its qualitative attributes.

> One of my main arguments is that the characteristic trait of a company in the German Mittelstand is not the size of its workforce or the numbers on its balance sheets, but rather its corporate governance in a broad sense that encompasses both legal and sociocultural features.
>
> (Berghof 2006, p. 271)

What has not changed over time is the existence of Mittelstand as a socially embedded business conceit that has clearly identifiable characteristics, receives special consideration from the government and that generates unique outcomes in relation to other SMEs. Its ambiguity lies more in the quantitative definition, and less with the observable qualitative traits.

Six core attributes of Mittelstand firms

Much of Mittelstand research concentrates on the quantitative characteristics of the enterprises, while the qualitative characteristics generate the unique outcomes. It is in the qualities of these SMEs that we found it useful to separate out and apply the observations, experience and lessons from Mittelstand research to the Southern Norway context. We took the original characterisations of these firms and generalised the attributes, which were then broken down into specific traits that could be operationalised and analysed, either with quantitative data or through the collection of qualitative interview data. The observable attributes of the Mittelstand companies that we explored in relation to Southern Norway's firms are six-fold:

1. They have concentrated ownership (many are or began as family-owned firms).
2. They are relatively long-lived.
3. They have a flat organisational structure with high levels of devolved responsibility.
4. Their leadership is embedded in the community.
5. They build upon specialised and highly trained skills.
6. They have what we define as an engaged workforce.

In this more universal version of the Mittelstand firm, ownership is concentrated and often family based. They operate mostly in tight, business-to-business value chains. They have long-term and focused strategies, develop continuously with a heavy dose of incremental innovation and avoid high risk behaviour that achieves only short-term financial rewards. The owners and employees are personally connected to the firm and the community, and take a generational perspective on the firm's development. This enables a long-term, industrial perspective that underpins a profit sufficiency approach instead of profit maximisation. Leadership's responsibilities, authority and resources are well-balanced for strategic planning and for encouraging employee loyalty. Employer-employee relations are structured so as to facilitate co-operation and transparency in flat hierarchies. The work culture is characterised by inclusion and leadership and employees generally have a strong sense of

Table 13.1 Generalised attributes and traits of Mittelstand firms

Concentrated ownership	*Longevity*	*Flat organisational structure*	*Leadership embedded in the community*	*Specialised and highly trained skills*	*Engaged workforce*
Autonomous decision-making Strategic clarity Primary focus on the long term Management is well-versed (hands on) in the firm's core competencies	Ability to survive a wide range of business cycles Ability to adapt to changing market conditions Ability to incorporate technological change Niche focus	Vertical lines of communication are short Performance is transparent Clearly defined responsibilities Responsibilities match authority and resources Close contact along the value chain (embedded)	Leadership originates from the local community or is a long-term transplant with shared values. Social check on local power asymmetries Reputation is integral to success Socially embedded business success	Long employee retention rates Internalised competencies in core product(s) Internalised competencies in core processes Homegrown, experience-based competencies	Employee loyalty: firm more than just a job Subscribe to leadership's vision Adept at teaming and problem-solving Self-regulating workforce

mutual trust and loyalty. Unwritten norms are important and the culture is informal. This helps make the firms flexible and better able to communicate with customers on multiple levels.

Many employees began as apprentices, and have long experience in the branch and in their firm. The level of technical expertise is an important aspect of firms' unique advantages. The firms are integrated members of their region and treat their social responsibilities as moral obligations, not merely legal requirements. They protect their competencies and skills, and try to avoid layoffs or downsizing during tough times. This approach results in a loyal and dedicated labour force, with long experience and an ability to customise solutions for demanding customers.

Table 13.1 provides our taxonomy of the attributes and their associated traits. These two research reports did not address every factor in the table but represent the initial steps in building a more grounded understanding for regional firm success, and the initial steps in providing guidance based on this alternative perspective.

Project 1: crises, adaptation and growth

The initial research project, *Crisis, Adaptation and Growth – A Regional Analysis of Southern Norway* (2013) sought to understand what impact the global financial shocks had on major industries in the Agder region, what the underlying characteristics and trends were and how the firms and industries were positioned to move forward. The first portion of the report asked: How have the region's firms tackled the financial crisis, both as a whole and in different key branches, and have firms maintained their competitiveness? The question became no less relevant after the fall in oil prices in 2014 created a new economic challenge for part of the industry in Southern Norway.

Agder Research's portion of the report, the regional analysis of Southern Norway, was a part of Norges Handelshøyskole's (NHH) *Crisis, Adaptation and Growth* that analysed the international, national and regional effects of the crisis. For their contribution, Agder Research received financing from Skipskreditfondet, Aust-Agders fylkeskommune, Vest-Agders fylkeskommune and Kristiansand kommune. Agder Research's contribution to this report is composed of three parts that analyse different perspectives on the region. The three overall approaches taken in the report employ theory-building, quantitative data and qualitative data analysis. The major themes include an analysis of the business structure and trends for a selected portion of the region's industries, knowledge and innovation, and regional leadership and interaction in Agder. This review will draw primarily upon the first portion of the report.

Agder: a defined economic industrial region

The economic base of the Agder region of Norway, traditionally defined as the 30 counties of East and West Agder in Southern Norway, has certain characteristics that make it unique as a Norwegian region. Agder is the smallest region of Norway, with 5.7% of the population and 5.1% of the mainland area. Despite its relatively small physical size and population, it is the leading exporter of reworked products in Norway. Export from the Agder region has grown and remained strong throughout the period with only a brief interruption during the economic crisis in 2008–2009. The largest portion of this export is composed of traditional industries, namely smelting of metals, machinery and equipment. Agder alone makes up 33% of the total gross income of machinery and equipment production and over 20% of the total employment in these branches in Norway (NACE 28-29999). During the period 1997–2010, the gross product of the Agder region increased by 113.6% compared to 63.2% for all of Norway. This bifurcated growth raised the Agder region's portion of the national gross product from 8% to 10% over the same period.

The quantitative data from this project is composed of multiple variables, covering the empirical characteristics of 525 of Agder's firms in 12 separate branches from 2006 to 2011. The firms selected from these branches comprise a sample covering 74% of the total turnover in the region as well as 66% of total employment.

For all the selected firms there was an increase in operating income of 51%, where there has been a growth in employment of 40% from 2006 to 2011. The effect of the financial crisis on the level of activity did not appear to have been significant. The distribution of income among the branches has changed during the period, with the greatest change occurring in oil and gas, whose percentage of operating income in our sample grew from 27% in 2006 to 36% in 2011.

Concerning profitability, the picture is somewhat different. There are large variations between branches and big swings within branches in different years. The operating result for the group as a whole grew by 7% in the 2006–2011 period, while the increase in the result before tax is closer to 0% in the same period. The margins have been pressed.

The indicators connected to value show that the total book value has increased by 82% in the 2006–2011 period. There is an increase in all of the indicators in the analysis related to machine and equipment, ships, rigging and other equipment, recorded R&D and the book value of patents. There has been an increase in aggregated capital equity in the period with the largest positive change in the oil and gas industry.

Even though many of the firms on the region fall into the more generalised small- and medium-sized firm category, Mittelstand is not about turnover, profit or employment size, but how the firm operates. It is the way these firms are led, managed, produce and develop and how they anchor their production in technological knowledge and skilled craftsmanship that is critical (Simon 1996). The ability to combine knowledge about the market, technology and the firm's resources is the central dynamic. We have identified six characteristics of Mittelstand firms, and in the reports explored whether they could be found in the firms and sectors under study.

Concentrated ownership: Concentrated ownership, especially family ownership, has often been asserted to be an important explanatory factor for long-term thinking and planning in the Mittelstand model. We observed a large element of concentrated ownership among the firms we studied. In all branches, with the exception of finance, the percentage of firms that have a single owner, with more than 34% of stock (thereby possessing veto rights by law) is over 80%. In seven of the branches studied in the *Crisis, Adaptation and Growth* report, the percentage of concentrated ownership is over 90%. Family ownership is relatively widespread, especially in tourism, leisure boating, shipping, wood processing and in the mechanical industry. Two branches stand out for their large presence of international ownership: the processing industry and the oil and gas sector. Currently, these also score highly on the industrial and concentrated ownership scale. The most important factor is not which country the owner comes from; rather, it is that the firm has autonomy, latitude and the opportunity to operate with a long-term perspective.

Longevity (age): Longevity or age of a firm in an open economy is a consequence of the company's ability to adjust to changes. A Mittelstand firm does not think in quarterly or annual report terms, but in generational terms. The traditions and history a long-lived company carries with it can influence strategy, as well as how people work and how they innovate. With the exception of four sectors, the average age of the firms is over 20 years. The exceptions, as expected, were in the newer sectors of data and telecommunications, the service industry, culture and building and construction. The sectors with the highest longevity are: the processing industry with a median age of 39 years, leisure boating at 38 years, mechanical engineering at 32 years and food and tourism and wood processing at 20 and 29 years median age respectively. In the finance sector and the oil and gas sector individual firms of long duration exist that raise the average.

Flat organisational structure: The report drew on other research on the "Norwegian Model" that indicates that firms in Norway are typified by flat structures with short communication lines from the floor to the top and fostering a high degree of involvement by employees. We found flat organisational structures with short distances between the leaders and the floor, short and open lines of communication internally and along the value chain and inclusion of all levels in product and process development. As a result of these initial findings, we included a series of questions related to this factor in the follow-on report that focused specifically on the mechanical industry sector.

Firms are anchored in their local communities: Mittelstand firms are integrated into their local communities. Leadership is often found locally, shares regional values and attitudes and is concerned with the company's role in the local community. The survey indicated that business leaders in Southern Norway believed that the leadership and the employees should all have the same wage increases. In addition, these business leaders, to a greater degree than their Rogaland counterparts, believed that employment should be protected at the expense of firm profit. Leadership in these firms is socially integrated, and a part of the same milieu as the other employees: that the firm is anchored in the local community.

Specialised and high competency: Core competencies were developed internally with an emphasis on high degrees of knowledge and experience-based skills connected to both the products and the processes. The description given aligns with the Mittelstand and Hidden Champions models. Similar descriptions are given by multiple local oil and gas firms in the regional media and on their web pages. Our hypothesis was that there are similar characteristics in other firms in Southern Norway, especially in traditional industries such as wood processing, the mechanical industry, oil and gas and the leisure boat industry. Furthermore, this focus on core competencies underpinned firm success in this branch, and presented one of their biggest challenges to future development in the region.

Engaged workforce: Inclusion and active participation is a strong element in Norwegian corporate culture. Hidle and Normann (2008) provided evidence that leaders in Southern Norway were focused on employee inclusion at all levels, and supported allowing them to give voice to their points of view. The same survey also indicated that leaders in Southern Norway are less likely than in neighbouring Rogaland to believe that employee participation will block the ability to make decisions.

These findings support the assertion that the Norwegian model, based on equality, short distance from the floor to the top, transparency, personal responsibility and a shared, deeply rooted work ethic imbued with a continuous improvement mentality, reflects many of the core socio-cultural aspects that typify Mittelstand firms in Germany. Hidle and Normann's (2008) research found that these types of attitudes and values were more strongly held than in the rest of the country. Southern Norway's business leaders were more open to other cultures, and more willing to change than leaders in Norway as a whole.

Project 2: mechanical engineering in Agder

The second report, *The Mechanical Industry in Agder: Status, Challenges and Proposals for Action*, was commissioned by Southern Norway Kompetansefond and Aust-Agder as a direct result of the findings and implications of the first report. The critically important mechanical industry in the region was potentially under threat. The theoretical underpinnings developed in the *Crisis, Adaptation and Growth* report served as the foundation for carrying out the quantitative and qualitative analyses that resulted in conclusions in three categories: (1) concerning the trends in the industry, (2) concerning the strengths, weaknesses, opportunities and threats the firms face and (3) proposals each for the firms, the branch and for changes in the constraints they face.

Mechanical engineering represents the largest proportion of turnover and employment of the Agder industries. Production of machines and equipment is the largest category of mechanical engineering in Agder, and the firms that comprise this category represent 40.7% of total operating income and 61.2% of the total operating result for category 28 in all of Norway in 2013.

Industry in Southern Norway as a whole has shown positive development over the past 15 years in both value added and export terms. The analysis performed by Agder Research in the project *The Mechanical Industry in Agder: Status, Challenges and Proposals for Action* in 2013 revealed a divergence of results within the mechanical industry. While some firms have had solid growth and returns, often driven by demand from the oil and gas industry, other firms are fighting for survival. In the companies studied, the average operating margin fell from 6.4% in 2006 to 2.8% in 2012. The tougher market crystallised the winners and losers, and the least competitive firms are struggling.

Mechanical engineering in Southern Norway faces extreme competitive pressures, and higher wage and salary costs create added pressure when they are set up against firms from lower cost countries. A relatively strong Norwegian currency position adds even more pressure. From 2002 to 2012 the hourly wage cost in Norway measured in common currency grew by 2.6% per year more than that of Norway's trade partners. This evolution meant that the average hourly wage cost for Norwegian industry was 70% higher than the trade-weighted average of our EU trade partners.

A high degree of dependency by mechanical engineering in Southern Norway on oil related customers makes the sector vulnerable to significant falls in oil prices and the consequent decrease in oil and gas development investments.

In order to engage a relatively broad and representative spectrum of firms across the four industrial codes, we contacted the Lister Alliance (LA) and Sørlandsporten Technology Network (STN) to conduct in-depth, onsite interviews. The interviewees were members of each firm's leadership and the interviews lasted from 1 hour 30 minutes to 3 hours each.

The interviews provide a solid basis from which to extract qualitative information. There are both collective observations and unique experiences that deepen our understanding of the firms and the challenges they face. The report generated five specific recommendations for action that created serious interest from actors in the region. One firm leader went so far as to say that the conclusions and recommendations were akin to a strategy document for his firm.

General overview and characteristics

The sector has several characteristics and trends that typify the firms, the customers and the markets wherein they operate.

The firms involved in this study began primarily as family owned firms. In several cases the same entrepreneur started multiple companies within the same branch, which bore the organisational and cultural imprint of those founders. Like typical German Mittelstand firms, these firms are primarily located in nonurban areas spread throughout Southern Norway. This has important implications for the firm's culture, leadership, skill base and logistics. On the surface, these traits impact these firms in several different ways. The importance of these firms to their communities is greater than it would be in a more populous, urban environment as they are relatively large in terms of local employment and tax revenues. Any loss involving these companies could have a deep impact on both the economies and societies of the surrounding communities. This feeling of local significance and responsibility, expressed by the leadership representatives to whom we spoke, underpins a deeper commitment to the locale than mere profit maximisation or good public relations. In every instance, even the transplanted leaders identified closely with their local community.

The location where the firm originally was established invariably owes as much to the founder's connection to the area (Krugman 1991) as to the availability of skills, raw materials and transport. The desire to succeed in the current location was palpable. The leadership invariably felt a close personal connection to the region and to the workers at the site. In the few cases where significant movement was planned or underway, or where employees needed to be let go, the reticence and even pain at the decisions that had to be made ran deep.

Although the predominant descriptions of the firms' relationships to their communities were positive, many of the firms felt undervalued for their competency and importance by their local communities.

What do firms see as their biggest threats?

Most of those interviewed had a very clear understanding of the characteristics and trends that relate to their firm's development, as well as the ever increasing challenges they face within their industry and from operating from the high-cost Norwegian market. This high level of self-awareness, one could even say hyper-awareness, contributes to the "burning platform" mentality that was clearly evident in almost every interview. In the short and medium term, this sense of urgency appears to fuel a proactive willingness to change products, markets, processes and, less often, organisational forms and has encouraged the development of a strong problem-solving culture. On the downside, as a consequence of this urgency, putting out fires appears to take more energy, focus and resources than is desirable.

The biggest threats identified by the firms in this branch can be categorised into four broad groups. They are: (1) costs, (2) skills, (3) quality and (4) customers. The cost factor in Norwegian production of all types is an underlying theme that is well documented in the international evaluations of the Norwegian market, as well as in concerns expressed from Oslo. The interviews universally and adamantly confirmed this concern within the region. The pay structure and wage trends are so daunting for small businesses in this branch that it limits new job creation and makes production in Norway, despite the qualitative advantages the firms possess, less attractive and profitable. As seen in Figure 13.1, the cost of labour is growing faster than for international competitors. Domestic influences cited for this decrease on returns to labour are fuelled both by the fact that wage growth is outstripping productivity growth, and by the fact that increasingly higher wages are necessary to compete with the regional offshore sector.

This dynamic is one that can be compounded by matters out of the individual firm's control. The primary example was the exchange rate. Only one leader mentioned that they were employing more sophisticated techniques for limiting this exposure, while another contended that their whole off-shoring of production was an effort to capture gains from producing abroad in lower cost markets while selling predominantly to Norwegian customers and securing a stable, strong currency on the income side.

The second threat specified was the availability of skilled labour. This threat goes beyond just the obvious cost aspect of attracting qualified people. Recruiting good candidates to the less urban areas of Southern Norway is a challenge that has proven to be daunting to many of the firms. In addition to finding the right people and getting them to relocate to or stay in the region, there are the further aspects of training and retaining.

The third threat facing firms in the region concerned the durability of the quality advantage. Quality is usually presented in terms of strength, but it is one that is under pressure for the firms in the region. High quality is the

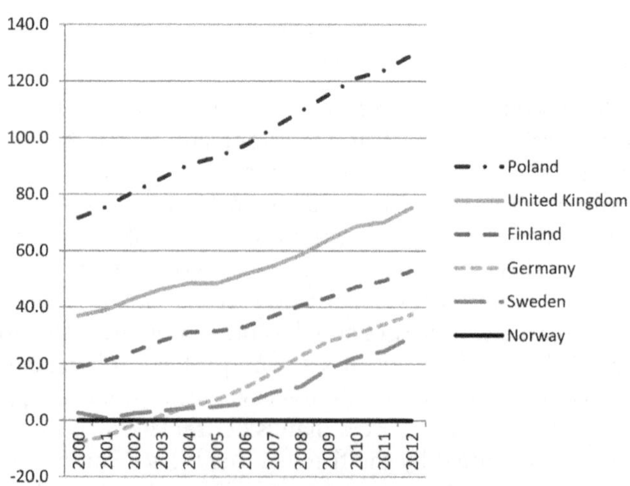

Figure 13.1 Year on year growth in the absolute gap in unit labour costs

Source: Calculations using OECD statistics.

single most cited of the reasons among those interviewed to explain what allows many of the firms to continue to produce in Norway. The threat to this advantage was explained to us on two different levels. On the one level, low cost suppliers from other countries, including China, Turkey and Poland, were unable to consistently meet the quality demands that the local producer had for inputs to their products. This resulted in expensive, time consuming rework and in some cases rejection. Ironically, this leads to the second level threat which involves low-cost producers who are getting too good at what they do. As increasing amounts of work are shipped abroad and local firms train their international suppliers to the appropriate standards, the complex combination of skills, experience, know-how and knowledge that underpins this Mittelstand level of quality is also building up among potential or actual competitors. Some feel that they are sowing the seeds of their own destruction.

The fourth and final threat mentioned consistently has to do with the customers. The threat comes from the reliance on a few large, demanding customers during times of crisis or slow growth. This policy is generally seen as positive, allowing a firm to specialise, meet the evolving needs of their key clients and increase quality. The recent crisis highlighted the potential weakness of this approach: shocks to these customers were passed on to the suppliers in the form of cancelled orders, no new orders or demands for price cuts on existing or new orders. In order to address this weakness, a few firms are trying to expand into complementary markets by developing, for example, onshore products and uses for their offshore products or skills, or vice versa. Developments are tied to existing core competencies within the firm. Almost all the firms are satisfied with their ability to sell to, and meet the needs of, their existing customer base. Quite a number of the leaders we spoke to were less certain about their ability to generate new sales and find new markets. Finally, a couple of the firms we talked to had good bellwether indicators that their orders would increase or decrease. In many cases the timing and scope of the recent crisis was not signalled well in advance to the firms. This lack of information heightened uncertainty during the crisis and impacted their ability to respond or compensate.

Firms' history, ownership and business models

Most of the companies studied began as family owned firms embedded in the region. As such, they appear to be viewed as part of the fabric of the local community. This connection between the owner and the location came up repeatedly. The leaders interviewed were very familiar with the history of the firms they worked for, and had strong, positive feelings about the role that that history played in arriving at their current situation. They knew, or knew the story of, the company's founder(s) and changes in the company's fortunes and direction that resulted from key events or decisions. The clear impression given was that this history was both personal and relevant to the leadership as well as to the workers. The narrative is a part of the collective culture of the factory. The business model is seen as an integral part of the firm's culture and is perceived to have evolved organically out of the firm's history, and in many cases is the result of a few key turning points. The pivotal events mentioned were of three types: (1) there was a change in ownership or generation, (2) there was a significant change in leadership or (3) a bankruptcy occurred. These transitional experiences often served as the impetus for initiating changes in product mix or market focus, or led to organisational changes. The sense was that, even after the most traumatic change, a bankruptcy or near bankruptcy for example, there was continuity that tied today's firms to the people, products and decisions that got them to where they are. In most cases the interviewees maintain that the owners have had and currently have a clear strategy for where they want to go with the company, and share this strategy with the board of directors and the leadership. The strategy has not been one centred on short-term profit maximisation, but rather has focused on product development, process optimisation, personnel development, workplace safety and adaptation to the demands of the market. Significant amounts of capital had to be tied up in order to produce these products and to deliver the relatively meagre margins, and this happened because of owner commitment. The goal is not only successfully producing and selling a good product, but successfully producing that product in the community where the factory is located.

The ownership is concentrated and involved. In a significant number of cases the owner is part of the leadership or is involved on a daily basis in the operation of the firm. Questions and problems between the owner and the leadership, and the leadership and the rest of the facility, could be dealt with either in person or with a phone call. In every case, there seemed to be a very close fit between responsibility, authority and resources. This means that the owners who did keep themselves at a distance delegated the decision-making authority and financial resources to those in the organisation that were responsible to deliver.

Leaders felt that concentrated ownership led to several positive results. Strategy development often involved elements of or all of the leadership and this increased the understanding, acceptance and ownership of the strategy. The support and latitude that the owner gave the leadership in pursuing the chosen strategy was steady and rooted in trust, and this made the job easier. Resources often followed and matched the strategy. The impression given in these interviews was that the firms were decisively led with a significant amount of accountability expected from the leadership.

Organisations were primarily described as flat. Several of the other firms had recently gone through restructurings in order to streamline and decrease hierarchy. There are two dominant types of organising among these producers. The first is set up with roughly three levels. The first level has operators and specialists with a senior or a foreman who also works on the floor. The second level incorporates elements of the leadership and associated support staff, usually engineers and a limited number of sales personnel. Finally, there is a board of directors and owner. The second organisational structure centres on organising around projects. This structure is used when there are few individual production runs that involve elements of design, customisation and support for installation and commissioning. The project is managed from start to finish, and often has significant changes made by the customer underway.

These firms are a product of their historical contexts. The core competencies have developed over time, and involve both high quality, proprietary products or customised methods, solutions or services that can be rigged to meet the customers' needs.

The strategic decisions that helped these companies evolve into their present forms fall into four types: (1) firms limited their product line to focus on fewer products they excelled at producing, (2) firms defined their markets more narrowly, often (but not exclusively) shifting their focus towards offshore parts or support, (3) firms developed a unique mixture of product, support and know-how customised to a few large customers' needs and (4) new firms have been set up, often linked to the original one, designed to develop a related product or service that was beyond the scope of the original company. In practice, these strategies are not mutually exclusive.

What is the role of leadership in firm development?

The different leaders seemed to possess many similar personal qualities and represented a tight grouping of leadership styles. This should not be surprising, given the prevalence of common owners or former owners, similar start-up histories, the similarity in processes and customer demands and the shared culture from which they are drawn. In broad strokes, they seemed decisive, results-oriented and engaged, taking a personal pride in their firm's accomplishments and ability to navigate even tough economic conditions. There was almost no avoidance or blaming behaviour voiced, often noting that "we probably could have been better at . . . " whatever failure or challenge was being discussed. The leaders we spoke to felt they had both the latitude and resources to do their job. They felt accountable not only to the owner, but in most cases to their employees and to the surrounding community. Leadership positions were often filled through internal promotion and a deep understanding of the product, production process and target market was the leading factor in filling positions, instead of formal advanced education. Familiarity with the people, products and process was evident in most of the factory walk-throughs. It was stated repeatedly that the accumulation of this knowledge and the ability to make sound decisions and eventually lead was rooted in a long process of working within the firm or in closely related industry. Another crucial quality many of the firms mentioned, both for leaders and all other employees, was "fit". The ability to fit in and work as part of a team is considered essential to success. Lines of communication are short, and decisions are communicated quickly and clearly.

In almost every factory, there appeared to be a flurry of activity under way in addition to daily production that is in some way driven by leadership's desire not to stand still and simply continue with business as usual, even if that business is going well. This impulse to change could not be successfully translated to the floor, however, without a competent workforce that is willing to learn, modify and implement these programmes.

What are the firms' competitive advantages?

The competitive advantages that the firms discussed varied from firm to firm, market to market and customer to customer. These five elements were brought up repeatedly: (1) quality, (2) flexibility, (3) speed, (4) dependability and (5) service.

Quality is a factor that is often discussed as the reason for Southern Norway's industrial success. What does that encompass? Quality often involves specific or high-spec raw materials that are used in the production process, such as specific grade metals or high end, dependable components. It also involves other factors such as know-how in handling and working with the materials, control of the production process, traceability of errors and testing and provable standards. Each of these topics came up in conjunction with what the firms' viewed as critical advantages for meeting their customers' quality demands.

Flexibility is mentioned as a factor that is critical to the customer and which provides firms with an advantage. Flexibility involves the ability to customise the product to specific customers' needs. In order to meet this ever growing need, a number of the firms have been expanding their design capabilities and ensuring that the engineers, and in some cases workers, stay in contact with the customer. A critical element of this flexibility is the willingness and ability to incorporate changes after production is set in motion, especially in the larger project type situations. Several firms are working hard to upgrade their capabilities and trying to build on their ability to propose alternate/better solutions to the customer before a problem arises or before asked.

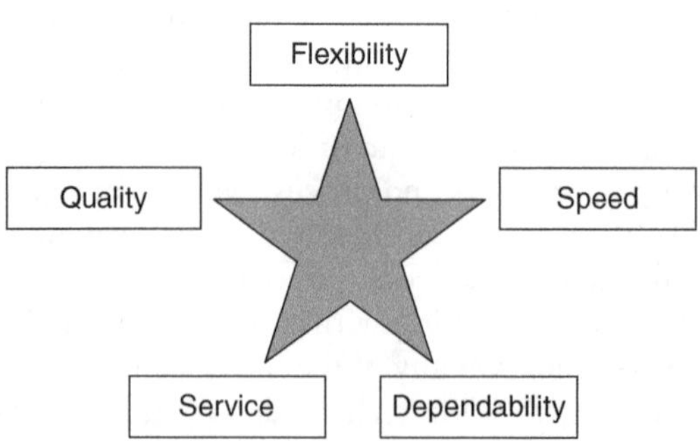

Figure 13.2 Competitive advantages for mechanical engineering firms

Speed primarily centres on the ability to get the product from the factory to the customer in the shortest time possible, or provide support to minimise downtime. As firms focus on becoming lean across their whole supply chains, they do not want large holdups developing because of a lack of inventory and customers are pressed to minimise turnaround time on orders. A number of the products are usually parts of much larger jobs, and may not be ordered until they are needed, or cannot be fully designed until the job reaches a given stage. Once the specs are known, the product must be delivered on time to prevent costly overruns.

Dependability is also one of the characteristics that came up in many of the discussions. Dependability often meant the reputation of the firm to provide a consistently superior product. The products often were not of the highest complexity or state of the art in any discernible way; they were more often robust and fit to a specific need. The production processes were often complex and required unique skill sets. In some cases, this product even bore the mark of the supplier in order to assure end users further up the line. In another vein, dependability meant that they were able to deliver on time and in full. That did not always mean quickly, but it meant on schedule.

The final advantage that came up many times in the interviews can be labelled service. The service discussed here was available all along the interactions with the customer. The goal for a good number of the firms we interviewed was to be a complete provider in the product range. That meant support in design, problem-solving, project management and commissioning and aftermarket maintenance and support.

Recommendations

The challenges uncovered and presented in these two reports must be addressed if the firms are to survive. Many of the firms have durable Mittelstand characteristics. In these strengths, there exists the potential for these firms to survive and grow in the future. There are also inherent weaknesses and threats that must be tackled in order to deal with them in an efficient and adequate manner. As the cost-gap grows and the quality-gap shrinks, the need for radical innovation grows in many regional firms. This requires strategic changes that can have sweeping consequences for the firm's business model and the way in which the firm pursues its development. Weak and falling profitability in many of the firms indicates that significant efforts are required in the near term.

Agder Research generated five actionable proposals that could be pursued by individual firms. The proposals need to be seen in context, and require that the firms develop further, integrate and configure their resources and competencies in a new manner. Because the threat picture is in continuous flux, the proposals are part of a continuous and dynamic process. These five specific proposals fell under the following categories: (1) focused differentiation,

(2) identify profitable niches, (3) develop proprietary brands, (4) optimisation of the production process and (5) enhance competencies.

In addition to these recommendations, the report advised the two existing networks to enter into a closer formal arrangement that would intensify their co-operation and would increase their ability to learn from one another and other successful networks in the region, and to prioritise their goals vis-à-vis the political system.

Is it relevant to apply the concept of Mittelstand to Norwegian companies?

In both reports we were looking at a limited period of time for these companies, and drawing conclusions or making generalisations must take this into account. There is intense financial distress in the markets these actors are dependent upon, and it hit them in two key areas of weakness for Mittelstand firms: their exposure to external capital vagaries because of undercapitalisation, and their exposure to global markets.

Agder Research concluded that many, if not most, of the firms shared clear parallels with the German Mittelstand firms. There are many indications that the Mittelstand model can provide valuable insight into how local firms work, why they succeed and what policies have the greatest chance of having a positive impact. This new approach to the nature of the firms within the "black box" generates measurable variables, testable hypotheses and concrete recommendations for reproducing success, and has generated new research questions that have engaged the interest of local stakeholders. In terms of building a robust or resilient region, the models and the learning they have generated offer guidance to firms that are struggling with falling margins, show a path to evolve from a regional actor to a global market leader and can play a role in helping policy-makers focus on the correct policies to aid in sustainable growth and community well-being. This theoretical framework, centred on the meso and micro socio-cultural characteristics of the region's business and work environments, and built on German Mittelstand research, offers a more relevant, bottom-up approach for the study of businesses in Southern Norway than one finds in the more ubiquitous Anglo-American textbooks.

- Understanding the business model is not limited to the size or finances of the firm.
- These firms have helped imbue the region with the necessary characteristics to make the Agder region resilient.
- It is important to engage the subjects under study in this type of research.

The reports have received widespread exposure within both the regional private and public sectors. A new report on Hidden Champions is now in process and will be presented during 2016.

The next steps in this process are two-fold. The first has already begun with a new round of research and in depth interviews with the Mittelstand firms identified as Hidden Champions. The second is to look more closely at the known weaknesses that threaten Mittelstand firms and to engage other actors relevant to these challenges in the discussion of how to help insulate these firms from their greatest weaknesses while allowing them to exploit their strengths.

The value of applying the Mittelstand concept

These two linked research projects are positive and significant examples of how regional political leadership, firms and research institutes can work together to generate actionable research. The interplay of new generalisable theoretical approaches that provide new perspectives on different levels of analysis and authors new questions, with grounded quantitative data collection, and supplemented with in-depth, structured qualitative input, offers a roadmap for the link between theory and practice. The results of the research have enjoyed wide regional exposure and have raised Agder Research's profile as an active contributor to regional and firm strategic development. The research agenda that has arisen out of these projects is helping to frame the next round of research questions and has the potential to aid in questions about public and private resource allocations, business models, regional and national policies and key transmission lines for economic and social disruption.

There are two primary reasons for including these reports and treating them as a single case within the context of this book. The first is that they provide an example of the importance of understanding the role of applied social sciences to the regional knowledge system. Second, these reports clearly demonstrate the value of using different tools, approaches and levels of analysis at different stages of knowledge accumulation.

The two connected reports discussed in this chapter reflect a relatively seamless example of theoretical development going hand-in-hand with commissioned grounded research and concrete policy proposals. The result is the generation of knowledge on several levels meeting diverse goals. The agenda is ongoing. The reports have proven themselves relevant to policymakers, who have a deeper understanding of the social impact of the industries and their needs, to networks in the industry who are refining their goals and structure and to the firms themselves who have a more specified understanding of their strengths and weaknesses and what these mean for their future competitiveness. Progress is being made both in the effort to generalise the nature of the Mittelstand firm away from a singularly German construct, and in bringing to bear the extensive public policy experience Germany has collected in this realm over the years. In addition, the new questions being asked locally are evolving from mainly economic ones to those concerning the socially embedded nature of business success, its sustainability and the roles and scope of public-private co-operation.

Part IV

Influencing regional social practice

In this part we present projects that have had the intention of influencing regional practice. Of course there is no sharp distinction between understanding, explaining and influencing regional practice, and most chapters in this book have elements of all three. However, some research projects are more defined in terms of change than others.

In Chapter 14: Getting China-ready the case is about supporting a local tourism destination management organisation in southern Norway. In relation to Chinese outbound tourism to the Nordic countries, the argument in the chapter is that commissioned research can be a way to assist the tourism industry into changing the marketing of a region by understanding how to communicate place in symbolically more appropriate ways. Thus the researcher can bridge the knowledge of global tourists' cultural background, taste and preferences in order for the local tourism industry to adapt in relevant ways.

In Chapter 15: Business models for new experiential services the case is the development of an art event centre. The researchers work from a model of service innovation, and try through a process to adjust and implement this model in practice.

In Chapter 16: Commitment to sustainability in Agder the case is about an initiative to increase CSR (corporate social responsibility) awareness among industry at Agder. The chapter argues that the research project has contributed to development of more CSR awareness and initiatives at Agder.

In Chapter 17: Universities' external relations the case is some research done in relation to the development of the TTO offices at the university. The research in this case tried to investigate into how employees at the university regraded external engagement. The research project found that the new regional university was about to adopt the same institutional pattern that are found in an older university, thus limiting the possibility for this new university to represent new collaborative forms.

14 Getting China-ready

Sarah Holst Kjær

Adopting a new perspective in tourism

Marketing a regional tourism destination to different groups of global travellers can be viewed as an act of diplomacy. One needs to target and narrate certain local signs, symbols and metaphors, while avoiding others. Choosing one's marketing story means understanding how the presentation is received by members of other cultures. Tourism marketing is not only crucial to the tourism industry itself, but spills over into how other sectors located at the destination will be perceived by foreigners. Thus, tourism marketing of a destination needs to be targeted in culturally relevant ways, in order to appeal to the nationalities one wants to attract. Not only pleasure-tourists but also technical visitors such as workforces, business investors or business owners obtain tourism information when choosing one region over another for their outbound engagements. Since destination management organisations (DMOs), also named 'visit-organisations', produce marketing and branding campaigns targeted to different tourist groups, they can be regarded as important key players in the symbolic production of a region.

In this chapter I discuss the touristic processes of southern Norway to attract a new and growing market of the upper-middle class Chinese outbound, business and leisure, traveller. Norwegian destination adaptation and tourism marketing as the symbolic production of a region is to present and discuss how ethnographic research and knowledge, obtained by the study on different consumer segments, in this case Chinese visitors' cultural and social background, can support the development of a regional tourism industry. 'Tourism' is mainly an instrument for two things: a developmental tool for rural regions to become self-sufficient, whenever there is a possibility for residents not to be able to become part of the 'ordinary' workforce. In addition, tourism is a tool for a nation to brand and market its export products on a global market.

The region of southern Norway is not dense with cultural and natural heritage sights compared to, for example, Southern-European destinations. Still, it has natural, farm, 'food-secure' and environmental features; some urban heritage areas and sporadic experience-arranged attractions and sights which can be viewed as quite attractive in a more and more polluted world, especially the Chinese. The region can be viewed as a countryside region. Thus, based on nature, ocean, beach, mountain, farm and village-related places which, at the time of the investigation, were not fully planned and arranged as attractions to tourists in general and Chinese visitors in particular. Tourism destination management was thus important to strategically 'fill in the gaps' of roads, places, sceneries and tourist attractions in a way which would be considered interesting to the nationalities the region wanted to attract and collaborate with. But how could southern Norway work to become China-ready? What would the purpose for this region be and what needed to be done in order to create relevant tourism marketing and destination adaptation?

At the time of the investigation, it was estimated that China produced one third of the world's goods (Nolan 2012). To an extent, this left Europe out-sourced, and with a need to develop new strategies on earning more on leisure and tourism activities. The approach of the European Union has thus been to focus on the development of recreational instead of productive space. Tourism-scapes, presenting greenness, sustainability, cultural and post-industrial heritage and regional tradition have in general been a way to identify 'Old Europe' as responsible and with a sustainable profile. The goal of attracting visitors from far-away places is the result of globalisation. Europe has become dependent on handling this new position. Even the smallest acts of understanding the visitor, or having local-global intercultural competence, can be regarded as effective when approaching a large outbound travel market such as the Chinese (Kjær 2015).

The research case presented focuses on how to mature a destination in the Nordic rural region, in order to make the right decisions on whether or not to adapt to a Chinese market. Through the collaborative work of different DMOs in southern Scandinavia, I will especially focus on how the Norwegian marketing processes were supposed to be informed by empirically founded cultural information on Chinese preferences, tastes and habits. The goal of the investigations was to provide regional tourism marketing with cultural understandings in order to adapt the Nordic destination into the preferences of a possible future Chinese outbound travel market.

Idealistically speaking, destination marketing is a result of destination management. This means that marketing and destination adaptation – the practice of turning local resources into customised and targeted experience-products – should be closely connected. This chapter, though, will not discuss the implementation of Chinese consumer knowledge to the field of local tourism practice. I focus on the process of collecting cultural information of a future travel group, understanding how the local tourism and non-tourism industry perceived working towards a new market, and evaluating how one could instrument the cultural knowledge on Chinese outbound tourism into a customised narrative and brand of the Nordic rural countryside.

It is possible for a destination to have many, and possibly also conflicting, symbolic narratives in order to facilitate different markets. It is related to great financial risk to develop, adapt and market a destination for future groups of tourists, instead of focusing on the groups already tailored for. Therefore, the local society must support the decision of approaching new markets, by viewing itself as a strategic part of the destination narrative. Tapping into the potential of communicating in relevant ways with new groups of labour, investors and business owners, needs to be viewed as the actual reason for destination marketing. As an instrument for business to business-to-business relations, destination adaptation to certain nationalities can therefore be regarded as an important act of diplomacy.

I want to move the focus from 'just' discussing how a region can work to attract more visitors in order for the tourism industry to become better at creating a profit. Instead, I want to investigate the tourism industry as an instrument for marketing a destination. The branding of a region can be understood as a way to create a symbolic narrative which, strategically, is meant to support the region aiming at creating new markets.

Developing understanding of Chinese tourism

The case in this chapter consists of two research-projects, namely:

1. An interregional research project named Chinavia II (2013–2014), funded by the European Union's regional development fund. In this project I conducted ethnographic research, investigating Chinese visitors and their perceptions of southern Scandinavia, especially southern Norway.
2. An experimental business-innovation project named VRI-Chinavia (2013), supported by The Research Council of Norway. Here, management from different local tourism and non-tourism businesses which, for different reasons, could have an interest in approaching the Chinese outbound travel market, were interviewed. Business areas ranged from commercial and non-commercial experience attractions to larger oil companies, metal factories and members of the chamber of commerce.

Both research projects were commissioned by the local DMO, Visit Southern Norway. A DMO is not supposed to act like an organisation with its own goals, as its job is to serve the tourism industry. Still, as the Danish tourism researcher Matias Thuen Jørgensen (2012) explains, a DMO is also measured against the number of tourists it can actually attract through its international marketing campaigns. Hence, as project owners, the DMO was not only responsible for the marketing of its private business-members' experience-products and the public investors' regions, cities and towns. It was also responsible for providing its members with relevant and educational information on current market conditions and trends. Collaborating on these types of research projects was a way for the industry to get research financed and have research-based knowledge applied in the field of practice.

A DMO needs to inform their usual stakeholders, the local tourism industry and the public decision makers, of the possibilities of a new market situation in Nordic regional tourism: To aim at a global travel and tourism segment like the Chinese, rather than working towards the neighbouring markets, as the industry mainly did at the time, meant professionalising all parts of the industry with intercultural competences and cultural consumer and lifestyle knowledge. By doing this, the goal was to be more qualified in matching and adapting the region's existing experience-products to a new consumer group.

The visit-organisation wanted to understand in what way and whether or not to approach the Chinese outbound travel market. How 'China-ready' was the region of southern Norway to approach this market? Were local companies ready to adapt and invest? In addition, it was important to find out whether or not Chinese outbound travellers, either pleasure- or business-seeking, would find any appealing features about the region. Would there be possible affinities so strong that Chinese travellers actually would create significant travel-traffic to the destination?

Approaching a new and foreign market is associated with high-risk investments. It is also expensive to do the necessary research in order to qualify one's decisions. Furthermore, it is difficult to tell where capital will go next, and how capital will find its new sources of profit (Thrift 2008). The regional tourism industry was presented, by me and my two collaborative Chinese researchers, whom I subcontracted for the project, with the idea that if a destination attracted a little percentage of the Chinese outbound travellers, the impact could be significant, as the market would continue to grow. Chinese outbound travel was well above the general global increase in total tourism numbers. Still, on a firm-level, the destination needed to do an 'inventory' of its experience-production and resources in order to analyse whether it would be worthwhile adapting the industry to fit the needs of Chinese consumers. Many of the local tourism businesses were small-scale and would not have the capacity to serve large number of tourists. This meant that they needed to facilitate in other ways: by scaling up prices, creating relevance or collaborating with others or providing different products in a joint experience-package chain. In order to reduce investments, the travel packages should be based on already existing experience products. But they needed to be reassembled, re-narrated and re-packaged in a targeted way, adapting the destination to its possibly future leisure consumers.

According to the World Tourism Organisation, by 2020 there will be over 100 million Chinese outbound tourists. This will account for over 6% of the world's travellers, making China an important market to tap into (Petersen 2009). In 2013, Visit Norway counted in 97,000 Chinese bed-nights in Norway. In 2008 this number was only half the size. Similarly, Visit Denmark counted in 2013 151,749 Chinese bed-nights in Denmark and had furthermore the ambition to increase the number of bed-nights to 175,000 in 2015 by moving Chinese tourists away from the capital and into the Danish countryside. Statistics show that the new Chinese middle class was on the rise, referring to the year 2010 where Europe received close to 3.8 million Chinese visitors and the year 2012 where 80 million Chinese people visited destinations around the world. This made Chinese outbound visitors the global travel industry's number one growth-segment (Kjær 2015).

Hence, the argumentation of why it was important to work towards the Chinese market, create targeted marketing material, support the brand-process by 'excavating' the destination potential and apply new Nordic metaphors and ultimately adapting the tourism industry, was primarily economic. It was the assumption that the rapid development and huge potential of a Chinese source market eventually would be felt in regional Scandinavian travel destinations. If the region wanted to be part of that 'first wave' of Chinese leisure and business visits, a targeted and strategic approach was needed. Understanding the Chinese travel motivations, habits, customs and lifestyle-ideals meant understanding how to provide for the Chinese cultural ways and getting the local tourism business ready to facilitate their tastes and preferences.

The commissioning of the project meant that the research problem, methods and target groups were fixed. The commissioned research aimed at establishing a firm knowledge base of the Chinese outbound travel market by interviewing Chinese visitors about their opinions of the southern Norway region. The aim was to identify a regional experience-product potential – what kind of countryside experience and leisure products did the Chinese middle class travel consumer want in southern Norway? Thus, the research aim was to carry out an analysis of the regional potential and through this, provide strategic recommendations for future China efforts in the region.

New research questions would arise from the process of investigating the approach to the Chinese outbound travel market. Based on ethnographically collected observations and interviews both from Chinese and Norwegian informants and, in addition, providing Visit Southern Norway with previous study on Norwegian and Chinese habits, preferences, tastes and symbolic understandings in order to form this knowledge base, different kinds of suggestions linked to inter-cultural relationships would emerge.

We found that 'the Nordic model' – the organisation of everyday family-life, democracy and consensus – corresponded with Chinese ideals of harmony and balance. We put the Chinese approaches of travelling in Norway into a general inventory. This list was meant to avoid dislikes and convert likes into experience-product suggestions, matching accommodation, food and drink, culture heritage sites, points of interests, educational elements and even the 'most-enjoyed' organisation of attraction sights which had been perceived as appealing to the Chinese travellers. The overall emotional strategy when doing destination adaptation – selecting experience-products over others – was to create the least possible tension and maximise comfort and security by suggesting suitable and correct tourism information and experience-products, using understandable metaphors, signs and symbols.

What was found the most suited and attractive experiential features in the local geography, and in order to fit this particular local-global encounter, were approached in the collected qualitative material and investigated through culture analytical theories originating from trend-studies and consumer behaviour studies. Analysis of social and individual emotions such as sharing, loyalty, comfort, security and affinity were also highly important perspectives, because many tourists travel for existential purposes. In addition, an understanding of Chinese presuppositions such as cultural imaginations about and practices of being in the Nordic landscape were investigated. The Chinese perception of access to information about cultural heritage sights, restaurants' food offers, availability of public transportation and shopping and souvenir-offerings were also analysed in a total-experience perspective.

Knowing what is 'suitable' meant interviewing and doing participant observation in order to understand how the Chinese visitors associated from the unfamiliar to the familiar and vice versa. Thus, collecting, mapping and analysing the attitudes of and opinions on southern Norway, the Chinese informants provided us with the research-based suggestions on how to market southern Norway, as a part of one transgressing experience package product using metaphors of 'the North' (the Nordic region). Attempting to leave aside all self-perceptions of southern Norway which, from a domestic market viewpoint, was perceived as a sunny destination, the North as a cold and unapproachable place was in many ways the Chinese outbound travel market's only reference.

In the context of the Northern countries' capacity to become attractive in a global tourism market, competing with other nations and making travellers stay longer, what needed to be developed was the rural and regional countryside outside of the larger Nordic capitals. 'Filling in the dots' between capitals meant creating a nation-crossing, experience package-tour with supporting marketing material which promoted the Nordic countries as one single experience-product. This product, aimed at the Chinese urban upper-middle class – a money-strong consumer group who had the means to travel to far-away and exotic destinations like the Nordic region – were familiar with the collective metaphor of 'the North', because this metaphor was their own. In a regional perspective, being part of the North seemed perhaps excessive, but the Chinese were used to grandeur and super-size and part of their travel habits involved including as many meaning-making experiences and countries in one trip as possible (Bui, Wilkins & Lee 2013). In the project, 'the North' therefore not only signified a natural (and cold) territory stretching to the cape of the north to the cape of the south in Norway and even further down south to Denmark and with Greenland to the west and Finland to the east. It also defined the attempt to produce a global marketing brand which sold a destination through the Chinese's preconceptions and place mythologies.

As a result, a marketing approach, namely creating a campaign or Chinese symbolic narrative of the North, was part of the output. Advice on how this narrative should inform the local tourism industry into adapting the region's experience-products, services and attractions to match the Chinese visitor was given back to the industry in a research report. Suggestions on travel packages experiences which corresponded with the Chinese positive preconceptions of and affinities about the Nordic region, presentations and scientific publications were also the result of the research.

Research methods

In an applied market-ethnography like this, the project owner Visit Sørlandet outlined how the research should focus on interviewing Chinese visitors and members of the local tourism and non-tourism industries. The questions were fixed: how could the destination adapt to, develop marketing strategies and define a new market direction? The public good could benefit from the research findings, but to begin with they were part of a decision-making process on whether or not to make regional investments and collaborations.

We thus investigated the 'regional potential' by qualitative ethnographic methods, both by interviewing Chinese visitors about their opinions and attitudes towards the local tourism industry and by doing participant observation, following the natural logic of travelling: How was the Chinese visitor guided to different attractions? How were places, services and experiences communicated? Focusing on a total experience, from leaving home to returning home again, the entire journey should, at its best, be well-designed, thought-through and themed as a learning opportunity, as 'a grand tour'.

We 'hung out' as tourists would do, doing participant observation and looking for ways to adjust the experience at a place in order to fit the ideals of a Chinese total experience: having a busy schedule with access to the right kind of food, transport and experiences and preferably doing more countries in one journey. In our ethnographic participant observations at 18 tourism establishments, ranging from hotels, restaurants, shopping streets, heritage museums, theme parks and public recreation areas an experience test tour included general and specific knowledge on Chinese outbound travelling.

Our ethnographic research team, consisting of Chinese and non-Chinese researchers, speaking and not speaking Mandarin, did an experience test tour which, to some extent, also included interviewing management at the tourism attractions. What was the 'regional potential of approaching the Chinese market' when viewed on a firm-level?

We also interviewed non-tourism actors. The region had business-to-business contact with the Chinese employees, students and investors. We wanted to ask how the adaptation and marketing of the region could facilitate the region's business-to-business and intercultural encounters. Hence, the regional non-touristic Norwegian-Chinese companies who employed Chinese, or were owned by Chinese investors, were invited in, but seemed reluctant to communicate our call for interview participants. Mostly our requests went through the businesses' human resource departments and here one did not want to cause any displeasure to the owners or employees. For validity purposes, though, it is not unusual in ethnographic trend-studies like this, to have a small number of 'early birds', or first comers, to 'predict' and locate future trends. The small number of informants corresponded with the novelty of Chinese tourism in southern Norway, and in Norway in general.

Sixteen Chinese visitors were identified, and they were group-interviewed in 2013 in Mandarin and English language. The informants were presented with touristic pictures of different countryside experiences, e.g. visiting cultural history museums, doing nature-based activities; coastal, farm, mountain and cabin-life, self-drive and camping in the countryside. They were also shown photos of food dishes, festivals and shopping. They were invited to freely elaborate and associate about their own experiences, the (lack of) accessibility to and information about the places and their likes and dislikes.

It became clear that urban well-educated informants, such as biologists, engineers, web-designers, experts within mechatronics and philosophers, could inform the industry with creative insight. Their position as visitors and employees staying in southern Norway at the time of the interview, illustrated the idea that misplacement can be an innovative and co-creative resource. The informants were able to transfer knowledge from other places when they discussed the region as a destination and they drew upon a Chinese upper middle class imagination of a good lifestyle: what would a suitable work-life balance look like and how could family and individual leisure life be defined in an ideal world? In this regard, the Chinese visitors were unique sources of expertise, providing global consumer experience of the regional tourism and leisure realities.

The Chinese informants had two to seven years of experience with living in Norway. From the interviews, we wanted a clearer definition of the mythical metaphor of the North. How could the metaphor be transformed into corresponding experience-products? The question was, whether Norwegian countryside-sensations such as peace and quiet, contemplation, purity, freshness, cleanliness and a health-, food- and activity-based lifestyle would be something of a natural liking, or affinity, to the Chinese, urban, well-educated, experienced, but possibly also busy and knowledge-desiring Chinese. In relation to the capacity of the regional tourism industry, we also wanted to know about the Chinese preferences for travelling alone, in pairs as friends, in smaller inter-generational family groups or larger groups.

When interviewing these well-educated visitors in southern Norway they were leisure consumers who offered co-creative ideas for new products in the regional tourism industry. The Chinese visitors provided great insight into how leisure interactions could improve or change. The impact of ethnological identity-markers: lifestyle; habits, routines, age, gender and (ethnic) culture, and how these affected leisure experiences and consumer needs, was important to the industry. This qualitative information could enrich the work routines and organisational structure in the local tourism businesses and ultimately, the interviews could help clarify what kind of emerging trends the destination would have to take into consideration in order to approach the Chinese market (Mariampolski 2006).

Applying previous research

In a touristic perspective, the work and life of a region is considered balanced when service-jobs, for example found in the tourism industry, support the needs of the upper-middle class workforce in high-skilled positions. What has often been theorised thus is how the tourism and experience industry can develop the status and reputation of a destination. In order to improve a place, tourism development has thus, in a regional context, been viewed as effective when creating a strong symbolic status of a destination. Tourism thus has often been instrumentalised to improve the 'soft' everyday leisure and culture activities of a region, while, at the same time, being a way to create a livelihood for small- and medium-sized businesses. This has in addition been the goal in many regional developmental strategies during the last decade all over Europe (Aronsson 2007; Löfgren 2001).

What has not been fully realised, though, is how regional tourism is not only an industry in itself, but also a cross-sector activity. This means that tourism can be viewed as a way to create intercultural competences in local-global encounters and, across nations, smooth cultural relationships in both tourism and non-tourism business-to-business affairs.

In a late-capitalist global world, people, investments and business ownerships move. This makes it even more important for a region to use touristic marketing and branding in order to present oneself in relevant and attractive ways in order to promote new investments (Ren & Ooi 2013). A region's instrument to handle local-global business-to-business relations and establishing a productive intercultural encounter can thus work through the tourism industry's practices of destination marketing and destination adaptation.

In a new global world order, things can easily be perceived as out of order and people as misplaced. In fact, 'globalisation' – ideally defined as free flow of information, things, people and services – turns many (late) modern ways of organising tourism upside down. Norwegian-Chinese relations are only at starting point and it is still a little strange to find a Chinese temple hotel in the Swedish countryside, in Älvkarleby. Still, it is now (almost) standard, that Scandinavian ethnologists interpret the Others' specific cultural semiotics as self-evident ways of understanding the We. It is also becoming even more ordinary to decipher local knowledge, far-away from home, in order to perform better in outbound business relations (Kristoffersen 2008).

From previous studies on Chinese outbound travel patterns and consumer preferences we learned how other nations already had adapted their tourism industry. Thus the regional tourism industry's (non-existing) 'China-efforts' were analysed in relation to the already established Chinese travel market in New Zeeland and Australia. What could we learn from these Western destinations? These countries were popular because of their proximity to China, but we were also able to learn from these countries because of a (to Norway) similar natural landscape with plentiful of nature-based attractions. New Zeeland and Australia had a warmer climate and more inexpensive accommodation and service-offerings, though (Pan & Laws 2003; Yu & Weiler 2001).

The research team looked for comparative research at destinations where Chinese outbound travellers already had previous experiences, and possibly also had developed different preferences they would compare the Nordic region with. Consequently, the assumption was that after having explored China's neighbouring Western countries and the cultural heritage sights of European (and the Nordic) capitals, eventually, the Chinese traveller, and his or her family, would want to experience the tranquillity of small rural villages, coast-, cabin- and country-life. At least, this was the travel-pattern we found in previous research (see e.g. Yu & Weiler 2001).

In a late-modern marketing and branding perspective, the cross-national experience-package tours were stylised through personalised and descriptive storytelling. Even Chinese non-academic literature was consulted, since it could correspond with a Chinese 'coming of age' story which corresponded with the Chinese traveller's documented desire for the individualistic, educational and existential features, 'the grand tour', which also had made self-drive tourism amongst Chinese travellers very popular. Thus, the suggested marketing material could imitate a small piece of grand tour travel literature organised through self-drive on 'a road less travelled' where notions of freedom, choice of nature-based activities and culture-heritage learning were promoted. In order to frame the marketing campaign in a Chinese relevant way, *Journey to the North* was chosen by the Chinese speaking part of the research team. The campaign's name was meant to refer to the Chinese imaginations of a Nordic region by associating to an extremely famous novel, and on the Chinese school curriculum, *Journey to the West* from the 16th century Ming Dynasty, credited the author Wu Cheng'en.

Because this was a study on a possible future market, we followed the definition of a 'trend' which means tendency, something about the future and tomorrow which has been 'planted, moulded and nurtured' by what is happening in the present. The American trend-analysts Janine Lopiano-Misdom and Joanne De Luca (1997, p. xi) remind us that:

> There are no crystal balls or big secrets to unfold. To get there: to be ready for the big explosion of tomorrow, we just need to look at what is brewing today in the progressive micro-cultures . . . – those thinkers and doers who move in individual mind-set.

Thus, the few numbers of Chinese travellers we interviewed can be understood as first-movers. As representatives of a future trend, their behaviours and attitudes were relevant on at least two levels for the regional tourism industry. They were co-creators evaluating their experiences with, adapting and improving the touristic products, attractions and destinations, and, as first-mover marketers, making the Chinese informants aware of the destination and by this stimulating their (possible) social media habits of posting exotic and far-away experiences of the North, could also provide the region with valuable word-of-mouth destination marketing.

The theoretical perspectives in the project informed the research process in circular ways. We needed to know about Chinese travel-patterns, cultural assumptions and leisure preferences in order to do the interviews. But we also needed to modify theory obtained from other destinations and context in order to understand the Nordic conditions. In this process, tourism as an intercultural encounter also means studying oneself.

Previous ethnological and anthropological research on what it means to conduct tourism business, being part of Norwegian identity, customs and habits and providing the 'best' of the available resources also needed to be included in a intercultural encounter perspective.

The locals meeting the visitors, and vice versa, can expose 'us' as much as it exposes 'them'. An intercultural encounter can be defined as a way to describe the conflicts which sometimes occur when the visitors' manners and ways are understood as strange and demanding by the locals. In contrast, the visitors, as in this case often well-off and metropolitan, can view the locals as simple-minded, not having an educated sense of quality, taste and correct (class and nationality informed) behaviour (Löfgren 1999). The relational structures in an intercultural encounter can hence result in numerous local-global hinders to perform regional tourism business well.

Results

To even get to the point of experiencing regional attractions in a satisfactory way, there were a great number of barriers which needed to be overcome. The Chinese visitors' experience of southern Norway resulted in many requests regarding guidance through tourism information, marketing, service and attraction sight design. In addition, the infrastructural situation – completing a full journey through friction free public transport, checking in and out of hotels, restaurants and locating activities – was difficult.

What in general is viewed as 'normal', namely that destinations are 'home-blind' or perform poorly when it comes to viewing themselves from an exoteric perspective, was even more problematic when perceived from a nationality speaking a completely different language and not having any preliminary cultural reference-points. Our empirical investigations of 'the Chinese experience of southern Norway' made us able to define two different sets of contesting sensibilities: southern Norway was perceived as the most boring, cold and unsophisticated place they had ever experienced, and southern Norway was considered the purest, cleanest and most balanced place they had ever seen. In the following discussion I will analyse these and other utterances and opinions originating from the Chinese interview-material.

In addition, we interviewed local tourism- and non-tourism actors in order to see how 'China-ready' the region was, or wanted to be. Here I will give some rich empirical examples of how the local-global encounter was evaluated from a southern Norwegian perspective. In an interview with the head of tourism destination management in the Norwegian town of Arendal, the manager defined some reasons why planning and organising a business-to-business relationship between Norway and China would be important. There was already regional potential for actually taking the intercultural relationships seriously, she argued:

> We have, to the best of my knowledge, no Chinese tourists arriving. We have never had a request for guiding, and we do not have any tourism-information written in Mandarin. There are, as far as I know, no local tour operators working towards the Chinese market. The county council has not been focusing on this market, but it might happen in the future since several companies located in the region – e.g. National Oil Well, Aker Pusnes/MacGregor, Teamtec – either are owned by, or have very close business relations with, Chinese industries.
>
> (interview, M. Lunøe Rand, 17 May 2014)

The head of tourism destination management thus viewed the future visitors in the perspective of already established business-relations. Norwegian-Chinese affairs were thus not just working on a touristic level, but could also affect the non-touristic industry.

Aiming at the Chinese market might be viewed on a larger scale. As an official way to perform culture and business exchange, the manager of the Kristiansand Chamber of Commerce and responsible for international business explained:

> At the moment the chamber of commerce does not give China a particular focus, but I plan to make it a theme in the nearest future. There are quite a lot of relations in the region. Technological companies, sport chains, graphic companies: some have Chinese owners. I thought we were too different to establish business-relations and the opposite has happened: the Chinese have done massive investments here. China is also beginning to become a high-cost country. Those, who succeed in China, know a lot about China. Trust is very important. In my work we try to attract high-competence migrant workers: technical visitors, especially within the oil and gas sector. The Chinese company owners

> a very interested in the local business life in general and of how to transfer knowledge and competences from here to China in order to do various construction projects. Many of the companies are world-wide businesses, so things are not so peaceful and quiet as it might seem. We have a lot to offer the businesses in terms of leisure-activities, but it is a challenge to communicate our assets. The biggest challenge in recruiting and keeping a foreign workforce is 'draw back': the spouse doesn't get a job and wants to go home. People with a high education are often married to people with a high education and here there are not perhaps matching opportunities for both. The regional tourism strategy to work towards the segment of families and children is great for the industry, we think. We have to see to that family-life works in every aspect. Migrant workers do not just go home at night: they need something more. If I could decide, I think that all businesses should create leisure and culture programmes and experience packages for their visitors. This material would be useful, when we recruit future Chinese employees: before accepting the job, they would know what the family could do in its spare-time. At the local high-school the youngsters for instance take Chinese lessons. This is because their parents work in an international environment or because the young people themselves see that the Chinese market is interesting. We should also teach Chinese from an earlier stage, I think.
>
> (interview, O. P. Sunde, 14 June 2014)

Tourism business owners from the regional tourism industry were, as earlier mentioned, also interviewed. Based on the industry's limited experience with this particular market, we learned that the regional countryside could and should not compete with the experiences the Chinese already had at home. A local theme park owner said:

> Have you travelled in China and have you visited all their magnificent sights, you will know that nothing in Scandinavia can compete with this. In this sense we are monkeys in the West. Manhattan is nothing! We cannot impress them with our cultural sights, factories, fine buildings or road constructions: they already have that on a much more sophisticated scale. But! They are not after, what they already have: they want something new.
>
> (interview, V. Hansson, 11 January 2014)

'Being proud' of what a Norwegian tourism establishment could offer, was an initial condition for the industry to perform experience-adaptation to the Chinese market. The Nordic countries should not, as the theme park owner explained, compete with what the Chinese already had but instead offer something new. In his mind, the Chinese market was a great business opportunity which could be exploited. The theme park owner continued:

> If there is one group of tourists which is really important to customise for, it is the Chinese. Really! . . . We had the Chinese ambassador visiting our business and had set the table for 50 guests inside the mountain here. We served plenty of fish and seafood and had planted 'friendship-trees' and lilies everywhere. It was all very beautiful and we were very pleased serving our guests. We tried to get to local newspaper to cover the event, but they were not interested. We posted a little on Facebook but could have had a lot more out of it, media-wise.
>
> (interview, V. Hansson, 3 January 2014)

When it came to the Chinese outbound travelling, the regional attractions had almost no clear overview or consumer behaviour knowledge on how to approach the market. The industry presented some ways of coping, though, wanted to give 'the best' of what it could offer.

A café owner at a nature-heritage park in the town of Kristiansand explained:

> We once had a gigantic travel group from a cruise ship visiting our café. There was a queue as long as I don't know. The concept was that each passenger was going to have a freshly baked waffle and we baked and baked. I think we only priced the waffle 10 NOK to the travel company and we earned nothing compared to the work load, because we wanted everything to be made by hand and served fresh. This was just too much of a pressure on our capacity and probably it wasn't much fun for the Chinese tourists waiting in line either!
>
> (interview, F. M. Moe, 6 January 2014)

The adaptation of regional tourism experiences must consist of an appropriate level of relevance: meaning and information, aimed at the Chinese market. Besides the interviews with the Chinese visitors and the ethnographically designed experience test tour, the local tourism businesses had almost no Chinese consumers to test the industry's performances up against. The research linked local tourism and non-tourism businesses together, testing regional boundaries and different interests. It was evident from the interviews that tourism and non-tourism actors in the region shared the common goal of working towards understanding the Chinese as an employee, leisure consumer and business owner. In order to do this, it is important to understand that modern Chinese (business) culture is about establishing relationships, both by socialising and negotiating business transactions. Understanding the cultural value of building a relationship through tourism can be very important in a Norwegian-Chinese relationship.

Destination adaptation and intercultural encounters

So how could, or should, the region of southern Norway strategically and practically put itself on 'the Chinese map'? What was the main argument for communicating with a new Chinese market and how can we understand local tourism and non-tourism actors' reasoning about (not) making the region China-ready?

First of all, Chinese social and emotional customs, rituals and habits need to be transformed into actual ways of conducting the touristic encounter, also understanding that the Norwegian ideals of social balance and consensus will meet a much more hierarchical way of organising: being inside or outside, the social fabric. Handling relationships in ceremonial ways and as ritualistic important, being proud of what one can offer, is, to start with, very important in both regional tourism and non-tourism business transactions (Kristoffersen 2008).

Part of the economic argumentation was developed by interviewing both tourism and non-tourism actors on how Norwegian-Chinese relations could benefit from a targeted, experience-product place-brand of the North. Hence, the goal was to discuss how destination adaptation, aimed at Chinese consumers, could improve the intercultural encounters which the region already, on different levels, participated in. Through an applied cultural analysis of the Chinese travellers, their class-based cultural values, social norms, habits, routines and aesthetical preferences, destination adaptation would not only be more qualified, this knowledge could in general also be useful to all regional actors engaged in local-global affairs. Tourism development – destination adaptation and destination marketing – was a way to promote the region to foreign business partners, investors, owners and employees. In this sense, the non-touristic industry depended on tourism marketing and developmental strategies in order to become attractive in a global market competition.

'Destination adaptation' can be defined as an understanding of both the cultural and natural means of matching and managing resources in relation to the tourism business' life cycle, handling rejuvenation, maturity or decline. The English tourism management researcher John Swarbrooke (2000, p. 218) argues that, in other words, adaptation is:

> about attractions using the resources and variables they control (for example the organisation and the product) in such a way that they achieve their goals and objectives. It is all about exploiting opportunities and neutralising threats . . . this means being proactive and dynamic.

Returning to the theme park owner, was he a future trendsetter within regional destination adaptation? Was he producing tourism products, using the resources and market knowledge he had, aiming at a new market in relevant ways? In many ways the event he had created, serving a seafood dinner inside the mountain to the ambassador, was a celebration and a spectacular marketing event, at least, and hopefully, in the Chinese media. Consulting marketing-theories he did things right: he served a celebrity, a popular ambassador, which is a very useful way to get media-attention. He furthermore matched the Chinese likings of freshly cooked seafood with easily available local resources, and he posted the event on social media, but more could have been done, he stated.

The theme park owner had differentiated his experience-product and had customised it but was he China-ready? Creating these specialties, could he keep up if a flow of visitors, unexpectedly, started to show? What about the other experiences he provided at the theme park: did they support this customised event? In case of a second visit, had he aimed at accumulating data on consumer opinions and behaviours, in order to improve the experience?

At least, he had learned something about the region's participation in a value-chain: the local newspaper was disinterested in covering the event. In addition, in order to destination adapt, a tourism business also needs to make an inventory of its existing experience-products and resources examining how easy or difficult, inexpensive or costly, it will be to target the taste of the Chinese consumers. The next step will be convincing the rest about the destination: travel companies; tourism marketers and media; hotels; transport; restaurants, need to support the effort of the individual business.

The Norwegian café owner found the opportunity to serve waffles which are sweet cakes shaped as a heart, baked on pancake dough and served with brown cheese, strawberry jam and sometimes white sugar. The heart-shaped waffle can be understood as an esoteric symbol of Norwegian cultural and social emotions: it connotes the transaction of familiarity and work as a sign of something Norwegians are very proud of, namely the social reciprocal system where guests, when eating the waffle, are invited to become an equal part of the social fabric. One will find the waffle dish at every social opportunity in Norwegian society: when ending the work week on a Friday in the canteen; when celebrating Saturday at the sports club or at the church bazaar or when shopping in main street. One can thus be sure to be served a waffle when celebrating everything from national holidays to children's birthdays parties (Døving 2003). By this service the café owner invited the Chinese visitors to celebrate the togetherness of Norwegian society. Hence, by this cultural act, he wanted to provide a great service and give the best a Norwegian could think of.

Nothing was wrong with this business transaction when considered in the context of Norwegian identity-making and everyday life 'household-gifts' transactions. In an intercultural encounter, however, the wheat-based dessert was unfortunately not very attractive to Chinese consumers. From the interviews with the Chinese visitors we discussed the food available in regional attractions. One female exclaimed: 'Please, no more hot-dogs and waffles!'

Everything unhealthy is not part of the Chinese ideal holiday, the other informants agreed. On the contrary, in a Chinese mind-set, a holiday should make you fresh, healthy and strong. Hot dogs, pizza and waffles, industrialised convenience food which Scandinavian families 'allow' themselves during a vacation or accept, because it is difficult to find anything else, were probably the worst a tourism establishment could serve a Chinese guest.

When interviewing the tourism business owners, the difficulty of supplying a huge and unknown market was the management's primary worry. The businesses had little capacity, both in service-performance and product-adaptation. While exploring the possibilities of a new travel market in the region, the commissioned research also started creating awareness: how could the industry prepare itself and convince the rest of the destination to provide suitable touristic experiences for Chinese travellers?

Co-creation and attraction site design

'Co-creation' can be defined as a way for unusual partners to create something together. A part of this applied method, e.g. consumers developing an industry's products, is also to remember that when it comes to service and experience consumption the traveller is a 'live co-producer'. In a tourism-setting, services and experiences are being performed not only by the establishment but also by the engaged consumer who wants to be part of this enactment. A business should therefore be very interested in creating the right conditions for a consumer to participate in the service or experience moment, because this participation is a great part of the product (Prahalad & Ramaswamy 2004).

The Chinese visitors asked for 'more comfort' in the cold and stormy climate. But how could this consumer need assist co-creation? In the interviews, the visitors asked for opportunities to 'enjoy the sunshine in the restaurant'; 'sit [in furniture with blankets] on a big grass lawn'; 'see the sea-view'; 'make a barbeque' and have access to 'entertainment equipment for children'. All this was part of Chinese holiday-ideals and something they, from their previous travel-experiences in other countries, would expect to have provided for at tourism attractions.

The Chinese visitors were used to spending all day at one attraction, doing all sorts of activities and consuming a mix of experiential elements: from culture heritage to popular culture. This desire did not necessarily fit the European place-aesthetics where special features of a location need to originate from 'a limited but distinct part of history and tradition' (Arlt 2006). The Nordic 'untouched' way of experiencing, e.g. nature-based attractions, is highly influenced by a political planning-ideal: many Europeans correspondingly appreciate a non-manipulated, non-pre-arranged and non-commercialised destination design (Jivén & Larkham 2003). Nordic rural nature has thus been idealised as a 'virgin ground' of off-grid areas with no conveniences, services, public transportations, internet-connections or Wi-Fi zones, which, in a European mind-set, should be explored through physical maps and bodily movements, hunches, feeling and sensing, engaging with the landscape (Kjær 2011). As a response to this untouched place-aesthetic ideal, one informant said, 'Places in Norway aren't planned like tourist attractions'.

When asked about Norwegian experiences and attractions, one female biologist exclaimed: 'It is so boring here. Get a hobby or go mad!' A male engineer said:

> I really want to know more about culture. But the Norwegians cannot be very proud of their heritage, because nowhere am I able to read about it on the Web: neither in English or Mandarin. The museums are never open, and it is impossible to find out which bus will take you there.

Some of the Chinese visitors would define Norway as 'cold and primitive' and remarked 'Who would ever want to live here?' One would soften the opinion and say, 'It isn't as cold as I expected'. All informants focused on the 'cute wooden houses', exotic because everything is built of stone in China, but were the houses comfortable to stay in, they would ask. They were all fascinated with experiencing the natural scenery. One commented on the mountain landscape surrounding a ski-destination in southern Norway: 'I have never seen such thick snow before'.

The informants' wordings were based on comparison to other places in the world, better or worse. In this sense the informants were experienced and their attitudes were important as co-productive resources which could help the industry to develop targeted experience-products.

What is clear from these utterances is that the Chinese experience of the region had variations, but some Chinese cultural, geographical and social perceptions – such as the experience of a cold climate, (lack of) friendly attitudes, the cleanliness and the beauty of nature – were consistent themes.

In the perspective of an intercultural encounter, the visitors presented social preferences of being in a crowd and having a good time, referring to Chinese ideals of 'warmth' and 'togetherness'. Could, or should, a cold and isolated place like the Nordic region, create comfort and cosiness in order to adapt? These bodily sensations were important to the Chinese visitors, but in Northern-European context, a great Norwegian countryside experience was about engaging with the extreme, harsh (and uncomfortable) forces of nature in order to produce and maintain 'good health'. The ideal of a 'fresh spirit' was closely connected to the experience of being in a cold climate.

Habits of health were not only important when designing experience-products at tourism establishments, these habits also said a great deal about which local resources were considered valuable and, in this sense, could be refined into e.g. souvenirs or even export products aimed at the Chinese market.

From a Chinese perspective, the most desired experience-products involved nature and health-related aspects. In the rural geography, there were plenty of things which connoted mental harmony found in 'nature and spiritual beliefs' or physical health found in the purity of the environment. 'It's so blue here!' one person said. In Chinese perception, the colour blue refers to a high quality in environmental sustainability. A 'fresh ambience' and activities such as 'fishing, rafting, cycling, cooking and picking fruits' not vegetables, because the soil is 'too dirty', and wanting a 'fish and sea food dining' included attractive regional raw products such as 'fish-oil', 'seaweed', 'salmon' and locally produced beer. All these things were attached to Chinese likings and preferences and could be transformed into possible micro-experiences. Referring to larger Chinese ideals on balance and harmony, these things were considered very important aspects of being a traveller in the North. Still, for the regional tourism industry to realise that these natural features in themselves were not tourism-products, but instead needed to be commoditised, shaped, packaged and organised in different ways in order to match the Chinese consumer, could nevertheless become difficult. The ideal of a raw and untouched nature is often objectifying experience-products in a naturalistic way, considering 'the unprocessed' a selling point (Olsen 2007). Still, in order for the tourism industry to sustain, natural goods – for example, sceneries, landscapes or freshness, need to be commoditised.

Destination branding and the symbolic production of a region

When the investigation was undertaken, the Nordic region could not compete on a global scale with other European destinations, their iconic cities and classic cultural heritage. The Nordic region had many natural attractions but few heritage sites and in general needed to develop its destinations to a certain standard, for instance because 'the Chinese are very aware of whether a site is on UNESCO's list' (Jørgensen 2012, p. 114). Because the Chinese are trained in 'extreme consumerism' and therefore understand 'tourism destinations *as* branded commodities' (Arlt 2006, p. 199) the money-strong, upper-middle class outbound traveller is thus expecting a themed, visualised and narrated geography which immediately can be identified as a destination.

When trying to establish a productive regional-global relationship, the rural Nordic region, which has a low level of cultural heritage sights, needs to produce attractiveness and meaningfulness in other ways. By participating in the investigation, the regional tourism and non-tourism industry had found it important to manage the visitor experience. Still, the process of marketing and branding the destination through adapting actual experiences and resources seemed difficult.

Destination marketing and destination branding, take the point of departure in a narrative and symbolic idea which has to be concretised into a place: materiality and products in order to be considered a real and relevant description of a region by the target group (Ren & Ooi 2013). 'Branding' can therefore refer to the process of selecting and packaging relevant products and places of a destination in order to fit the consumer's specific habits, routines and social emotions. Still, when branding strategically, this can create issues relating to the identity-making of a region. Do 'we' become something we want to be, when we are co-created by outsiders? Should not identity-creation rise from residents and their (sub-cultural) forms of expressions? Or should identity instead rise from corporate society and ideas produced here?

In tourism history, the stagnation and reinvention of a place is not new (MacCannell 1976). Experiences can be repackaged, re-narrated and re-performed with the intention of foregrounding certain sensations, histories and events, while leaving others aside. Several stories and place brands can easily be connected to the same topography, live side by side and contest each other. Some brands might even be perceived as more historically correct than others. In a culture history perspective, southern Norway has had several place brands, circulating identity-ideas about pirates, poets, migrants; timber- and wooden boat-production; religion or even the southern feeling of summer (Hundstad 2009). One can argue that these themes all say more about those who invented them, than about the exact natural features and authentic events of the destination. In this sense, a place brand can be viewed as 'playful identity-work' providing a local sense of community (Johnsen 2010).

Hopefully these destination brands have marketed the region to intended target groups. Often, though, they are esoteric images of how a region would like to perceive itself. In a global market situation, a region nevertheless needs to differentiate the destination and compete with others by having the most interesting identity. Place branding is about modifying the perceptions of a larger audience. Different people will have different perceptions of a destination, still the 'arrival of globalisation' has made a regional identity even more blurred, which makes it important to control and arrange what a region stands for. Thus, a brand is a way of (re)capturing oneself while, at the same time, activating an audience's imaginations in positive ways (Ren & Ooi 2013).

In Chinese preconceptions 'the North' was the only geographical metaphor they knew before actually being in the surroundings. They filled the sign with experiences of "clean" and "fresh air", they understood the 'ecological environment as quite good' the informants explained. The perceptions of Norway as being cold, natural and unapproachable did to some extend originate from thinking and feeling with the geography, but the destination was also thought of through Chinese imaginations and norms. The Chinese travellers were not familiar with the rough, cold and windy landscape. Instead they approached it through a symbolism of purity and freshness. It was an imagination which was available as a relationship-tool between body and place. The Chinese, stylistic figure of the North helped the Chinese travellers being linked to the landscape in, to them, understandable ways. Based on association with other places of the world, the interviews showed that the Chinese experience of southern Norway was founded in the cold climate; the cleanliness and the beauty of nature.

Adapting to the Chinese consumer could be difficult. Still, it could also be an opportunity to follow the ideals of destination adaption which is to produce meaningful experiences by theming and designing the surroundings. The aim of tourism development is to create totality. The German tourism geographer Wolfgang Georg Arlt (2006) argues that the Chinese outbound tourism experience should be regarded as symbolic or as

> a total imagery which – at first hand – is not bodily sensed, but rather understood through visualisation and the totality of thematic. When approaching the Chinese market, one needs to think as a 'brand-creator who designs a total world' or an imagined community. In the mind of the Chinese consumer, there are 'no limits to consumption.'
>
> (Arlt 2006, p. 198)

When communicating a destination to this particular group of visitors a total experience needs to be in focus.

One way to offer totality could hence be through treating the place as a branded commodity, i.e. connecting myth and materiality to match the desires of refreshing health and spirit through the Nordic landscape. In order to create an appealing perceptual and sensuous environment, a branded narrative meant carefully choosing parts of the region's culture and landscape which could make up for the entirety, leaving aside the irrelevant things which did not support the brand. Or, as the Dutch experience economists Boswijk, Thijssen and Peelen (2007) clarify, a branded or themed destination is about the elimination of unproductive clues in the experience design. When creating cohesion or entirety in an environment, it needs to correlate both with the actual consumer experience and his or her imagination.

How to get China-ready?

Destination branding, marketing and adaptation are important components in destination management. It would of course be of great disappointment to visitors, if the DMO's marketing campaign did not resemble the geography it was marketing. Thus, in this research project, creating awareness in the tourism industry about potentially new travel trends and investigating how the Chinese metaphor of the North could function as a way to adapt the industry's already existing experience-products to match a new market was analysed.

In a market-ethnography the project owner decides what needs to be known. In order for a destination marketing organisation, like Visit Sørlandet, to brand the region in targeted ways, I have discussed how regional touristic images of food, sceneries and attractions appeared in the eyes of the Chinese consumer and how, it was suggested, adapted through knowledge on consumer behaviour and through processes of co-creation.

I have analysed how the region of southern Norway were perceived as a symbolic place of 'the North' which, in addition, and though the qualitative interviews with Chinese travellers and local tourism and non-tourism industry actors, was given substance either through consumer desires or consumer disappointments, and as ways of co-producing destination adaptation and destination branding.

The interviewed visitors were well-educated metropolitans who were 'only' consumers and had no expert-knowledge on experience-product design. They nevertheless provided useful insights on how to approach a Chinese upper middle-class consumer. Not every effort made by the regional tourism industry was discussed in flattering terms by the Chinese informants and not all regional tourism and non-tourism business actors could identify the potential of aiming towards a new global market. The touristic narrative of the North needed in addition, to be created with carefully chosen parts which could make up for the positive Chinese imagination of the entirety. Promoting a good, balanced and healthy lifestyle and presenting pure, natural scenery were some of the signs and symbols which could fill the metaphor with content.

The process of creating an appealing destination brand based on the intentions of smoothing intercultural encounters, trying to host and please outsiders, their tastes and imaginations in order for them to like us, is a highly sophisticated process where actual and imagined materiality need to correlate. In order for a destination to create a successful image, backstage-collaboration between many different regional actors' needs to be linked and the efforts need to be marketed through the Other's affirmative place-mythologies.

In destination adaptation it is important to rethink oneself, allocating what is already available to what the consumer wants in order to lower the investments. When defining a new way of perceiving a region, anything can potentially be transformed to a great and meaningful experience.

We found that southern Norway, representing the countryside outside the larger Nordic cities, needed to be creative in how to rethink itself *as* a brand commodity in order to approach a local-global intercultural relationship presented by the Chinese visitors, business owners and foreign investors in the region. I have thus discussed the possibility of the tourism businesses to match their already existing services, experiences and raw-products to what this particular consumer group would prefer. Leaving aside markers of self-identity, such as the sweet waffle or the aesthetics of an untouched natural landscape, it became clear from the interviews that many elements of Chinese travel-making in the Nordic countryside are both possible and appreciated if just the communicating tools of destination adaptation and destination branding are designed in suitable ways.

Adapting local tourism products to new and emerging markets is a high-risk enterprise. One needs to investigate and find the touch points – the right matches – between experience-products and the tourists' preferences.

For example, it would be too demanding for each tourism business to work individually. Hence, working together on a destination level, connecting to the region's other businesses, private and public institutions, is vital in order for the tourism industry to perform successfully. This chapter discusses how a region's tourism and leisure industry – the marketing and delivery of experiential services and products – needs to be acknowledged as the destinations' and country's communicative and targeted image towards new markets. In this way, investments in tourism industry innovations are a practice which should concern all sectors of local society.

Doing research-based tourism development – understanding consumers' preferences and adapting a destination to these cultural needs for meaning – should reduce industry risks. When capitalising on Chinese outbound tourism in the Nordic rural regions, commissioned research can be a way for a region to understand itself as part of a larger destination. Sharing consumers in a common value chain with neighbouring countries, applied research hence assists the development of cross-collaborative business models of regions and nations.

15 Business models for new experiential services

Tor Helge Aas and Geir Jørgensen

Business models

A business model represents the business logic (Casadesus-Masanell & Ricart 2010) or the theory of the business (Drucker 1994) by defining the way an organisation generates and captures (economic) value (Teece 2010). Although business models have always existed as a foundation for economic behaviour, they did not receive much attention in academic literature before the 1990s (Coombes & Nicholson 2013). This attention was in part driven by the emergence of the Internet, and the need for new and innovative business models to capture value from e-businesses (Amit & Zott 2001).

Since then the topic has also received attention in other areas of business management, and in particular in the area of innovation management. This is not surprising because the potential value of a new product or a new service remains latent until it is commercialised in some way via a business model (Chesbrough 2010). Thus, the development and design of business models is now acknowledged as a critical part of new product or new service development (NSD) projects in commercial for-profit businesses (Chesbrough & Rosenbloom 2002).

In this chapter we will discuss whether formal design of business models may also be useful when non-commercial, non-profit organisations develop new products and services. In particular, we investigate, through an applied research project, whether the use of a particular business model design tool called "Business Model Canvas" (BMC) (Osterwalder & Pigneur 2010) was useful in a particular case. The case was a NSD project conducted by a performing arts centre located in the largest city in southern Norway. This chapter aims to discuss the experiences from the research project, both from a business model design perspective and from a research method perspective. The chapter demonstrates that it is possible to combine academic research in the innovation management area with providing constructive managerial advice.

Applying business models in the cultural sector

Research approach and procedure

As indicated in the introduction, this chapter is based on a single case study concerning a performing arts centre located in a city in southern Norway.

This centre was the home of the regional theatre, the regional symphony orchestra and the regional opera, and the centre was the host of an array of cultural events. These events were provided by a combination of permanent employees and temporary hired freelance art practitioners (for example actors). The centre had about 140 permanent employees.

In June 2012, the performing arts centre contacted a so-called regional research broker because they wanted assistance from a research community. The research broker was funded by The Research Council of Norway (RCN) and the local county Council, and his role was to assist organisations located in the region, such as the performing arts centre, in defining their research needs. His role was also to assist in identifying relevant research teams, and he even had capital (from RCN and the local county Council) to fund small research projects (such as the project reported in this chapter).

In a meeting with the research broker, the performing arts centre explained that they were running a NSD project aiming to digitise cultural events. The research broker was told that the technical challenges in this project were manageable and well taken care of. However, how the new service could be implemented was more difficult to understand. With this background, the centre wanted assistance from a research community.

The research broker was able to identify a research team (i.e. the authors of this chapter) from the regional research institute (located in the same city) interested in innovation management and business model design, and a meeting between the research team and the performing arts centre was arranged the same month. The performing arts centre was represented by five people in this first meeting; three from the project team and two from the administration. In the meeting, the challenges related to realising the value potential of the project were discussed. The main question from the point of view of the performing arts centre was how the new service (digitised events) could be commercially implemented and targeted in a way that would be financially sustainable, and at the same time provide valuable experiences for the audience. During the meeting, it was agreed that it would be worthwhile to test whether the use of the BMC tool could help in solving this challenge by designing a sustainable business model for the new service. A research project aiming to test the usefulness of the BMC tool was defined and initialised.

To assess the managerial usefulness of using BMC in the case organisation we deployed a qualitative research approach with so-called strong intervention (Jönsson & Lukka 2007). During the research process we (i.e. the two researchers authoring this chapter) worked together with employees in the case organisation. We acted in part as active participants and in part as observers and interviewers in this process. From a scientific point of view, it was perceived as an advantage that the case organisation had not previously used any formal business model design methodology. Consequently, the findings of this study were not influenced by any effects of previously applied formal business model design methodologies.

The research progressed through three steps. First, to design the business model for the new service, a workshop was arranged. The project manager (from the case organisation) was responsible for selecting participants for the workshop and he searched for and selected participants with various roles in the organisation. As a result of the selection process, nine employees from the case organisation were selected and all of these participated in the workshop. The participants included both representatives from administrative, technical and artistic management from the theatre, the symphony orchestra and the opera. The two researchers (authors of this chapter) facilitated the workshop. The researchers participated actively in the workshop by introducing the BMC tool to the participants and by asking the participants essential questions, and in some cases also by helping the participants find solutions. The workshop lasted 1 day and was arranged in June 2013, approximately one year after the initial meeting. The reason for this time lag was that the project team in the performing arts centre wanted to be sure that the technical solution was solid before discussing business models. In June 2013 the project team had decided upon a technical solution and had tested this several times.

The second step of the research process was an in-depth group interview where the researcher (first author of this chapter) asked the participants questions about the relevance and usefulness of the BMC tool. The interview was arranged in November 2013 and lasted 4 hours. Four employees representing key administrative and technical management roles participated in the interview. The researcher used an interview guide during the workshop process, and the workshop was recorded and transcribed.

The third step of the research process was conducted a bit more than one year after the second step, in January 2015. In this step we wanted to see whether the business model resulting from step 1 had actually been implemented, and if so why or why not. To assess this, we interviewed the project manager in the performing arts centre. The interview lasted for approximately 1 hour 30 minutes, and it was recorded and transcribed. We used the same interview guide as in step 2 during this interview. The research procedure is summarised in Table 15.1.

Results of step 1: design of Business Model Canvas

In summary the nine building blocks of the BMC resulting from the first workshop had the following characteristics[1]:

- Customer segments: The primary customer segment targeted (by the new service) is potential users who, for various reasons, such as age, health or illness, are unable to experience the events in the performing arts centre. This includes users in institutions such as hospitals and retirement and nursing homes. Such priorities are in line with the mandate of the performing arts centre, which is to bring cultural experiences to the residents in the region.

Table 15.1 The research procedure

Research step	*Date*	*Method*	*Outcome*	*Participants*
0	June 2012	Initial meeting	Research question and research approach agreement	Research broker, research team and five participants from the case organisation (administrative, technical and project management)
1	June 2013	Workshop: BMC design	Design of BMC	Research team and nine participants from the case organisation (administrative, technical, artistic and project management)
2	November 2013	In-depth group interview	First assessment of BMC usefulness	One researcher and four participants from the case organisation (administrative, technical and project management)
3	January 2015	In-depth interview	Second assessment of BMC usefulness	One researcher and project manager from case organisation

- Value propositions: The new digital service provides cultural experiences to people present in a social community, although these are not able to be present in one of the physical auditoriums in the performing arts centre. This means that the performing arts centre will stream the events to partner institutions (hospitals, retirement homes) where groups of people are present.
- Channels: The performing arts centre will establish agreements with relevant institutions (hospitals, retirement homes) and these institutions will be the most essential part of the distribution channel. The establishment of suitable facilities in each partner institution is essential to ensure high quality events.
- Customer relationships: It is important to establish relationship with relevant institutions. Because the service provided is experience based, the technical facilities and dedicated super users in the institutions targeted are important. Therefore, it is necessary with tight customer relationships to ensure quality and protect reputation.
- Revenue streams: Today the performing arts centre is funded by three sources: (a) public funds, (b) ticket revenue and (c) sponsorships. The new service will not generate new revenue from users, but will strengthen public actors' willingness to future funding because the new

service is a good response to the mandate given by the public funders. It could also increase the attractiveness of the performing art centre as a sponsor object among companies that want to promote themselves as socially responsible.

- Key resources: The human resources required to produce the events include performing artists, technicians in charge of audio and video and administrative resources that are responsible for sales, support and the training of super users in institutions.
- Key activities: There are four main activities: (a) artistic production in the form of concerts, theatre, operas or musicals, (b) technical production providing the necessary infrastructure, (c) digital production, which includes operating the infrastructure and a server park and (d) the administrative production, including marketing and sales.
- Key partnerships: The most important partners can be divided into four main groups: (a) institutions where the potential users are located, (b) broadband providers, (c) external suppliers of equipment and d) personnel to the technical and digital production.
- Cost structure: The costs of the new service are related to artistic, technical, administrative and digital production. Many of the major cost drivers (e.g. artistic and technical production and in part administrative costs) are so-called "sunk costs". Costs directly associated with the digital output are fully variable and exclusively linked to the new service.

During the first workshop (research step 1) we noted that the participants were able to reach an agreement relatively quickly in most of the dimensions of the canvas. We therefore asked the participants if they had already discussed these topics, and they confirmed that a lot of the same issues had arisen already during the initial technical development and testing. For example, when deciding what type of recording equipment to use they had to discuss who the audience should be, and what level of recording quality they would demand. Thus, a lot of important business model decisions had actually been taken implicitly during the technical development stage. Nevertheless, the workshop participants stated that these decisions were often taken in an ad-hoc manner without having the overview provided by the BMC. Thus, the visualisation of the business model dimensions and their connection was new to them.

Results of step 2: first assessment of the usefulness of the Business Model Canvas tool

In the second research step, the effects and antecedents of using the BMC tool were discussed. The informants who participated in the group interview in the second step agreed that the business model that was developed in the first workshop was enabling progress in the ongoing service innovation project.

The following quote from one participant illustrates this: "You may say that the BMC model we developed is a pleasant confirmation that this project is on the right path".

The participants further claimed that the BMC work would be an important basis for decision making in the project. For example, one participant argued: "There will be some decisions now in the near future related to how we proceed after the pilot phase of the project, and insight provided by the BMC work will enable us to make these decisions".

The informants also drew attention to the copyright issue. This is an important issue in relation to the specific service innovation project discussed here, due to the fact that this project is essentially about providing artistic events to people other than those physically sitting in the audience at the performing arts centre. The BMC work was not sufficient to get in the depths of this issue, but the BMC design gave, according to participants, a better basis to discuss copyright issues related to streaming services in general.

Our findings also suggested that the implementation of the BMC tool had had effects on the organisational level. In relation to this, the workshop participants informed us about ongoing work related to improving innovation- and project-practices in the case organisation. One informant described this work like this: "We will continue to stunt and being creative . . . , but we want a little more structure in what we do, especially in relation to such major strategic projects like this service innovation project".

The workshop participants believed that in the future, it may be necessary to integrate the BMC tool in project and innovation activities at the performing arts centre. The participants noted, however, that it was very important that the tool is implemented in a way that does not harm the creative early phase of innovation projects. When asked if the BMC tool will be used in other projects in the performing arts centre, one informant for example stated:

> The service innovation project about digitalisation should strictly speaking not exist, but it has been allowed to live because some enthusiasts have been allowed to work with it . . . These enthusiasts have come forward and said "I really burn for this project. Please allow me to work on it . . . " As a result they were allowed to spend time on the project . . . So if the question is if we are going to use this methodology in all possible contexts, I will answer a resounding no. Our way of working and our way of exploiting the artistic and technical resources in this house, it is like we have a tolerance and openness to good ideas. So, it is like if someone comes with a good idea the managerial response is often: "Yes, try to figure it out . . . " I think that it is important that we continue to work this way. But later in the innovation process, when the project requires either a lot of time or a lot of money to go forward, then I think the BMC tool may help.

The service innovation project had existed for a relatively long time before the first BMC workshop was arranged. Before the first workshop the project team had partly focused on testing different technical solutions, and they had also discussed various possible business models without making use of a particular structured business model development methodology. In fact, during the technical development process they had implicitly also taken several important business model decisions, as mentioned earlier. Nevertheless, when asked whether participants believed that the first workshop was held too late in the project, the answer was no. The participants felt that the timing was favourable. One participant for example stated:

> I think the first workshop was arranged at the appropriate time. Had it been arranged earlier we had not been able to answer the questions you asked . . . I think we had to test the concept in a pilot phase . . . I do not think I had wanted this business model work earlier in pilot phase as a kind of premise . . . I think it was important for the result that we were allowed to fumble a bit in the beginning.

Another participant stated:

> I agree very much that the first workshop should not have been arranged earlier. I think it has something to do with the type of business we are. We are a creative business that starts new processes without always knowing where it will end. I think if we had tried to figure out all the business model things too early, we would perhaps have stopped the project. We had probably seen so many challenges and obstacles that we would had said; "OK, we will wait a bit." Instead we said; "Yes, we can try this. It sounds like fun . . ." In this case I actually think that this is an important reason for the progress.

One participant wondered if the reason for this may lie in the type of business the performing arts centre is:

> I might have a feeling that this may be different for us as partly publicly funded institution than it is for a purely private business, because we have the opportunity to go into such a pilot phase. If this had been a purely commercial project, it may be that it had been important to conduct the business modelling in the beginning to test out if this was a sustainable way forward.

In the first workshop personnel with many different roles in the case organisation (i.e. artistic, technical and administrative management) participated, as mentioned earlier. The composition of this team was also seen as an essential condition for the success of the workshop. One participant for example stated:

> When we decided who should participate in the workshop, we thought we should have someone from the project-team, plus some managers who are a little bit more peripheral to the process. I think this composition of participants is important. It is necessary to have someone who is able to raise some critical questions, because if they are not present in such a workshop setting, when should they ask these questions?

Another participant confirmed the importance of including interdisciplinary and different functional roles in the business model design work:

> It was important from a project point of view that the top management participated . . . In addition we thought it was important to include personnel that will be involved in the operation of the new service, for example production manager, technicians and musicians.

There was some discussion among the workshop participants whether also potential customers/users (such as a pilot institution) should have been included in the first workshop. There were arguments both for and against this. All agreed that user involvement was important for the project, but most participants felt the BMC workshop should be an internal work shop.

To summarise, we may state that on the whole the participants were satisfied with the BMC tool. However, during the discussion in the second workshop it became clear that several participants felt that the name of the tool perhaps should be modified when used in a similar context. Participants for example expressed: "For us it would be an advantage if the tool is not called 'business model'. It should be called 'operational model', or another more neutral term, I think " and "We should not use monetary expressions, such as business model, in my view, because the results of this process should be communicated also to persons other than business people." They also stated:

> The term "business model" is perhaps a bit misleading since we are in part a publicly funded enterprise. The tool might have been called something else since we do not do business in the normal sense. Still, even though we are in part a publicly funded enterprise, I will say that the methodology as such is very relevant for us.

Results of step 3: second assessment of the usefulness of the Business Model Canvas tool

A bit more than one year after the second step we visited the performing arts centre again and interviewed the project manager. On the whole the findings of this research step confirmed the findings of research step 2. At this stage the project was almost finished, and several tests had been run to ensure that the technical solutions were solid. Discussions with customers and users had also confirmed that the business model derived in research step 1 was feasible. The project manager still stated that the deployment of the BMC tool had been useful, especially in helping to visualise the business model in a clear manner. This visualisation had been useful when discussing the project internally, but also when discussing the project with external actors. In fact, the BMC had for example been successfully used during the discussions with the (prospective) customers.

How to apply business model design

Business model design processes and tools

The management literature suggests a number of different tools that may assist managers in designing business models during new service or new product development processes. One example is the tool suggested by Johnson (2010) called *seizing the white space*. He suggests that the design of a business model includes the definition and specification of four building blocks:

1 the customer value proposition
2 the profit formula
3 the key resources; and
4 the key processes.

Another example is a tool suggested by Zott, Amit and Massa (2010). They perceive business models as the "activity systems" businesses implement to exploit their business opportunities, and suggest a framework with three business model design elements:

1 content (what activities should be performed?)
2 structure (how should they be linked and sequenced?); and
3 governance (who should perform them, and where?).

Zott, Amit and Massa (2010) also suggest four important "design themes" that drive value:

1 novelty (adopt innovative content, structure or governance)
2 lock-in (build in elements to retain business model stakeholders, e.g. customers)
3 complementarities (bundle activities to generate more value); and
4 efficiency (reorganise activities to reduce transaction costs).

A third business model design tool example is the tool focused in this chapter, namely the BMC tool suggested by Osterwalder and Pigneur (2010). It is suggested by the authors that the business model design process has the following order:

1 customer segments
2 value propositions
3 channels
4 customer relationships
5 revenue streams
6 key resources
7 key activities
8 key partnerships
9 cost structure.

They write:

> A business model describes the rationale of how an organisation creates, delivers, and captures value . . . business model can best be described through nine basic building blocks that show the logic of how a company intends to make money . . . The nine building blocks in BMC are; customer segments (an organisation serves one or several customer segments: value propositions (an organisation seeks to solve customer problems and satisfy customer needs with value propositions), channels (value propositions are delivered to customers through communication, distribution, and sales channels), customer relationships (customer relationships are established and maintained with each customer segment), revenue streams (revenue streams result from value propositions successfully offered to customers), key resources (key resources are the assets required to offer and deliver the previously described elements . . .), key activities (. . . by performing a number of key activities), key partnerships (some activities are outsourced and some resources are acquired outside the enterprise), and cost structure (the business model elements results in the cost structure).
>
> (Osterwalder & Pigneur 2010, pp. 14–17)

Although the BMC tool has been adopted by an increasing number of businesses, its managerial usefulness has been evaluated surprisingly few times in objective empirical research studies (Fritscher & Pigneur 2014). The few existing empirical BMC evaluations focus on a limited number of sectors, including particularly the manufacturing sector and the software services sector (Eppler, Hoffmann & Bresciani 2011; Lucassen, Brinkkemper, Jansen & Handoyo 2012).

To a large extent these sectors produce and deliver value propositions with a tangible and homogeneous nature, and the production and consumption of the value propositions (i.e. products and services) delivered by these sectors often happen as two independent processes. In light of this we argue that the value propositions delivered by other parts of the service sector, such as the cultural sector, are very different.

Organisations in the cultural sector often deliver value propositions in the form of experiences. These experiences often have an intangible and heterogeneous nature and they are often consumed and produced at the same time, often with the audience (customers) physically present in the auditorium (Zeithaml, Parasuraman & Berry 1985). Furthermore, the creation of customer value and customer experiences in this sector is not only a consequence of interactions between the organisation and the customer, but also a consequence of interactions between customers (Zomerdijk & Voss 2010). Consequently, the value propositions delivered by organisations in this sector are often difficult or impossible to store.

Furthermore, Caves (2000) suggests that organisations in the cultural sector often experience particularly high demand uncertainty. The mission of organisations in the cultural sector is often also different from the mission of pure for-profit organisations. The consequence is that organisations in the cultural sector have a tendency to develop "art for art's sake" and not for economic value generation (Caves 2000). In the resource dimension organisations in the cultural sector often need employees with diversified skills, and there is also often a particularly strong relationship between the skills of the employees and success (Caves 2000).

We recognise the characteristic features of the cultural industry, and argue that because this industry differs substantially in several dimensions from the industries which have been the focus of prior empirical business model design research, it is not obvious that current findings and normative business model design guidance are relevant for the cultural industry. From an academic point of view this literature gap is concerning, particularly due to the general importance of the cultural industry for regional development (Lindeborg & Lindkvist 2013). The present study contributes in filling this gap in the literature.

Lessons from a business model design perspective

The results from our empirical investigation indicate that use of the BMC tool can be helpful also when organisations in the cultural sector take decisions during innovation processes. Thus, we may conclude that the implementation of BMC may have similar potential effects when implemented in organisations in the cultural sector as when implemented in other sectors, such as the software or manufacturing sectors.

Thus, the potential positive effects of a BMC implementation do not seem to be negatively affected by the characteristics of the cultural sector. In fact, based on the empirical findings from our case, it rather appears to be opposite, i.e. the description of a relevant business models in general, and the use of BMC in particular, seems to be particularly important during innovation processes in cultural organisations. Our findings indicate that the factors complicating innovation management in this sector, for example the facts that the value proposition is intangible, that the demand is uncertain and that the skills of the employees are particularly important may become more manageable when using a structured framework such as BMC during the innovation process. In other words; the effects of BMC deployment on managerial decisions may be even more positive in this sector than in other sectors.

The results also indicate, however, that these positive effects do not appear automatically. Our findings suggest that there are at least two conditions that should be met to be able to release the positive effects on managerial decisions in cultural organisations. First, our findings indicate that it may be essential that the organisational culture is taken into account when BMC is implemented. In our case organisation the participants for example argued that it was important that the BMC tool was not introduced at an early stage because this would arguably have disturbed the ongoing creative process. We believe it is true that a creative organisational culture is often present in cultural organisations (Jeffcut & Pratt 2002). We do question, however, if this really implies that tools such as BMC should not be used in an early stage of innovation projects. In fact, our case organisation implicitly had to take a number of business model decisions in an early stage, and perhaps these decisions could have been dealt with more efficiently if an explicit tool such as BMC had been used. Nevertheless, what we believe is the important lesson from this, is that tools such as BMC must be implemented with caution, and in accordance with the mindset of the organisational members.

Second, our results indicate that it may be crucial to select appropriate participants when the BMC tool is deployed. The participants in the case organisation were both personnel that had detailed knowledge of the ongoing project, as well as general administrative, technical and artistic managers. Our findings suggest that this contribution from different functions in the organisation was essential for successful BMC design in our case organisation. We believe that this second condition may be explained by the nature of cultural services. In most cases, the production of cultural services is often dependent on employees with diversified skills and diversified skills are therefore also probably needed when cultural organisations design new business models.

Lessons from a research method perspective

The experiences reported in this chapter are the results of an applied research project initiated by the case organisation, i.e. an organisation in the cultural sector. They contacted the research community because they needed assistance in deciding how a new service under development could be commercially implemented and targeted in a way that would be financially sustainable and at the same time provide valuable experiences for the audience.

Indeed, the chosen research approach was affected by this very specific need from the case organisation. The challenge, from a research point of view, was that although the need stated by the case organisation had high relevance from a practitioner's point of view, it had limited relevance from a scientific point of view. Thus, to make the project interesting not only from a practitioner's perspective, but also from a scientific and academic research perspective we (i.e. the researchers) had to search for an approach that could simultaneously satisfy both needs.

The idea that an empirical evaluation of the usefulness of the BMC tool in the context of cultural industries could satisfy both needs came from the researchers. The research ambition and approach was communicated to the case organisation, and they accepted this approach as long as we would also be able to provide advices on how the new service under development could be commercialised.

Thus, we may state that the research approach was a compromise between the needs of the case organisation and the needs of the researchers. In addition, the fact that the financial funds allocated to the project were very limited, also affected the research approach. One consequence of this situation was that the scientific method we chose had limitations. From a scientific point of view, it would for example had been an advantage if we had been able to follow the case organisation much more closely during the entire implementation of the service innovation project. Perhaps would it also have been an advantage to follow similar processes in other organisations. In sum this would have enabled us to get a better understanding of what activities and decisions taken during innovation processes that bring organisations closer to using sustainable business models. With this insight, we would most likely had been able to be more specific when suggesting how the BMC tool could or should be integrated in NSD processes.

Nevertheless, although the study did have methodological limitations, we believe that the study was able to provide some interesting insights related to business model design (see the previous section), in addition to assisting the case organisation in their project. It should also be noted that the case organisation would in fact not have given us access to the case if we had not been willing also to assist them in their project. At the same time, we would not have been able to provide the new scientific insight if the case organisation had not been willing to deploy a specific business model design tool such as BMC. Thus, in our opinion, the study demonstrates that to combine scientific research in the management area with managerial consultancy may be valuable both from an academic point of view and a practitioner's point of view. This is especially true if both the research community and the case organisation are willing to be flexible and to compromise.

Crossing sectors

In this chapter, we have reported the experiences from a single case study where we tried to combine academic research on business model design with providing constructive managerial advice. Due to the fact that both the researchers and the case organisation were flexible and willing to compromise, the project was able to achieve the aims of both parts. From a research point of view, the findings suggest that factors complicating the management of business model design processes in the cultural sector, such as intangibility, may become more manageable when using a structured tool such as BMC. At the same time a practical outcome of the study was a concrete proposition of how a business model for a new service developed by the case organisations could look like. Although the study provided valuable results, we also acknowledge its limitations. We suggest that future research should continue the evaluation of BMC and other business model design tools in close collaboration with organisations.

The book discusses the role and challenges of applied research in regional knowledge systems by addressing the following research question (RQ): how is knowledge developed in a reflective reconstruction within a regional context, and what is the role of applied social science in this process? Our chapter contributes to this RQ by discussing the experiences from an applied research project where researchers from a regional research institute provided assistance to a regional performing arts centre during the NSD processes of the centre.

The project was initiated by the performing arts centre. This centre contacted a regional research broker because they wanted assistance from a research community in deciding how a new service under development could be commercially implemented and targeted. The research broker contacted the regional research institution and initiated the project. The project was funded from the VRI-programme and the county. Thus, the project was not funded through the basic funding of the research institute, and is therefore an example of commissioned research.

In commissioned research the researchers typically have limited freedom in defining the research objectives and designing the research process (see Chapter 1 in this book). This was also the case in this project. Nevertheless, in the case project the researchers were to some degree allowed to participate in designing the project. Thus, it may be stated that the definition of the objectives of the case project happened in collaboration between the researchers and practitioners at the performing arts centre.

The researchers used the opportunity to participate in defining the objectives of the project to suggest making the project interesting not only from the perspective of the performing arts centre, but also from a more general scientific and academic research perspective. Based on this the researchers from the research institute and the practitioners from the performing arts centre were able to agree upon a research design that would satisfy both needs. In the case this compromise increased the project's impact on the more general scientific knowledge development.

During the project the researchers acted in part as active participants. They facilitated the process and also provided suggestions on what tools that could be used during the process. The researchers did not have a normative agenda towards practice during the process. Instead they observed how the participants used the suggested tools and evaluated the usefulness of the tools through in-depth interviews. The chapter demonstrates that it is possible to combine academic research with providing constructive managerial advice if the researchers and the practitioners are willing to be flexible and to compromise.

Note

1 See Aas and Jørgensen (2013) for more details.

16 Commitment to sustainability in Agder

Stina Torjesen and Karen Landmark

The corporate social responsibility project at Agder

In this chapter we look closer at a regional initiative called CSR Agder. CSR Agder was a project-based co-operation on corporate social responsibility (CSR) and sustainability, which involved actors from the private and public sector, as well as Agder Research (AR) and University of Agder (UoA). This project exemplifies the idea of Triple Helix. The project lasted for 4 years and ended in 2013. This chapter outlines the origins of the project, key initiatives, collaboration and possible outcomes. It also presents material on how three key regional industrial actors work related to CSR and sustainability.

The project provided an important arena for conversations on sustainability. It allowed actors to forge a shared conceptualisation of sustainability as one where, in a long-term scenario, 'business as usual' was highly risky. Moreover, and importantly, it also allowed the participants to generate a shared understanding of sustainability as a possible source of value creation and business survival. The latter point is relevant for this book: a central function of the project was to develop a shared sense of appropriateness around the notion that it was acceptable to make money when and while addressing sustainability. Finally, the project also allowed for new research to be initiated; this was research that was funded by regional government agencies, and undertaken in close collaboration with regional companies.

It is not easy to measure how deeply rooted sustainability is in the regional knowledge system. However, we believe that the applied research project CSR Agder allowed the actors to forge a shared conceptualisation of sustainability as one where in a long-term scenario 'business as usual' is highly risky, and also one where sustainability could be understood as a possible source of value creation and business survival. The participants welcomed the emphasis on business survival and shared value: and it was particularly helpful to arrive at these insights collectively, so that participants were assured that due attention to the business case was appropriate. This collective realisation may, arguably, have strengthened the companies' commitment to sustainability, and supported knowledge development into the regional knowledge system.

A regional initiative towards corporate social responsibility

Theoretical perspectives

Two themes from the literature hold particular relevance for our chapter: the reasoning behind corporate social responsibility initiatives, and debates about the likely scale and pace of change as society and business attempt to transition towards sustainability. The literature on CSR looks at the role of business in society from the firm level perspective. At its core lies the question of what impacts companies may have on society, either positive or negative, and the extent to which, and how, companies need to address, or even utilise further, these impacts. There are at least three ways to think about the role of companies in relation to society.

The first perspective holds that companies should constrain or adjust their behaviour so that this conforms to prevailing social norms or distinct ethical frameworks. From this perspective companies are seen as facing a set of ethical expectations that go beyond pure legal requirements. These ethical requirements can be formulated differently, depending on which type of ethical reasoning one may want to adopt (i.e. utilitarian, Kantian or other) or depending on what type of social norms would prevail in a given context. Seen from an Integrative Social Contract Theory perspective, for example, the moral consensus in many societies has shifted, so that companies are not only expected to focus on producing goods and services at reasonable prices, but also to address other issues, including environmental footprint, provision of decent work throughout a company's supply chain or the consequences of work and management patterns in a company on racial or gender inequality. Companies need to adhere to what is expected by society (ethical responsibilities) and also, ideally, contribute to society through additional charitable acts (philanthropic acts). Importantly, this strand in the literature acknowledges that the ethically imposed restrictions or additional contributions that companies allow for may, in some cases, result in additional costs or missed business opportunities.

The second perspective argues that companies will improve their risk management if they engage with social actors to 'do good'. This perspective finds that 'doing good' will be costly, but that such activities are nevertheless justified because they can 'integrate companies into the social fabric of local communities' in a way that 'strengthen social bonds' (Fombrun, Gardberg & Barnett 2000). Moreover, and crucially, engaging with non-profit actors and communities will build 'reputational capital', which in turn may strengthen a company's ability to 'negotiate more attractive contracts with suppliers and governments, to charge premium prices for its products, and to reduce its cost of capital' (Fombrun et al. 2000, p. 1). Here, even if there are tangible and immediate costs associated with CSR, these are likely to pay off in the long run, even if these benefits will be hard to measure in quantitative terms.

The third perspective stresses that companies can transform social problems into business opportunities. This implies attempting to solve critical social challenges while simultaneously seeking to increase the profitability of the firm. A number of writers have contributed to this strand in the literature. Harvard professors Michael E Porter and Mark R Kramer hold a particularly prominent position due to their widely referred concept of Creating Shared Value (CSV) (Porter & Kramer 2011). Here, all social and environmental challenges facing local or global communities constitute potential business opportunities that should be addressed at the strategic management level and as part of forging competitive business strategies. Given the profound social and environmental challenges facing communities across the globe, Porter and Kramer predict that CSV will 'drive the next wave of innovation and productivity growth in the global economy'. In more detailed terms CSV may entail strategies to re-conceive products and markets so that these can solve social or environmental problems; re-defining productivity in the value chain by increasing the social, environmental and economic performance of supply chain members; and fostering local cluster development in areas where key suppliers are located.

There is relatively little scholarly consensus in the field of CSR, and the ethical vs. the strategic understanding is a major division in the field. Indeed, one can label CSR as an essentially contested concept. These scholarly divisions form a stark contrast to the consensus making process that materialised in the course of the regional project. However, we will later argue that this third perspective was acknowledged by all the participants in the project CSR Agder, but still most of all a theoretical perspective, not used actively to change their business at the time span of the project.

CSR Agder: a regional response to global challenges

The project CSR Agder was initiated in 2008 against the backdrop of global insecurity, finance crises and rising awareness of the negative consequences of climate change. Business as usual became a risky option and more and more actors were looking for new paths forward. At this time several regional actors expressed the importance of better knowledge about the benefits of CSR for Agder as a region, and for private and public organisations operating in and from Agder.

One initiative from UoA joined forces with another initiative taken in co-operation by AR and a private communication firm in Kristiansand. In addition, both regional counties started to put sustainability on the agenda and looked for ways of taking practical measures. In addition, NHO (confederation of Norwegian enterprises) and LO (The Labour Union) had both elevated CSR on their agendas, while Innovation Norway had just started its own CSR programme. It made good sense to join forces, and they did, facilitated by Agder Research and funded initially by all actors involved. The project CSR Agder started its trial period in 2009, and worked to build a base for a more long-term and goal based project.

The project involved a number of different companies that had, at the outset, different outlooks on CSR and also different levels of commitment to CSR. Some companies were close to consumer markets (clothing, amusement, food) and were partially concerned and motivated by present or likely future customer expectations. Other companies (renewable energy and large industrial plants) were more concerned over potential future changes to the business context due increased attention to environmental concerns. At least one of these companies formed part of a large multinational company where, at the head quarter level at the time of our project, CSR was promoted as a major concern for all business operations.

In the early phase of the project, much time was spent on knowledge generation through arranging workshops with prominent external sustainability experts and internal discussions. The research team played a central part in selecting who should speak, defining the themes and highlighting relevant literature. The research team also conducted what was referred to as 'faglig fasilitering' (can be translated to knowledge-based facilitation). 'Faglig fasilitering' resembles ideas in the Action Research field, in particular, if we understand action research as a process of trying out theories in real life, with real people, in real situations as a mutual learning process in a mutually acceptable ethical landscape. However, the project was not designed as an action research project to begin with, but in hindsight we see that this could have added some important dimensions.

Later, as part of the main project more formal arrangement 'fagforum' was launched in 2011 and consolidated its position as an important meeting point in 2013. Meetings were held at the venues of one of the members in the forum, and the agenda for the day was set by the project in collaboration with companies that were hosted. A key aim was to collectively build capacity on the theme of sustainability/innovation/CSR. Companies were each other's critics and supporters. During each visit, one of the companies was challenged to present their work on corporate responsibility

Table 16.1 Vision and goals set in 2010

Vision	Agder as a region known for its research based and continuous work on CSR in all its organisations
Main project goal	Create a network of key actors for promoting CSR in a way that supports green growth, innovation and development of the region
Through	Increasing the regional knowledge of how organisations implement and use CSR as a driver for change
	Use CSR as a mean of co-operation between regional business and institutions

and sustainability, focusing on areas they considered to be challenging. The project group subsequently gave advice and feedback, and further discussed the way forward. A key theme in much of the presentations and discussions was increasing awareness that 'business as usual' was not an option. EYDE members have in our opinion approached this challenge in a manner consistent with theories of industrial clusters. Companies in the same cluster often have different customers and products but share many needs, challenges, resources and frameworks. Collaboration to acquire new knowledge and opportunity for joint reflection on the long-term strategic consequences are typical benefits that cluster members can take advantage of and which may strengthen the companies' individual competitiveness. It is useful for these companies to use the cluster as a forum for dialogue between businesses and for dialogue with the government and other external resources and actors.

The project also triggered research. One prominent initiative was a case study of three industrial actors. We will go on to highlight some key findings and relate these briefly to the relevant literature. A key emphasis of the case studies was to explore how the companies were able to create 'shared value': i.e. delivering social or environmental value to the region as well as economic value for the company.

The research found that the construction company Skanska has focused on being the best at delivering green buildings and has thus gained a competitive advantage, while major construction projects in the region have become more environmentally friendly. Dyreparken actively adheres to ethical issues relating to animal zoo, and has signed a long-term and effective co-operation with the relevant actors in the voluntary sector who share Dyreparken's objectives. The clothing company Stormberg has been among the first fashion brands in Norway who have published their supplier lists publicly and actively worked to improve safety and production conditions at its Asian subcontractors. This has given the company more stable supplies, as well as good long-term relationships with their suppliers.

Saint Gobain and Xstrata (now Glencore) is part of the EYDE cluster and had jointly with the other companies in the network identified energy and the environment as key focus areas. The aim was to solve environmental problems with their products and be international leaders in energy production. Saint Gobain and Xstrata, as members of EYDE Network, had used this forum to jointly identify key challenges related to environmental and resource shortages that may affect the companies' long-term strategies. Firms rely on central projections in academia and society. In particular, these firms engage with discourses centred on how current industry production, consumption and population growth continues to 9 billion people have a resource overuse corresponding to 2.5 Earths in 2050. Large-scale innovation and efficiency are needed in a variety of industry sectors in order to avoid such a scenario. Companies with long-term investment horizons, such as the processing industry in Agder, must take into account changes in market and business conditions that will result from this.

How to initiate corporate social responsibility

The project changed over the years it existed: starting as an open innovation area, where ideas and knowledge were shared, through a more introvert phase where these ideas were developed business case by business case in the 'fagforum' meetings, to yet another phase of trying to look more in-depth on four specific cases. The project founders and funders also played different roles throughout the project, some being more involved than others.

It is difficult to claim that the project initiated specific changes to regional plans, although it could be the case that the knowledge and capacity built into the project on the part of government actors will shape future planning processes.

Still, we can point to several initiatives in the region that put sustainability at its core. VRI-programme at Agder decided in 2011 to make sustainability a cross cutting standard in all their projects. This was decided in the context of the counties participation in and development of CSR Agder. The VINN plan (the regional plan for innovation and sustainable value creation 2015–2030) has also developed the content of sustainability for the region from something that was an add-on to something that is at the core of regional development.

The project involved all major government and business actors in the region that already were actively engaged in sustainability related activities and concerns. This unique and sustained gathering of major actors ensured that it became a prominent arena; indeed, it was one of the main arenas for conversations on sustainability to take place in the region during its time.

As mentioned earlier, it also allowed actors to forge a shared conceptualisation of sustainability as one where in a long-term scenario 'business as usual' is highly risky and also one where sustainability could be understood as a possible source of value creation and business survival. The participants welcomed the emphasis on business survival and shared value, and it was particularly helpful to arrive at these insights collectively, so that participants were assured that due attention to the business case was appropriate. This collective realisation may, arguably, have strengthened the companies' commitment to sustainability.

The research that was undertaken formed an important part of this collective realisation. The interviews undertaken and the final publication were important promoters of these perspectives. At the outset of the project the researchers and several of the key industry participants had 'conscious knowledge' (explicit knowledge held by the individual) of sustainability and also an interest in the 'business case' for sustainability. It may have been that case that the project helped create 'objectified knowledge' that is now shared among the organisations participating.

The role of applied research in initiating corporate social responsibility

The researchers in this project were highly involved and deliberately influenced practice. Scholarly theories and knowledge were provided so as to fit business interest and responsiveness to 'the business case for CSR'. In hindsight this provision of knowledge was selective; the third strategic perspective on CSR was prioritised over ethical perspectives by the researchers.

In this way the project points to the social nature of knowledge formation in two ways: It highlights the potential use of research and scholarly insights to help forge consensus among a range of different actors. It also highlights the role of researchers and the role of scholarly knowledge as building the case for appropriateness of particular business practices and business discourses. Our role as researchers or as informed facilitators in this project changed as the project developed. We started the project with a wish to enforce beliefs and to build consensus around the idea that business as usual is not an option. Our agenda was normative from the start, but throughout the project the roles around the table were in many ways equalised, meaning the parts informed each other and a common ground was established. The researchers brought boarder theoretical awareness, businesses contributed with their knowledge over real business constraints. The different parts of the project brought specific knowledge to the table, and through the process, new knowledge was developed building on insights from all parts.

Looking ahead we can note that the project ended in 2013, but work continues along other tracks: Parallel to the development of the project itself, the regional CSR/Sustainability discourse also developed. The public debate concerning sustainability is much more obvious and present in 2015 than it was in 2009 when the project started. Hence, all the involved parties now get sustainability input from a multiple of sources. We argue that in Agder in 2015, sustainability is recognised by many of the main regional actors as a driving force for business development and regional development.

For AR, sustainability has become a part of organisational strategies and goals and is today noticeable in several projects, crossing subject lines. Still, the organisation has not yet expressed that sustainability is a main driving force, making the organisation prioritise some projects over others.

Yet, by way of conclusion, we should stress the unique contributions and role of AR in putting sustainability on the regional agenda. The research institute undertakes applied research and is depended on external funding for their research activities. This was an important trigger of dialogue with a range of actors and it gave an incentive to invite in, and elicit support, from both government and business actors. In this way the necessity to generate funding became a virtue of some sort, helping to foster co-operation and a broad regional dialogue.

17 Universities' external relations

Hans Christian Garmann Johnsen, Roger Henning Normann and Rómulo Pinheiro

Universities' third task

Much attention has been given to the so-called third task of the university (OECD 2007a; see also Chapter 10 in this book). Some universities even brand themselves as 'innovative universities', highlighting their interactive role with business and society at large. There are external calls for stronger university-society co-operation. In Norway, as in many other countries, part of such efforts has been attempted formalised and organised as technology-transfer office (TTO). In this chapter we ask how a small university in a peripheral region can succeed with institutionalising the TTO function, how should the TTO function be organised, what are the internal barriers in the university for more external co-operation and to what extent this TTO function complements other external roles of the university.

The background for the case we present here is that the University of Agder (UoA), which is a relatively new, regional university, wants to take a role in supporting socio-economic development of Southern Norway. However, the university struggles to define this role and to develop strategies that would support it.

In analysing this, we identify two main and competing conceptualisations of how the university interacts with the region. These two correspond roughly to a major divide in the theoretical discussion on the social role of universities. On the one hand, there is the innovation, or *regional innovation* discourse, that emphasises the social, utilitarian and economic role of universities. On the other hand, there is the study of academic *institutionalisation*, which looks at how universities develop based on their generic disciplinary structure.

Our research of the social role of the UoA was initially much informed by the regional innovation discourse. Our qualitative research and quantitative interviews, revealed that there are many features of the university in compliance with the institutional discourse. In the discussion part of this chapter, we aim to bring these two discourses together and reflect on possible implications for policy, theory and practice in the form of a strategy for the university.

The background for this project was that UoA commissioned researchers, at Agder Research and Department of Work-life and Innovation (through the RIS Centre), to collaborate on a feasibility study relating to possible forthcoming restructuring of the TTO-function at the UoA. The design of the project was mainly done in a dialogue between the involved parties at the UoA in January 2011. The intention from the university was to get a new contract with The Research Council of Norway (RCN), so as to maintain its funding of the TTO function. The feasibility study should result in a draft of *different* organisational models for TTO functions at the university. The project had a short time span. The report was to be ready by June 2011. The researchers from the RIS Centre were also asked to develop a plan for implementation of the project.

The researchers used this 'freedom' to ensure that the quantitative and qualitative studies were designed in such a way that data from the project could also later be used in academic publications. The report that came out of the project contained theoretical outlines of discourses related to TTOs in addition to the data we had collected. This was interview data with academics and administrators within UoA, with regional stakeholders seeking to identify and take a role relating to the new TTO in the region, with TTO representatives abroad and in other parts of Norway as well as a quantitative survey mapping variations in external engagements of UoA employees (Normann & Johnsen 2011).

The report, which contained strategic assessments and relatively clear recommendations, was later used by UoA to develop a new and successful application for funding of the TTO function (the FORNY programme), as well as dedicating 1 man-year to TTO related functions in the UoA's administration. The researchers later used the data collected in the project as foundations for academic conference chapters and publications. By 2016 the new TTO organisation has been established.

The disciplinary variety of external engagement by the University of Agder

The policy discussion about TTOs is not entirely new. It goes back more than three decades. The systematic focus on commercialisation of university knowledge was institutionalised in the United States via the 'Bayh-Dole Act' from 1980, and equivalent legislation in many other EU countries in the 1990s. Norway enacted this type of legislation only in 2003, in spite of the fact that university-industry collaborations go back to the mid-1990s (Gulbrandsen & Nerdrum 2009). TTO is primarily about securing the intellectual property (IP) rights to university research. In other words, the question of the university's knowledge has not only a social (open) side, but also a purely private side in the form of proprietary good (Slaughter & Leslie 1997). From this perspective TTOs can be viewed as an instrumental policy tool to increase productivity. This does not entail that the notion that universities should contribute with knowledge that directly benefits the market place/society at large is novel. The American 'land grant universities' which were established in the 1880s, belong to this category, as well as the German technical universities and the UK's civic ('red brick') universities established during the same period. In Norway, the Bergen-based Norwegian School of Economics (NHH) and the former Agricultural College (outskirts of Oslo) also fall into this category, while the more than 200-years-old ('classic') University of Oslo has, to a greater extent, been less oriented towards industry or 'the market' in its classic sense.

The notion of TTO is based on an assumption of a value chain, where research-based ideas can be developed into something that can be traded into the market place. However, before it can be commercialised, the idea must undergo many different phases, with each phase requiring special expertise and, to a certain extent, also different institutional support. In Norway, a government sponsored programme (FORNY) has aided such types of activities since the mid-1990s. Universities in Norway have chosen different models for this, and are also different in how far down in the value chain (degree of institutionalisation) they have engaged with technology transfers to the outside world.

More specifically, there are also many different discussions starting from technology transfer, to more systemic changes in university/society relations. Common to these discourses are that they imply stronger (tighter) interactions between research (science) and society. However, studies have indicated that the transfer of knowledge from university to business and society at large is a more complex process than what is described in the academic literature. Recent studies suggest that there are major challenges to efficiently and effectively organise such types of interactions and co-operative arrangements (Normann 2012; Normann & Johnsen 2013; Pinheiro, Benneworth & Jones 2012).

In contrast to the *instrumental perspective* which follows a logic of means ends rationality or outcomes (March & Olsen 2006), the *institutionalisation perspective* tries to understand the dynamics of university development from its generic feature of knowledge development, cultures and disciplines. Burton Clark's (1983) seminal work sheds light on the centrality of *knowledge*, the building block in which higher education systems are built upon, to the ways in which university activities and structures have traditionally been, and still are organised (Frank & Gabler 2006; Jencks & Riesman 2002). While reflecting upon the challenges associated with efforts geared towards generating normative statements about the purpose or *raison d'être* of universities, Clark (1983) contends that, if or when there is a shared purpose within a given local setting or organisation, it emerges from the forming of academic groups (and individual loyalties) around bodies of knowledge or *disciplines*, with functioning objectives arising from the interplay between 'the organisation of people' and 'the organisation of knowledge'.

Dressel and Marcus (1982) define an *academic discipline* as a systematic way of organising and studying a given phenomenon. According to them, disciplinary structures are composed of *five* basic components, namely:

- a substantive component; encompassing assumptions, variables, concepts, principles and relationships;
- a linguistic component; upon which core disciplinary elements are identified and key relationships defined and explored;
- a syntactical component; i.e. the continuous searching and organising process leading to the further development of the discipline;
- a value-component; based on shared commitments on content (what) and methodologies (how);
- a conjunctive component; shedding light on the relationship between distinct disciplinary fields.

It is the unique interaction of the elements mentioned earlier that provides each discipline with its 'distinctive character'. To date, the most famous (and polemic) debate around the differences amongst disciplinary fields was triggered by C.P. Snow's memorable (1959) lecture on the conflict between the natural sciences and the arts/humanities (Snow 2012). Amongst other aspects, a controversial distinction between the 'culture of science' and the 'culture of intellectuals' was advanced. Snow's account has received numerous criticisms. Becher (1981, p. 122), for one, claims that Snow's dichotomy is 'crude and damaging' and that it does not account for 'the activities and aspirations of those who inhabit the [complex] worlds of different disciplines'. According to Clark (1983), each academic discipline possesses a unique *knowledge tradition* or categories of thought. Associated with this aspect are distinct *codes of conduct*, i.e. agreed upon templates of appropriate behaviour, what neo-institutional scholars like March and Olsen (2006) term as 'the logic of appropriateness'. Disciplines influence the values and norms of individuals through socialisation or indoctrination processes (Parry 2007), hence creating scientific communities 'of men who share a paradigm' (Kuhn 1970, cited by Clark 1983, p. 76). Despite their undeniable influence, sociologists like Clark (1983) contend that disciplinary cultures are hard to pin down, not only because they are vaguely sensed by their members, but also because they are barely perceived by outsiders.

The role of disciplines

When it comes to attempts at defining what a discipline *is* and *does*, five distinct positions have been identified (Krishnan 2009). From a *philosophical perspective*, academic disciplines are directly associated with problems related to the organisation of knowledge and how it relates to reality. The issue of 'unity' versus 'plurality' (dis-unity) is of paramount importance in this regard. From a more traditional philosophical perspective academic disciplines are simply conceived as particular branches of knowledge which, taken together, form the whole or unity of knowledge that has been created by the efforts of distinct, yet inter-related scholarly communities. Yet, this conceptualisation does not take into account that academic disciplines reflect the dilemma that our knowledge of the world is, to a large degree, split into a large number of branches. Proponents of 'plurality' views of knowledge (and science for that matter), argue that boundaries between disciplinary fields exist because this creates some level of coherence in terms of theories, concepts, and methods, thus allowing for the testing and validation of hypothesis according to agreed-upon scientific rules. The latter tend to differ from discipline to discipline, hence making them to some extent incompatible.

The *sociological perspective* tends to approach academic disciplines from the viewpoint of the sociology of work, with professionalisation and the division of labour as core dimensions. Following this line of thought, disciplines are then treated as a particular form of division of labour within science, and as a crucial aspect of the *institutionalisation* and *professionalisation of science*. Professionalisation increases the competition amongst disciplinary groups over limited financial resources, influence, autonomy and status, and tends to exacerbate distinct values and belief systems (Clark 1983), in turn, contributing to both a sense of unity (amongst equals) and fragmentation, i.e. the rise of sub-cultures and a silo mentality. Academic professions or disciplines 'are thus identified as the main power blocs in the academic environment with the most homogeneous and professionalised disciplines exerting most influence in universities and the scientific community' (Krishnan 2009, p. 29).

The *historical perspective* sheds light both on the continuity (*institutionalisation*) of disciplines and the discontinuity (*de-institutionalisation*) from obsolete practices and ways of thinking. Historians are keen to investigate the wider societal context and the overall (macro-level) conditions that influence the development of a given disciplinary field. For example, within the realm of the social sciences, a whole range of new disciplines were institutionally established during the late 19th and early 20th century, including sociology, anthropology, psychology, political science and economics (Krishnan 2009). Evolutionary patterns have been observed. In the cases of anthropology and psychology, the disciplines split from their parent fields of natural history (former) and philosophy and medicine (latter). Historical inquiries point to a kind of natural 'life cycle' for disciplines, with development patterns moving from *formation* to *eclipsing* and later *decline*, albeit not necessarily in a deterministic fashion.

From a *management perspective*, disciplinary department structures are seen primarily as an organisational problem and a way of marketing knowledge.

> Universities need to position themselves on the higher education and science market by recruiting and retaining suitable personnel that can acquire and promote marketable new knowledge in the form of attractive courses, technological or business application and policy development – all of which are important sources of income and reputation for universities.
>
> (Krishnan 2009, p. 37)

The rise of 'strategic science regimes' in tandem with the need for greater organisational responsiveness and flexibility are resulting in novel structural combinations, as illustrated by the predominance of interdisciplinary (teaching and research) units tasked with knowledge- production, transmission (transfer) and application or innovation. The seeming combination of (global) *excellence* and (local) *relevance* (Perry & May 2006) is putting a premium on knowledge production of the so called 'mode-2' type (Nowotny, Scott & Gibbons 2001). This tends to transcend disciplinary boundaries and adopt an increasingly external, societal outlook (i.e. focus on impact).

Finally, the *anthropological perspective* conceives of academic disciplines in terms of the cultural (universal) practices that aid their original creation, maintenance and survivability. In such situations, practitioners belong to different 'academic tribes' inhabiting and defending different 'knowledge territories', distinguishing themselves through self-created cultural practices and specific values. Each discipline is characterised by its own *subculture*, clearly identifiable by a common vocabulary. According to Becher (1981, p. 114), *language* 'helps to unite groups of people, partly at least because it reflects shared values and serves to reinforce them'. There are substantial internal variations across specific disciplinary fields. For example, with respect to their apparent vulnerability to outside forces, it is argued that, in their work, social scientists and humanists are more susceptible to political and/or world views when compared to their natural sciences peers. Similarly, differences have been detected both *across* and *within* professional fields from medicine to law to engineering, in line with their normative orientations or dominant *ethos* (teaching, research, service) and the work-patterns of a given profession.

Disciplinary cultures

Amongst social science scholars interested in the dynamics of higher education systems, Tony Becher's seminal work on *disciplinary cultures* has, over the years, received considerable praise and attention (Becher 1981, 1987, 1994; Becher & Trowler 2001; Neumann & Becher 2002).

Lattuca and Stark (1994, p. 404) argue that Becher's work provides a considerable body of knowledge supporting the thesis of enduring epistemological differences. Scholars like Parry (2007) have recognised Becher's work on academic tribes and territories as 'a landmark overview of academe'.

In contrast, others have criticised Becher's work for its over-emphasis on the socialisation aspects (epistemological features) of disciplines in explaining the behaviour of academics, in detriment of organisational, cultural and ideological characteristics of particular contexts and the interests and understandings of actors in them (Trowler 1997). Naturally, it is worth bearing in mind that Becher's original conclusions were limited to two national higher education systems (UK and US) and a few dominant institutions, and that the (national and international) higher education landscape and the academic profession have changed considerably in the last three decades.

A major aspect of this body of work lies on the assumption that the *cultural* and *cognitive* aspects of disciplines are tightly intertwined. Becher proposes a categorisation or typology based on *four* distinct disciplinary groupings, organised along the following dimensions: *hard* vs. *soft*; *pure* vs. *applied*. Amongst other aspects, the author describes in detail the knowledge orientation and the cultural traits associated with each one of the disciplinary groupings.

Regarding 'soft' knowledge domains, *soft-pure* scientific inquiry was best characterised by considerable heterogeneity amongst disciplinary fields. Generally speaking, however, it is pointed out that the role of external interests (e.g. political agencies) across the social sciences appears to be stronger than is the case in the humanities, the natural sciences or even the technical professions (Becher & Trowler 2001). As for the research agendas surrounding *soft-applied* knowledge, it is claimed that their predominant features lie on the relative susceptibility to non-academic interests such as those emanating from professional associations, governmental agencies and/or groups of clients. The permeation of external interests in the primary activities of academe was found to be a significant factor in the overall degree of autonomy enjoyed by a given discipline.

Beecher and Trowler (2001, p. 177) comment that 'value attached to directly useful knowledge is related to broader cultural considerations, and varies over time and place', and that 'there are countervailing tendencies amongst elite applied scientists towards achieving independence from external influence by favouring the more theoretical, less instrumental aspects of the domain'.

We may thereby conclude that these taxonomies and classification provide us with other types of expectations as regards university/society

Table 17.1 Broad disciplinary groupings

Hard, pure	*Soft, pure*
Abstract reflective	Concrete reflective
Natural sciences	Humanities and social sciences
Hard, applied	*Soft, applied*
Abstract active	Concrete active
Science-based professions	Social professions

Source: Based on Becher (1994, p. 152).

interactions, then was the case in the more instrumentalistic, regional innovation discourse.

Our case: University of Agder and the Agder region

In this chapter we focus on the interplay between knowledge-related (sub-disciplinary) dimensions and patterns of external engagement at the sub-unit level of the UoA. The university was founded in 2007, although it has developed (amalgamation) from five previous educational institutions that date back about 40 years. In spite of its distinct historical path, institutional profile and institutionalised traditions as, primarily, an education-centered establishment, academic postures across UoA sub-units differ somewhat, thus shedding light on the complexities associated with the interplay between epistemological dimensions and more locally-routed (contextual) aspects in both the 'inner' (private) and 'outer' (public) lives of academic units.

In 2009, R&D-personnel at the university produced 295 publication points (0.58 points per R&D man-year). In 2013 this had increased to 568 points (0.96 points per man-year), a 93% rise. Here, UoA distinguishes itself from the other Norwegian Universities. The mean for the period in the sector is a 15% increase (excluding UoA).

Another development concerns the growth in R&D personnel. In 2007 there were 521 employees working in academic positions at UoA. By 2013, this had increased to 590, a 13% growth (similar to that of the sector as a whole). The number of R&D-personnel with a doctorate has also grown. In 2007 220 of the UoA employees held a doctorate; in 2013, this had increased by 20%, to 264.

Maybe the most radical change is the University's attractiveness as a study place. Back in 2007, when it was still as a university college it enrolled 7,757 students. In 2013 this number increased to 11,030 students, a 42% rise. In 2014, there were on average 19.4 students per R&D-employee at the UoA, the most amongst all the 'new' Universities (University of Nordland 17.4, and University of Stavanger 14.3). The five 'old' universities had in 2014 between 6.8 and 7.9 students per R&D-position.

Interesting changes have also happened regarding patterns of external co-operation and resource dependencies. If we operationalise the latter as 'external funding' and 'research revenue', we see that in 2009 UoA generated NOK 33 million from RCN and the EU (NOK 58,000 per research FTE). By 2013, this had dropped to NOK 25.5 million (NOK 43,000 per research FTE). For UoA, this represents a 25% *decrease* in external funding per research FTE in the period. If we compare this to the developments at the other universities in Norway in the period, we find a 15% *increase* in external funding per research FTE (excluding UoA).[1]

This represents a puzzle; why did UoA's employees generate greater amounts of external funding back when there were fewer people with a doctorate, and when the university was still a college? In order to understand

Table 17.2 Best use of knowledge in conjunction with public agencies and/or private companies

	Commercialised. a product or service	*Contribute to increased productivity*	*Contribute to organisational renewal*	*Increase others' expertise*	*Increasing ethical awareness*	*Increasing democratic competencies*	*Provide a better basis for decisions*	*Increase learning ability*	*Contribute to entertainment and experiences*	*Provide better health*	*Contribute to the social debate*
Department of Engineering	22.9%	20.0%	3.9%	9.7%	6.1%	2.1%	8.1%	8.1%	11.4%	2.2%	4.4%
Department of Information and Communication Technology	20.0%	8.0%	5.3%	4.6%	1.2%	2.1%	4.1%	3.6%	8.6%	2.2%	2.9%
Institute of Health and Nursing	5.7%	8.0%	11.8%	11.1%	19.5%	6.3%	10.6%	8.1%	2.9%	33.3%	10.9%
Department of Public Health and Sports Nutrition	5.7%	6.0%	1.3%	5.6%	2.4%	0.0%	2.4%	5.4%	2.9%	24.4%	6.6%
Department of Nordic and Media Studies	5.7%	2.0%	5.3%	10.6%	8.5%	18.8%	9.8%	10.8%	22.9%	4.4%	14.6%
Department of Religion, Philosophy and History	5.7%	4.0%	5.3%	5.6%	13.4%	14.6%	7.3%	3.6%	11.4%	2.2%	8.0%
Department of Music	5.7%	4.0%	3.9%	3.2%	4.9%	4.2%	3.3%	3.6%	11.4%	4.4%	2.2%
Department of Natural Sciences	5.7%	4.0%	3.9%	3.7%	1.2%	4.2%	3.3%	2.7%	5.7%	6.7%	2.2%
Department of Mathematical Sciences	5.7%	4.0%	3.9%	6.9%	2.4%	4.2%	5.7%	9.0%	5.7%	2.2%	6.6%
Department of Psychosocial Health	2.9%	0.0%	3.9%	3.7%	11.0%	6.3%	3.3%	6.3%	2.9%	8.9%	4.4%
Department of Languages and Translation	2.9%	2.0%	1.3%	2.8%	1.2%	2.1%	0.8%	3.6%	0.0%	0.0%	2.2%
Department of Pedagogic	2.9%	4.0%	11.8%	6.0%	8.5%	8.3%	4.9%	9.0%	5.7%	2.2%	6.6%
Department of Visual and Theatrical Subjects	2.9%	0.0%	0.0%	2.8%	3.7%	4.2%	0.8%	2.7%	8.6%	4.4%	2.2%
Department of Working Life and Innovation	2.9%	8.0%	9.2%	5.1%	2.4%	4.2%	6.5%	4.5%	0.0%	0.0%	3.6%
Department of Economics	2.9%	12.0%	11.8%	6.0%	2.4%	6.3%	13.0%	6.3%	0.0%	0.0%	6.6%
Department of Teacher Education	0.0%	0.0%	1.3%	0.5%	1.2%	2.1%	0.0%	0.0%	0.0%	0.0%	0.0%
Department of Sociology and Social Work	0.0%	2.0%	3.9%	2.3%	4.9%	2.1%	4.1%	2.7%	0.0%	0.0%	3.6%
Department of Information Systems	0.0%	8.0%	6.6%	4.2%	3.7%	2.1%	4.9%	5.4%	0.0%	0.0%	5.1%
Department of Political Science and Management	0.0%	4.0%	5.3%	3.2%	1.2%	4.2%	4.9%	2.7%	0.0%	2.2%	4.4%
Number of replies (total)	35	50	76	216	82	48	123	111	35	45	137

Table 17.3 Co-operation with public and/or private entities for the following activities

	R&D[1]	*Com*[2]	*Stud*[3]	*Run*[4]	*Exch*[5]	*Guest*[6]	*Sup*[7]	*Pro*[8]	*Cour*[9]	*MS*[10]	*ME*[11]	*Best*[12]	*Restr*[13]	*Adm*[14]
Department of Music	3.8	2.8	2.8	2.0	2.8	3.0	3.5	2.0	3.3	3.3	2.8	2.3	2.0	2.8
Department of Languages and Translation	2.5	F	2.5	3.0	2.5	2.3	1.8	1.6	2.6	2.1	2.0	1.0	1.6	1.7
Department of Public Health and Sports Nutrition	3.0	2.0	2.0	2.9	1.8	1.8	2.2	2.0	2.8	1.8	1.1	1.0	1.3	1.7
Department of Mathematical Sciences	3.1	2.0	2.6	3.0	2.0	2.4	2.1	1.7	2.4	1.6	2.3	1.1	1.2	1.3
Department of Psychosocial Health	3.1	1.8	2.4	3.4	3.4	3.1	2.9	2.1	2.8	2.1	2.2	1.4	1.9	1.8
Department of Political Science and Management	2.8	1.8	3.4	3.2	2.0	3.0	2.0	2.3	3.3	1.5	1.5	1.3	2.5	1.6
Department of Sociology and Social Work	3.9	1.6	2.1	2.6	1.8	2.8	2.2	2.2	2.4	1.8	1.2	1.0	1.0	1.5
AVERAGE	3.2	1.5	2.3	2.7	2.1	2.4	2.2	1.9	2.6	1.7	1.7	1.2	1.5	1.7
Department of Nordic and Media Studies	2.8	1.5	2.1	2.8	2.1	2.3	1.8	1.5	2.4	1.6	1.9	1.2	1.5	1.9
Department of Natural Sciences	2.6	1.5	2.8	2.8	1.4	1.9	2.3	1.6	2.8	1.7	1.7	1.0	1.2	1.3
Department of Engineering	3.2	1.5	2.4	2.6	1.7	2.4	2.7	1.8	2.2	1.7	1.4	1.2	1.3	1.4
Department of Education	3.8	1.4	2.4	3.4	1.9	2.6	1.3	1.3	3.1	1.1	1.3	1.2	1.1	1.7
Department of Health and Nursing	3.6	1.4	2.3	2.4	2.9	2.4	2.1	2.7	2.9	2.4	2.4	1.1	1.7	1.9
Department of Information and Communication Technology	3.2	1.4	1.6	1.8	1.5	1.5	2.5	1.6	1.8	1.2	1.2	1.1	1.0	1.0
Department of Religion, Philosophy and History	2.8	1.3	1.9	2.9	1.8	2.4	1.2	1.1	2.8	1.1	1.4	1.2	1.4	1.8
Institute for Visual and Theatrical Subjects	1.8	1.3	1.7	2.5	1.4	1.5	1.4	1.7	2.1	1.5	1.0	1.0	1.0	1.0
Department of Economics	2.9	1.3	2.1	2.9	2.1	2.3	2.5	2.1	2.6	1.4	1.4	1.4	1.6	1.9
Department of Information Systems	3.1	1.1	2.1	2.6	2.6	3.1	3.4	3.0	2.0	2.3	2.0	1.1	1.9	1.6
Department for Working Life and Innovation	4.3	1.0	2.2	2.9	2.4	2.7	2.5	1.9	2.8	1.9	1.4	1.1	1.9	2.2

Note: Average score per department (scale 1–5; 5 = very important; 1 = not important). Categories: (1) Research and development; (2) Commercialisation of research and/or development results (sorting variable); (3) Development of study and course programmes; (4) Run courses or lectures; (5) Exchange of students from the university to the public and/or private entities; (6) Guest lectures by people from the public and/or private entities; (7) Supervise Bachelor, Master or PhD thesis written in collaboration with, or on behalf of public and/or private sector; (8) Other projects undertaken by students in collaboration with / on behalf of the public and/or private entities; (9) Courses and/or teaching; (10) Mobility of students of UoA; (11)Mobility of graduates from UoA; (12) Contribute to business establishment; (13) Contribute to restructuring or reorganisation; (14) Contribute with administrative and/or managerial support.

this, we were allowed to make a survey questionnaire amongst UoA staff. The response rate for the survey was 49%, covering 61% of the academic staff. Next, we present the data (answers) emanating from the survey, grouped along departmental or sub-disciplinary units. Tables 17.2 and 17.3 present the results.

Disciplinary diversity in interaction

The overall finding from our study was that there are great varieties in the form of external engagement across departments at the university. Some findings from the earlier Table 17.3 should be pointed out. For example, we see that when posed with the question *'How do you think your knowledge can best be used in conjunction with public agencies and/or private companies?'* the bulk of the answers are in the group 'increase others' expertise'. The second largest response comes in the group 'contribute to public debate'. We note that the highest scores on commercialisation of products and services, come from the Department of Engineering and Department of Information and Communication Technology. To the question 'Co-operation with public and/or private entities' for the following activities, the highest scores emanate from the Department for Working Life and Innovation, Department of Sociology and Social Work, Department of Music and Department of Education in respect to 'Research and Development'. When we link this to 'commercialisation of research' and/or development results', somewhat surprisingly, the Department of Music scores highest in the sample. More interestingly, perhaps, is that the table shows the diversity of interaction forms and intensity. For example, the Department of Psychosocial Health scores low on 'Research and Development', but scores highest as regards 'External Courses' and 'Students Exchange'.

Based on the fact that there is this diversity in interaction patterns across disciplines at the university, our report to UoA's leadership suggested three possible models to increase its regional impact:

- Model A: the institutional model (build-up of activity at the university). Emphasising that commercialisation of research-based knowledge is a core activity for the university in line with research and teaching. There is a huge untapped potential that can be exploited by targeted investment at the university;
- Model B: the network model (contract/organisational co-operation between institutions). Incubator and the start-up milieus in the region are small and fragmented. The university can help to establish larger and more robust academic environments through initiating co-operation, creating a neutral platform of idea-development as institutional divides developing ideas from investing activities;

- Model C: the market model (launching of operation to another institution). The potential for commercialisation of knowledge is small. It is important for UoA to focus on research and teaching because external actors can manage statutory tasks on behalf of the university.

Following our recommendations, the university management tried to combine models *A* and *B*. It strengthened its internal organisation for research development, and it has engaged in organisational development in its wider regional networks with the intention of pooling resources and increasing efficiency. Deliberately, it has not chosen *model C*, i.e. leave it to external partners to drive the innovation and commercialisation activity more or less independent of the university.

Earlier, we presented two theoretical perspectives; *instrumental* perspective and the *institutional* perspective. While instrumental perspective takes regional development as its point of departure, and (normatively) asks how higher education can contribute to knowledge development in the region, the institutional perspective emphasises the different knowledge development processes at the disciplinary level. Thus, whereas the former perspective is outer-oriented and geared towards the market/society, the latter is inner-oriented towards science/knowledge/academia.

Becher's findings across the natural and social sciences as well as the humanities are of particular relevance. Natural scientists (e.g. physicists) were found to play an active role in issues of science policy, 'partly, perhaps, because they tend to be "flexible people, ready to turn their attention to other things", but partly also because they recognise that it is important to win public support for their activities' (Becher 1990, p. 17). Historians were thought to have learnt how to accommodate both their own ideals and external realities, 'they are sensible people, politically (with a small p)' (Becher 1989, p. 275). Finally, sociologists were perceived as being 'highly politicised, guilty of indoctrinating students, and "very left"' (Becher 1981, p. 110).

Thus, how disciplines interact with society, we argue, is *not* so much a matter of a local/regional practice, but instead of *learned codes* (norms, values, beliefs, identities) within the disciplines themselves. In other words, from the perspective of sociology of science/knowledge (Merton 1973), our empirical findings lend support towards the importance attributed to the socialisation, both early on (educational training) and on the job (departmental units), of relatively autonomous professionals (knowledge) workers, such as academic communities (Dingwall & Lewis 2014).

Can research influence practice?

In this study, we had both a narrow focus on how a university can transfer knowledge, and, on the other hand, a broader focus on knowledge development between university and region. We have argued that our data supports a broader perspective of knowledge interaction between university and region, but does the data support either the instrumental perspective of the institutional perspective?

It is fair to say that our empirical findings support some of the arguments found in the institutional literature on how disciplines develop. However, we have not been able to map out our data exactly so that it matches Becher's typology. One reason for this is that UoA is a rather young university with many applied fields of research. It does not have strong departments of basic research. Neither is it strong in the field of the natural sciences. However, this in itself makes our findings even more interesting, as we would expect that disciplines would mean less on such a university setting when compared to traditional universities characterised by well-established disciplinary demarcations. We found clear and strict disciplinary divides within a new, regionally-embedded university with many applied fields of knowledge/research. This indicates a strong institutional effect of the knowledge domains (disciplines).

In our report to the university, we communicated this insight and argued that it should have implications, even for the TTO organisation. Rather than a TTO, we argued for a knowledge transfer function that had a broader mandate to support regional and external engagement by the departments based on their disciplinary differences. Realisation of this idea is yet to be seen.

Note

1 Data from: http://dbh.nsd.uib.no/.

Conclusion

Applied social science research in the regional knowledge system

Hans Christian Garmann Johnsen, Elisabet S. Hauge, May-Linda Magnussen and Richard Ennals

The learning involved in writing this book

For the authors co-writing this book about knowledge, the writing process itself has produced knowledge that is both useful and important. Clearly, all academic writing involves, or at least *should* involve, some kind of learning. The learning in this book process has, however, been different from what is involved in writing an article for a scientific journal, or a book chapter in an anthology. In such writing, one positions one's "piece of knowledge" amongst the knowledge contributions of others engaging in a debate within a discipline or a research field. This means that even if there are differences between what the researchers engaging in a certain scientific debate research on, and how, and also disagreements on ontological and epistemological issues between them, these differences and disagreements will also have some limitations to their range, even if this range will vary amongst disciplines and research fields. This undoubtedly has its advantages. Gathering a diverse group of researchers and have them discuss something they all have in common, as we have done in this book, is however also productive. It simply produces another kind of knowledge; a knowledge that is both useful, and also quite urgent to bring forward at this point of time in Norwegian research history.

The reader of this book cannot have avoided noticing that its authors do not all belong to the same discipline or engage in the same research field. However, also within Agder Research, most of the time we work with those of our colleagues closest to our own research fields and disciplines; the ones who agree with us on basic ontological, epistemological and methodological issues. Many of us also spend a considerable amount of time collaborating and discussing with researchers outside our own organisation and region, while at the same time spending much time working closely with "practitioners" outside our own organisation, contributing to the social changes we are writing about in this book. All in all, this leaves *little time* and *few arenas* for academic discussions involving all academic staff at Agder Research. In addition, we have up until now lacked a *common language* for talking across disciplines and research fields in a productive manner; in a manner which may produce collective knowledge that we as an organisation need to advocate the common interest we and our partners have in developing our region towards becoming more socially, economically and environmentally sustainable.

At the beginning of the process of writing this book, the considerable diversity between the authors' research took much of our attention, and even seemed a bit overwhelming. However, we regard this diversity as healthy because it shows that we as researchers respond to diverse needs for knowledge with producing diverse knowledge instead of doing "one-size-fits-all" exercises. Also, the great variety in research approaches and outcomes between the authors has stimulated reflection in the process of writing the book. To be able to "talk" with each other, we have had to step further back from our everyday research and development activities than we usually do, and to address epistemological and ontological questions in a more fundamental and explicit manner than we often have to. We can say that the authors have had to position their research in a bigger research "map" than we usually need to position it in. We have had to move further away from the map than we usually do, in order to get the bigger picture, and reflect on our own and others' parts in it. We have had to position our research and development activities in what we in this book call the "regional knowledge system". While the dimensions and categories in this concept (as in any other concept) oversimplify the complex social reality of applied research, we no doubt needed to simplify in order to be able to talk about our research across the great variety of disciplines and research fields. Also, these dimensions and categories gave us a language to speak in, and to disagree in.

However, writing a book not merely aiming at showing this diversity, but also focusing on what we all had in common: namely doing applied social science research in the Agder region, the similarities between our research and development activities gradually became more visible. Moreover, we gradually developed a *collective knowledge* that we need, not only to sustain ourselves as an organisation, but to continue developing the Agder region using research. On an almost everyday basis, the authors of this book *see* the impact of our research on development and innovation processes in the region. We could say that we *see* the knowledge society, the way we define it, in action, being central parts of it ourselves. Obviously, this impact of our research has to do with the scientific quality of it. Another important prerequisite for making research matter is, however, knowledge about the production and dissemination of such knowledge in itself. Between ourselves, the authors of this book hold what is, in the process of co-writing this book, becoming *collective knowledge* on doing applied social science in close collaboration with representatives from public, private and civil sector in the Agder region. Doing applied research *that matters* is a form of competence in itself, but a competence or a form of knowledge that has low visibility, and is seldom articulated by central actors in the region we work in. This fact, coupled with a government push towards fewer and bigger research communities, and the universities' low ability to do the kind of research and development projects that we engage in, have made us realise how timely this book project is in today's Norway.

The way we see it, applied research closely tied to local and regional needs for change, is under threat in Norway today. For the authors, this not only constitutes a personal threat, but also a threat for the region. The way we and our partners see it, we not only contribute towards societal changes, but towards *necessary* societal changes. Having a vivid and sustainable regional economy is fundamental for the future of the region, and so is having an environment that it is possible to work and live in. Having a society that utilises its human resources in a good way is also an essential part of creating a region which is attractive to work and live in, and which is sustainable in the long run. Co-writing this book, we have not only become aware of knowledge we have in common, but have only to a small degree put this into words together. We have also become aware of a common engagement that both comes from doing our research, and is also needed in order to make our research matter. We not only *know* a lot about the social, economic and environmental development in our region. We also *care* about what happens here, also because we work and live here and engage in the social relations we do our work in. Writing this book has become a part of putting this knowledge and this engagement out there, in the region.

Some overall findings across the chapters in the book

In this book, applied research is seen as a vital part of the infrastructure for economic and social development, in the region and beyond. In Norway, a network of regional research institutes, doing mostly applied research, was established before the foundation of a new generation of regional universities. One can say that that income from oil and gas was invested in building a sustainable future. In this book we have tried to address the issue of how applied social science research contributes to knowledge development in a regional knowledge system. It has been organised in four parts.

In Part I we presented the context of the discussion, the region; studies that deliberately aimed to influence regional policy. Common to these studies is that they related to policy frameworks and discourses in the region.

Chapter 1: Developing a sustainable business model in a changing economy is a critique of the traditional institutional model for applied research. It shows how complex the relation is between being relevant, and at the same time having a high academic level.

Chapter 2: Why Norway has to develop its own innovation policy discusses how to measure the cause and effect of innovation. It is a critique of the linear model. Absorptive capacity implies a communicative organisation.

Chapter 3: Knowledge transfer in different regional contexts argues that there is a configuration of institutions that impacts the policy options.

Chapter 4: Collective knowing argues that the development process between research and practice (policy) is a long-term process of both constructing knowledge, but also developing relations, trust, mutual understanding and ability to reflect and consider new knowledge. The chapter argues that this happens often in conflict ridden environment.

Part II was mainly about understanding regional practice. These were studies that predominantly had an interpretive perspective.

Chapter 5: Opening or reproducing understanding argues, in line with Chapter 4, that the relation between research and practice is a process that takes time and involves values and conflicts. The researcher cannot avoid standing in a contested field. Time is important, as are the informal deliberation and negations that happen backstage. The researchers can easily come into a legitimacy crisis. The chapter considers three traditions of engaged research: the pragmatic, the dialogical and the critical.

Chapter 6: Social integration of refugees presents a critique of theorising and use of theoretical categories to understand particular contexts. The chapter calls for a more holistic approach to research.

Chapter 7: Comparative reflection argues that the experience of the researcher has a crucial impact on what the researcher will be able to understand, see and interpret in the field.

Chapter 8: Phenomenology of music students argues that a development process, like the education of musicians and the subsequent development of entrepreneurship in art, has to consider the process by which students develop ability, skills and interests in pursuing such a strategy. The chapter uses the term "projecting" as a way to describe what goes on at a psychological level in such processes.

Chapter 9: Power and knowledge argues that there often is a dominant discourse, and that the researcher needs to consider if they want to challenge this discourse. Being a researcher in particular fields implies going into a field of power.

Part III of the book presented studies that mainly aim at explaining regional practice. Common to these studies is that they had a proactive ambition to say something about causes, with important and decisive dimensions for social development.

Chapter 10: Network ties between universities and cultural and creative industries tries to show how relation between researchers and practice is dependent on networks, and the type of position the individual researcher has in such networks.

Chapter 11: The usefulness of applied research discusses the role of the researchers in trial research proved on a network development.

Chapter 12: Regional knowledge infrastructure argues that a long-term effect of research engagement with practice, can produce both institutions and competence that bring both research and practice forward.

Chapter 13: The Mittelstand argues that as a result of researchers introducing a new concept, one is able to see dimensions in development that would otherwise not be obvious. Deeper insight into a phenomenon increases our understanding, and also our policy recommendations.

Part IV of the book presented studies that were very directly aimed at influencing and changing regional social practice. Common to these studies was that they had a strong normative objective.

Chapter 14: Getting China-ready discusses how the researcher engages in a process of constructing an identity for a region.

Chapter 15: Business models for new experiential services discusses how theory from one field can be transferred to another field. It argues that this transfer can lead to creative processes. The research can help assist the process.

Chapter 16: Commitment to sustainability in Agder argues that this has helped to create an arena to discuss CSR,thus conceptualising this in relation to a strategy for the region.

Chapter 17: Universities' external relations discusses the double role that researchers face when on the one hand assisting the university with a TTO strategy, and at the same time reflecting on the type of processes exist between science and society. It has turned out to be rather complicated to make policy recommendations, based on the findings of the research project.

A balancing act

We do not see the contributions in this book as representative of applied social science research in a strict sense. But we do argue that the projects presented in this book represent a variety of approaches and positions that cover a large part of the field of social science. We have tried to analyse the chapters according to some of the issues we discussed in the introduction.

Table C.1 Level of involvement and level of analysis

	Individual	*Social*	*Structural*
Involved	Entrepreneurial musicians (8)	Collective knowing (4) Action research (5)	
Engaged	Institutional ethography (6) Ethno-integration (7)	Women's network (11) Knowledge infrastructure (12) CSR Agder (16)	Academia and industry (10) Tourism development (14) Business model transfer (15)
Observer		Knowledge sharing (3) Power and knowledge (9)	New business model (1) Innovation policy (2) Mittelstand business (13) Universities' third role (17)

Table C.2 Confirmative or critical research

	Confirm, enforce	*Criticise, renew*
Cultural	Entrepreneurial musicians (8) Tourism development (14) CSR Agder (16)	Collective knowing (4) Action research (5) Institutional ethnography (6) Ethno-integration (7) Power and knowledge (9)
Institutional	Knowledge sharing (3) Women's network (11) Knowledge infrastructure (12) Mittelstand business (13) Business model transfer (15)	New business model (1) Innovation policy (2) Academia and industry (10) Universities' third role (17)

On the issue of different ways of relating to practice, we have among the chapters represented the positions presented in Table C.1 (in Tables C.1, C.2 and C.3 we do not use the chapter's name, rather we have put a label on each chapter, chapter number in brackets).

We have also tried to classify whether the projects in the chapters are critical or confirmative in relation to stakeholders and regional practice. We have seen it in relation to two dimensions: culture and institutions. Although these are not clearly distinct entities, it refers to either the softer (like opinions, attitudes) or the harder (like organisations, formal authority or physical barriers) aspects of regional practice. Table C.2 is our summary.

One of the questions we asked ourselves was if there were any systematic tendencies between ways of funding research in regards how to do research and to what extent research is confirmative or critical. We found no such pattern. Commissioned research can be critical, just as contributory funded research can be confirmative; however, we also made the point that by referring to more basic research, the researcher can develop his or her critical sense.

We put as a subtitle to this book: 'Balancing validity, meaning and convenience'. What we implied by that is that applied social science is done in a social field where the researcher has to balance these concerns. The different chapters show how the researchers have managed this balancing; what choices are made and how the research is adjusted to the social environment. Sometimes convenience concerns are of highest priority; other times, validity or meaning. We see no particular pattern in this, neither do we propose an ideal model for handling the different concerns. Our argument is that doing applied social science research is *a balancing act*.

The knowledge system

In many ways this is a book that describes a multitude of situations, projects, research perspectives that happens in a specific research milieu. In a first view, Chapters 1–17 might seem like a fusion of different research projects that are written out as individual descriptions of ongoing and finalised research projects. The chapter contributions might also be read in an alternative way; independently or seen as a group of perspectives on the same phenomenon; the process of knowledge development.

As applied researchers we all have our special, expert fields. Expert knowledge is constantly evolving through new research projects, seminars, lectures and speeches, participating at professional conferences and writing scientific articles. Even though authors have contributed to this book project, it is obvious that not all of them have the same expert knowledge in research topics such as the Mittelstand, women refugees, knowledge transfer in regions or Chinese tourists. At the same time the book is an example of how different researchers prefer and activate different research strategies and methods. But, this is exactly one of the book's learning and focus points; the process of knowledge development is unique and multitudinous. Experiences cutting across researchers' daily lives stimulate new knowledge, competence and wisdom. With a platform in the researchers' expert fields, discussions have been lifted among the book project participants.

In our daily lives as applied researchers these are topics that we seldom have time to reflect upon, especially together in workshops and in discussion groups. A research milieu might easily appear as a block of flats, where the neighbours seldom meet and share and discuss specific information. A book project like this has opened the opportunity for such knowledge sharing and discussion. The single researchers were challenged to reflect upon their own contribution to a broader research field than their own expert field; the process of knowledge development, which is the platform for applied research role in the knowledge society.

Centre: periphery dimension

What we see in Norway (and in the EU) is a centralisation of the knowledge development process. One important policy path in the Norwegian society is building bigger unions of knowledge institutions. Policy added implement that accepted research institutes has to consist of more than 20 man-years to achieve basic grant from The Research Council of Norway. As a result, universities and research institutes have started an irreversible process of merging into bigger units. Merging institutes of research actors differs. In some occasions research institutes agree on merging with universities or university collages, in other situations research institutes merge with other complementary research institutes.

Democratise the process of the knowledge society by activating and involving citizens

The concept of the knowledge society has for a long time been an important term in EU policy, national policy and regional policy. But what does it actually mean? In such policy documents, the meaning of the concepts tends to be rather blurred and ambiguous, and it is difficult to judge whether we have or are now living in a knowledge society or not. On one hand, discussion often concerns what it means to be a member of the ongoing knowledge society. On the other hand, the discussion is about knowledge development for the future. The knowledge society is claimed to be about making a solid platform for future generations, and not just building a society that is *good enough* here and now. This understanding makes the concept of the knowledge society a continuous process.

> In a knowledge society, although knowledge is a main resource for development, we should not expect to have knowledge about everything. . . . we should be more concerned with the process of producing knowledge, because we are so dependent upon it.
>
> (Johnsen 2014, p. 1)

Developing the knowledge society is broader than building an infrastructure of research institutions and universities. The concept of knowledge is abstract and dynamic. Developing the knowledge society is a long-term common project that involves all of society participants. It is about understanding knowledge as a social process, highly influenced by power and policy, which involves and influences all of society's inhabitants/members. Developing knowledge is thus not restricted to an absolute structure of what is correct or false knowledge. In the process of realising the knowledge society, research institutes have an important role as gate keepers. The regional social science research institutes are platforms where different society actors' knowledge and lived experiences are accumulated.

In this process researchers are not totally objective or neutral. Doing research is also about getting "dirty hands", in the sense that the researcher interacts with the field of research at the same time as they have or build (hopefully in-depth) background knowledge about the phenomenon studied. The single book chapters are examples of researchers having a specific field of interest, at the same time as the individual authors are at different stages within their academic career and in their personal knowledge development process. In addition to being involved as researchers in different study fields, also researchers are influenced by power and policy when engaging within a specific field of research. The individual chapters therefore attempt to disclose the process of how new knowledge was designed and derived. One by one the individual chapters highlight how knowledge development is a unique process. Each chapter, both independently and collectively, provides examples of how knowledge is context-sensitive and timely. Research results are normally presented as academic time-limited snapshots of observed phenomenon, footprints such as articles, books and book chapters. The snapshots are nevertheless parts of a long evolutionary process that continues after the footprints are left behind in the collective process of realising the knowledge society.

Applied social science and the regional knowledge system

In the introduction we presented our meta perspective and a model for the main dimensions of a *regional knowledge system*. In concluding this book, it is relevant to ask what we can learn from the 17 cases we have presented on the development of a regional knowledge system.

We asked in the introduction: how is knowledge developed in a reflective reconstruction within a regional context, and what is the role of applied social sciences in this process? There is no simple answer to this question. The different chapters give each some part of the answer. Table C.3 illustrates that the cases in this book cover the majority of the knowledge creating situations that are set out in the table. Many of the cases might have been positioned in more than one category; however, as this is not a representative study, we present it merely as illustrating our argument. The table thereby shows that applied social science research can take many different roles and influence knowledge development in different ways.

One might argue that this is a rather vague conclusion of the present study. However, implicit in our formulations is that even if we cannot claim that we have presented a representative and comprehensive analysis

Table C.3 Applied social science research in the regional knowledge system

	Power: the social position or role dimension	*Beliefs: the dispositional dimension*	*Position: the interactive-situational dimension*	*Institutions: the knowledge-institutionalisation dimension*
Individual, explictit knowledge	Academia and industry (10) Business model transfer (15)	Entrepreneurial musicians (8)		
Collective, explicit knowledge	Innovation policy (2) Mittelstand business (13)	Tourism development (14)	Knowledge infrastructure (12)	Universities' third role (17) New business model (1)
Individual, implicit knowledge		Ethno-integration (7)	Action research (5) Power and knowledge (9)	
Collective, implicit knowledge	Women's network (11)	Institutional ethnography (6)	Knowledge sharing (3) Collective knowing (4)	CSR Agder (16)

of applied social science research in a regional knowledge system, we do argue that we have pointed at some of the major forms in which knowledge is developed and used in a region in the interplay between applied social science research and practice. Nobody can predict how knowledge will develop. Rather, knowledge development is a result of many different knowledge elements, some of which contradict each other. Other research institutes and academic departments could benefit from undertaking similar exercises. Talking to each other as researchers is a good preparation for communication with the wider world.

References

Aas, T. H. & Jørgensen, G. (2013). *Kilden digital: Forretningsmodell for streaming av kildens forestillinger*. Kristiansand, Norway: Agderforskning.

Abu-Lughod, L. (2006). The muslim woman: The power of images and the danger of pity. *Eurozine*. Retrieved from http://www.eurozine.com/articles/2006-09-01-abulughod-en.html

Agranoff, R. (1998). Partnerships in public management: Rural enterprise alliances. *International Journal of Public Administration, 21*(11), 1533–1575. doi: 10.1080/01900699808525360

Albach, H. (1999). Medium-sized firms in Germany – a perspective on their strategic orientation. In WHU Koblenz – Otto Beisheim Graduate School of Management (Ed.), *Structure and dynamics of the German Mittelstand* (pp. 101–115). Heidelberg, Germany: Physica Verlag.

Alvesson, M. & Sköldberg, K. (2009). *Reflexive methodology – new vistas for qualitative research* (2nd ed.). London, UK: Sage Publishing.

Amdam, R. (2005). *Planlegging som handling*. Oslo, Norway: Universitetsforlaget.

Amit, R. & Zott, C. (2001). Value creation in E-business. *Strategic Management Journal, 22*, 493–520.

Andersen, K. V., Hansen, H. K., Isaksen, A. & Raunio, M. (2010). Nordic city regions in the creative class debate – putting the creative class thesis to a test. *Industry and Innovation, 17*(2), 215–240. doi: 10.1080/13662711003633496

Andersen, N. A. (2003). *Discursive analytical strategies: Understanding Foucault, Koselleck, Laclau, Luhmann*. Bristol, UK: Policy Press.

Ardichvili, A., Cardozo, R. & Ray, S. (2003). A theory of entrepreneurial opportunity identification and development. *Journal of Business Venturing, 18*(1), 105–123.

Arlt, W. G. (2006). *China's outbound tourism*. London, UK: Routledge.

Arnesen, T. & Riseth, J. Å (2008). Konfliktfylda naturskyddsprosesser i Norge. In C. Sandström, S. Hovik & E. I. Falleth (Eds), *Omstridd Natur* (pp. 83–104). Umeå, Sweden: Boréa Bokförlag AB.

Arnstein, S. R. (1969). A ladder of citizen participation. *Journal of the American Institute of Planners, 35*(4), 216–224.

Aronsson, L. (2007). Kartor över kulturella ekonomier. In Lars Aronsson (Ed.), *Kulturell ekonomi. Skapandet av värden, platser och identiteter i upplevelsesamhället* (pp. 16–39). Pozkal, Poland: Studentlitteratur.

Arowosegbe, J. (2014). African studies and the bias of Eurocentricism. *Social Dynamics, 40*(2), 308–321.

Asheim, B. (2009). Guest editorial: Introduction to the creative class in European city regions. *Economic Geography, 85*(4), 355–362. doi: 10.1111/j.1944-8287.2009.01046.x.

Asheim, B. & Gertler, M. (2005). The geography of innovation. In J. Fagerberg, D. C. Mowery & R. R. Nelson (Eds.), *The Oxford handbook of innovation* (pp. 291–317). Oxford, UK: Oxford University Press.

Asheim, B., Coenen, L., Moodysson, J. & Vang, J. (2007). Constructing knowledge-based regional advantage: Implications for regional innovation policy. *International Journal of Entrepreneurship and Innovation Management, 7*(2), 140–155.

Aslesen, H. W. & Isaksen, A. (2007). New perspectives on knowledge-intensive services and innovation. *Geografiske Annaler Series B-Human Geography, 89B*(1), 45–58.

Aslesen, H. W. & Isaksen, A. (2014). Klynger for enhver pris? Kunnskapsbaser og innovasjonssamarbeid. In H. C. G. Johnsen & I. Amundsen (Eds), *Forskning møter praksis: Perspektiver på arbeidsliv og innovasjon i kunnskapssamfunnet* (pp. 44–60). Kristiansand, Norway: Portal Akademisk.

Bathelt, H., Malmberg, A. & Maskell, P. (2004). Clusters and knowledge: Local buzz, global pipelines and the process of knowledge creation. *Progress in Human Geography, 28*(1), 31–56. doi: 10.1191/0309132504ph469oa

Becher, T. (1981). Towards a definition of disciplinary cultures. *Studies in Higher Education, 6*(2), 109–122.

Becher, T. (1989). *Academic tribes and territories: Intellectual enquiry and the cultures of disciplines*. London, UK: Society for Research into Higher Education.

Becher, T. (1990). The counter-culture of specialisation. *European Journal of Education, 25*(3), 333–346.

Becher, T. (1994). The significance of disciplinary differences. *Studies in Higher Education, 19*(2), 151–161.

Becher, T. & Trowler, P. (2001) *Academic tribes and territories: Intellectual enquiry and the culture of disciplines*. Buckingham, UK: Society for Research into Higher Education & Open University Press.

Bennett, C. J. & Howlett, M. (1992). The lessons of learning: Reconciling theories of policy learning and policy change. *Policy Sciences*, 25(3), 275–294.

Berger, P. & Luckmann, T. (1991) [1966]. *The social construction of reality: A treatise in the sociology of knowledge*. Harmondsworth, UK: Penguin Books.

Berghoff, H. (2006). The end of family business? The Mittelstand and German capitalism in transition 1949–2000. *Business History Review, 80*(2), 263–295.

Berkes, F. (2007). Adaptive co-management and complexity: Exploring the many faces of co-management. In D. Armitage, F. Berkes & N. Doubleday (Eds), *Adaptive co-management: collaboration, learning and multi-level governance* (pp. 19–38). Vancouver, Canada: UBC Press.

Berkes, F. (2009). Evolution of co-management: Role of knowledge generation, bridging organizations and social learning. *Journal of Environmental Management, 90*(5), 1692–1702. ISI: 000264634400003.

Berkes, F. & Folke, C. (1998). Linking social and ecological systems for resilience and sustainability. In F. Berkes & C. Folke (Eds), *Linking social and ecological systems: management practices and social mechanisms for building resilience* (pp. 1–27). Cambridge, UK: Cambridge University Press.

Bitard, P., Edquist, C., Hommen, L. & Rickne, A. (2008). Reconsidering the paradox of high R&D input and low innovation: Sweden. In C. Edquist & L. Hommen

(Eds), *Small country innovation systems: Globalization, change and policy in Asia and Europe* (pp. 237–280). Cheltenham, UK: Edward Edgar.

Björkell, S. (2008). Resistance to top-down conservation policy and the search for new participatory models. In J. Keulartz, & G. Leistra (Eds), *Legitimacy in European nature conservation policy: Case studies in multilevel governance* (pp. 109–126). Heidelberg, Germany: Springer.

Bond, S. (2011). Negotiating a 'democratic ethos': Moving beyond the agonostic-communicative divide. *Planning Theory, 10*(2), 161–186.

Boschma, R. & Frenken, K. (2009). Some notes on institutions in evolutionary economic geography. *Economic Geography, 85*(2), 151–158.

Boswijk, A., Thijssen, T. & Peelen, E. (2007). *The experience economy: A new perspective.* Amsterdam, the Netherlands: Pearson Education Benelux.

Bourdieu, P. (1980). *The logic of practice.* Stanford, CA: Stanford University Press.

Brunner, R. D. & Steelman, T. A. (2005). Beyond scientific management. In R. D. Brunner, T. A. Steelman, L. Coe-Juell, C. M. Cromley, C. M. Edwards & D. W. Tucker (Eds), *Adaptive governance: Integrating science, policy, and decision making* (pp. 1–45). New York, NY: Colombia University Press.

Bryman, A. (2008). *Social research methods.* Oxford, UK: Oxford University Press.

Bui, H. T., Wilkins, H. C. & Lee, Y. S. (2013). The 'imagined west' of young independent travellers from Asia. *Annals of Leisure Research*, 16(2), 130–48.

Bøgh Holmen, R. & Fjose, S. (2014). Value added and ripple effects from the node cluster. Menon Report 5/2014. Oslo, Norway: Menon.

Caplan, P. (2009). Understanding modernity/ies: The idea of a moral community on Mafia Island, Tanzania. In K. Larsen (Ed.), *Repositioning and changing ideological and material circumstances among the Swahili on the East African Coast.* Uppsala, Sweden: Nordiska Afrikainstitutet.

Carr, W. & Kemmis, S. (1986). *Becoming critical: Education, knowledge and action research.* London, UK: The Falmer Press.

Casadesus-Masanell, R. & Ricart, J. E. (2010). From strategy to business models and onto tactics. *Longe Range Planning*, 43(2), 195–215.

Caves, R. E. (2000). *Creative industries: Contracts between art and commerce.* Boston, MA: Harvard University Press.

Chapain, C., Clifton, N. & Comunian, R. (2012). Understanding creative regions: Bridging the gap between global discourses and regional and national contexts. *Regional Studies, 47*(2), 131–134. doi: 10.1080/00343404.2013.746441

Chesbrough, H. (2010). Business model innovation: Opportunities and barriers. *Long Range Planning, 43*(2), 354–363.

Chesbrough, H. & Rosenbloom, R. S. (2002). The role of the business model in capturing value from innovation: Evidence from xerox corporation's technology spin-off companies. *Industrial and Corporate Change, 11*(3), 529–555.

Clark, B. (1983). *The higher education system: Academic organization in cross-national perspective.* Berkeley, CA: University of California Press.

Clarke, J. & Holt, R. (2010). Reflective judgement: Understanding entrepreneurship as ethical practice. *Journal of Business Ethics, 94*(3), 317–331.

Cohen, W. & Levinthal, D. (1990). Absorptive capacity: A new perspective on learning and innovation. *Administrative Science Quarterly, 35*(1), 128–152.

Coleman, J. S. & Coleman, J. S. (1994). *Foundations of social theory.* Harvard, MA: Harvard University Press.

Comte, A. (1988) [1830]. *Introduction to positive philosophy.* Cambridge, MA: Hackett Publishing.
Comunian, R., Faggian, A. & Jewell, S. (2011). Winning and losing in the creative industries: An analysis of creative graduates' career opportunities across creative disciplines. *Cultural Trends, 20*(3/4), 291–308. doi: 10.1080/09548963.2011.589710
Cooke, J. & Kothari, U. (2001). *Participation: The new tyranny?* London, UK: Zed Books.
Cooke, P. & Leydesdorff, L. (2006) Regional development in the knowledge-based economy: The construction of advantage. *The Journal of Technology Transfer, 31*(1), 5–15.
Coombes, P. H. & Nicholson, J. D. (2013). Business models and their relationship with marketing: A systematic literature review. *Industrial Marketing Management, 42*(5), 656–664.
Cornwall, A. (2009). New narratives of women's empowerment. Audio presented at Sussex Development Lecture at the University of Sussex. Retrieved from http://www.ids.ac.uk/go/news/new-narratives-of-women-s-empowerment.
Cowell, R. & Owens, S. (2011). *Land and limits: Interpreting sustainability in the planning process* (2nd ed.). Oxford, UK: Routledge.
Crewe, E. & Harrison, E. (1998). *Whose development? An ethnography of aid.* London, UK: Zed Books.
Cunningham, S. D., Cutler, T. A., Hearn, G. N, Ryan, M. D. & Keane, M. A. (2004). An innovation agenda for the creative industries: where is the R&D? *Media International Australia Incorporating Culture and Policy: Quarterly Journal of Media Research and Resources, 112*, 174–185.
Damvad. (2012). *Evaluering av basisfinansieringen til norske forskningsinstitutter som omfattes av retningslinjene for basisfinansiering.* Oslo, Norway: Damvad.
Daugstad, K. (2011). The participatory dimension in nature conservation processes: Examples of ideology and practice from Norway. In M. Jones & M. Steneke (Eds), *The European landscape convention: The challenge of participation.* Heidelberg, Germany: Springer.
Daugstad, K., Svarstad, H. & Vistad, O. I. (2006). A case of conflicts in conservation: Two trenches or a three-dimensional complexity? *Landscape Research, 31*(1), 1–19. ISI: 000239845600001
Davies, S. (2011). Regional resilience in the 2008–2010 downturn: Comparative evidence from European countries. *Cambridge Journal of Regions, Economy and Society, 4*(3), 369–382.
Deetz, S. (1992). *Democracy in an age of corporate colonization: Developments in communication and the politics of everyday life.* Albany, NY: University of New York Press.
Deiaco, E., Hughes, A. & McKelvey, M. (2012). Universities as strategic actors in the knowledge economy. *Cambridge Journal of Economics, 36*(3), 525–541.
Dietz, T., Ostrom, E. & Stern, P. C. (2003). The struggle to govern the commons. *Science, 302*(5652), 1907–1912. ISI: 000187174000041
Dingwall, R. & Lewis, P. (Eds). (2014). *The sociology of the professions: Lawyers, doctors and others.* New Orleans, LA: Quid Pro Books.
Dressel, P. L. & Marcus, D. (1982). *On teaching and learning in college: Reemphasizing the roles of learners and the disciplines.* San Francisco, CA: Jossey-Bass.
Dreyfus, H. L. (1991). *Being-in-the-world: A commentary on Heidegger's 'Being and Time', division 1.* Cambridge, MA: MIT Press.

Drucker, P. (1994). The theory of the business. *Harvard Business Review*, September–October, 95–104.

Døving, R. (2003). *Rype med lettøl: En antropologi fra Norge*. Oslo, Norway: Pax.

Edelman, M. & Haugerud, A. (2005). Introduction. In M. Edelman & A. Haugerud (Eds), *The anthropology of development and globalization: From classical political economy to contemporary neoliberalism* (pp. 1–74). Malden, MA: Blackwell.

Eikeland, O. (2007). Why should mainstream social researchers be interested in action research? *International Journal of Action Research, 3*(1/2), 38–64. Retrieved from http://search.ebscohost.com/login.aspx?direct=true&db=sih&AN=25977309&site=ehost-live.

Elling, B. (2008). *Rationality and the environment: Decision-making in environmental politics and assessment*. London, UK: Earthscan.

Ellison, A. P. (2001). *Entrepreneur and the transformation of the global economy*. Cheltenham, UK: Edward Elgar Publishing.

Engelen, E., Keulartz, J. & Leistra, G. (2008). European nature conservation policy making: from substantive to procedural sources of legitimacy. In J. Keulartz & G. Leistra (Eds), *Legitimacy in European nature conservation policy: Case studies in multilevel governance* (pp. 3–21). Heidelberg, Germany: Springer.

Ennals, R. & Gustavsen, B. (1999). *Work organization and Europe as a development coalition*. Amsterdam, the Netherlands: John Benjamins Publishing.

Eppler, M. J., Hoffmann, F. & Bresciani, S. (2011). New business models through collaborative idea generation. *International Journal of Innovation Management, 15*(06), 1323–1341.

Escobar, A. (1995). *Encountering development: The making and unmaking of the Third World*. Princeton, NJ: Princeton University Press.

Escobar, A. (1997). Anthropology and development. *International Social Science Journal, 49*(154), 497–515.

Espelien, A. & Gran, A. B. (2011). *Kulturnæringens betydning for norsk økonomi: Status og utvikling (2000–2009)*. Nr. 9/2011. Oslo, Norway: Menon.

Etzkowitz, H. & Leydesdorff, L (Eds). (1997). *Universities and the global knowledge economy: A triple helix of university-industry-government relations*. London, UK: Continuum.

Etzkowitz, H. & Leydesdorff, L. (2000). The dynamics of innovation: from national systems and 'mode 2' to a triple helix of university–industry–government relations. *Research Policy, 29*(2), 109–23.

EU. (2009). Challenging futures of science in society – emerging trends and cutting-edge issues. Report of the MASIS Expert Group set up by the European Commission. Retrieved from http://ec.europa.eu/research/science-society/document_library/pdf_06/the-masis-report_en.pdf.

European Commission. (2013). Commission staff working document: Developing an indicator of innovation output. Retrieved from http://ec.europa.eu/research/press/2013/pdf/staff_working_document_indicator_of_innovation_output.pdf.

European Commission. (2014) Innovation union scoreboard. Retrieved from http://europa.eu/rapid/press-release_IP-14-198_en.htm.

Fagerberg, J. (2005). Innovation. A guide to the literature. In J. Fagerberg, D. C. Mowery & R. R. Nelson (Eds), *The Oxford handbook of innovation* (pp. 1–26). Oxford, UK: Oxford University Press.

Falleth, E. I. & Hovik, S. (2008). *Lokal forvaltning av store verneområder – erfaringer fra fire forsøk*. Oslo, Norway: NIBR – Norsk institutt for by- og regionforskning.

Ferguson, J. (1990). *The anti-politics machine: 'Development', depoliticization, and bureaucratic power in Lesotho*. Cambridge, UK: Cambridge University Press.

Fingleton, B. Garretsen, H. & Martin, R. (2012). Recessionary shocks and regional employment: Evidence on the resilience of U.K. regions. *Journal of Regional Science, 52*(1), 109–133.

Flood, R. L. (2001). The relationship of 'systems thinking' to action research. In P. Reason & H. Bradbury (Eds), *Handbook of action research* (pp. 133–144). London, UK: Sage Publishing.

Florida, R. (1995). Toward the learning region. *Futures, 27*(5), 527–36.

Florida, R. (2003). Cities and the creative class. *City & Community, 2*(1), 3–19. doi: 10.1111/1540–6040.00034.

Florida, R., Mellander, C. & Stolarick, K. (2008). Inside the black box of regional development–human capital, the creative class and tolerance. *Journal of Economic Geography, 8*(5), 615–649. doi: 10.1093/jeg/lbn023.

Flyvbjerg, B. (1998a). Habermas and Foucault: Thinkers for civil society? *British Journal of Sociology, 49*(2), 210–233.

Flyvbjerg, B. (1998b). *Rationality and power: Democracy in practice* (S. Sampson, Trans.). Chicago, IL: University of Chicago Press.

Flyvbjerg, B. (2002). Bringing power to planning research – one researcher's praxis story. *Journal of Planning Education and Research, 21*, 353–366.

Folke, C. (2006). The economic perspective: Conservation against development versus conservation for development. *Conservation Biology, 20*(3), 686–688. ISI: 000238313200021.

Fombrun, C. J., Gardberg, N. A. & Barnett, M. L. (2000). Opportunity platforms and safety nets: Corporate citizenship and reputational risk. *Business and Society Review, 105*(1), 85–106.

Foucault, M. (1980). *Power/knowledge: Selected interviews and other writings 1972–1977*. Brighton, UK: Harvester Press.

Frank, D. J. & Gabler, J. (2006). *Reconstructing the university: Worldwide shifts in academia in the 20th century*. Stanford, CA: Stanford University Press.

Freire, P. (1996). *Pedagogy of the oppressed*. Harmondsworth, UK: Penguin Books.

Freire, P. (2008a). *Pedagogía de la Autonomía: Saberes necesarios para la práctica educativa*. Buenos Aires, Argentina: Siglo XXI.

Freire, P. (2008b). *Pedagogía de la Esperanza: Un reencuentro con la pedagogía del oprimido*. Buenos Aires, Argentina: Siglo XXI.

Fritscher, B. & Pigneur, Y. (2014, June). Business model design: An evaluation of paper-based and computer-aided canvases. Paper presented at the Fourth International Symposium on Business Modeling and Software Design, Luxembourg.

Frykman, J. & Gilje, N. (2003). *Being there: New perspectives on phenomenology and the analysis of culture*. Lund, Sweden: Nordic Academic Press.

Fuller, S. (2002). *Social epistemology*. Bloomington, IN: Indiana University Press.

Gaglio, C. M. & Katz, J. A. (2001). The physiological basis of opportunity identification: Entrepreneurial alertness. *Small Business Economics*, 16(2), 95–111.

Gardner, K. & Lewis, D. (1996). *Anthropology, development and the post-modern challenge*. London, UK: Pluto Press.

Geertz, C. (1973). *The interpretation of cultures: Selected essays*. New York, NY: Basic Books.

Gibbons, M., Limoges, C., Nowotny, H., Schwartzman, S., Scott, P. & Trow, M. (1994). *The new production of knowledge: The dynamics of science and research in contemporary societies*. London, UK: Sage Publishing.

Giddens, A. (1984). *The constitution of society*. Cambridge, UK: Polity Press.

Gipuzkoa Sarean. (2015). San Sebastian, Basque Country: Provincial Council of Gipuzkoa.

Gladwell, M. (2008). *Outliers. The story of success*. Harmondsworth, UK: Penguin Books.

Goddard, J. & Vallance, P. (2013). *The University and the city*. London, UK: Routledge.

Godin, B. & Gingras, Y. (2000). The place of universities in the system of knowledge production. *Research Policy, 29*(2), 273–278.

Greenwood, D. J. & Levin, M. (1998). *Introduction to action research: Social research for social change*. Thousand Oaks, CA: Sage Publishing.

Grönholm, S. (2009). Governing national parks in Finland: The illusion of public involvement. *Local Environment: The International Journal of Justice and Sustainability, 14*(3), 233–243. Retrieved from http://www.informaworld.com/10.1080/13549830802692955.

Gulbrandsen, M. & Nerdrum, L. (2009). University-industry relations in Norway. In J. Fagerberg, D. Mowery, Verspagen, B. (Eds), *Innovation, path dependency, and policy: The Norwegian case* (pp. 297–326). Oxford, UK: Oxford University Press.

Guribye, E. & K. Hidle (2013). *Læreres hjelperoller i voksenopplæringen. FoU-rapport nr. 5, 2013*. Kristiansand, Norway: Agderforskning.

Gustavsen, B. (1992). *Dialogue and development: Theory of communication, action research and the restructuring of working life*. Assen, the Netherlands: Van Gorcum.

Gustavsen, B. (2005). Innovation and action research. *International Journal of Action Research, 1*(3), 267–289.

Gustavsen, B. (2007). Research responses to practical challenges: What can action research contribute? *International Journal of Action Research, 3*(1/2), 93–111.

Haaland, H. (2008). Narrating history, negotiating rights: A discussion of knowledge, land rights and matters of identity in Madjadjane Mozambique (PhD thesis). Ås, Norway: Noragric.

Habermas, J. (1971) [1968]. *Knowledge and human interests*. London, UK: Beacon Press.

Habermas, J. 1974 [1964]. *Theory and Practice*. London, UK: Heinemann.

Haddeland, E. (2013). *Bedre integrering på dagsorden*. Retrieved from http://www.lyngdalsavis.no/gammel/nyheter/1207/.

Hajer, M. A. (2003). A frame in the fields: Policymaking and the reinvention of politics. In M. A. Hajer & H. Wagenaar (Eds), *Deliberative policy analysis understanding governance in the network society* (pp. 88–112). Cambridge, UK: Cambridge University Press.

Hansen, H. P. (2007). Demokrati og naturforvaltning – en kritisk sociologisk-historisk analyse af nationalparkudviklingen i Danmark (PhD thesis). Roskilde, Denmark: Roskilde University.

Harding, A., Scott, A., Laske, A. & Burtscher, C. (Eds). (2007). *Bright satanic mills: Universities, regional development and the knowledge economy*. Aldershot, UK: Ashgate.

Hauge, E., Pinheiro, R. & Zyzak, B. (2013). *Samarbeid mellom akademia og kreative næringer: En kvalitativ analyse i Agder-regionen*. Kristiansand, Norway: Agderforskning.

Hayek. F. A. (1976) [1949]. The facts of the social sciences. In F. A. Hayek (Ed.), *Individualism and economic order* (pp. 57–76). London, UK: Routledge and Kegan Paul.

Healey, P., de Magalhaes, C. & Madanipour, A. (1999). Institutional capacity building, urban planning and urban regeneration projects. *Futura (Journal of the Finnish Society for Future Studies), 18*(3), 117–137.

Hearn, G., Cunningham, S. & Ordoñez, D. (2004). Commercialisation of knowledge in universities: The case of the creative industries. *Prometheus, 22*(2), 189–200. doi: 10.1080/0810902042000218364.

Heidegger, M. (1996). *Being and time: A translation of Sein und Zeit*. Albany, NY: State University of New York Press.

Hidle, K. & Normann, R. H. (2008). Leadership attitudes in southern Norway: Analysis of values held by the regional leaders in the business, public and political sectors in the Agder region. Project report no. 24/2008. Kristiansand, Norway: Agderforskning.

Hillier, J. (2003). Agon'izing over consensus: Why Habermasian ideals cannot be 'real'. *Planning Theory 2*(1), 37–59.

Hills, G. E., Lumpkin, G. T. & Singh, R. P. (1997). Opportunity recognition: Perceptions and behaviours of entrepreneurs. *Frontiers of Entrepreneurship Research, 17*(330–344), 168–182.

Hjemdahl, K. M. (2011). Twisted field working, fighting for the relevance of being connected. *Ethnologia Europaea, 41*(1), 65–79.

Hjemdahl M. K., Hauge, S. E & Lind, E. (2007). *Festivaler på Sørlandet: Kultur i kraftformat*. Kristiansand, Norway: Agderforskning.

Hobart, M. (1993). *An anthropological critique of development: The growth of ignorance*. London, UK: Routledge.

Holt, R. (2008). Using activity theory to understand entrepreneurial opportunity. *Mind, Culture & Activity, 15*(1), 52–70.

Holy, L. & Stuchlick, M. (1983). *Action, norms and representations: Foundations of anthropological inquiry*. Cambridge, UK: Cambridge University Press.

Holzner, B. (1968). *Reality construction in society*. Cambridge, MA: Schenkman.

Holzner, B. & Marx, J. H. (1979). *Knowledge application: The knowledge system of society*. Boston, MA: Allyn and Bacon.

Horwitz, F. M., Heng, C. T & Quazi, H. A. (2003). Finders, keepers? Attracting, motivating and retaining knowledge workers. *Human Resource Management Journal, 13*(4), 23–44.

Hovik, S. & Reitan, M. (2004). National environmental goals in search of local institutions. *Environment and Planning C, Government and Policy, 22*(5), 687–700.

Howell, S. (2011). Antropologiens uutholdelige letthet. *Norsk Antropologisk Tidsskrift* 22(3/4), 167–180.

Hundstad, D. (2009). Regionsbygging i sør. In Bjørg Seland (Ed.), *Regionen. historiske perspektiver, aktuelle utfordringer* (pp. 59–88). Kristiansand, Norway: Høyskoleforlaget.

Huxham, C., Vangen, S., Huxham, C. & Eden, C. (2000). The challenge of collaborative governance. *Public Management: An International Journal of Research and Theory, 2*(3), 337–358. doi: 10.1080/14719030000000021.

Hylland-Eriksen, T. (2004). *What is anthropology?* London, UK: Pluto.

Ingold, T. (Ed.). (2011). *Redrawing anthropology: Materials, movements, lines.* Surrey, UK: Ashgate.

Innes, J. E. & Booher, D. E. (2010). *Planning with complexity: An introduction to collaborative rationality for public policy.* Oxford, UK: Routledge.

Isaksen, A. & Karlsen, J. (2010). Different modes of innovation and the challenge of connecting universities and industry: Case studies of two regional industries in Norway. *European Planning Studies, 18*(12), 1993–2008.

Isaksen, A. & Karlsen, J. (2012a). What is regional in regional clusters? The case of the globally oriented oil and gas cluster in Agder Norway. *Industry and Innovation, 19*(3), 249–263.

Isaksen, A. & Karlsen, J. (2012b). Combined and complex mode of innovation in regional cluster development: Analysis of the light-weight material cluster in Raufoss, Norway. In B. Asheim & M. D. Parili (Eds), *Interactive learning for innovation: A key driver within clusters and innovation systems* (pp. 115–136). Basingstoke, UK: Palgrave Macmillan.

Isaksen, A. & Nilsson, M. (2013). Combined innovation policy: Linking scientific and practical knowledge in innovation systems. *European Planning Studies, 21*(12), 1919–1936.

Isaksen, A. & Trippl, M. (2014). *Regional industrial path development in different regional innovation systems: A conceptual analysis.* Lund University, Sweden: CIRCLE-Center for Innovation, Research and Competences in the Learning Economy.

Jackson, M. (1996). *Things as they are: New directions in phenomenological anthropology.* Bloomington, IN: Indiana University Press.

Jakobsen, S.-E. & Lorentzen, T. (2015). Between bonding and bridging: Regional differences in innovative collaboration in Norway. *Norsk Geografisk Tidsskrift – Norwegian Journal of Geography, 69*(2), 80–89. doi: 10.1080/00291951.2015.1016550

Jeffcutt, P. & Pratt, A. C. (2002). Managing creativity in the cultural industries. *Creativity and Innovation Management, 11*(4), 225–233.

Jencks, C. & Riesman, D. (2002). *The academic revolution.* New Brunswick, NJ: Transaction Publishers.

Jensen, M. B., Johnson, B., Lorenz, E. & Lundvall, B. Å. (2007). Forms of knowledge and modes of innovation. *Research Policy, 36*(5), 680–693.

Jivén, G. & Larkham, P. J. (2003). Sense of place, authenticity and character: A commentary. *Journal of Urban Design, 8*(1), 67–81.

Johnsen, B. E. (2010). Iscenesatt sjøfartshistorie på sørlandske sommerfestivaler og spel. In B. E. Johnsen & K. Pabst (Eds), *Formidling: Bruk og misbruk av historie* (pp. 135–174). Kristiansand, Norway: Høyskoleforlaget.

Johnsen, H. C. G. (2001). Involvement at work: A study of communicative processes and individual involvement in organizational development (PhD thesis). Copenhagen, Denmark: Samfundslitteratur.

Johnsen, H. C. G. (2014). *The new natural resource: Knowledge development, society and economics.* Farnham, UK: Gower Publishing.

Johnsen, H. C. G. & Ennals, R. (Eds). (2012). *Creating collaborative advantage: Innovation and knowledge creation in regional economies.* Farnham, UK: Gower Publishing.

Johnsen, H. C. G. & Normann, R. H. (2004). When research and practice collide: The role of action research when there is a conflict of interest with stakeholders. *Systemic Practice and Action Research, 17*(3), 207–235.

Johnsen, H. C. G., Knudsen, J. P. & Normann, R. (2014). Action research strategies at the 'third place'. *International Journal of Action Research, 10*(2), 235–257.

Johnsen, H. C. G., Torjesen, S. & Ennals, R. (2015). *Higher education in a sustainable society*. Heidelberg, Germany: Springer.

Johnson, M. (2010). *Seizing the white space: Growth and renewal through business model innovation*. Boston, MA: Harvard Business Press.

Jones, O. (1995). Lay discourses of the rural: developments and implications for rural studies. *Journal of Rural Studies, 11*(1), 35–50.

Jönsson S. & Lukka, K. (2007). There and back again: Doing interventionist research in management accounting. In Chapman, C. S., Hopwood, A. G. & Shields, M. G. (Eds), *Handbook of management accounting research* (vol. 1) (pp. 373–397). Oxford, UK: Elsevier.

Jørgensen, M. T. (2012). Catering to the dragon. Is the Danish tourism sector 'China ready'? (master's thesis). Department of Culture and Global Studies. Aalborg University, Denmark.

Karlsen, J. (2010). Regional complexity and the need for engaged governance. *Ekonomiaz, 74*(2), 91–111.

Karlsen, J. & Larrea, M. (2012). Emergence of shared leadership in the Basque Country. In M. Sotarauta, I. Horlings & J. Liddle (Eds), *Leadership and change in sustainable regional development* (pp. 212–233). London, UK: Routledge.

Karlsen, J. & Larrea, M. (2014). *Territorial development and action research: Innovation through dialgoue*. Farnham, UK: Gower.

Karlsen, J., Isaksen, A. & Spilling, O. R. (2011). The challenge of constructing regional advantages in peripheral areas: The case of marine biotechnology in Tromsø, Norway. *Entrepreneurship & Regional Development, 23*(3), 235–257.

Keast, R. & Mandell, M. P. (2013). Network performance: A complex interplay of form and action. *International Review of Public Administration, 18*(2), 27–45. doi: 10.1080/12294659.2013.10805251.

Kincheloe, J. L. & McLaren, P. (2005). Rethinking critical theory and qualitative research. In N. K. Denzin & Y. S. Lincoln (Eds), *The Sage handbook of qualitative research* (3rd ed.) (pp 279–313). Thousand Oaks, CA: Sage Publishing.

Kingsbury, H. (2001). *Music, talent, and performance: A conservatory cultural system*. Philadelphia, PA: Temple University Press.

Kjær, S. H. (2011). Kystturisme, fyrtårne og romantisk oplevelsesdesign. *Kulturella Perspektiv: Svensk Etnologisk Tidskrift,* 2(20), 21–32.

Kjær, S. H. (2015). Den digitale rejse: Digitaliseringsprojekter i kulturavsindustrien. *Kulturella Perspektiv: Svensk Etnologisk Tidskrift, 3–4*(2), 53–64.

Koppenjan, J. F. M. (2007). Consensus and conflict in policy networks: To much or too little? In J. Torfing & E. Sørensen (Eds), *Theories of democratic network governance* (pp. 132–152). Basingstoke, UK: Palgrave Macmillian.

Krishnan, A. (2009). What are academic disciplines? Some observations on disciplinarity vs interdisciplinarity debate. ESRC National Centre for Research Methods: NCRM Working Paper Series. Retrieved from http://eprint.ncrm.ac.uk/783/1/what_are_academic_discipline.pdf.

Kristoffersen, H. (2008). *Det nye kina: Kinesisk handel, kultur og politikk*. Oslo, Norway: Universitetsforlaget.

Krugman, P. (1991). Increasing returns and economic geography. *Journal of Political Economy, 99*(3), 483–99.

Lachapelle, P. R. & McCool, S. F. (2005). Exploring the concept of 'ownership' in natural resource planning. *Society and Natural Resources, 18*(3), 279–285.

Laclau, E. (2005). *On populist reason*. New York, NY: Verso.

Laclau, E. & Mouffe, C. (2001). *Hegemony and socialist strategy: Towards a radical democratic politics*. London, UK: Verso.

Lam, A. (2005). Organizational innovation. In J. Fagerberg, D. C. Mowery & R. R. Nelson (Eds), *The Oxford handbook of innovation* (pp. 115–147). Oxford, UK: Oxford University Press.

Landström, H. (2005). *Pioneers in entrepreneurship and small business research*. Heidelberg, Germany: Springer.

Larsen, K. (2008). *Where humans and spirits meet: The politics of rituals and identified spirits in Zanzibar*. New York, NY: Berghahn Books.

Lattuca, L. R. & Stark, J. S. (1994). Will disciplinary perspectives impede curricular reform? *The Journal of Higher Education, 65*(4), 401–426.

Lester, R. & Sotarauta, M. (Eds). (2007). *Innovation, universities and the competitiveness of regions*. Helsinki, Finland: Tekes.

Levin, M. (Ed.). (2002). *Researching enterprise development: Action research on the cooperation between management and labour in Norway*. Amsterdam, the Netherlands: John Benjamins Publishing.

Lewin, K. (1951). *Field theory in social science: Selected theoretical papers*. New York, NY: Harper.

Lindeborg, L. & Lindkvist, L. (2013). *The value of art and culture for regional development: A Scandinavian perspective*. London, UK: Routledge/Taylor & Francis Group.

Long, N. (2001). *Development sociology: Actor perspectives*. London, UK: Routledge.

Lopiano-Misdom, J. & De Luca, J. (1997). *Street trends: How today's alternative youth cultures are creating tomorrow's mainstream markets*. New York, NY: HarperBusiness.

Lorenz, E. (2011). Regional learning dynamics and systems of education and training: A European comparison. *Journal of the Knowledge Economy, 2*(4), 481–506.

Lorenz, E. & Valeyre, A. (2006). Organizational forms and innovative performance: A comparison of the EU-15. In E. Lorenz & B.-Å. Lundvall (Eds), *How Europe's economies learn: Coordinating competing models* (pp. 140–160). Oxford, UK: Oxford University Press.

Löfgren, O. 1999: *On holiday: A history of vacationing*. Berkeley, CA: University of California Press.

Lucassen, G., Brinkkemper, S., Jansen, S. & E. Handoyo. (2012). Comparison of visual business modeling techniques for software companies. In Cusumano, M. A., Iyer, B. & Venkatraman, N. (Eds), *Software business* (pp. 79–93). Heidelberg, Germany: Springer.

Luhmann, N. (1996). *Social systems*. Stanford, CA: Stanford University Press.

Lund, J. (2015, 14 September). Omstilling – til hva da? (Renewal – to what?). *Aftenposten*, p. 3.

Lundvall, B.-Å. (2010). Scope, style, and theme of research on knowledge and learning societies. *Journal of the Knowledge Economy, 1*(1), 18–23. doi: 10.1007/s13132–009–0007–6.
Lundvall, B.-Å. & Borrás, S. (1997). The globalising learning economy: Implications for innovation policy. Report from DG XII, Commission of the European Union.
Lundvall, B.-Å. & Johnson, B. (1994). The learning economy. *Journal of Industry Studies, 1*(2), 23–42.
Lundvall, B.-Å., Vang, J., Joseph, K. J. & Chaminade, C. (2009). Innovation system research and developing countries. In B.-Å. Lundvall, K. J. Joseph, C. Chaminade & J. Vang (Eds), *Handbook of innovation systems and developing countries: Building domestic capabilities in a global setting* (pp. 1–30). Cheltenham: Edward Elgar Publishing.
Lydesdorff, L. (2006). *The knowledge based economy*. Bacon Raton, FL: Universal Publishers.
MacCannell, D. (1976). *The tourist. A new theory of the leisure class*. New York, NY: Schocken Books.
Magnussen, M.-L. & Svarstad, C. (2012a). NEW Facts forprosjekt: Karlegging av kvinner i prosess- og olje-/gassindustri på Sørlandet. Prosjektrapport nr 10/2012. Kristiansand, Norway: Agderforskning.
Magnussen, M.-L. & Svarstad, C. (2012b). NEW Facts hovedprosjekt: Videre analyser av av kvinner i prosess- og olje-/gassindustri på Sørlandet. Prosjektrapport nr 15/2012. Kristiansand, Norway: Agderforskning.
Magnussen, M.-L. & Svarstad, C. (2013). Kvinner i prosess- og olje-/gassindustri på Agder. In H. Stousland & H. Witsø (Eds), *Likestilling 2013: Kunnskap og innovasjon på Agder* (pp. 93–115). Kristiansand, Norway: Portal Akademisk Forag.
Mandell, M. & Keast, R. (2007). Evaluating network arrangements: Toward revised performance measures. *Public Performance & Management Review, 30*(4), 574–597. doi: 10.2307/20447651.
March, J. G. (1991). Exploration and exploitation in organizational learning. *Organization Science, 2*(1), 71–87.
March, J. G., & Olsen, J. P. (2006). The logic of appropriateness. In M. Moran, M. Rein & R. Goodin, (Eds), *The Oxford handbook of public policy* (pp. 689–708). Oxford, UK: Oxford University Press.
Mariampolski, H. (2006). *Ethnography for marketers: A guide to consumer immersion*. Thousand Oaks, CA: Sage Publishing.
Martin, R. & Sunley, P. (2006). Path dependence and regional economic evolution. *Journal of Economic Geography, 6*(4), 395–437. doi: 10.1093/jeg/lbl012
Mazzucato, M. (2013). *The entrepreneurial state: Debunking public vs. private sector myths*. London, UK: Anthem Press.
McCann, P. & Ortega-Argilés, R. (2013). Smart specialization, regional growth and applications to European Union cohesion policy. *Regional Studies, 47*, 1–12. doi: 10.1080/00343404.2013.799769.
McGuigan, J. (2009). Doing a Florida thing: The creative class thesis and cultural policy. *International Journal of Cultural Policy, 15*(3), 291–300. doi: 10.1080/10286630902763281.
Meadowcroft, J. (1999). Planning for sustainable development: What can be learned from the critics. In M. Kenny & J. Meadowcroft (Eds), *Planning sustainability* (pp. 12–39). London, UK: Routledge.

Meadowcroft, J. (2007). Who is in charge here? Governance for sustainable development in a complex world. *Journal of Environmental Policy and Planning, 9*(3–4), 299–314.

Meld. St. 18 (2012–2013). (2013). *Lange linjer– kunnskap gir muligheter.* Oslo, Norway: Kunnskapsdepartementet.

Merleau-Ponty, M. (1994) [1962]. *Phenomenology of perception.* London, UK: Routledge.

Merton, R. K. (1973). *The sociology of science: Theoretical and empirical investigations.* Chicago, IL: University of Chicago Press.

Miles, M. B., Huberman, A. M. & Saldaña, J. (2014). *Qualitative data analysis: A methods sourcebook* (3rd ed.). Los Angeles, CA: Sage Publishing.

Mohanty, C. T. (2003). *Feminism without borders: Decolonizing theory, practicing solidarity.* Durham, NC: Duke University Press.

Mohanty, C. T., Russo, A. & Torres, L. (1991). *Third world women and the politics of feminism.* Bloomington, IN: Indiana University Press.

Mouffe C. (1999). Deliberative democracy or agonistic pluralism? *Social Research, 66*(3), 745–758.

Mouffe, C. (2005). *On the political.* Oxford, UK: Routledge.

Moulaert, F. & Nussbaumer, J. (2005). The social region: Beyond the territorial dynamics of the learning economy. *Urban and Regional Studies, 12*(1), 45–64.

Murdoch, J. & Pratt, A. C. (1993) Rural studies: Modernism, postmodernism and the 'post-rural'. *Journal of Rural Studies, 9*(4), 411–427.

Nahapiet, J. & Goshal, S. (1998). Social capital, intellectual capital, and the organizational advantage. *The Academy of Management Review, 23*(2), 242–266.

Nelson, R., Howden, M. & Smith, M. S. (2008). Using adaptive governance to rethink the way science supports Australian drought policy. *Environmental Science & Policy, 11*(7) 588–601.

Neumann, R. & Becher, T. (2002). Teaching and learning in their disciplinary contexts: A conceptual analysis. *Studies in Higher Education, 27*(4), 405–417.

Nielsen, B. S. & Nielsen, K. A. (2006a). *En menneskelig natur – aktionsforskning for bæredygtighed og politisk kultur [A human nature – action research for sustainability and political culture].* Copenhagen, Denmark: Frydenlund.

Nielsen, K. A. & Nielsen, B. S. (2005). Kritisk-utopisk aktionsforskning: Demokratisk naturforvaltning som kollektiv dannelsesproces [Critical utopian action reseach: Democratic nature management as social learning]. In T. B. Jensen & G. Christensen (Eds), *Psykologiske og pædagogiske metoder: Kvalitative og kvantitative forskningsmetoder i praksis* (pp. 155–180). Copenhagen, Denmark: Roskilde Universitetsforlag.

Nielsen, K. A. & Nielsen, B. S. (2006b). Methodologies in action research – action research and critical theory. In K. A. Nielsen & L. Svensson (Eds), *Action research and interactive research: Beyond practice and theory* (pp. 63–88). Maastricht, the Netherlands: Shaker Publishing.

Nielsen, K. A. & Nielsen, B. S. (2007). *Demokrati og naturbeskyttelse – dannelse af borgerfællesskaber gennem social læring – med møn som ekempel.* Copenhagen, Denmark: Frydenlund.

Nielsen, K. A. & Svensson, L. (Eds). (2006). *Action research and interactive research: Beyond practice and theory.* Maastricht, the Netherlands: Shaker Publishing.

Nielsen, K. A., Elling, B. & Jelsoe, E. (2010). *A new agenda for sustainability.* Farnham, UK: Ashgate.

Nolan, P. (2012). Is China buying the world? *Challenge, 55*(2), 108–118.
Nonaka, I., Toyama, R. & Konno, N. (2001). SECI, Ba and leadership: A unified model of dynamic knowledge creation. In I. Nonaka & D. Teece, *Managing industrial knowledge: Creation, transfer and utilization* (pp. 13–43). London, UK: Sage Publishing.
Normann, R. H. 2012. The collaborative steering dilemma of network based development. In H. C. G. Johnsen & J. R. Ennals (Eds), *Creating collaborative advantage: Innovation and knowledge creation in regional economies* (pp. 91–101). Farnham, UK: Gower.
Normann, R. & Johnsen, H. C. (2011). *Mulighetsstudie for 'technology transfer office' – funksjonen ved Universitetet i Agder*. Kristiansand, Norway: Agderforskning.
Normann, R. H. & H. C. G. Johnsen (2013). Developing the 'third place' – the collaborative roles of universities in territorial knowledge creation. In R. Sugden, M. Valania & J. R Wilson (Eds), *Cooperation and leadership in academia* (pp. 197–215). Cheltenham, UK: Edward Elgar Publishing.
Normann, R. H. & Vasstrøm, M. (2012). Municipalities as governance network actors in rural communities. *European Planning Studies, 20*(6), 941–960. Retrieved from http://dx.doi.org/10.1080/09654313.2012.673565.
NOU. (2012). *Utenfor og innenfor – Norges avtaler med EU*. Oslo, Norway: Utenriksdepartementet.
NOU. (2016). *Ved et vendepunkt: Fra ressursøkonomi til kunnskapsøkonomi – produktivitetskommisjonens andre rapport [At a turning point: From resource economy to knowledge economy]*. Oslo, Norway: Finansdepartementet.
Nowotny, H., Scott, P. & Gibbons, M. (2001). *Re-thinking science: Knowledge and the public in an age of uncertainty*. Cambridge, UK: Polity Press.
Nustad, K. G. (2003). *Gavens makt: Norsk utviklingshjelp som formynderskap*. Oslo, Norway: Pax Forlag.
OECD. (2005). *Building competitive regions: Strategies and governance*. Paris, France: OECD.
OECD. (2007a). *Higher education and regions: Globally competitive, locally engaged*. Paris, France: OECD.
OECD. (2007b). *Economic Surveys: Norway*. Paris, France: OECD.
OECD. (2010). *Regions matter: Economic recovery, innovation and sustainable growth*. Paris, France: OECD.
OECD. (2014). *OECD factbook 2014: Economic, environmental and social statistics*. Paris, France: OECD Publishing. Retrieved from http://dx.doi.org/10.1787/factbook-2014-en.
OECD. (2015). *Hvordan gjør Norge det sammenliknet med andre land?* Retrieved from http://www.oecd360.org/norway.
Oliver, C. (1991). Strategic responses to institutional processes. *Academy of Management Review, 16*(1), 145–179.
Olsen, K. 2007. Kultur som ressursgrunnlag. In S. Lynges (Ed.), *Kultur og turistattraksjoner: Jakten på det norske, jakten på opplevelser* (pp. 43–59). Oslo, Norway: Universitetsforlaget.
Osterwalder, A. & Pigneur, Y. (2010). *Business model generation*. Hoboken, NJ: Wiley.
Ostrom, E. (1990). *Governing the commons: The evolution of institutions for collective action*. New York, NY: Cambridge University Press.

Pan, G. W. & Laws, E. (2003). Tourism development of Australia as a sustained preferred destination for Chinese tourists. *Asia Pacific Journal of Tourism Research, 8*(1), 37–47.

Parry, S. (2007). *Disciplines and doctorates*. Dordrecht, the Netherlands: Springer.

Pedler, M., J. Burgoyne & Brook, C. (2005). What has action learning learned to become? *Action Learning, 2*(1), 49–68.

Perkmann, M., Tartari, V., McKelvey, M., Autio, E., Broström, A., D'Este, P. D. & Sobrero, M. (2012). Academic engagement and commercialisation: A review of the literature on university–industry relations. *Research Policy, 42*(2), 423–442. doi: 10.1016/j.respol.2012.09.007.

Perry, B. & May, T. (2006). Excellence, relevance and the university: The 'missing middle' in socio-economic engagement. *Journal of Higher Education in Africa*, 4(3), 69–92.

Petersen, S. L. (2009). Chinese tourists' travel motivations and their resultant preferred travel activities (master's thesis). Esbjerg, Denmark: Department of International Tourism and Leisure Management, SDU.

Pinheiro, R. (2013). Bridging the local with the global: Building a new university on the fringes of Europe. *Tertiary Education and Management, 19*(2), 144–160. doi: 10.1080/13583883.2013.782063.

Pinheiro, R. & Hauge, E. (2014). Global scripts and local translations: The case of cultural and creative industries (CCIs) in Norway. *City, Culture and Society, 5*(2), 87–95. doi: http://dx.doi.org/10.1016/j.ccs.2014.05.007

Pinheiro, R., Benneworth, P. & Jones, G. A. (2012). *Universities and regional development: A critical assessment of tensions and contradictions*. London, UK: Routledge.

Pløger J. (2004). Strife: urban planning and agonism. *Planning Theory, 3*(1), 71–92.

Popper, K. R. (1979). *Truth, rationality and the growth of scientific knowledge*. Frankfurt am Main, Germany: Vittorio Klostermann.

Porter, M. E. & Kramer, M. R. (2011). The big idea: Creating shared value. *Harvard Business Review, 89*(1), 2.

Powell, W. W. & Grodal, S. (2005). Networks of innovators. In J. Fagerberg, D. C. Mowery & R. R. Nelson (Eds), *The Oxford handbook of innovation* (pp. 56–85). Oxford, UK: Oxford University Press.

Prahalad, C. K. & Ramaswamy, V. (2004). *The future of competition: Co-creating unique value with customers*. Cambridge, MA: Harvard University Press.

Primoziz, D. T. (2001). *On Merleau-Ponty*. Belmont, CA: Wadsworth.

Pålshaugen, Ø. (2004). How to do things with words: Towards a linguistic turn in action research? *Concepts and Transformation, 9*(2), 181–203.

Pålshaugen, Ø. (2007). On the diversity of action research. *International Journal of Action Research, 3*(1/2) 9–14.

Pålshaugen, Ø. (2014). Dialogues in innovation: Interactive learning and interactive research as means for a context sensitive regional innovation policy. *International Journal of Action Research, 10*(2), 213–234.

Rankin, K. (2002). Social capital, microfinance, and the politics of development. *Journal of Feminist Economics, 8*(1), 1–24.

Rankin, K. N. (2003). Cultures of economies: Gender and socio-spatial change in Nepal. *Gender, Place and Culture, 10*(2), 111–129.

RCN 2014. *Det norske forsknings- og innovasjonssystemet – statistikk og indikatorer*. Oslo, Norway: The Research Council of Norway.

Reason, P. & Bradbury, H. (Eds). (2001a). *Handbook of action research participative inquiry and practice.* London, UK: Sage Publishing.

Reason, P. & Bradbury, H. (2001b). Introduction: Inquiry and participation in search of a world worthy of human aspiration. In P. Reason & H. Bradbury (Eds), *Handbook of action research: Participative inquiry and practice* (pp. 1–14). London, UK: Sage Publishing.

Regional Development Plan Agder 2020. (2013) *Kristiansand, Norway: East and West Agder County Councils.* Retrieved from http://vaf.no/planer/regionplan-agder-2020/.

Reitan, M. (2004). Politicisation and professional expertise in the policy of nature conservation. Local Environment: *The International Journal of Justice and Sustainability, 9*(5), 437–450. Retrieved from http://www.informaworld.com/10.1080/1354983042000255342.

Ren, C. & Ooi, C. S. (2013). Auto-communicating micro-Orientalism: Articulating 'Denmark' in China at the Shanghai Expo. *Asia Europe Journal, 11*(2), 129–145.

Revans, R. W. (1980). *Action learning: New techniques for managers.* London, UK: Blond & Briggs.

Rittel, H. & Webber, M. (1973). Dilemmas in a general theory of planning. *Policy Sciences, 4*, 155–169.

Rodrigues, M. J. (2002). *The new knowledge economy in Europe: A strategy for international competitiveness and social cohesion.* Cheltenham, UK: Edward Elgar Publishing.

Roe, E. (1991). Development narratives or making the best of blueprint development. *World Development, 19*(4), 287–300.

Rosenfeld, S. A. (1997). Bringing business clusters into the mainstream of economic development. *European Planning Studies, 5*(1), 3–23.

Roy, A. (2010). *Poverty capital: Microfinance and the making of development.* New York, NY: Routledge.

Rugkåsa, M. (2012). *Likhetens dilemma: Om sivilisering og integrasjon i den velferdsambisiøse norske stat.* Oslo, Norway: Gyldendal Akademisk.

Sandström, C., Hovik, S. & Falleth, E. I. (2008). *Omstridd natur – trender & utmaninger i nordisk naturforvaltning.* Umeå, Sweden: Borea Bokförlag AB.

Saxenian, A. (1994). *Regional advantage: Culture and competition in Silicon Valley and Route 128.* Cambridge, MA: Harvard University Press.

Schütz, A. (1972) [1932]. *The phenomenology of the social world.* London, UK: Heinemann Educational Books.

Schwartz, D. & Tödtling, F. (2011). Regional innovation systems. In P. Cooke & B. T. Asheim (Eds), *Handbook of regional innovation and growth* (pp. 455–466). Cheltenham, UK: Edward Elgar Publishing.

Shane, S. (2000). Prior knowledge and the discovery of entrepreneurial opportunities. *Organization Science, 11*(2), 448–469.

Shane, S. & Venkataraman, S. (2000). The promise of entrepreneurship as a field of research. *Academy of Management Review, 25*(1), 217–226.

Simmie, J. (2012). Path dependence and new technological path creation in the Danish wind power industry. *European Planning Studies, 20*(5), 753–772.

Simmie, J. & Martin, R. (2010). The economic resilience of regions: Towards an evolutionary approach. *Cambridge Journal of Regions, Economy and Society, 3*(1), 27–43.

Simon, H. (1992). Lessons from Germany's midsize giants. *Harvard Business Review*, March–April, 115–123.

Simon, H. (1996). You Don't Have to be German to be a 'Hidden Champion'. *Business Strategy Review, 7*(2), 1–13.

Simon, H. (2009). *Hidden champions of the 21st century: Success strategies of unknown world market leaders.* New York, NY: Springer.

SINPRO 2020. (2014). *Report from the Foresight Process.* Mandal, Norway: SINPRO.

SINTEF. (2015). *Universitetssamarbeidet.* Retrieved from http://www.sintef.no/universitetssamarbeidet1/.

Slaughter, S. & Leslie, L. L. (1997). *Academic capitalism: Politics, policies, and the entrepreneurial university.* Baltimore, MD: Johns Hopkins University Press.

Smith, D. E. (2005). *Institutional ethnography: A sociology for people.* Lanham, MD: Altamira Press.

Smith, D. E. (1999). *Writing the social.* Toronto, Canada: University of Toronto Press.

Snow, C. P. (2012). *The two cultures.* Cambridge, UK: Cambridge University Press.

Steyaert, P., Barzman, M., Billaud, J. P., Brives, H., Hubert, B., Ollivier, G. & Roche, B. (2007). The role of knowledge and research in facilitating social learning among stakeholders in natural resources management in the French Atlantic coastal wetlands. *Environmental Science & Policy, 10*(6), 537–550. ISI: 000249286600005.

Stoller, S. (2009). Phenomenology and the poststructural critique of experience. *International Journal of Philosophical Studies, 17*(5), 707–737.

Storper, M. (1997). *The regional world.* New York, NY: The Guilford Press.

Stringer, L. C., Dougill, A. J, Fraser, E., Hubacek, K., Prell, C. & Reed, M. S. (2006). Unpacking 'participation' in the adaptive management of social ecological systems: A critical review. *Ecology and Society, 11*(2), 39. Retrieved from http://www.ecologyandsociety.org/vol11/iss2/art39/.

Svensson, L. & Nielsen, K. A. (2006). Action research and interactive research. In K. A. Nielsen & L. Svensson (Eds), *Action research and interactive research: Beyond practice and theory* (pp. 13–44). Maastricht, the Netherlands: Shaker Publishing.

Swarbrooke, J. (2000). *The development and management of visitor attractions.* London, UK: Elsevier.

Søndergaard, D. (2000). Destabiliserende diskursanalyse: Veje ind i poststrukturalistisk inspireret empirisk forskning. In Haavind H. (Ed.), *Kjønn og fortolkende metode: Metodiske muligheter i kvalitativ forskning* (pp. 60–104). Oslo: Gyldendal Akademisk Forlag.

Teece, D. J. (2010). Business models, business strategy and innovation. *Long Range Planning, 43*(2–3), 172–194.

Teece, D. J., Pisano, G. & Shuen, A. (1997). Dynamic capabilities and strategic management. *Strategic Management Journal, 18*(7), 509–533.

The Research Council of Norway. (2009). *Utredning om videre utforming av regionale forskningsfond.* Oslo, Norway: Forskningsrådet. Retrieved from http://www.forskningsradet.no/no/Om_instituttsektoren/1254000564607.

The Research Council of Norway. (2012). *Evaluering av de tolv regionale forskningsinstituttene.* Oslo, Norway: Forskningsrådet. Retrieved from http://www.forskningsradet.no/no/Om_instituttsektoren/1254000564607.

The Research Council of Norway. (2014a). *Instituttsektoren – forskningsrådets strategi 2014–2018.* Oslo, Norway: Forskningsrådet. Retrieved from http://www.forskningsradet.no/no/Om_instituttsektoren/1254000564607.

The Research Council of Norway. (2014b). *Årsrapport 2013 primærnæringsinstituttene nøkkeltall, instituttpresentasjon og bruk av basisbevilgningen.* Oslo, Norway: Forskningsrådet. Retrieved from http://www.forskningsradet.no/no/Om_instituttsektoren/1254000564607.

The Research Council of Norway. (2014c). *Regionalt arbeid: Forskningsrådets policy for 2014–2018.* Retrieved from http://www.forskningsradet.no/servlet/Satellite?c=Page&pagename=ForskningsradetNorsk%2FHovedsidemal&cid=1175003277667&querystring=Regionalt+arbeid.+Forskningsr%C3%A5dets+policy+for+2014%E2%80%932018+&spell=true&filters=cssitename%2C%21ForskningsradetEngelsk%2C%2Clangcodes%2Cno&isglobalsearch=true&configuration=nfrsearchersppublished.

The Research Council of Norway. (2014d). *Utdyping av retningslinjenes grunnleggende krav til institutter for at de kan gis statlig basisfinansiering.* Retrieved from http://www.forskningsradet.no/servlet/Satellite?c=Page&pagename=ForskningsradetNorsk%2FHovedsidemal&cid=1175003277667&querystring=Utdyping+av+retningslinjenes+grunnleggende+krav+til+institutter+for+at+de+kan+gis+statlig+basisfinansiering&spell=true&filters=cssitename%2C%21ForskningsradetEngelsk%2C%2Clangcodes%2Cno&isglobalsearch=true&configuration=nfrsearchersppublished.

The Research Council of Norway. (2014e). *Årsrapport 2013: De samfunnsvitenskapelige instituttene nøkkeltall, instituttpresentasjon og bruk av basisbevilgningen.* Oslo, Norway: Forskningsrådet. Retrieved from http://www.forskningsradet.no/no/Om_instituttsektoren/1254000564607.

The Research Council of Norway. (2014f). *Årsrapport 2013: De teknisk-industrielle instituttene nøkkeltall, instituttpresentasjon og bruk av basisbevilgningen.* Oslo, Norway: Forskningsrådet. Retrieved from http://www.forskningsradet.no/no/Om_instituttsektoren/1254000564607.

The Research Council of Norway. (2014g). *Årsrapport 2013: Miljøinstituttene nøkkeltall, instituttpresentasjon og bruk av basisbevilgningen.* Oslo, Norway: Forskningsrådet. Retrieved from http://www.forskningsradet.no/no/Om_instituttsektoren/1254000564607

Thissen, M., van Oort, F., Diodato, D. & Ruijs, A. (2013). *Regional competitiveness and smart specialization in Europe: Place-based development in international economic networks.* Cheltenham, UK: Edward Elgar Publishing.

Thrift, N. (2008). *Non-representational theory: Space, politics, affect.* London, UK: Routledge.

Toulmin, S. E. & Gustavsen, B. (1996). *Beyond theory: Changing organizations through participation.* Amsterdam, the Netherlands: John Benjamins Publishing.

Tödtling, F. & Trippl, M. (2005). One size fits all? Towards a differentiated regional innovation policy approach. *Research Policy, 34*(8), 1203–1219. doi: 10.1016/j.respol.2005.01.018.

Tripathy, J. & Mohapatra, D. (2011). Does development exist outside representation? *Journal of Developing Societies, 27*(2), 93–118.

Trowler, P. (1997). Beyond the Robbins trap: Reconceptualising academic responses to change in higher education (or . . . quiet flows the don?). *Studies in Higher Education, 22*(3), 301–318.

Tsoukas, H. (1996). The firm as a distributed knowledge system: A constructionist approach. *Strategic Management Journal, 17*(S2), 11–25.

Vanthillo, T. & Verhetsel, A. (2012). Paradigm change in regional policy: Towards smart specialisation? Lessons from Flanders (Belgium). *Belgeo, 1–2*(1). Retrieved from http://belgeo.revues.org/7083.

Vasstrøm, M. (2014). Rediscovering nature as commons in environmental planning: New understandings through dialogue. *International Journal of the Commons, 8*(2), 493–512.

Vasstrøm, M. & Normann, R. H. (2014). Role transformations in collaborative R&D-projects as reciprocation between research, practice and policy. *International Journal of Action Research, 10*(2), 184–212.

Vatne, E. (2013). Den spesialiserte leverandørindustrien til petroleumsvirksomhet: Omfang og geografisk utbredelse i NorgeSNF-rapport, 2(13), 1–49. Bergen, Norway: Samfunns- og næringslivsforskning. Retrieved from http://www.snf.no/Admin/Public/Download.aspx?file=Files%2FFiler%2FPublications%2FR02_13.pdf.

Wallevik, H. (2012). The complexity of generalisation: A phenomenological approach to economic affairs among women in Zanzibar Town (PhD thesis). Ås, Norway: Noragric.

Whitehead, A., Cornwall, A. & Harrison, E. (Eds). (2007). *Feminisms in development: Contradictions, contestations and challenges*. London, UK: Zed Books.

Whitehead, A., Cornwall, A. & Harrison, E. (2008). *Gender myths and feminist fables: The struggle for interpretive power in gender and development*. Malden, MA: Blackwell.

Whyte, W. F. (1991). *Participatory action research*. Newbury Park, CA: Sage Publishing.

Willig, R. (2007). *Til forsvar for kritikken*. Copenhagen, Denmark: Hans Reitzels Forlag.

Winther, M. B. & Svendsen, G. L. H. (2012). 'The rotten banana' fires back: The story of a Danish discourse of inclusive rurality in the making. *Journal of Rural Studies, 28*(4), 466–477. doi: 10.1016/j.jrurstud.2012.05.003.

World Economic Forum. (2014). *The global competitiveness report 2014–15*. Retrieved from http://www3.weforum.org/docs/WEF_GlobalCompetitivenessReport_2014–15.pdf.

Yu, X. & Weiler, B. (2001). Mainland Chinese pleasure travelers to Australia: A leisure behavior analysis. *Tourism Culture & Communication, 3*(2), 81–91.

Zachrisson, A. (2009). The designation of Fulufjället national park: Efficient co-management through downward accountability? *Local Environment: The International Journal of Justice and Sustainability, 14*(3), 259–271. Retrieved from http://www.informaworld.com/10.1080/13549830802693177.

Zack, M. H. (2005). The strategic advantage of knowledge and learning. *International Journal of Learning and Intellectual Capital, 2*(1), 1–20.

Zeithaml, V. A., Parasuraman, A. & Berry, L. L.(1985). Problems and strategies in service marketing. *Journal of Marketing, 49*(4), 33–46.

Zomerdijk, L. G. & Voss, C. A. (2010). Service design for experience-centric services. *Journal of Service Research, 13*(1), 67–82.

Zott, C., Amit, R. & Massa, L. (2010). Business model design: An activity system perspective. *Long Range Planning, 43*(2/3), 216–226.

Index